THE BOOK OF THIRTY CENTURIES

THE MACMILLAN COMPANY
NEW YORK · BOSTON · CHICAGO
DALLAS · ATLANTA · SAN FRANCISCO

MACMILLAN AND CO., LIMITED
LONDON · BOMBAY · CALCUTTA
MADRAS · MELBOURNE

**THE MACMILLAN COMPANY
OF CANADA, LIMITED**
TORONTO

Hebrew University "Dead Sea Scroll"
Isaiah lvii. 17 — lix. 7

Photograph by courtesy of Professor E. L. Sukenik, Museum of Jewish Antiquities, Hebrew University, Jerusalem, and of *The Hebrew Biblical Encyclopaedia*.

Approximately two-thirds actual size.

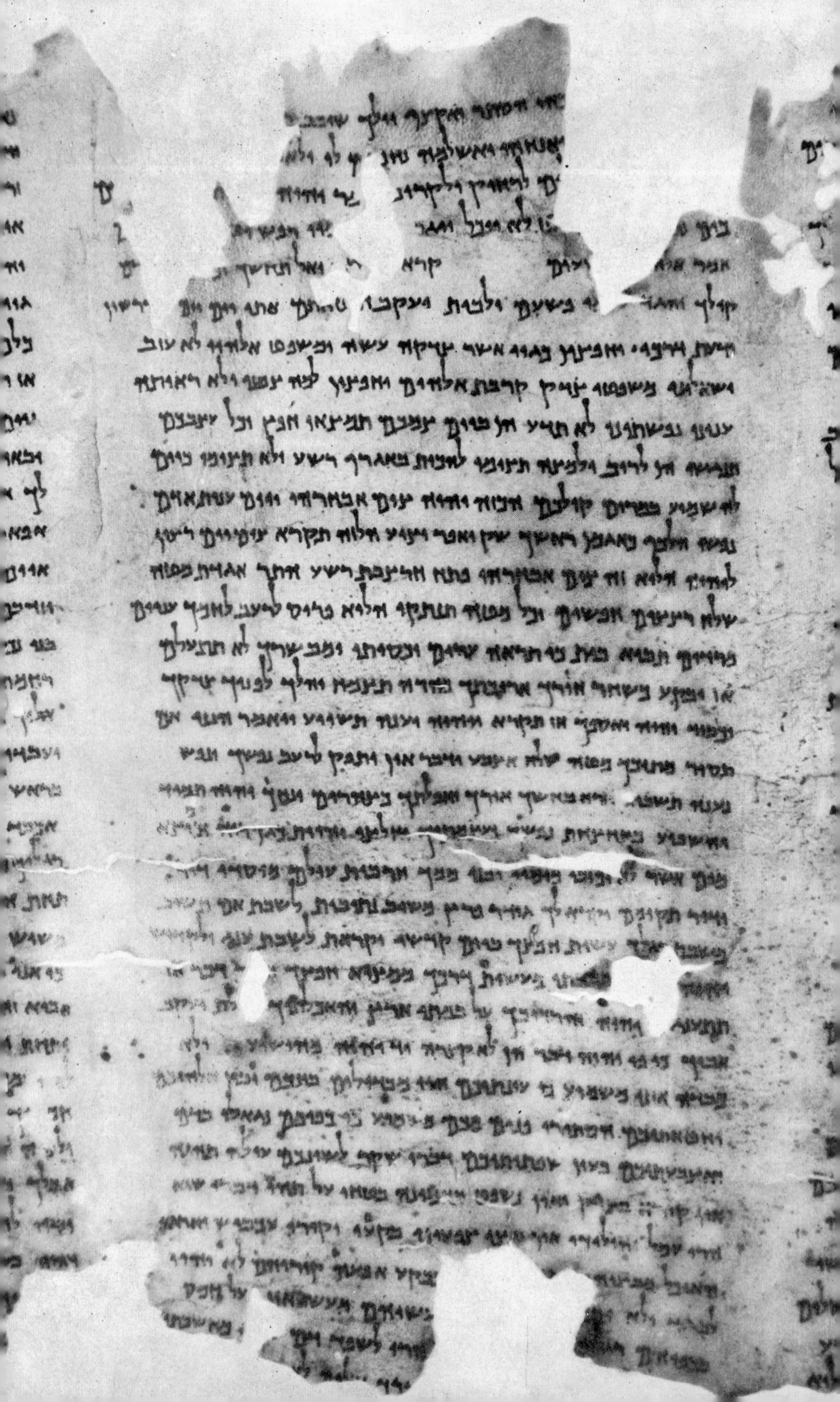

THE BOOK

OF

THIRTY CENTURIES

AN INTRODUCTION

TO MODERN STUDY OF THE BIBLE

BY

STANLEY RYPINS

New York

THE MACMILLAN COMPANY

1951

Scriptural passages, under authorization of The Macmillan Company, are cited, as a general rule, from *The Modern Reader's Bible* — the English Revised Version as edited by Richard G. Moulton; departure from this practice, whenever dictated by the interpretative procedure, is invariably indicated.

From each of the following copyrighted translations quotations are used by permission: *The Holy Scriptures,* copyrighted 1917 by The Jewish Publication Society of America; *The Bible: An American Translation,* by J. M. Powis Smith and Edgar J. Goodspeed, copyrighted 1931 by the University of Chicago; *The Holy Bible: A New Translation,* by James Moffatt, copyrighted 1922, 1935 by Harper and Brothers and 1950 by James Moffatt; *The Revised Standard Version of the New Testament,* copyrighted 1946 by The International Council of Religious Education.

TO

E. A. LOWE

in gratitude

for his illumination,

during memorable hours Oxonian,

of the ways of a scribe with his pen.

"And they read in the book, in the law of God, distinctly; and they gave the sense, so that they understood the reading."

Neh. viii. 8

"He that giveth answer before he heareth,
It is folly and shame unto him."

Prov. xviii. 13

PREFACE

The Book of Thirty Centuries, conforming consistently to accepted requirements of Biblical scholarship, and attempting to meet the exacting expectations of the Scripturally Learned, is nevertheless primarily designed for the average intelligent reader whose critical equipment does not include a knowledge of either Hebrew or Greek. Punctilious attention to transliteration and translation will, it is believed, insure for the alert reader a relatively easy comprehension of every phase of the presentation. Material which, because of its linguistic or other character, is likely to interest the specialist alone has been relegated, if immediately relevant to the exposition, to the foot of the page, or, if less urgent, to the terminal Notes, the body of the text being thus arranged for uninterrupted and readily assimilable reading.

For generous privileges courteously granted, contributory to the preparation of this study, my thanks are due to the official custodians of Biblioteca Apostolica Vaticana; Bibliothèque Nationale; the Bodleian Library; the British and Foreign Bible Society Library, London; the British Museum; the Jewish Theological Seminary of New York City, the John Rylands Library; Pembroke College Library, Cambridge; the Pierpont Morgan Library; Princeton University Library; the New York Public Library; the Smithsonian Institution; Union Theological Seminary of New York City; Universitäts Bibliothek, Basle; University Library, Cambridge; and the Zurich Stadtbibliothek.

For welcome and helpful advice in the fields of their special competence I am under deep obligation, gratefully acknowledged, to two of my colleagues in the College of the City of

New York: Professor A. S. Halkin, for expert and painstaking review of the chapters on Old Testament revision; and Professor Bernard D. N. Grebanier, for practised evaluation of other chapters with reference particularly to matters of form.

To my wife, Evelyn, I am indebted — polite understatement — not only for unflagging assistance in the wearisome labor of preparing the manuscript for publication, but, on a superior plane, for sensitive and penetrating criticism of the work by which it has greatly benefited at every step toward its fruition.

"Reader," wrote Cotton Mather at the close of his *Magnalia Christi Americana*, "Carthagena was of the mind, that unto those *Three Things* which the Ancients held Impossible, there should be added this *Fourth*, to find a Book Printed without Errata's." Although every care has been taken in the production of *The Book of Thirty Centuries* to provide an example of that Fourth Impossibility, the author, entertaining no expectation of having achieved that miraculous goal, wishes here, in advance, to express his gratitude to any diligent reader who, discovering an error or errors, whatsoever their character, kindly troubles to call them to his attention.

S. R.

New York City,
August 30, 1950.

FOREWORD

KOHELETH, the Preacher, long since lamenting the endless making of many books, would surely have been confirmed in his literary cynicism had he foreseen, what today is sufficiently plain, that, of myriad volumes, only a remnant effectively survive the ages, and of those few only a handful exercise more than a fleeting influence over the thinking and conduct of mankind. Indeed, with respect to contemporary western culture, the number of books undeniably momentous in their prolonged and universal authority is reducible ultimately to but two. These paramount twain, the products of widely separated eras, are *The Holy Bible* of multiple inspiration, and *The Origin of Species* from a single individual's scientific pen. Although to this pair of dissimilar, if not antagonistic, works every reader will hasten, with inevitable eclecticism, to add a select few of his own, no one reasonably aware of the quality of our current civilization will be able to eliminate either the epochal contribution of Charles Darwin and his successors or the enduring impress of Psalmist, Prophet, Evangelist and Apostle. The effective impact — whether for good or for evil — of *The Origin of Species* upon modern thought and action has, in the scant century of its existence, been equalled by no book since the dawn of Christianity. The all-pervading influence of the Bible — likewise, some may hold, for good or for evil — has for the thirty centuries of its history been unrivalled. This being the case, an easy and familiar grasp both of Scripture and of Darwin — whether or not agreement be with either or both — is basic to modern man's cultural orientation. A man may read and speak half a dozen tongues, may excel in a given field of knowledge or activity, but unless his educational background be both Scriptural and evolutionary his cultural credentials remain deficient.

Said the great nineteenth-century scientist Huxley — than whom Darwin had no abler advocate: "Take the Bible as a whole; make the severest deductions which fair criticism can dictate for shortcomings and positive errors; . . . there still remains in this old literature a vast residuum of moral beauty and grandeur . . . this Book has been woven into the life of all that is best and noblest in English history; . . . it is written in the noblest and purest English, and abounds in exquisite beauties of mere literary form; . . . it forbids the veriest hind who never left his village to be ignorant of the existence of other countries and other civilizations, and of a great past, stretching back to the furthest limits of the oldest nations in the world." This evaluation of Scripture in the nineteenth century possesses equal validity in the twentieth. The ascendancy, however, of scientific education — for which Huxley, it may be said, and his associate, Herbert Spencer, were primarily responsible — has so impoverished contemporary academic offerings in the languages and literatures of the cultures from which our own has largely evolved, that today, except within limited professional circles, not only is Latin — for more than a millennium the universal medium of polite letters and learned communication — relegated to pharmaceutical usage or legal jargon, and the elegance of Greek restricted, in the main, to its alphabetical essence in the designation of anything-but-Hellenic fraternal associations, but the Bible, even in English translation, is so far removed from uses other than liturgical that Scriptural references, injudiciously spoken, often fall upon unresponsive ears.

Many modern readers of the Scriptures in English probably find themselves in the position of the late Roger Fry who, "at an age when [he] could understand scarcely any of [the Bible], became so familiar with the words, . . . learned to take them so much for granted, that . . . the too familiar words refused to bite

on the imagination, [requiring] many years of forgetfulness before the Bible became as it were depolarized, so that one could
really get into some sort of contact with the various authors."
Of those who, reading the Bible only in English, try, by writing
books about its literary excellence, to effect an intellectual *rap-
prochement* with authors of Books as difficult as Revelation or
Job, some have yet to discover that no translation — including
the King James Version — accurately conveys in its every passage either the primary sense or the aesthetic flavor of the
original. With reference to this critical astigmatism, distinction
between the Old Testament and the New is merely one of
degree. For thorough appreciation of Gospel or Epistle, as ensuing pages attempt to make clear, familiarity with Greek —
particularly that of the first century — is fundamental. Pre-
requisite to something better than superficial understanding of
the Old Testament, even more than mastery of post-classical
Greek is essential for fullest comprehension of the New, is a
knowledge of Biblical Hebrew. Readers of the Old Testament
in its original language are only too well aware of the numerous
passages which elude lexical, grammatical or syntactical analysis, and yet, reading smoothly enough in an accommodating
translation, convey nothing of their inherent difficulties to those
who depend solely upon the Bible in English. When, despite
deftness of translators, unintelligibilities of the Hebrew text remain transparently such even in English versions, and, notably
in the post-exilic writings, "verse after verse makes no sense at
all," it is natural, and certainly refreshing, to have such passages
bemoaned as "discouraging reading." Discouragement of a different kind — one stimulus to the writing of this book — arises
from the willingness of an admirable contemporary classicist,
who would on no account tolerate a study of Virgil or Homer
by one who commands neither Latin nor Greek, to venture
critical appraisal of Isaiah, Amos, Ezekiel, Hosea or Jeremiah
without that acquaintance with Hebrew idiom which, throughout the Old Testament, and above all for comprehension of the
difficult prophetic writings, is assuredly indispensable. Indiffer-

ence of this character to the discipline of Semitic linguistics is largely responsible, no doubt, for the common but entirely untenable claim that the Bible of King James — from which its most enthusiastic admirers are compelled, for elucidation at least of Proverbs, Ecclesiastes, Song of Songs and Job, to turn to later Versions — is as accurate in its translation as it is supreme in its acknowledged perfection of Jacobean English.

The decline in humanistic studies consequent upon the rise of Darwinism, though from some points of view regrettable, is not without its compensation even for Biblical studies. Evolutionary thinking, originally confined to questions biological, has with remarkable rapidity penetrated into numerous other departments of twentieth-century thought. Instability, now held to be characteristic of all things included within the domain of the physical sciences, is likewise considered typical of all things human. Not only "the great globe, yea, all which it inherit, shall dissolve," but, pending that comfortably remote event, all creations of the world's dominant though transient inhabitant, man — his legal and juridical systems, his forms of social organization, his philosophic and religious concepts, his standards of ethics and beauty — constantly undergo perceptible modification toward some unperceived end. This dynamic condition, recorded by Heraclitus and his school alone among the ancients, is today, as a result of Darwin's sweeping vision, commonly perceived wherever thought is free. Many, accordingly, among modern Biblical scholars find it rewarding to examine Scripture, in a manner unknown to previous generations, as a slowly-developed expression of changing human institutions, reflecting their gradual transformation, as society made leisurely progress, into something which men of good will earnestly hope will be still further transformed. Such is the point of view from which the following chapters are written. They may be read — ample provision to that end having been made — without a knowledge of Hebrew or Greek; whatever value these chapters possess can, however, be assimilated only by those who, no longer walking in pre-Darwinian darkness, have seen a great light.

CONTENTS

ABBREVIATIONS

Ac.: Acts of the Apostles
A.J.V.: *The Holy Scriptures* (O.T.), Philadelphia, 1917
Am.: Amos
Aram.: Aramaic
Arm.: Armenian
A. R. V.: *American Revised Version* (1901)
A. S. V.: *American Standard Version* (1901)
A. V.: *Authorized Version* (1611)
Babyl.: Babylonian Talmud
B. A. S. O. R.: *Bulletin American Schools of Oriental Research*
Boh.: Bohairic
Chr.: Chronicles
Cod(d.): Codex (codices)
Col.: Colossians
Cor.: Corinthians
D: Deuteronomist
Dan.: Daniel
Deut.: Deuteronomy
Diat.: Diatessaron
E: Elohist
Eccl.: Ecclesiastes
Ecclus.: Ecclesiasticus
Egypt.: Egyptian
Eph.: Ephesians
Est.: Esther
Eth.: Ethiopian, Ethiopic
Eus.: Eusebius, bp. of Caesarea
Ex.: Exodus

Ezek.: Ezekiel
Ezr.: Ezra
Gal.: Galatians
Gen.: Genesis
Gk.: Greek
Gth.: Gothic
Hab.: Habakkuk
Hag.: Haggai
Heb.: Hebrews
Hex.: Hexateuch
Hist. Eccl.: *Historia Ecclesiae*
Hkl.: Harkleian Revision Syr. N. T.
Hos.: Hosea
I. C. C.: *International Critical Commentary*
Is.: Isaiah
J: Yahvist
Jas.: James
JE: Yahvist and Elohist
Jer.: Jeremiah
Jn.: John (Gospel of)
Jo.: John (Epistle of)
Jon.: Jonah
Josh.: Joshua
J. Q. R.: *Jewish Quarterly Review*
Judg.: Judges
Kgs.: Kings
Lam.: Lamentations
Lat.: Latin
Lev.: Leviticus
Lk.: Luke (Gospel of)

LXX: Septuagint
Mac.: Maccabees
Mal.: Malachi
Meg.: Megillah (Mish. treatise)
mg.: margin
Mic.: Micah
Mish.: Mishna
Mk.: Mark (Gospel of)
MS(S.): manuscript(s)
Mt.: Matthew (Gospel of)
M. T.: Massoretic Text
Neh.: Nehemiah
N. T.: New Testament
Num.: Numbers
O. Lat.: Old Latin
O. Syr.: Old Syriac
O. T.: Old Testament
P: Priestly document
Patr. Gr.: Migne, *Patrologiae Cursus Completus, Ser. Graeca*
Patr. Lat.: Migne, *Patrologiae Cursus Completus, Ser. Latina*
Pet.: Peter
Phil.: Philippians
Phm.: Philemon
Prov.: Proverbs
Ps(s.): Psalm(s)
Psh.: Peshitto
Rev.: Revelation
Rom.: Romans

R. S. V.: *Revised Standard Version* (1948)
R. V.: *Revised Version* (English)
Sah.: Sahidic
Sam.: Samaritan
Sam.: Samuel
Sanh.: Sanhedrin (Talmudic treatise)
Shab.: Shabbat (Talmudic treatise)
S. of S.: Song of Songs
Syr.: Syriac
Syr. C.: Curetonian Syriac (Gospels)
Syr. H.: Jerusalem Syriac (lectionary)
Syr. S.: Sinaitic Syriac (Gospels)
Thess.: Thessalonians
Tim.: Timothy
Tit.: Titus
T. R.: *Textus Receptus*
U. L. C.: University Library, Cambridge, Eng.
Vulg.: Vulgate
v (v).: verse(s)
Yad.: Yadayim (Talmudic treatise)
Yer.: Jerusalem Talmud
Zech.: Zechariah

CHAPTER I

Transmission of the Text

"Remember the days of old, Consider the
years of many generations."
                              Deut. xxxii. 7

THE Bible — wretchedly printed, badly edited, inadequately translated — is yet the most arresting of anthologies. Composed by many authors of unequal creative and intellectual power, at widely separated intervals during approximately a thousand years, these collected writings constitute a select "library," the various books of which reflect the literary, social and religious genius of the people who laid the ethical foundation of western culture. Originally unrelated works, each complete in itself, these ancient compositions, as competent authorities[1] agree, circulated at first as independent productions. Placed, eventually, between the covers of a single volume, these histories, legends, narratives, essays, poems, laws, maxims, letters, theophanies, rhapsodies and orations comprise, in the case of the New Testament, a post-classical Greek Miscellany, and, in that of the Old Testament, a Hebrew anthology. Only as such can these writings be called *a book*.[a]

[a] In this study, the term *Bible* or *Scripture(s)* is regularly employed to include everything Biblical from Genesis through Revelation; *i. e.*, the Old Testament, the Apocrypha and the New Testament. Whenever one of these major divisions is under separate consideration it is referred to specifically by its appropriate title. This, it is hoped, will avoid a common inconsistency.

1

Recognition of the composite character of *one* portion of this anthology is embedded in the word, of Greek origin, *Pentateuch*; that is, the *five books* (Genesis, Exodus, Leviticus, Numbers, Deuteronomy). Jewish students, to this day, commonly refer to these first five books of the Bible by the Hebrew word for *five* [ḤāMēš — חמש].[b] Our word *Bible*, in the original Greek form from which it is derived, was a plural: τὰ βιβλία — the books.[c] The plural sense is still preserved in the familiar term, the *Scriptures*. In current English usage, *the Bible*, unmistakably singular, means *the* Book — the Book of all Books; just as, to the American mind, *the* Constitution signifies, without further elaboration, the basic Federal Charter.

Biblical writings, both the Hebrew and the Greek, have come down to us from ancient times in manuscript form. No early manuscript, however, is known which contains the entire Bible, nor, indeed, all of both Testaments, the Old and the New.[2] Even the printing press, multiplying Bibles by the millions, and in all languages, has, incredibly enough, and long ago, produced only a single edition of the *complete Bible in its original tongues*.[3] The incomplete or mutilated state of manuscripts which have survived from an antiquity in which the printing press was undreamed of creates but one of the several problems of Biblical palaeography. A full comprehension of those problems depends upon a clear understanding of the techniques of the professional scribe and the character of his transcription. This subject, fundamental as it is to Biblical scholarship, we shall examine in a subsequent chapter.

[b] The vocalization of this, the simplest inflectional form of the cardinal number *five*, is commonly modified, with reference to the Five Books of Moses, either to ḤUMaš or to ḤUMMaš. For system of transliteration employed, *v. infra*, p. 63, note t.

[c] To Byblos (a Phoenician town — now the Syrian village Gebal — to which Egypt exported papyrus and from which the Greeks purchased it) the Greeks owe, first, their word for *papyrus* (βίβλος; thus always Herodotus), and, second, their word (βιβλίον) for that which was made of papyrus, a book. The plural of this neuter noun, βιβλία, construed erroneously as a feminine singular, gave rise to the English *Bible*. Cp. *milliner*, from Milan; *parchment*, from Pergamum.

Manuscripts — portable documents written by hand — made their earliest known appearance in the Mesopotamian Valley, in the form of clay tablets, more than four thousand years ago. The cuneiform or wedge-shaped script employed by scribes of the Sumerian, Akkadian, Vannic, Hittite, Assyrian and Babylonian epochs was skillfully impressed with a tool called a *stylus* upon the smoothed surface of small blocks of soft clay, which were then exposed to the heat of the sun to bake and to harden into permanent, brick-like records. Of the many thousands of such documents on sun-baked clay which have survived the vicissitudes of four millennia, some are of immediate and vital importance to Biblical scholarship, as will be seen later in this study. Mesopotamian clay, as a medium for writing, was eventually superseded, as civilization shifted its center, by the much more convenient but more perishable Egyptian papyrus — a thin, light, flexible, ink-absorbing sheet of moistened, hammered and sun-dried layers of Nile reed slices — from which comes our English word *paper*. The stylus, concurrently, was supplanted by the split reed (*calamus*) or quill, prototype of the modern steel pen. On papyrus, too, although not so abundantly as upon clay, there have been preserved miscellaneous writings with which the student of the Bible must concern himself. But by far the largest quantity of available ancient Biblical documents was written on leather, parchment or vellum especially prepared for the purpose from the skins of cows, goats, or sheep. Such skins, sewn together in long strips, and rolled up on a wooden core or roller for convenience in handling or storage, were the "books" of pre-Christian centuries and the official records of medieval monarchs.[d]

Specimens of these rolls, in large numbers, may be examined in the archives of European governments — pipe rolls, close rolls, patent rolls, calendar rolls, *coram rege* rolls — or, more accessibly, in every synagogue. No synagogue is without its "ark" [ארון — 'arôn] in which is enshrined its richly-clad copy

---

[d] A linguistic vestige of this technique survives in *muster-roll, roll-call* and in *sheepskin* colloquially used for *diploma*.

or copies of the Five Books of Moses, hand-written in black, non-metallic ink upon strips of leather or parchment, rendered durable with lime and gall nut, wound around two wooden rollers (one attached to *either* end of the strip) to form what is commonly called in English *the Scrolls.* Five other Books of the Old Testament — Ruth, Ecclesiastes, Song of Songs, Lamentations and Esther, the last most frequently a manuscript unto itself — are invariably referred to in Hebrew as *rolls* [מגלות — MeGiLLÔth].[e]

It was not until the second century of the Common Era (or possibly a trifle earlier) that manuscripts were first stitched together in something resembling pamphlet or book form. Thus assembled, a manuscript is known as a *codex.* Of these manuscripts — scrolls and codices alike — unrecorded hundreds have perished. Fire, water, wear and tear, vandalism and war sufficiently account for the loss of large numbers. Under the oppression of Antiochus Epiphanes in the second century B. C. — a tyranny out of which sprang the heroes of the Apocrypha, Judas Maccabeus and his brothers — many Hebrew Biblical scrolls must have been destroyed. The Hebrew manuscripts of the Old Testament, moreover, suffered an additional and even more effective destruction, any copy worn or soiled through use being rejected as no longer acceptable [פסול — PāSUL] for ceremonial purposes, and, if not laid away to be forgotten in the synagogal storeroom, piously protected from profanation by burial beside the body of a great or good man.[4] In the case of manuscripts of the Pentateuch — that portion of the Old Testament known in Hebrew as the Law [תורה — TÔRAH], which universally stands first in sacerdotal importance in Jewish worship — burial was obligatory if in one column of the text as many as four errors were discovered,[f] or if in the entire body of the Torah there was found a single mistake in the designation of those sections [פרשיות —

[e] Superb examples of such *megilloth* — beautifully illuminated, and housed, for their preciousness, in exquisitely wrought silver containers — may be seen in various museums, notably in that of the Jewish Theological Seminary of New York City.

[f] This regulation applied also to the roll of Esther.

ᴘᴀʀᴀšɪʏʏÔᴛʜ] which were "open" [פתוחה — ᴘᴇᴛʜᴜḥᴀʜ] or "closed" [סתומה — sᴇᴛʜᴜᴍᴀʜ].⁵ The inevitable consequence of this pious biblioclasm is that — except, as will appear, for one recent find — no extant Hebrew roll or codex of any major part of the Old Testament is of great antiquity; nor until just yesterday did it seem in the least likely that anything other than mutilated fragments of truly ancient copies would ever be recovered.

Such Hebrew Biblical manuscripts as have survived intact owe their preservation in part to their lodgment in the synagogal depository or *genizah* [גניזה],ᵍ or, as shown by recent discovery, in some place of concealment and security. From such a *genizah* at Kaffa in the Crimeaʰ came the splendid collection of forty-two rolls now housed in the public library of Leningrad. From the *genizah* of the Karaiteⁱ synagogue in Fostat (Cairo, Egypt) there was brought back to England, in 1896, by Dr. Solomon Schechter, a rich collection of Biblical manuscripts which are now preserved in the library of Cambridge University. Other Hebrew Biblical manuscripts finding a permanent home, centuries earlier, in European libraries, have thereby escaped destruction. In the Vatican Library alone, by the year 1756, there were Hebrew manuscripts to the number of five hundred and twelve,⁶ of which thirty-nine were Biblical, and at the present

---

ᵍ This word, meaning "hidden" in Hebrew, is customarily applied to a cemetery in which timeworn, heretical or disgraced Hebrew books or papers have been secreted; so that, as it has been said, a *genizah* "serves the double purpose of preserving good things from harm and bad things from harming." *Cf. Babylonian Talmud*, translated into English, ed. I. Epstein, London, 1935–1949, *Megillah* 26ᵇ and *Yoma* 12ᵇ.

ʰ This *genizah*, located on the ground floor behind the ark of the synagogue, was entered from the outside of the building through an opening so tiny that only a very small boy could effect his way into it. Its contents were removed, about the year 1840, by the Russian Karaite archaeologist, Abraham ben Samuel Firkovitch, to whom the Leningrad library is indebted for a large part of its notable collection. Kaffa is also known as Theodosia or Feodosia.

ⁱ The Karaites, a Jewish sect founded, under Mohammedan influence, by Anan ben David in the eighth century, claimed, not without exaggeration, that their religious observances were based directly upon the text of the O. T. rather than upon rabbinical doctrine.

time the total number of Hebrew manuscripts in European and American collections, now catalogued and available to scholars, is well above sixteen thousand, of which more than fifteen hundred are Biblical.[j]

None of these many manuscripts, however, as Biblical records go, is ancient. Although palaeographers find it reasonably easy to identify, from the type of penmanship or character of the ink, the country in which a Hebrew manuscript was written, the present state of Hebrew palaeography (unlike that of Latin or Greek, to which we come subsequently) is unfortunately so undeveloped that no accurate determination of the date of an undated Hebrew manuscript is possible on the internal palaeographical evidence alone. The marked distinctions (particularly in the Rabbinic and cursive[7] characters) between Hebrew manuscripts of Syrian, Persian, Egyptian, Yemenite, Greek, Italian, Spanish, French, German, or other origin, are useful as an indication rather of provenance than of chronology. By far the greater number of these manuscripts, of which there are many,[k] are late copies, of the twelfth to the sixteenth century.[1]

Among Hebrew Biblical works the contemporary dating of which is unquestioned, the oldest is the manuscript of the Latter Prophets at Leningrad, Codex Babylonicus Petropolitanus, finished, according to its colophon,[8] in the year 916. The Vatican Library possesses two Hebrew Biblical codices of slightly earlier and identical dating, *Anno Mundi* 4600, equivalent to A. D. 840. One of these two is a codex,[9] dated on the last of its one hundred

---

[j] At the British Museum, 165; the Bodleian Library, 146; Bibliothèque Nationale, 132; the Vatican Library, 40; University Library, Cambridge, 32; at Leningrad, 146; Parma, 118 (*exclusive of* some three hundred-odd assorted Prophets, *megilloth*, Psalters, and Hagiographa); Vienna, 24; Berlin, 14; the Jewish Theological Seminary of New York City, about 100; the Hebrew Union College, Cincinnati, approximately 50.

[k] As far back as 1759, Benjamin Kennicott, in his *State of the Printed Hebrew Text of the Old Testament*, Oxford, listed nine whole Biblical Hebrew manuscripts in England, and eighty-two elsewhere.

[1] Throughout this study, the centuries of the Common Era are cited without the grammatically barbarous specification, *A. D.*, which, meaning "in the *year* of the Lord," is logically inapplicable to *centuries*. Pre-Christian centuries are invariably indicated as such.

and seventy folios, containing the Books of Deuteronomy, Ruth
and Esther; the Song of Songs, Ecclesiastes, Lamentations; and
those selected readings from the Prophets, both the Former and
the Latter,[m] known as the *Haftarot* [הפטרות — HAPHṬARÔTH].
The other — Assemani, No. VI, of four hundred folios, dated
on folio 395 — consists of the Hagiographa and the Former and
Latter Prophets. At Cambridge University there is a manuscript dated A. D. 856, the trustworthiness of which date, however, is maintained by only one scholar. At Oxford, Codex
Laudianus of the Old Testament (all except a large part of
Genesis) is dated by Kennicott in the tenth century. At Parma,
de Rossi[10] dates manuscript No. 634 (Leviticus xxi. 19 —
Numbers i. 50) in the eighth century; others ascribe it to the
tenth or later centuries. In the possession of the Karaite community of Cairo there is a codex now containing only the
Former and Latter Prophets. This manuscript, written by Moses
ben Asher[n] at Tiberias, was completed, according to a colophon
at the end of the Minor Prophets,[o] eight hundred and twenty-
seven years after the destruction of Jerusalem, which is to say,
by Jewish reckoning, A. D. 895.[11] An undated vellum manuscript of the Pentateuch in the British Museum (MS. Oriental
4445), written three columns to a page, in a hand — depending
from the ruled lines — identical with that of Codex Babylonicus
Petropolitanus, but with the probably contemporary infra-linear
vowel-pointing[12] commonly associated with the school of Tiberias, is thought to be of a slightly earlier period: "probably written
about the middle of the ninth century."[13] A date earlier than

[m] Former Prophets: Josh., Judg., Sam., Kgs. Latter Prophets: Is., Jer.,
Ezek., and Minor Prophets; *v. infra,* note o.

[n] Moses ben Asher (the elder), a Massorete who flourished at Tiberias the
latter half of the ninth century, was the father of Aaron ben Moses ben Asher
(the younger) whose transcription of the Old Testament, written A. D. 922
but no longer extant, became the progenitor of succeeding generations of
codices. *V. infra,* p. 44, note ii.

[o] The twelve Prophets, Hosea — Malachi, are traditionally, although inappropriately, called Minor only because their books are shorter than the three
which, in the Jewish tradition, comprise the Major group: Isaiah, Jeremiah,
Ezekiel. The A. V. makes Daniel a fourth Major Prophet.

that cannot with confidence be assigned to any known Hebrew
Biblical codex. Claims of manuscripts of earlier date have from
time to time been made, but have all been shown to be inconsistent with the available evidence or based upon deliberate
falsification or forgery. The oldest known Hebrew manuscript
of any major portion of the Old Testament heretofore available
to editors of the Bible, is no earlier, it is to be remembered, than
the ninth century.

Until very recently, a single fragmentary Hebrew text discovered in Egypt has been recognized as a survival of far greater
antiquity — possibly from the late-Maccabean era.ᵖ This fragment consists of twenty-four lines, written on only one side of a
papyrus sheet, as if it were originally part of a roll. It contains
a variant form of the Deuteronomic Decalogue — with notable
departures from the Massoretic Text, many of them unique —
followed *immediately* by Deuteronomy vi. 4 (the šema' — שמע),
and is therefore not a relic of some Pentateuchal roll, but a
portion, in all probability, of a lectionary for ritual purposes.
This rare document, now at the library of the University of
Cambridge, is known, in acknowledgment of its donor, Mr. W.
L. Nash, into whose possession it came in 1901, as the Nash
Papyrus. Dating, it is at present believed, from the earlier half
of the first pre-Christian century, its antiquity is surpassed only
by four extant Greek Biblical fragments — a translation of a
portion of Deuteronomy¹⁴ — and, it may tentatively be held,
by some of the Hebrew and Aramaic Biblical scrolls and frag-

ᵖ Dating of the Nash Papyrus throws some light upon the uncertainties of
Hebrew palaeography. In 1903, it was "safely" assigned by S. A. Cook (in
Proceedings of the Society for Biblical Archaeology, XXV, Jan. 1903, p. 51) "to the
second century of this era . . . the first quarter of that century . . . the most
probable." In 1937, this date was lowered considerably by W. F. Albright
(*Journal of Biblical Literature*, LVI, p. 172) to "not later than about 100 B. C."
In *Bulletin of the American Schools of Oriental Research* for Feb. 1949 (p. 23, n. 65ᵃ)
Professor Albright raises the date about half a century; and more recently, in a
private communication, is kind enough to state that he is "now inclined to
date it [Nash Papyrus] rather after than before 100 B. C. but in no case after
about 50 B. C."

ments discovered allegedly by Bedouin, in 1947 and 1948, in a cave at 'Ain Fashkha near the northern end of the Dead Sea.

These ancient documents, some of which, including an Isaiah scroll, were acquired in 1948 by St. Mark's Syrian Orthodox Convent in the Old City of Jerusalem, and others of which, also containing a scroll of Isaiah, came the same year into the possession of Hebrew University on Mt. Scopus, Jerusalem,�q

�q Acquisition of these scrolls, variously reported by officials of the American Schools for Oriental Research, St. Mark's Syrian Orthodox Convent, and Hebrew University, remains something of a mystery [*cf.* John C. Trever, "The Discovery of the Scrolls," in *The Biblical Archaeologist,* XI, No. 3 (Sept. 1948), pp. 46–57; Mar Athanasius Y. Samuel, "The Purchase of the Jerusalem Scrolls," *ibid.,* XII, No. 2 (May 1949), pp. 26–31; E. L. Sukenik, מגילות גנוזות, Jerusalem, Bialik Foundation, 1948; H. L. Ginsberg, "The Hebrew University Scrolls from the Sectarian Cache," in *Bulletin of the American Schools of Oriental Research,* 112 (Dec. 1948), pp. 19, 20]. As first announced (over the telephone, Feb. 18, 1948) to Dr. Trever of the American Schools of Oriental Research by the late Father Butros Sowmy of St. Mark's, five of the MSS. had been found not by Bedouin in a cave but by himself in the course of cataloguing the books of the Syrian Orthodox Convent [Trever, *op. cit.,* p. 46]; and, as Professor Solomon Zeitlin of Dropsie College for Hebrew and Cognate Learning is at pains to point out [*Jewish Quarterly Review,* XXXIX, No. 4 (April 1949), p. 356], "Neither Sukenik nor the members of the American Schools of Oriental Research ever saw the Bedouin . . . They only heard about them from the Syrians." The three "rough-looking Bedouins" who are reported by the Syrian Archbishop-Metropolitan of Jerusalem and Transjordan to have "appeared with some very dirty rolls, several of them wrapped in dirty cloth with a black substance on them" [*The Biblical Archaeologist,* XII, No. 2, p. 27] were dismissed, through an "unfortunate error," without being brought into his presence, by one of his faithful subordinates who, unaware that they had been sent for and were eagerly awaited, "was firm and sent them away." Negotiations by Professor E. L. Sukenik, Director of the Museum of Jewish Antiquities, Hebrew University, for his purchase of scrolls were conducted — through the barbed-wire barricade with which in November 1947 Hebrew University was necessarily protected — with two merchants, one a Christian the other Mohammedan, both from Bethlehem. Not until some weeks after conclusion of this transaction through the barrier did one of the librarians at Hebrew University, recalling that two members of the staff had long since (either August or October) been shown five scrolls at the Syrian Convent, apparently companions of those at Hebrew University, disclose that fact for the first time to Dr. Sukenik [*cf.* G. Ernest Wright in *The Biblical Archaeologist,* XII, No. 2, p. 34]. The conflicting accounts of the "discovery"; the vagueness and meagerness of early reports of what had been found, reducing the scholarly

have, with but one dissenting voice,[15] been pronounced, first on palaeographic and subsequently on other grounds, of pre-Christian origin. The Isaiah scroll, apparently oldest of the St. Mark's collection, "cannot," according to a distinguished authority, "be later than about 100 B. C., and it probably belongs to the second half of the second century B. C."[16] Even earlier is the dating of this scroll by another eminent scholar, who, on the precarious basis of evidence provided by a reproduction of column thirty-three alone, refers it to "the first half of the second century B. C. E."[17] Palaeographic examination of the entire

---

world to "inferences"; the failure of reputable scholars, first, when "there was delivered unto [them] the book of the prophet Isaiah," to identify it at sight, then, whether for financial or other considerations, to arrange an expert investigation of the 'Ain Fashkha cave prior to its "unauthorized excavation" by two personages whose names, although admitted to be privately known, are still withheld from the public [*B. A. S. O. R.*, 114 (April 1949), p. 8]; neglect, so far, to have the ink of the scrolls submitted to chemical analysis; the inability of Father Yusef, of the Syrian Convent, after sleeping with a companion (a merchant) one August night in the cave, to rescue the only complete jar he said he found there because "it proved too heavy to carry in the heat" [*The Biblical Archaeologist*, XII, No. 2, p. 28]; the statement of Professor O. R. Sellers [*B. A. S. O. R.*, 114, p. 8] that "The full story of the cave has not yet come out" — these, together with reportorial overtones indicative of unfortunate tensions, combine to make, in the words of Professor G. Ernest Wright of McCormick Theological Seminary [*The Biblical Archaeologist*, XII, No. 2, p. 35], "a fantastic story, at first almost impossible to believe." Some extenuation of the procedures may be found in the fact that, at the time of appearance of the still unidentified Bedouin with their "find," Palestine was war-torn and Jerusalem a divided city.

However mysterious the transactions, St. Mark's acquired five MSS.: a nearly complete Isaiah, a Commentary on Habakkuk, two rolls of a sectarian manual of discipline, and, so far as can be ascertained until unrolling of the MS. is effected, a "Lamech Apocalypse" in Aramaic. Included in this acquisition were three fragments of Daniel: portions of i. 10–16, ii. 2–6, and iii. 23–30, the verses subsequent to ii. 3 being, as in the M. T., in Aramaic. Hebrew University purchased six MSS.: a fragmentary and mutilated Isaiah (portions of the last twenty chapters and fragments of earlier chapters), four rolls of "Thanksgiving Psalms," and one to which Professor Sukenik has given the title "War of the Sons of Light with the Sons of Darkness." Publication of these documents, now in progress, includes, to date, besides Sukenik's previously mentioned מגילות גנוזות, only *The Dead Sea Scrolls of St. Mark's Monastery*, Vol. I, New Haven, 1950, ed. by Millar Burrows with the assistance of W. H. Brownlee and John C. Trever.

manuscript prompts a third student of the St. Mark's Isaiah to assign it, with some circumspection, to "about 125–100 B. C." and to identify it, "with the possible exception of the Greek fragments of Deuteronomy," as *the oldest existing manuscript of the Bible in any language.*"[18] Somewhat greater antiquity may, however, with further palaeographic study, have to be conceded either to the mutilated Isaiah scroll at Hebrew University — closer, it appears, to the Massoretic Text than the St. Mark's Isaiah — or, more probably, to sundry Pentateuchal fragments, possibly of considerably earlier date, recovered, not through Bedouin and Syrian intermediaries but laboriously and painstakingly from the floor of the cave at 'Ain Fashkha, by competent archaeological excavators, in February 1949.[19] Of these precious relics of perhaps two millenia ago, some fifty-nine, written in Hebrew, include a single fragment of Genesis, two of Judges, several of Deuteronomy; and four — in that earlier Phoenician script from which the Hebrew characters were developed[20] — preserve sections of the central and basic portion of Leviticus known as the Code of Holiness.[21] Should these four Levitical fragments prove to be earliest of all surviving Biblical documents, or the claim of either one or both of the 'Ain Fashkha Isaiah scrolls to pre-Christian origin be securely established,[r] the fact unfortunately would still remain that,

---

[r] Evidence supplementary to the purely palaeographical in dating these Biblical documents is, at the present limited stage of ancient Hebrew palaeography, particularly desirable. Opposition to the Hellenistic dating comes primarily from Professor Zeitlin who, maintaining "the very first attempt at a commentary" to have been Targum Jonathan, produced after the second destruction of the Temple, A. D. 70, vigorously contends that "it is absolutely certain that the Commentary on the Book of Habakkuk, found in the . . . cave, could not have been written during the Second Commonwealth" in Hellenistic times; and who, suggesting the "likelihood that [all] these Scrolls came from the *geniza* storehouse," their "discovery" at 'Ain Fashkha being a "hoax," asserts without reservation that "It is certain [the scrolls] do not belong to the pre-Christian period" [*cf. J. Q. R.*, XXXIX, pp. 359, 360 and XLI, pp. 1–58; *cf.*, further, Joseph Reider, "The Dead Sea Scrolls," in *J. Q. R.*, XLI (July 1950), p. 70: "the most likely date for these manuscripts might be the third or fourth Christian century."]. In support of the Hellenistic dating, much has been made of the age of the jars in which, presumably for long

fragments excepted, for editors of all but one of the Old Testament Books — Isaiah — no Hebrew manuscript earlier than the ninth century is yet available.

The serious critical problems[22] raised by this relative "modernity" of the Hebrew record of ancient historical events — such as the Exodus from Egypt, which occurred some two thousand years previously — are rendered less crucial by the testimony of the surviving translations of the Old Testament, especially those into Greek, the manuscripts of which were

---

centuries, the 'Ain Fashkha scrolls — like the documents mentioned at Jer. xxxii. 14 — were protected from deterioration. Such "urn-burial" of MSS. being a well-attested practice, it need cause no surprise [*cf. Assumption of Moses*, in R. H. Charles, *Apocrypha and Pseudepigrapha of the Old Testament*, Oxford, 1913, Vol. II, p. 415; R. de Vaux, "La grotte des manuscrits hébreux," in *Revue Biblique*, Vol. 56, No. 4 (Oct. 1949), pp. 591, 592; Frank M. Cross, Jr., "The Scrolls in the Hebrew University," in *The Biblical Archaeologist*, Vol. XII, No. 2, p. 38]. What is surprising, however, is the extraordinary shape of the protective jars — two whole specimens of which are now a prize of the Museum of Jewish Antiquities, Hebrew University — their profiles being unduplicated by those of any known vessel of any period of Hellenistic ceramics [cp. de Vaux, *op. cit.*, p. 588 with C. C. McCown, *Tell en-Nasbeh, etc.*, Berkeley and New Haven, 1947, *passim*]. Father de Vaux concludes from this circumstance [*op. cit.*, p. 595] that the jars — of which there were originally, it appears from the shards, at least fifty — were all manufactured at the same time, in a single pottery, and were expressly designed for the purpose of safely concealing a library among which the 'Ain Fashkha scrolls were numbered. The date of these jars, assigned by the learned Dominican scholar to the second century B. C., or "à la rigueur du début du Ier siècle" [*op. cit.*, p. 596], is held to establish the time subsequent to which none of the concealed rolls could have been written. Justification for this conclusion resides precariously enough in the profusion of the unusual receptacles and the assumption that they were especially ordered for a specific function on a particular occasion in an ascertainable epoch. Between any given vessel and its contents there need obviously be no chronological connection. Late medieval MSS. could well enough have been sealed into an early Hellenistic urn, had one survived the intervening centuries. Any number of MSS., ancient or medieval, could have been deposited in specially prepared containers of Roman origin. For storing away the eleven MSS. so far recovered, only two of the supposedly Hellenistic jars need have survived, each being proportioned to accommodate comfortably at least six documents of the size of St. Mark's Isaiah. Fifty jars thus designed and thus utilized as a documentary depository — whether of Hellenistic or post-Christian manufacture — would have housed some three hundred rolls, a collection sufficiently comprehensive to awaken incredulity.

transcribed several centuries earlier than any extant Hebrew codex. Of the several Greek versions, the translation most important in the transmission of the Scriptural text — the earliest — is known as the Septuagint.[23] Comprised of both the canonical and the apocryphal books of the Old Testament, and produced during the third and second centuries B. C., the Septuagint has survived in well over three hundred parchment or vellum manuscripts, none of which, however, is of pre-Christian times. Some thirty of these codices, the earliest, are uncials:[s] manuscripts the characters of which are all large letters detached one from another. The best known exemplars are bound together with the Greek New Testament,[t] in magnificent vellum codices, now most treasured among rare library items. None is of earlier date than the middle of the fourth century.

Septuagintal Greek uncial manuscripts of the *fourth* century are exactly two: one, known since 1481[u] to have been in the Vatican Library, and therefore called Codex Vaticanus;[v] the

[s] Latin, *uncialis*, inch-high (from *uncia*, an inch), with reference to letters, *large*; known also as majuscules. These date from the fourth to the tenth centuries. Manuscripts of later date (ninth — fifteenth centuries) in which the letters are smaller and tend to join together, are called cursives or minuscules. In some manuscripts these two types are merged in a transitional script, Roman Half-uncial, as in the MS. of St. Hilary on the Trinity (written prior to A. D. 509) at St. Peter's, Rome.

[t] MSS. of N. T. are considered separately; *v. infra*, pp. 21 ff.

[u] MS. Vat. Gr. 1209. Thus first indexed in the manuscript catalogue of manuscripts in the Vatican Library in 1481. It is not known whence this codex came nor how it entered the Vatican collection. Removed for a few years to Paris — a spoil of Napoleon's wars — during which time it was examined by Johann Leonhard Hug, it was restored to the Vatican in 1815.

[v] Greek Biblical uncials were at first identified by descriptive titles, usually determined by location or ownership. Subsequently, as the scientific spirit pervaded humanistic studies, these titles were replaced, in 1908, by C. R. Gregory (following J. J. Wetstein) with capital letters of the alphabet — at first those of the English alphabet, then, these exhausted, those of the Greek. Further identification of the uncials, as continued by Ernst von Dobschütz and now by H. Lietzmann, is by a number the first digit of which is zero (minuscules are designated by Arabic numbers). For the Codex Sinaiticus, when it was given its distinguishing letter, nothing other than *aleph* (א), the first letter of the Hebrew alphabet, seemed appropriate. Most unfortunately,

other, discovered by Constantin Tischendorf, just over a century ago, in 1844, at the Greek Catholic monastery of St. Catherine on Mt. Sinai, and therefore known as Codex Sinaiticus.[w] Both of these codices, too precious for any other than a scholar's expert hands, have been made conveniently available for study in facsimile editions.[24] The Vaticanus was long inaccessible to scholars.[x] Today, the codex, dismembered for purposes of reproduction, and each pair of conjoint folios permanently mounted between sheets of glass, is available to qualified scholars.[y] Codex Vaticanus was written by three different scribes, and was twice corrected, once by a contemporary "proof-reader" [$\delta\iota o\rho\vartheta\acute{\omega}\tau\eta\varsigma$] and, again, by a scribe of the tenth-eleventh century. Codex

---

MSS. of the O. T., considered separately from those of the N. T. in the earlier periods of modern Biblical scholarship, were assigned letters already used for N. T. codices. In consequence we now confusingly employ at least seventeen letters (English and Greek) to identify entirely distinct manuscripts, the Septuagintal and those of the N. T. In only four major instances (ℵ, A, B, and C), and in the one minor case of Codex O, where the Septuagint and the N. T. are embodied in a common codex, does this confusion vanish. A further complication arises from identical designation by the Smithsonian Institution of two unrelated MSS. [Θ and W] as Washingtonianus I, and two others [*1219* and I (the ninth letter)] as Washingtonianus II. This study attempts to avoid confusion by distinguishing with italics the symbols for purely Septuagintal MSS. (Greek capital letters herein used as symbols of LXX MSS., are underlined). Letters used as N. T. symbols are in roman. ℵ, A, B, C, referring to both major Biblical divisions, are printed in type of a distinguishing font. [There is still another systematic method of identification, ignored here, promulgated by H. von Soden in his *Die Schriften des Neuen Testaments*, Berlin, 1902]. No such system identifies Hebrew MSS.

[w] For the story of its discovery *v. infra*, p. 15.

[x] When, in the middle of the nineteenth century, the Vatican Library had so far relaxed its previous policy as to permit inspection of this celebrated codex, scholars had to promise merely to collate difficult passages and not to copy the text before them. In 1844, the Vaticanus was available for nine hours to von Muralt. In 1845, the English scholar, Tregelles, after his pockets were searched and all writing materials removed, was allowed to examine the manuscript. Tischendorf was permitted to inspect the codex on three occasions: in 1843, for six hours; in 1866, for eighteen hours; and again in 1866, for eighteen hours. Naturally enough, when the Library authorities discovered that their irreproachable guest had so far forgotten himself as to transcribe some twenty pages, the privilege of collation was straightway withdrawn.

[y] Codex Vaticanus was recently made available to the present writer with the utmost courtesy.

Vaticanus, formerly thought to contain the entire Bible, Septuagint and New Testament both complete,[z] though originally no doubt unabridged, now lacks, of the Septuagint, almost all of Genesis, and parts of Psalms and of II Samuel; and, of the New Testament, five entire books and a portion of a sixth. [25]

Codex Sinaiticus, the major portion of which became, in 1933, one of the glories of the British Museum,[aa] was written by four copyists. It contains the New Testament complete, but has unfortunately suffered serious loss and mutilation in its Septuagintal portion. Some of its readings are unique. Corrections, in hands of the fifth to seventh centuries, probably made at Caesarea, the library of which contained as its chief treasure the *Hexapla* of Origen, [26] are of high critical value. A corrector's note at the end of Esther (at Leipzig) reads, in translation, as follows: "Collated with an exceedingly ancient copy which was corrected by the hand of the holy martyr Pamphilus; and at the end of the same ancient book, which began with the first book of Kings and ended with Esther, there is some such subscription as this, in the hand of the same martyr; *Copied and corrected from the Hexapla of Origen corrected by himself. Antoninus the Confessor collated it; I, Pamphilus, corrected the volume in prison through the great favor and enlargement of God; and if it may be said without offence it is not easy to find a copy comparable to this copy.* The same ancient copy differed from the present volume in respect to certain proper names." [27]

The discovery of Codex Sinaiticus, miraculously plucked out from the burning, is one of the most romantic tales of Biblical scholarship. When first recognized by the astonished Tischen-

---

[z] This error has the persistence of a superstition. See, for example, Ernest Sutherland Bates, who as recently as 1937, in his *Biography of the Bible*, cites the Vaticanus (reproduction facing p. 24) as "The oldest complete manuscript of the New Testament," a statement which might well have been made in connection with his account of Codex Sinaiticus.

[aa] In the British Museum, 347 folios. In Leipzig, at the University Library, 43 leaves, deposited by Tischendorf in 1845, are bound up to form Codex Friderico-Augustanus. In Leningrad, at the Society of Ancient Literature, there is a single additional leaf, and, in book bindings, fragments of two others. See Table C.

dorf, discarded leaves of this manuscript of the Septuagint (one hundred and twenty-nine of them) lay in a basket with other waste papers about to be used by the pious custodians of ecclesiastical property at St. Catherine as fuel for their fire. Two similar basketfuls, so Tischendorf was informed, had already been consumed. Where there is no vision, manuscripts, as surely as people, perish!

Forty-three of these vellum leaves providentially delivered from the flames, were secured by their scholarly rescuer for himself; but his "too lively satisfaction" having aroused suspicions as to the value of the discarded folios, the monks withheld the remaining eighty-six. His injunction on the monks to take "religious care" of these leaves, and of any other such Biblical relics as might come to light, had for Tischendorf, it may be certain, none of the ironic overtones possibly conveyed to the twentieth-century reader.

Upon his return from Mt. Sinai to Saxony, Tischendorf presented to the King, Friedrich Augustus, his precious forty-three folios, of which he immediately published an edition in photolithographic reproduction.

Revisiting the monastery on Mt. Sinai in 1853, Tischendorf failed in his endeavor to obtain possession of the eighty-six leaves he had previously been denied, or to unearth further portions of the codex. Six years later, however, his third visit to St. Catherine proved more fruitful. This time, although he carried a letter of introduction from the Tsar, it was only by "an entirely fortuitous circumstance" that, as he was planning his departure, he was shown "a bulky kind of volume, wrapped up in red cloth," consisting not only of those eighty-six leaves which, fifteen years previously, he had rescued from the waste basket, but of two hundred and sixty-one additional leaves, in the same script and without doubt from the same codex, containing parts of the Old Testament, the apocryphal Epistle of Barnabas, a part of the apocryphal *Shepherd* of Hermas, and the New Testament in its entirety. This volume of three hundred and forty-seven folios was subsequently, in 1869, through Tischendorf's instrumentality, presented by the monastery to its titular head, the Tsar. Thus this codex, shorn of a third of its original contents, reached the Imperial Library of St. Petersburg. Thus this codex, rivalled only by its contemporary at the Vatican, came subsequently into the possession of the government of the Union of Socialist Soviet Republics, which, after an abortive attempt to effect its sale in the United States for one million American dollars, finally consented, with no overt indication of reluctance, to sell it, in 1933, to the British Museum at half that price — £100,000. This sum was raised partly by the British people themselves, whose contribution in pennies and sixpences greatly exceeded the total required. Neither party to this extraordinary transaction has ever evinced dissatisfaction with its conclusion. It is thus by a curious irony of history that the British people owe to the Russian Revolution their possession of a Biblical codex than which none, not even that of the Vatican, is of greater antiquity or authority.

Septuagintal Greek uncial manuscripts surviving from the *fifth* century are six.[bb] Of these, the most nearly complete is the magnificent Codex Alexandrinus[cc] which preserves all of the Old Testament, except half a leaf of Genesis and portions of I Samuel and Psalms, and includes in its nearly complete Apocrypha the four Maccabean books — the second and third of which are lacking in both Sinaiticus and Vaticanus and the fourth of which also is wanting in Vaticanus. Before the Psalms there are inserted two non-Biblical items: the Epistle of Athanasius (*ob.* A. D. 373) to Marcellinus on the Psalter; a summary by Eusebius (*ob.* A. D. 340) of the contents of the Psalms. Following the Psalms there is an additional psalm (numbered 151) found in other early manuscripts, and a number of "canticles" — Biblical excerpts for liturgical purposes. This justly famous manuscript, like the Sinaiticus, contains all the Books

[bb] Possibly seven; *v. infra*, p. 19, note ff.

[cc] Codex A, at the British Museum. Presented to Charles I in 1627 by Cyril Lucar, Patriarch first of Alexandria, later of Constantinople. Traditionally held, with some palaeographic justification, to have come from Alexandria, whence its name. It was written, it appears, by five scribes.

of the New Testament[dd] and also, a great rarity, the apocryphal Epistle of Clement. The apocryphal Psalms of Solomon were once, as its table of contents shows, appended to the New Testament. Owing to inaccessibility of the Vaticanus, and to ignorance of the existence of the Sinaiticus, Codex Alexandrinus was the oldest available manuscript upon which, until recent times, Biblical editors could, and did, base their work.

Another fifth-century uncial Greek manuscript of the Septuagint is Codex Ephraemi (Codex C), once the property of Catherine de' Medici, now at the Bibliothèque Nationale. Its sadly mutilated Septuagintal portion — sixty-four leaves — consists now of parts only of Job, Ecclesiastes, Wisdom, Ecclesiasticus, and Song of Songs.[28] Like the three previously mentioned codices, it contains the New Testament — parts, at least, of every Book except two.[29] No ancient codex other than these four — B, ℵ, A and C — unites the New Testament with the Septuagint.[ee]

Codex Ephraemi is a palimpsest; that is, a manuscript from which the original writing has been sufficiently erased to permit its use for a second text, which sometimes, though by no means always, is written, for greater clarity, at right-angles to the first script. This procedure is indicative not only of the scarcity or value of parchment in medieval times, but in some instances, alas, of the cultural deficiency of the later of the two scribes. The obliterated text is occasionally, from a modern point of view, more valuable than that which is written over it. Such is the case of Codex *rescriptus* Ephraemi, whose precious fifth-century Biblical text was rubbed out to be supplanted in the twelfth century by a Greek translation from the writings of the fourth-century Syrian saint, Ephraem of Edessa, whose name the Codex now bears. Fortunately, vestiges of the erased writing of a palimpsest can frequently be detected by close scrutiny of

[dd] Lacking parts of three Books; *v. infra*, p. 22, and Table C.

[ee] With the insignificant exception of the fragmentary sixth-century Codex Dublinensis Rescriptus (Codex O). *Cf.* Table C and footnote v, *supra*, p. 13.

the document, or can be restored to legibility through infra-red or ultra-violet photography or by means of chemical treatment. With respect to ancient codices, it may perhaps be said, it is better to mar than to burn.

The four remaining Greek uncial manuscripts of the fifth century in which parts of the Septuagint are preserved are the British Museum Genesis (Codex *D*), rescued in shrunken and defaced condition from the fire which destroyed the Cottonian library in 1731; the Codex Ambrosianus at Milan (Codex *F*); the Codex Sarravianus (Codex *G*) distributed at Leyden, Paris, and Leningrad; and Codex Δ, at the Bodleian Library, consisting of fragments of the apocryphal Bel and the Dragon.

From the Septuagintal codices included in Table A two others of early date are especially noteworthy. One is the Codex Marchalianus (Codex *Q*), a sixth-century vellum manuscript of Egyptian provenance, now at the Vatican Library. It contains the Minor Prophets. The other is Codex Basiliano-Vaticanus (Codex *N*), an eighth or ninth-century work in two volumes, one of which, as its name indicates, is at the Vatican, and the second of which, formerly known as Codex Venetus (Codex *V*), is at St. Mark's, Venice. It contains the greater part of the Old Testament, and, in the Apocrypha, is rivalled by Codex Alexandrinus alone in having all four of the Maccabean books. Although seriously mutilated, this manuscript was used, together with Codex Vaticanus, as the basis of the Roman edition of the Septuagint issued in 1587.

Recent acquisitions of the Smithsonian Institution (Freer Collection) have enriched the United States with two considerable Septuagintal items on early vellum. Codex Washingtonianus I (Codex Θ), containing Deuteronomy and Joshua — all that remains of what was originally a complete Pentateuch — is a beautifully executed production, probably of the fifth century.[ff] Codex Washingtonianus II (Codex *1219*), of the sixth

---

[ff] H. A. Sanders, *The Old Testament Manuscripts in the Freer Collection*, Part I, New York, 1910, p. 13: "written not later than the fifth century, and I am inclined to date it in the first half of the century." Sir Frederic Kenyon, *Our*

or seventh century, consists now of one hundred and seven
fragmentary leaves of the Psalter.[gg]

No vellum Septuagints, as we have seen, ante-date the Sinaiticus and the Vaticanus of the fourth century. Papyrus copies,
mere fragments though most of them be, happily carry us back
still farther. From the second half of the third century come the
twenty-seven leaves of portions of Genesis in the Chester Beatty
Collection at London (P 962)[hh] and the parts of thirty-three
leaves — Amos i. 10 to Malachi iv. 4 — in the Freer Collection
at the Smithsonian Institution (Papyrus X; Freer Gk. MS. V).
From the first half of the same century, the third, come fragments of thirty-three leaves of Isaiah (P 965; Chester Beatty
VII), and fifty imperfect leaves (twenty-one of which are at
Princeton University) of portions of Ezekiel, Daniel and Esther
(P 967, 968; Ch. B. IX, X). Even earlier are the parts of fifty
leaves (of which twenty-eight are in a good state of preservation)
of portions of Numbers and Deuteronomy in the Chester Beatty
Collection (No. VI; P 963)[ii] which, the palaeographical evidence indicates, cannot have been written later than the middle
of the second century. The volume in which these pages were
originally bound — apparently, on bibliographic grounds, of
one hundred and eight leaves — is thus the earliest known
specimen of a papyrus codex;[30] and, with one exception, is the
earliest of surviving Septuagintal manuscripts.

The exception is comprised of four mutilated fragments of a
papyrus roll, consisting altogether of some fifteen scattered verses
of Deuteronomy.[31] For many centuries part of the wrapping of
a mummy, these fragments,[jj] discovered in 1936, are now a

Bible and the Ancient Manuscripts, New York, 1941, p. 73: sixth century. The
Smithsonian Institution's label reads fourth or fifth century, but without
sufficient justification for the earlier date.

[gg] Pss. cxlii. 5–cli. 6 are in a ninth-century hand.

[hh] Papyri are designated by number, preceded by P, as in the catalogue
initiated by Alfred Rahlfs and continued by Kappler.

[ii] The University of Michigan possesses a few fragments of the codex from
which these leaves are detached. See Table E.

[jj] Rylands Papyrus Greek 458; Rahlfs: P 957.

prize exhibit at the John Rylands Library in Manchester, England. The fine book-hand in which they are written, preserving for us the only extant pre-Christian Greek evidence for the text of the Old Testament, is confidently assigned by competent palaeographic authority to the second century B. C. [32] These fugitive relics of an ancient culture, like the recently discovered Hebrew Old Testament fragments, [33] are perhaps a century or more older than any considerable manuscript, in any language, of any part of the Bible; and they take us back unexpectedly to Egypt, to a period not more than a single century removed from the time when, at Alexandria, as tradition holds, the legendary "Seventy" made the first translation into Greek of the Hebrew Old Testament.

* * *

The extant manuscripts of the New Testament, in the original Greek, and on vellum, were written down at a time much closer to the events they record than was any surviving manuscript, Hebrew or Greek, of the Old Testament. There is, none the less, a considerable interval between the events of New Testament history and the earliest known recording.

The two New Testament vellum manuscripts of greatest antiquity, codices Vaticanus and Sinaiticus, as we have noted in connection with the Septuagint, date from the middle of the fourth century. The Vatican Codex (B) [34] lacks five entire books — I and II Timothy, Titus, Philemon, and Revelation — and of Hebrews it wants the closing portion, ix. 14–xiii. 25. [kk] It is evident from the disordered numbering of sections throughout the Pauline Epistles in the Vaticanus that, in its archetype, Hebrews occupied a unique position between Galatians and Ephesians — a peculiarity of Sahidic (Upper Egyptian) texts. The order in which the Pauline Epistles actually appear in this codex (and also in Codex ℵ) is that adopted by the Council

---

[kk] Revelation, and the end of Hebrews, have been supplied by a fifteenth-century hand.

of Laodicea, A. D. 363.[35] Hebrews, in this arrangement, instead
of following, as in the Received Text,[36] the Pauline Epistles, is
placed between II Thessalonians and I Timothy. For these, and
other considerations, there is a temptation to locate the origin
of the Vaticanus at Alexandria; but the evidence is inconclusive,
and there are grounds for thinking Caesarea equally probable.

Codex Sinaiticus, in its New Testament portion, provides the
earliest complete transcript of the five Books — I and II Timothy, Titus, Philemon, and Revelation — and of the fragment of
Hebrews which are wanting in its noble contemporary the
Vaticanus. The textual authority of so complete and ancient a
New Testament is presumably very great. Sinaiticus is especially impressive where in many characteristic readings it sub-
stantiates the text of the Vatican manuscript. Codex א, however,
"so lends its grave authority, now to one and now to another
[witness], as to convince us more than ever of the futility of
seeking to derive the genuine text of the New Testament from
any one copy, however ancient, and on the whole, trust-
worthy."[37]

Two fifth-century Biblical Greek uncials previously mentioned
with reference to the Septuagint contain a major portion of the
New Testament too. Codex Alexandrinus fails to be a complete
New Testament only through mutilation of three of the twenty-
seven Books — the Gospels according to Matthew and John, and
the second Epistle to the Corinthians.[38] Codex A shares with
Codex א alone among the early uncials the distinction of having
preserved the Book of Revelation in its entirety. It is unique in its
preservation of the apocryphal First Epistle of Clement, of
which it contains all but a single leaf.[11] Codex Ephraemi (C), in
the surviving one hundred and forty-five leaves of its New
Testament portion, rescues for the Biblical scholar parts of
twenty-five books — about two-thirds of the New Testament

---

[11] Codex A contains also a small apocryphal fragment, long held to be a
unique memento of a Second Epistle of Clement. This fragment, however, is
neither unique nor an epistle, but a moral exhortation or homily, as is shown
by its conclusion (lacking in A), now known from the MS. discovered in 1875
in a monastery at Constantinople by Archbishop Bryennios of Nicomedia.

altogether.[39] Two books, II Thessalonians and II John, have disappeared entirely.

Three more Greek uncial manuscripts of parts of the New Testament only have survived from the fifth century. These three, containing at no time any part of the Septuagint, are known as codices Bezae, Borgianus, and Washingtonianus I (W).[mm] Codex Bezae (D) — at one time the property of a monastery at Clermont; subsequently in the possession of Calvin's biographer, Theodore Beza, by whom it was presented in 1581 to the library of Cambridge University — is the earliest known example of a bilingual Biblical text. Corresponding to the original Greek of the left-hand pages of the opened volume is an Old Latin translation on those to the right. Codex Bezae is the best witness, and the oldest, among Greek manuscripts to the so-called "Western" text.[nn] It contains the four Gospels, Acts, and (in Latin only) three inconsiderable fragments of III John. Codex Borgianus (T), a Greek and Coptic bilingual text at the Vatican Library (College of the Propaganda Collection) consists now only of fragments (179 verses) of the Gospels according to Luke and John. Codex Washingtonianus I (W), found within recent years in Egypt, is now in the Freer Collection at the Smithsonian Institution. This important uncial manuscript, probably written in the land where it was discovered, consists of the four Gospels[oo] in the "Western" order: Matthew, John,

---

[mm] This MS. is possibly of the late fourth century. Of twenty-odd New Testament Greek uncials from the sixth-tenth centuries, the most important are: Basiliensis (E), Beratinus (Φ), Boernerianus (G_3), Claromontanus (D_2), Cyprius (K), Dublinensis (Z), Koridethianus (Θ), Laudianus (E_2), Laurensis (Ψ), Nitriensis (R), Petropolitanus (Π), Porphyrianus (P_2), Purpureus Petropolitanus (N), Regius (L), Rossanensis (Σ), Sangallensis (Δ), Sinopensis (O), Tischendorfianus (Λ), Washingtonianus II (I), Zacynthius (Ξ). See Table C.

[nn] *V. infra*, p. 150; also B. F. Westcott and F. J. A. Hort, *The New Testament in the Original Greek*, New York, 1881, *passim*. Codex D is apparently the MS. η quoted in the margin of the first Greek N. T. with critical apparatus, published by Robert Étienne in 1550. It was probably used some four years earlier, also, at the Council of Trent.

[oo] Complete except for Mk. xv. 13–38, and Jn. xiv. 25–xvi. 7. Mk. v. 31–xvi. 8 reflects the "Caesarean" text; *v. infra*, p. 150.

Luke, Mark. In some of its readings it is unique.[pp] In others it gives the oldest Biblical Greek corroboration of many readings known previously only in translations or in quotations by the Fathers.

The evidence of the Versions and of Patristic quotations, incomplete though it be, is frequently regarded as of greater textual authority than the early Greek uncials. The Old Latin translations in particular, repeatedly cited by the Fathers, indicate the existence, as far back as the second century, of New Testament texts which, in many passages, must have been different from those of the oldest surviving Greek vellum codices.[qq] Of such earlier Greek texts, long thought to be utterly lost, several interesting fragments have in recent years been brought to light. These are all papyri and, for the most part, appear to have been written in the third century. The most considerable of these fragile documents (P 46) consists of eighty-six leaves, fifty-six of which are in the Chester Beatty Collection,[40] and thirty of which belong now to the University of Michigan.[41] A second contemporary Chester Beatty papyrus (P 45) — parts of thirty leaves — preserves scattered remains of the Gospels and Acts. Another Chester Beatty papyrus (P 47), although only ten leaves, with one to four lines missing from the top of each page, is remarkable in that it consists of the oldest known text of Revelation (ix. 10–xvii. 2), which, it will be recalled, is not included in Codex Vaticanus. Greatest in antiquity, however, and therefore of extreme interest and value, is a single mutilated leaf from a papyrus codex (P 52; Rylands Papyrus 457) both sides of which contain verses from the Gospel according to John.[42] This tattered fragment from Egypt, first published[43] in 1935, is now in the possession of the John Rylands Library. Its date, confidently placed by competent authority in

---

[pp] *V. infra*, p. 326, note 19; p. 143, note t; p. 285, note tt.

[qq] Of the thirty-eight known vellum MSS. of the Old Latin Version, twenty-eight are copies of the Gospels; none contains all of the N. T. None is earlier than the fourth century.

the first half of the second century, sets it apart as the earliest known copy, in any language, of any part of the New Testament. [44] It comes, a thing of shreds and patches, to the assistance of twentieth-century Biblical scholarship from a time which can be but little more than a century after the Crucifixion. If at the time this fragment was written it was read in Upper Egypt where it was found, it testifies to the wide diffusion of early Christian doctrine.

Further back in time, and nearer to the events recorded in the New Testament, the evidence of roll or codex, on vellum or papyrus, does not go. We now turn our attention, accordingly, from the history of the transmission of the text of the Bible — the Old Testament as well as the New — to the much more exacting but rewarding study of the nature of that text.

CHAPTER II

The Nature of the Old Testament Text

"exceedingly zealous for the traditions of my fathers."
Galatians i. 14

THE Old Testament gives literary expression to a culture essentially Oriental, reflecting, particularly in the Pentateuch, a literary tradition characteristic of the early civilizations which in pre-Patriarchal times spread out from the Mesopotamian Valley. The Western Asia in which Abraham sojourned was dominated culturally, if not politically, by the powerful Babylonian Empire. Long before his day, and for centuries after, the established international language of commerce, of diplomacy, and of an extensive literature was Babylonian; and the hand in which that language was written was the very ancient and but recently deciphered script known as cuneiform.[a] The oldest portions of the Scriptures, if they were committed to

[a] Cuneiform, invented by the Sumerians, was used by the Semitic Babylonians as far back as 4500 B. C. Since 1841, when Longperier climaxed the work of Grotefend, Burnouf, Lassen, Rawlinson, *et al.* on the trilingual cuneiform inscriptions of Persia by producing the first modern translation of a short Assyrian text, such progress has been made in Assyriology that a vast body of cuneiform documents, some of which possess Biblical significance, has been made available in English translation. *Cf.* A. J. Booth, *The Discovery and Decipherment of the Trilingual Cuneiform Inscriptions*, London, 1902; also William R. Harper (ed.), *Ancient Records of Assyria and Babylonia*, Chicago, n. d.; and Morris Jastrow, *Hebrew and Babylonian Traditions*, New York, 1914.

writing prior to the introduction of the Phoenician alphabet into Palestine,[b] must have been originally in the vernacular Hebrew expressed in cuneiform characters;[c] and even in their present familiar form exhibit a text derivative, it occasionally appears, from a prototype influenced by the language and written in the script of ancient Babylon.[d] The Old Testament, emerging from the cultural isolation in which it long appeared to stand, is now seen to be significantly associated with the general history and literature of the ancient Oriental world; and the Bible — especially in its earliest Books — acquires an historical and sociological enrichment if viewed in the light of its reflection, however qualified, of Babylonian culture.[1]

At what time and in what manner cuneiform was superseded by the much more manageable North Semitic[e] consonantal alphabet known as Phoenician has yet to be determined. This script, from which our own is ultimately derived, was employed in its early form by Phoenicians, Samaritans and Hebrews alike. Alphabetic Hebrew writing, in ink, using the twenty-two Phoenician consonants, was commonly used in Canaan and the surrounding territories as far back as the fourteenth century B. C.;[f] and recent discoveries in Israelite Palestine establish the

[b] In the sixteenth or seventeenth century B. C.; perhaps even earlier. *Cf.* William F. Albright, *From the Stone Age to Christianity*, Baltimore, 1940, p. 11.

[c] *Ibid.*, p. 12; also A. H. Sayce, Introduction to H. E. Naville's *Discovery of the Book of the Law under King Josiah*, London, 1911, p. viii. Closely allied to Hebrew, the Semitic language of Canaan — as is now well known from the Tel-el-Amarna tablets, from inscriptions on Canaanite seals, and from the documents discovered by Claude F. A. Schaeffer in 1929 at Ras Shamra — was likewise in some early instances written in cuneiform.

[d] Sayce, *ibid.*, p. ix. In Gen. xiv. 14, for example, the word ḤĀNĪKH (חניך), used here, and here only in the O. T., to denote Abraham's bodyguard, is merely a transliteration of a Babylonian word of identical meaning in a cuneiform document found at Taanach, near Megiddo, Palestine.

[e] North Semitic, indigenous to the region north of Arabia, from Syria on the west to the upper Valley of the Euphrates on the east, reached out as far as Asia Minor, Phoenicia, Palestine, Moab, Egypt, North Africa, and the chief cities of the Eastern Mediterranean shores and islands. *Cf.* G. A. Cooke, *A Text-book of North Semitic Inscriptions*, Oxford, 1903, p. xvii.

[f] *Cf.* C. F. A. Schaeffer, *The Cuneiform Texts of Ras Shamra-Ugarit*, London, 1939, p. 57. Canaanites and Phoenicians, so far as language and cultural tradi-

fact that writing was sufficiently practised in Shiloh in the time of David (tenth century B. C.) for the King to require a staff of secretaries. [2] A Hebrew inscription of five lines in these Phoenician characters, discovered in 1922 on the sarcophagus of Ahiram, King of Byblos, though dating from the twelfth or thirteenth century B. C., is of less interest to the Biblical scholar than the considerably later Aramaic record, in the same script, of the war of Mesha, King of Moab, with Ahab, King of Israel. The "Moabite Stone," now in the Louvre, upon which this record is inscribed, dates from the early years of the ninth century B. C.[g] A more recent example of this early form of Hebrew writing was cut — about 700 B. C.— into the wall of the rock-hewn tunnel at Jerusalem which conveys water from the pool of Siloam. This aqueduct was bored from either end; and the juncture of the two opposed excavations, surprisingly accurate for that epoch, is commemorated by an inscription. The same script is found also on Jewish coins from the Maccabean period to the Bar Kochba Rebellion of the second century, and in the Samaritan Pentateuch,[h] of which, however, no copy is known of earlier date than the tenth century.

Palestinian Jews, after the Babylonian exile (597–539 B. C.) were undoubtedly a bilingual people, speaking and writing not only their native Hebrew but also Aramaic,[i] the closely related tongue which, by that period, had become the principal lan-

---

tion went, were one people. *Cf.* William F. Albright, *Archaeology and the Religion of Israel*, Baltimore, 1942, p. 68.

[g] *Cf.* II Kgs. i. 1 and iii. 4 ff. See Mark Lidzbarski, "Eine Nachprüfung der Mesa-inschrift," in *Ephemeris für semitische Epigraphik*, I. 1 ff., Giessen, 1902. Shortly after discovery of the Moabite Stone in 1868 at Dibon, in Moab, east of the Dead Sea, the disturbed Bedouin of the district attempted to prevent its removal. By the drastic technique of heating and afterwards cracking the stone with a shower of cold water, they shattered it into numerous fragments; but, with the aid of a facsimile — a squeeze — which fortunately had been previously taken, nearly all of the text has been properly reassembled.

[h] The Samaritans, in their Pentateuch, retained and cherished the Phoenician script, from which they have never departed, as one of the evidences that theirs was the true faith. *V. infra*, p. 157, note c.

[i] *Cf.* II Kgs. xviii. 26.

guage of Syria and Mesopotamia and even of Jewish colonists as far removed as southern Egypt. From the old Phoenician consonantal alphabet the Aramaic scribes had meanwhile, by natural modifications, developed a characteristic script of their own. Abandoning the early form of Phoenician writing, the Aramaic-speaking Jews gradually adapted the newer Aramaic script to Hebrew itself, creating, in the course of the adaptation, the now familiar "square" letters in which the Hebrew Old Testament is to this day universally transcribed or printed. Jewish tradition, concurred in by early Christian authorities, attributes the invention of this Aramaic or "square" alphabet to Ezra, first of the Sopherim;[j] but, although it is conceivable that this "ready scribe in the Law of Moses" may have had some influence in this direction, it was not until long after the fifth century B. C. in which he flourished that the new characters were fully developed. It is commonly held that their introduction was primarily for the purpose of beautifying the sacred text. The "square" script, in any case, was at first employed, like the Coptic of the Egyptian priesthood, or the Latin of the pharmaceutical chemist of today, only by a limited circle of scribes into whose mysteries it was the part of wisdom for the average son of man not to inquire.

The "square" characters, owing to their incorporation in the Hebraic arcana, have been the least modified letters of all Semitic alphabets. Perhaps most contributory to this unusual alphabetical stability was the ancient injunction[3] against writing

---

[j] The sôpheRIM [סופרים] or scribes were originally merely people who knew how to write, royal archivists such as are referred to in II Sam. viii. 17; later, men learned in the Torah whose primary function was to read the Law aloud and to interpret it to the people. Hence the title became practically synonymous in post-exilic times with *men of wisdom*. Basically, however, and certainly in post-Biblical times, the Sopherim were simply accomplished professional penmen who earned a notoriously poor living either by the secretarial work of a notary public or by multiplying copies of the Scriptures or the texts of ceremonial paraphernalia. Adept in this work though the scribes became, the Talmudic account (*Yoma* 38[b]) of Ben Qamzar who could so manipulate four pens at one time as to write a four-lettered word with one stroke can be hardly more than a pious pleasantry.

any letter of the Hebrew Scriptures without leaving clear
parchment all around it. The use of ligatures, forbidden by
this rule, is one of the commonest causes in other languages
of transformation of original letter-design. The stability of the
Scriptural letters undoubtedly prevented deterioration, but unfortunately it also precluded desirable improvement. Remarkable achievement though this Aramaic alphabet was, its inventor
left much to be desired. Whatever his genius, he was apparently
not fully aware that the prime requirement of his twenty-two
consonants should have been that they be instantly and easily
distinguishable one from the others; and that the pattern of his
characters, to be satisfactory and practical, should have seized
on and exploited those "essential points in which letters differ." [4]
This criterion can hardly be held to have been observed with
letters of such similarity as ב and כ; נ and ג; ם and ס; ר, ך, and
ר; ה, ח, and ת; ו, ז, י, and ן. The "tittle" which is all that
distinguishes a *beth* [ב] from a *kaph* [כ] is, like other features of
the script, so small as to necessitate the use of Hebrew fonts of
large size. The printer of Hebrew books has little if any need
for type smaller than standard pica (12-point). The writer of
Hebrew manuscripts requires plenty of space and a most discriminating pen. To the scribe, the injunction not to depart from
his original by so much as a *jot*[k] or a *tittle*, was a literal necessity.
Hebrew writers of today, impatient of such barriers, employ an
alphabet which, though unligatured, flows readily in cursive
manner. Familiarity with the sacred text, and an indifference
to eye-strain, make possible, of course, the relatively rapid
reading of the vowel-less square writing of the Hebrew Old
Testament. Yet, as students of Biblical palaeography are constantly aware, textual variants which are the result merely of
mistaking one Hebrew consonant for another of nearly identical
form occur more frequently in Hebrew manuscripts than in
those written in Latin or Greek. [5]

Ease in reading and correctly interpreting the manuscripts
written in square writing was further hampered by the custom

[k] *I. e., yodh* (י), the smallest character in the Hebrew alphabet.

of separating words by a space only infinitesimally greater than the width of a hair or a thread which the scribes were instructed to leave between individual letters. Poetry, moreover, as in manuscripts of other ancient languages, was transcribed continuously as prose. The opening verses of Genesis, if thus written in English, would present the following appearance:

```
INTHEBEGINNINGGODC
REATEDTHEHEAVENAND
THEEARTHNOWTHEEART
HWASWITHOUTFORMAND
VOIDANDDARKNESSUPO
NTHEFACEOFTHEDEEP
```

Written without the vowels, as in the Hebrew text, the same verses would appear in this still stranger form:

```
NTHBGNNNGGDCRT
DTHHVNNDTHRTH
NWTHRTHWSWTHT
FRMNDVDNDDRKN
SSPNTHFCFTHDP
```

Extraordinary regulations were ultimately formulated by the rabbis for the professional scribes in their effort to obtain transcriptions of this consonantal text as nearly accurate as possible. In addition to the rule against ligatures previously mentioned, the Talmud meticulously enjoins the copyists against certain undesirable practices, and carefully specifies numerous obligatory procedures in the transcription of the Scrolls. Some of these regulations are obviously of a purely psychological nature, designed to impress the scribe with the sacrosanct character of his task. "My son," Rabbi Ishmael is reported in the Talmud[6] as cautioning a scribe, "be careful in thy work, as it is a heavenly work, lest thou err in omitting or in adding one jot, and so cause the destruction of the whole world." Before copying the Pentateuchal scroll a scribe had first to wash his whole body and to assume the garb appropriate to Jewish ritual; he was permitted to write the Tetragrammaton [יהוה — Y H V H] — the incommunicable name of God — only with a tried pen which would not spatter the sacred letters; and, should a king address him while he was writing them, the scribe was under sacred obligation completely to ignore the claims upon his attention of temporal majesty until he had completed the divine name. Nothing, not even a *yodh*, might be written from memory; and the text from which he made his copy had to be first certified by the rabbis as authentic. Minute instructions of a more practical nature were laid down for the scribe to follow with respect to the permissible number of lines to a column, the number of letters to a line, the quality of the parchment and its ruling, the formula of the ink, the spacing of letters, words and sections, and the use of such features as verse marks or final and capital letters. To what extent accuracy of transcription was secured by these various provisions will be seen in a subsequent chapter. [7]

The most accurate transcription of a purely consonantal text cannot relieve it of obscurities. Ancient Hebrew shares with the records of other Semitic languages a disconcerting ambiguity which arises from the lack of characters to express in writing the vowel sounds of the spoken tongue. In the many parallel passages of the Old Testament which depend directly one on the other, or which are derived from a common source, there occur numerous differences whose explanation is found only in the uncertainties of the ancient consonantal orthography. [8] The letters of any alphabet are, of course, nothing more than conventionally accepted symbols approximately representative of certain sounds. The want of such symbols with which to represent the vowel sounds is a serious deficiency. Even with such vowel symbols as are available in our contemporary English alphabet of twenty-six letters, the difficulties of translating the spoken word to a fully satisfactory written form are such as to have necessitated the invention and use of the international phonetic alphabet. Hebrew grammarians, unfortunately, have so far not availed themselves of this phonetic instrument.[1] In a consonantal script, to be certain, ambiguities may often, although not always, be resolved through the context. Of the many possible words derived, for instance, from the two consonants *M* and *D* (in the middle of a hypothetically vowel-less English sentence) the reader will probably be able to select that which the writer intended. There can be little hesitation between MiD and MuD; MaD and MeaD or MeeD; MoDe, MaDe, MooD, MaiD. It is apparent that, in the same hypothetical consonantal English sentence, the letters P L C S may be vocalized to read indifferently PaLaCeS or PLaCeS. With what confidence then, will an imaginary palaeographer of the future, unacquainted, let us conjecture, with the sentimental musical *mores* of an ancient American culture, interpret the newly-discovered consonantal relic M D P L S R S N D P L C S, the vocalization of which exhibits either the first line of a folk song believed to have been entitled "Home, Sweet Home," or, equally well, a fragment of some lost Jeremiad in which the primitive American people are berated for their "MaD PLeaSuReS aND PLaCeS!"

Textual ambiguities, in a Hebrew written with consonants alone, are frequently real and perplexing. The three-letter word משל [M š L], for example, may be either the verb *to rule* or the noun *a proverb* according to which of the thirteen possible vowels are supplied. The consonants רגל [R G L] with one set of vowels mean *to slander*; with another set, *a foot*. The triliteral ספר [S Ph R] may be read *to count*, *to declare*, *a scribe*, or *a book*. Variously vocalized, זכר [Z Kh R], to borrow an illustration from St. Jerome,[m] becomes *to remember*, *a memorial*, or *a male*; and the

---

[1] In the Grammars of Gesenius, Davidson, Weingreen, and Wallenrod, and the Primers of Mannheimer and Reichler, *pathaḥ* is given as the equivalent of the letter *a* in Sam, fat, had, bard, what, and far; *qameṣ gadol* is represented by the *a* (or, for Ashkenazic, *o*) in psalm, calf, yard, father (shore), arm (old), and fall; *qameṣ qatan* by the *o* in cot, on, top, born, and son.

[m] *Commentarium in Isaiam* (xxvi. 14), *Opera omnia studia ac labore Dominici Vallarsi*, 11 Vols., Venetiis, 1766–71, Vol. IV, col. 353: "Nec terrere nos debet, quare LXX *masculum*, & caeteri Interpretes *memoriam* transtulerunt, quum

ubiquitous דבר [D B R], depending on the vowels employed, and the context, signifies, among several dozen things, *word, speaker, pasture, pestilence, matter, promise, commandment, death,* and *he spoke.*[n] The meaning of מצלות [MɛṢiLLÔth] is not necessarily *bells,* as translated in Zechariah xiv. 20; but may also be *depths, bottom* [MɛṢuLÔth], and has been so vocalized by Aquila and by later Biblical commentators.[9] The word rendered *the bed* [המטה — HAMMiTTAH] in Genesis xlvii. 31 requires but a vowel change to mean *the staff* [HAMMATTĒH] as in the Peshitto, and is justifiably so translated in Hebrews xi. 21, which follows the Septuagint. This and other early Versions often illuminate obscure portions of the Old Testament, and make sufficiently clear that certain passages which in the Hebrew are apparently wrong are only cases of mistaken vocalization. In some instances where the translation and the received Hebrew text vocalize the consonants differently, one reading is as acceptable as the other.[o]

---

eisdem tribus literis, ZAY [*sic*], & CHAPH & RES, utrumque scribatur apud Hebraeos. Sed quando *memoriale* dicimus, legiter [*sic*] ZACHAR [*sic*], quando *masculum* ZOCHOR [*sic*]. Et hac verbi ambiguitate deceptum arbitrantur Saul, quando pugnavit contra Amalech et interfecit omne masculinum eorum [I Sam. xv]. Deo enim praecipiente, ut deleret omnem *memoriam* Amalech sub coelo, ille pro memoria, non tam errore, quam praedae seductus cupidine, *masculos* interpretatus est."

[n] Jerome, *Comm. in Jeremiam* (ix. 21), *op. cit.*, IV, 909: "Verbum Hebraicum, quod tribus literis scribitur, DALETH, BETH, RES (vocales enim in medio non habet) pro consequentia & legentis arbitrio, si legatur DABAR, *sermonem* significat; si DEBER, *mortem*; si DABBER [*sic*], *loquere.*" *Comm. in Is.* (ix. 8), *op. cit.*, IV, 136: "Apud Hebraeos DABAR, quod per tres literas scribitur consonantes DALETH, BETH, RES, pro locorum qualitate, si legatur DABAR, *verbum* significat, si DEBER, *mortem* & *pestilentiam.*" *Comm. in Hab.* (iii. 5), *op. cit.*, VI, 640: "Pro eo quod nos transtulimus *mortem*, in Hebraeo tres literae positae sunt, DALETH, BETH, RES, absque ulla vocali, quae si legantur DABAR, *verbum* significant, si DEBER, *pestem.*"

[o] *Cf.* D. Chwolson (tr. T. K. Abbott), "The Quiescents (or vowel-letters) הוי in Ancient Hebrew Orthography," in *Hebraica*, VI, 2 (Jan. 1890), *passim.* Something faintly analogous to this linguistic obscurity occurs, occasionally, in English. The variant factor, in our language, cannot, of course, be the indispensable and always written vowels, but may be the shifting accent. In English, by way of illustration, the letters i-n-v-a-l-i-d indicate, as the unwritten accent is supplied either for the first syllable or for the second, *a sick person* or the adjective *worthless.* English, however, with all its difficulties, offers no con-

In order to reduce the uncertainties of a text in which vowels found no visual representation, post-Biblical Hebrew writers gradually evolved some grammatical[p] and alphabetical innovations. Their increasing familiarity with Greek may have been a contributory influence. Even earlier — probably before the exile — the necessity of guarding against gross misunderstandings may have been realized.[10] The earliest refinement in textual clarification, whatever the date of its origin, was alphabetical: the three "quiescent" consonants, *he* [ה], *vav* [ו], and *yodh* [י], which, in early Hebrew, were never used in the middle of words or at their end, were arbitrarily but not always consistently introduced into words by the transcribers or editors[11] to serve as long — unchangeably long — vowels. Still so used, they are known as the vowel-letters, or vocalic consonants, or *matres lectiones*.[12] The use of ה and ו as terminal vowel-letters to differentiate inflectional forms, was an early improvement.[q] Somewhat later, certainly by the fourth century, the vowel-sounds in the middle of words was indicated by an intercalated *yodh* [י] or *vav* [ו]. This practice, though helpful, was never general,[r] as the deviations of manuscripts with respect to this point, a source of contention even among later medieval Jewish scholars, adequately demonstrate. Earlier scholars, the Massoretes,[13] attempted to establish precisely what words were to be written with vowel-letters and what words without; they succeeded, however, only in selecting from the divergent manuscripts the

---

fusion comparable to that of the regular verb in Hebrew, which frequently exhibits as many as ten different inflectional forms, each pronounced in its own distinctive way, but all *spelled with identical consonants*.

[p] In Mishnaic Hebrew, *e. g.*, after the first century, particles were introduced to express the genitive relation and others; and the reflexive conjunctions were employed in place of the passives.

[q] In ancient texts, before the custom arose of expressing terminal vowel-sounds by the vocalic consonants, no distinction was made in the Imperfect between the written forms of the singular and the plural of the third person masculine; nor, in the Perfect, between the singular and plural of the third person masculine and feminine.

[r] The Samaritan and Massoretic recensions of the Pentateuch differ particularly in this regard.

readings they considered most nearly correct, and were naturally unable, on the basis of the variant spellings, to formulate a systematic orthography.

The metamorphosis of the three quiescent consonants into vowels, though manifestly a step in the direction of textual clarification, was no preventive of misinterpretations and variant readings in passages where vowel-letters were not in question. "Nothing is more certain," states Driver, "than that . . . corruptions of different kinds found their way into the text of the Old Testament." [14] Difficulties in corrupt Hebrew passages may frequently be cleared up by the early translations — that of the Septuagint particularly — when their readings, based upon Hebrew manuscripts older by several centuries than those underlying the present text, are not only consonantally justifiable but in themselves highly probable. [15] Where the Septuagint and the Samaritan Pentateuch agree as to readings which differ from those of the corresponding passages in the later received Hebrew text, the conclusion is legitimate that archetypal manuscripts containing the readings of those two early Versions must at one time have existed, and were probably familiar to the Jews in Palestine prior to the second destruction of their Temple, A. D. 70. In one ancient Greek Version, that of Lucian, [16] there are renderings not found elsewhere, which, in certain passages, "presuppose a Hebrew original self-evidently superior" to that of the commonly accepted text. [17] Comparison of parallel passages clearly reveals many inconsistencies in the Scriptural books which are due solely to scribal failure correctly to interpret the consonantal source. [18] In Tannaitic literature of the second century Jewish writers came to the conclusion, held by them to be inevitable, that the ancient reading of several passages of Scripture must have varied from that which was then known. [19]

In earlier times the Biblical text was apparently treated with a certain degree of freedom. "No one looked with any great concern to the preservation of the individual letter of the alphabet . . . the earlier age went forward to its task with great freedom ... it even went so far as to alter the text itself, at times through a mere change of pronunciation, at times through the alterations of individual letters, yes, even of whole words, in order to resolve some difficulty of dogma or eradicate expressions derogatory to national esteem, modesty, or the moral sense."²⁰ Proper names, for instance, were now and then purposefully modified;ˢ "bless" was euphemistically substituted for "curse" in association with God;²¹ Jerusalem was changed, for priestly reasons, from a "righteous city" (עיר הצדק) to a "city of destruction";ᵗ whole words were inserted or omitted;ᵘ and to the Sopherim are admittedly due no less than eighteen deliberate textual alterationsᵛ for the removal of indelicate expressions or the elimination of apparent impieties.

ˢ Cp. the substitution of "Bosheth" (*i. e.*, "shame" — בשת) for "Baal" (בעל) in Ishbosheth (II Sam. ii. 8) for Eshbaal (I Chr. viii. 34, 35); Mephibosheth (II Sam. ix. 6) for Merib-baal (I Chr. viii. 34, 35).

ᵗ Is. xix. 18: עיר ההרס. *Cf. Jewish Encyclopedia*, VIII. 368. It is interesting, in connection with the preceding discussion (*v. supra*, p. 30), that this expression, exhibiting a confusion of *he* (ה) with *ḥeth* (ח), was taken as עיר החרס by Jerome, with the consequent reading "city of *the sun*" in the Douay translation.

ᵘ The Massoretes (*v. infra*, p. 40) sanctioned ten insertions (קרי ולא כתיב): at Judg. xx. 13; Ruth iii. 5, iii. 17; II Sam. viii. 3, xvi. 23, xviii. 20; II Kgs. xix. 31, xix. 37; Jer. xxxi. 38 (M. T. 37), l. 29; and eight omissions (כתיב ולא קרי): at II Sam. xiii. 33, xv. 21; II Kgs. v. 18; Ruth iii. 12; Jer. xxxviii. 16, xxxix. 12, li. 3; Ezek. xlviii. 16.

ᵛ These eighteen Decrees of the Scribes (ṬIQQUNE-SÔPHeRIM — תיקוני סופרים), sanctioned subsequently by the Masorah [*cf.* Masorah at Num. xii. 12 in Yemen MSS. Or. 1379, Or. 2349, and Or. 2365 in the British Museum], elude accurate specification. Not to be confused with the scribal emendations discussed below (p. 51), these "decrees" — as listed in C. D. Ginsburg's translation (London, 1865, p. 28) of Jacob ben Ḥayyim's Introduction to the second edition (1524–25) of Daniel Bomberg's Rabbinic Bible (*v. infra*, p. 176) — are, in the R. V., except as noted, the following:

1. Gen. xviii. 22, Abraham stood yet *instead of* Jehovah stood yet.
2. Num. xi. 15, my wretchedness *for* thy wretchedness.
3. Num. xii. 12, his (its) mother's *for* our mother's.
4. Num. xii. 12, the (its) flesh *for* our flesh.
5. I Sam. iii. 13, a curse upon themselves *for* a curse upon Elohim (so LXX).
6. II Sam. xvi. 12, look on the wrong done unto me (A. V.: look on my affliction) *for* see with his eye (A. J. V.: look on mine eye).
7. I Kgs. xii. 16, unto their tents *for* unto their gods.
8. II Chr. x. 16, unto their tents *for* unto their gods.

By the beginning of the second century, the consonantal Old Testament, vowel-letters included, had become fairly well fixed and, there can be little doubt, closely approximated the now-established text. To this, the Greek version of Aquila, [22] made in the first half of the second century, sufficiently testifies. Supplementary testimony occurs in the *Mishna* — the second-century written Code of the Oral Law; in its later amplification, the *Gemara*; in the Aramaic paraphrases of the Hebrew text called the *Targumim*; and in the writings of Origen in the third century and of Jerome in the fourth. Inasmuch as fluctuations in the form of the text are still shown by the Greek version of the *Book of Jubilees*[w] in the first century, it is the critical consensus that the fixation of the Hebrew consonantal text was ac-

---

9. Job vii. 20, to myself *for* to thee.
10. Job xxxii. 3, condemned Job *for* condemned Elohim.
11. Ps. cvi. 20, their glory *for* my glory.
12. Lam. iii. 20, my soul is bowed down within me *for* thy soul will mourn over me.
13. Jer. ii. 11, their glory *for* my glory.
14. Ezek. viii. 17, their nose *for* my nose.
15. Hos. iv. 7, their glory *for* my glory.
16. Hab. i. 12, we shall not die (A. V. and A. J. V.) *for* thou diest not (so R. V.).
17. Zech. ii. 8 (A. J. V. ii. 12), his eye *for* mine eye.
18. Mal. i. 13, what a weariness is it *for* ye make me expire.

In Ginsburg's *Introduction to the Massoretico-critical Edition of the Hebrew Bible* (London, 1897), however, item 7 above is omitted and items 3 and 4 coalesce into one, the total of 18 being here achieved by the inclusion of two additional "decrees" — one at II Sam. xx. 1, the other at Mal. iii. 8.

w A Midrashic commentary — the oldest known — on Genesis and a part of Exodus. Written from the strictest Pharasaic point of view, this work is sometimes referred to as *The Little Genesis*. Previously known only through the Greek, Latin and Ethiopic versions (the last of which was translated into English and published at London by R. H. Charles in 1902, and generally held with Charles to have been originally written either in Hebrew or Aramaic during the reign of John Hyrcanus as high priest of the Jews, 135–105 B. C.) *Jubilees* is now known, through a five-line fragment recently recovered from the cave at 'Ain Fashkha in which the "Dead Sea Scrolls" were presumably found, to have existed at a time — possibly the fourth pre-Christian century — when Hebrew was still currently written in the ancient Phoenician script. *Cf.* R. de Vaux, "La grotte des manuscrits hébreux," in *Revue Biblique*, Vol. 56, No. 4 (Oct. 1949), p. 604. *V. infra*, p. 305.

complished some time after the translation of *Jubilees* was in circulation — probably subsequent to the fall of Jerusalem, A. D. 70, and prior to the production of the version of Aquila. For at least the Pentateuchal portion of the Bible, Jewish scholarship claims the fixed consonantal text to be as early as the third century B. C. but at the same time admits that "it took centuries to produce a tolerable uniformity among all the circulating copies," and also that "as late as the second century ... scholars found it necessary to warn against incorrect copies."[x] In the first century, while the Temple was still standing, some attempt, it appears, had been made to produce officially approved scrolls of the Pentateuch from which others could be copied. Three such standard scrolls, according to an account in the Jerusalem Talmud,[y] were deposited in the Court of the Temple, but even these three were identified by titles which acknowledge their textual variations. Outside of the Temple at Jerusalem, in centers of Jewish learning such as Sura, Nehardea or Tiberias where differences of diction and orthography had naturally developed in the course of time, each school preserved its traditional pronunciation and spelling in a standard codex of its own.[z] Whatever the archetype from which extant Pentateuchal manuscripts are descended, it was certainly no letter-perfect representative of the text as originally written.[23]

Interpretation of the Hebrew Old Testament which was current in the first four or five centuries of the common era,

---

[x] *Jewish Encyclopedia*, VIII, 366. In the earliest specifically cited MS. of the Pentateuch, the Asverus Scroll — a copy of which is said to have been removed by Titus from Jerusalem to Rome, after the second destruction of the Temple, and eventually presented to the Jews of that city by the liberal emperor Alexander Severus (reigned A. D. 220–235) — there were eventually discovered not less than thirty-two variations from the text which was later established. *Cf*. Ad. Neubauer, in *Studia Biblica*, iii. (1891), pp. 19–22.

[y] *Ta'anit* lxviii. 1. sēpheR me'ôn was so called because of its reading מעון instead of מעונה in Deut. xxxiii. 27; sēpheR za'aTUTI, because of זעטוטי instead of נערי in Ex. xxiv. 5; sēpheR HI', because of its nine passages, rather than eleven, reading היא with a *yodh*. *Cf. Jewish Encyclopedia*, III, 178.

[z] *Jewish Encyclopedia*, VIII, 370. Cp. the pointing לִישְׂרָאֵל [Leyisrā'ēl] of Codex Ben Asher (*v. infra*, p. 44) with the pointing לִישְׂרָאֵל [Lisrā'ēl] of Codex Ben Naphtali.

fairly well fixed though its text had become with respect to the consonants and the three *matres lectiones*, was still unnecessarily handicapped by the lack of an adequate set of written symbols for the various vowel-sounds. The elimination of this deficiency was perhaps the chief contribution of the school of Jewish scholars at Tiberias who, probably as early as the sixth century,[aa] began in a novel manner to protect what they considered the only true interpretation of the consonantal text. Devotion to Talmudic tradition conditioned every phase of their Biblical work, including traditional pronunciation. The Massoretes, as these scholars are called from the Hebrew word for tradition, MASÔRAH (מסורה), devised a system of dots and dashes — the vowel-points — which, written adjacent to the consonants, served as vowels. These vowel-points are faintly analogous to such diacritical marks as the macron or breve, the *umlaut*, *tilde* or *cedilla*. Scholars competent in Hebrew have no more occasion for the aid of these vowel-points than readers of English, beyond the primer stage, for diacritical indication of the length of the vowels. No scroll designed for synagogal use is written with the vowel-points. No rabbi requires them. "Pointed" manuscripts, however, for instructional or private purposes, abound; and printed Hebrew Bibles for general use are customarily supplied with this diacritical vocalization.

These Massoretic vowel-signs, it will be seen, constitute a second or a supplementary Hebrew alphabet. Taken by themselves, of course, unlike the twenty-two consonants, they can have no intelligible meaning. They serve but to remove ambiguity from the consonantal text which in itself was originally considered complete and intelligible. They record a pronunciation of the language which, transmitted orally from generation to generation, had become traditional. Inasmuch as tradition is not only memorial but also interpretative, vowel notation, resolving ambiguities, may be legitimately looked upon as a running commentary on the text. The phonetic system of the

---

[aa] Jerome (*ob.* 420) knew nothing of their phonetic system, nor is it mentioned in the Talmud (c. 500).

Massoretes is in reality a critical parasite as distinct from the consonantal host as is any commentary distinct from the work upon which it comments. In spite of this obvious fact, the vowel-points were long considered an integral part of the most ancient Hebrew documents, and, throughout the Middle Ages and during the Renaissance, the relatively late date of their invention was not as a rule admitted. Ultimately, in the seventeenth century, the critical labors of Louis Capell, the French Protestant scholar, and of Brian Walton, the English editor of the remarkable Polyglot Bible of 1657, established the lateness of the Massoretic pointing beyond further question.[bb] It is still none the less customary, although quite without critical justification, to condemn as an unwarranted emendation an entirely legitimate translation of the established consonantal text if it be vocalized otherwise than in the Massoretic tradition. The English Versions of the Old Testament — even, with an occasional exception,[cc] the Revised Version — instead of being independent translations of the consonantal text, are accordingly nothing other than a rendition of the interpretation of the Massoretes.

The Massoretes, or traditionalists, could, of course, do nothing other than perpetuate the pronunciation of the language *as it was known to them*. Their prime object was to petrify, so to speak, the solemn cantillation of the divine service *as it was practised in their time*. They were in all probability unaware, despite some available evidence to the contrary, that Hebrew, like all living tongues, had undergone changes of more than one kind in the centuries since the Scriptural texts were first written. They were

---

[bb] Capell published his *Critica Sacra sive de variis quae in sacris Veteri Testamenti libris occurrunt lectionibus* in 1650. Catholic theologians, disciplined in the wisdom of authoritative interpretation, were not troubled over the ambiguities of the unpointed Hebrew text as were scholars of a Protestant faith whose extreme doctrine of the inspiration, verbal infallibility, and sufficiency of Scripture seemed to require the support of readings certified to be written, and of pre-exilic vowels. For Walton's *Polyglot*, *v. infra*, p. 177, note f.

[cc] R. V., in Is. lix. 19, for example, departs from the Massoretic Text (כתיב — *it is written*) to translate the consonants differently pointed. *V. infra*, p. 219, note j.

not practised in the evolutionary approach of modern linguists. Even as recently as the eighteenth century, the foremost of our early English lexicographers, Dr. Samuel Johnson, could naively announce the purpose of his *Dictionary* to be "to fix the English language." Only that language is "fixed" which is dead. Hebrew had been uninterruptedly a spoken tongue for perhaps twenty centuries before its crystallization by the Massoretes. They could not possibly be certain, any more than can we, of the pronunciation of Hebrew in Solomon's day. From the days not long before Solomon's time, when there was no king in Israel, there comes at least one Biblical record of phonetic variation: *Shibboleth* as against *Sibboleth*.[dd] In still later, post-Biblical times, the Massoretes Ben Asher and Ben Naphtali differed as to the pronunciation of the name of Jacob's fifth son, Isaachar.[ee] In different Greek and Latin pre-Massoretic versions of the Old Testament, divergent transliterations of Hebrew words sometimes indicate differences of pronunciation,[24] either at various times or in separated localities. In our own time Hebrew — even liturgical Hebrew — is sufficiently alive to have differentiated its pronunciation into the Ashkenazic of German and Polish Jews and the

---

[dd] Judges xii. 6.

[ee] Ben Asher's pointing יִשָּׂשכָר [yisa(s)khaR], found in numerous MSS., is followed by the Soncino Hebrew Bible of 1488, and later editions. To Ben Naphthali (*v. infra*, p. 44) are attributed three different punctuations: (1) יִשַּׂשכָר [yissakhaR], occurring in Leningrad MS. No. 110 and approved by Moses ben Mocha; (2) יִשַׂשכָר [yisaskhaR], found in the Masorah Parva at Gen. xxx. 18 of B. M. MS. Or. 2626–28, and recorded at p. 102 of Simchah Pinsker's לקוטי קדמוניות, Vienna, 1860; (3) יִשָּׂשכָר [yissakhaR], the reading of Leningrad MSS. 49, 54, 57, 59, 70, *et al.* Kittel's *Biblia Hebraica* concurs with none of these punctuations of Ben Asher or Ben Naphthali, but adopts יִשָּׂשכָר [yissa(s)khaR], the reading of MS. Or. 4445, *et al.*, and of the Bibles of Felix Pratensis (1517) and Jacob ben Ḥayyim (1524–25; *v. infra*, p. 176). Furthermore, Kittel records a textual יִשַׂשכָר [yissaskhaR] and a marginal יִשָׂכָר [yissakhaR]; in addition both Codex Babylonicus Petropolitanus and B. M. MS. Arundel Or. 2 exhibit יִשָׂשכָר [yi(s)sakhaR]. Note the instances in which the second or third letter is left unpointed — an unusual feature in a pointed text. For the etymologies to which these variations may be traced, see Gen. xxx. 17–18, and Abraham Geiger, *Urschrift und Übersetzungen der Bibel*, Breslau, 1857, pp. 359 ff.

Sephardic of the Jewish communities of the Iberian Peninsula. It is an entirely untenable contention, widely maintained though it be, that the phonetics of monarchic or prophetic Hebrew are preserved in the pointed text of the Doctors of Tiberias with no essential alteration. What they did succeed in preserving was a publicly recited liturgical Hebrew with all its accumulated imperfections.

With this Massoretic modification of the Scriptural writings, textual stability of the Hebrew Old Testament was, as such things go, finally achieved. After their original textual outline could no longer be easily recovered, the Hebrew Scriptures were handed from generation to generation with a scrupulous insistence on accuracy of transcription unparalleled in the history of any other ancient books. But this guardianship of the text came too late. The damage had been done. This particular fence had been erected, as the proverbial barn door had been locked, after the loss had been sustained. The Massoretes — those "elementary schoolmasters," as Margolis[25] calls them — no doubt established a text considered authoritative for the last thousand years; but the text they established — and of this there can be no reasonable question — embedded within its essentially sound matrix an element of fossilized corruption.[ff]

[ff] *Cf.* S. R. Driver, *Notes on the Hebrew Text of the Books of Samuel,* 2nd ed., rev. and enl., Oxford, 1913, p. xxxiv. See, further, S. A. Cook, in *Proceedings of the Society of Biblical Archaeology,* XXV, Jan. 1903, p. 46: "the [Nash] papyrus is a genuine Hebrew text . . . a Hebrew Biblical fragment which differs more widely from the Massoretic Text than any known manuscript . . . these readings are so consistently supported by the Septuagint that they clearly cannot be regarded as due to the imagination or defective memory of a scribe . . . only one explanation seems possible. The scrupulous fidelity in the preservation and correct transmission of the Old Testament dates only from a certain period . . . a critical and unbiased study of such *earlier and independent* writings as the Septuagint, the Samaritan Pentateuch, the Book of Jubilees, etc., forces the conviction that the text has not always been in the fixed state in which it has come down to us, and has led to the commonly accepted opinion that the "Massoretic" text is but a stage, and that almost the latest one, in the history of the Old Testament text . . . . This view . . . accepted by the great mass of Biblical scholars . . . is duly stated by the cautious and sober band of critics who prepared the Revised Version of the Old Testament."

Textual corruption of Biblical manuscripts is recognized today to a degree undreamed of by scholars during the Middle Ages. But even those "humble scholars" the Massoretes were not unaware of that textual problem and, although they dared not alter a single consonant of any official copy of Hebrew Scripture, they devised expedients by which in other copies they could guide the reader away from error. One of these was the marginal note.[gg] According to the traditional commentary — the Masorah — of the Rabbinic Bible published by Daniel Bomberg[26] there are more than thirteen hundred and fifty such marginalia in the Old Testament. Some of these are hardly more than the *corrigenda* or *errata* in a modern book; others indicate adoption by the Massoretes of readings at variance with the consonantal text. Beyond these recognized marginalia all the known Hebrew Biblical manuscripts adhere, with only slight scribal deviations, to a basic textual pattern. From the standard codices of the various schools, the Massoretes eliminated, in the course of two centuries, all but two lines of descent. One of these lines, the Babylonian, culminated in the Codex Ben Naphtali, no longer extant, produced in the first half of the tenth century, by the Massorete Moses ben David ben Naphtali;[hh] the other, the Palestinian, attained its definitive state at about the same time, in Tiberias, at the hand of Aaron ben Moses ben Asher,[ii] and is therefore known as the Codex Ben Asher. Of these two, Codex Ben Asher ultimately established its ascendancy and became the recognized standard. Although all the known codices of the Hebrew Old Testament are lineal descendants of Codex Ben Asher, no surviving manuscript of the received

[gg] Of these notes there are three types: the relatively few insertions and omissions previously mentioned (*v. supra*, p. 37, note u) and the frequent instruction to read something other than the text itself. *V. infra*, p. 50.

[hh] *Fl.* at Tiberias (?) c. A. D. 890–940.

[ii] Author, also, of short treatises on grammatical subjects. With him the Masorah may be held to have closed. His MS. of the O. T., written A. D. 922, has disappeared. A *copy*, now at Leningrad, was made in A. D. 1009. The codex at Aleppo, formerly ascribed to Ben Asher, is a work by a later hand, not earlier than the twelfth century.

Hebrew text adheres consistently to the system of that imperfect archetype. Readings from Ben Naphtali insist upon breaking in. No printed edition of the Hebrew Old Testament[jj] bases itself exclusively on the one rival interpretation or the other.[kk] Printed Old Testaments, like the manuscripts before them, are one and all eclectic. [27]

[jj] Not even the most recent rabbinical translation into English: *The Holy Scriptures*, The Jewish Publication Society of America, Philadelphia, 1917 — referred to hereafter, as a matter of convenience, as the *American Jewish Version* or A. J. V. *Cf.* Preface of this version, p. ix, note.

[kk] Although the Massoretic Text generally follows Ben Asher's pointing, for example in such forms as לְיִשְׂרָאֵל [Leyisra'ēl], it adopts the pointing of Ben Naphtali in לִיקְהַת [Liqqehath] at Prov. xxx. 17 and elsewhere.

CHAPTER III

Revision of the Old Testament Text—I

"Behold, the false pen of the scribes hath wrought falsely."
Jeremiah viii. 8

THE text of the Old Testament, both in its Massoretic and in its Septuagintal forms, having come down to us with numerous scribal imperfections, the basic problem of the Biblical scholar is to ascertain, as closely as possible, precisely what the ancient authors originally wrote. This is the function of textual criticism, which attempts, as its sole aim, to establish the most nearly perfect text. Fundamental in character, it should precede studies of a literary or historical nature. Historically, whether in fields Biblical or non-Biblical, the process has been exactly the reverse, with a consequent accumulation of psychological resistance to the claims of the critics whose interest in the mind of an author impels a search for the very words with which that mind found expression. Such close examination of the Biblical text is frequently referred to, with a revealing invidiousness, as "the lower criticism."

Even in non-Biblical investigation, the way of the textual critic is none too easy. The mind of the man who wrote *Macbeth* certainly commands our worshipful admiration; one of its outstanding attributes is its ability to express itself in terms supremely and uniquely effective. Let the textual critic, however

46

expert and wary, illuminate an accepted Macbethian banality
with an entirely credible and well-founded substitution of a
dramatically superb *me* for an anti-climactic and limping *or*,
and few indeed will be found to overcome their psychological
inertia sufficiently to understand the evidence and to approve.[a]
It has taken over three hundred years for Hamlet's too too
"solid" flesh to become properly "sullied" — and that only in
limited academic circles — although the textual support of that
metamorphosis is more than ordinarily compelling, and the
psychological determinant of the Prince's behavior is thereby
effectively emphasized.[1] Equally slow to arrive, but so indis-
putable as to gain general acceptance, is the happy explanation
by A. H. Bullen of a line in Marlowe's *Tragical History of Doctor
Faustus* which for three centuries had baffled editors. In the first
edition of this play, Faustus, surveying the fields of learning and
dismissing them one after the other, is made to say [I. 12]: "Bid
Oncaymaeon farewell, Galen come." In the second edition, an
editor who must have been mindful of the *Oeconomica* of Aristotle, but whose respect for Marlowe's "mighty line" was certainly small, rashly changed this unintelligible passage to read:
"Bid Oeconomy farewell, Galen come." This, however, was not
wisdom; for, as all the world could see *as soon as it was pointed
out*, the puzzling *Oncaymaeon* of the first edition was nothing other
than an Elizabethan typesetter's attempt to spell out in English
the well-known Aristotelian phrase ὂν καὶ μὴ ὂν, "being and
not being" — Hamlet's familiar "to be or not to be."[2] But it
took a textual critic to establish this reading.

The Bible itself, in its printed English versions, is not free
from such textual ambiguities. In the King James Version of
1611, for example, a conspicuous confusion, more apparent than

---

[a] Despite a most brilliant demonstration that Shakespeare wished him to,
Macbeth still refuses to say (Act II, Sc. 1, ll. 63, 64)

> "Hear it not, Duncan, for it is a knell
> That summons thee to Heaven, *me* to Hell."

Cf. Samuel A. Tannenbaum, *Shaksperian Scraps and other Elizabethan Fragments*, New York, 1933, p. 97.

real, is the reading at Zechariah xi. 17: "Woe to the idol shepherd." This seeming substitution of *idol* for *idle* — a blunder conceivably aural in origin; perhaps the result of the compositor's "trying to carry too many words in mind at once" [3] — is in reality traceable to factors orthographic and semantic. This *idol* — unquestionably derived from the Massoretic Text [3] — though to the modern mind conspicuously lacking in sense, was, for the readers of Coverdale's Bible or that of Geneva, presumably accepted and intelligible as a variant of *idle*, which, in sixteenth-century adjectival usage, included the concept *neglectful of duty*, or *foolish* — as in Smith-Goodspeed — or *worthless*, the meaning adopted by Moffatt, the Revised Version and the American Jewish Version. Retention unto the present day of the obsolete *idol* by the Authorized Version is paralleled, as an instance of editorial inertia, by the Douay Version, which, abiding here by the substantive interpretation of the Vulgate — O pastor et idolum — continues to offer its readers "O shepherd and idol."

Undeniably attributable to the compositor is an error of another kind found in the same edition, the Authorized Version of 1611, at Exodus xiv. 10, where three full lines of text are repeated. [4] The following year, there appeared several octavo editions of the Bible, in one of which the repetition of these three lines still occurs. Omissions of portions of the text make certain other editions remarkable. An octavo Authorized Version of 1631 was indiscreet enough to drop the word *not* from the seventh commandment (Ex. xx. 14), an error which resulted in the suppression of the thousand copies thus printed and the imposition of a fine of £300 (a heavy one in those days) upon the printers. This impression — of which only four copies are now known, one at the New York Public Library — is in consequence distinguished as the "Wicked" Bible. An omission less serious in ethical implications but greater in scope is recorded by Sir Nicholas L'Estrange of Hunstanton in the following anecdote preserved in a British Museum manuscript: [5] "Dr. Usher, Bishop of Armath, being to preach at Paules Crosse and passing hastily by one of the stationers, called for a Bible, and had a little one of the London edition given him out, but when he came to looke for his text, *that very verse was omitted* in the print: which gave the first occasion of complaint to the king of the insufferable negligence, and insufficience of the London printers and presse, and bredde that great contest that followed, betwixt the university of Cambridge and London stationers, about printing of the Bibles."

Omissions, repetitions, mis-readings and other errors are, as one might expect, far less frequent in the printed Bible than in its manuscript forerunners. Centuries before the adoption of Massoretic regulations designed to preclude transcriptional inaccuracies, errors of various kinds, as we have already seen, had crept into the Scriptural texts. Though many of these were of little moment, some were of great importance; all, as they were noted, contributed to the development of the techniques of textual criticism.

One of the earliest devices employed by pre-Massoretic scribes for the purpose of calling attention to a difficult or rare or unacceptable reading was the PASĒQ [פסק] or note-line. This consisted simply of a vertical line inserted at the appropriate point into the text, like *sic* or *Nota bene*, and served, for one of several purposes,[b] to indicate that the reading was not the responsibility of the scribe, but was an accurate transcription of his copy. Of such note-lines there are no less than one hundred and two in the book of Job alone. Many of them indicate a word appearing nowhere else; others call attention to doubtful readings or unintelligible passages. These note-lines, it must be understood, constitute no correction of the text; but, as Kennedy has pointed out,[6] they were "an important and valuable preparation for later work by the Massoretes." Of genuine text-critical character, however, were the NEQUDÔTh [נקודות] or Extraordinary Points, of which there are only fifteen

---

[b] Among other uses of this mark was the separation of the Divine Name from an adjacent word which was deemed unseemly for such association; and, more importantly, the indication of poetic rhythm.

instances in the entire Old Testament — ten in the Pentateuch, four in the Prophets, and but one in the Hagiographa. These points were employed "to condemn, as spurious, the words or letters over which they were placed." [7]

Mention of these points in the Talmud, supplemented by references to "corrections" and "removals" of the scribes, throws some light upon the critical attitude toward the pre-Massoretic text. This early text, though probably "fixed" in approximately its present form by the second century, had certainly undergone considerable editorial revision. The Septuagint, three to four centuries earlier, was a translation "evidently made from a [Hebrew] codex which differed widely in places from the text crystallized by the Masorah." [8] This divergence is further corroborated by the evidence of the Samaritan Pentateuch and of several papyri discovered within the last century. Without a doubt, as already noted, [9] textual corrections of various kinds had been made in the ancestral documents, and these were corrections of no little significance. Furthermore, we come across notes on textual criticism of the Old Testament, usually as it was edited by Origen (c. A. D. 185–253), in the exegetical works of Christian commentators of the third and fourth centuries. All this evidence, considerable though it be, points to no critical editing of the Old Testament text as a whole. For that scholarly work the world had to wait another millennium.

In the meantime some well-written codex — possibly one of those preserved in the Court of the Temple — served as the standard from which copies might be made. Attention has been previously drawn [10] to the annotations (QERE — קְרִי)[c] introduced into such copies to indicate, among many other things, substitutions of readings other than those found in the standard text. In some instances, very probably, such substitutions, of earlier date, are evidence of variant readings in manuscripts no longer extant. In others, they indicate what was felt by Jewish authorities to be the "necessity of replacing erroneous, difficult,

---

[c] This verb — an Aramaic imperative, sometimes inadvisedly vocalized קְרַ (QERI) — may be best rendered "to be read."

irregular, provincial, archaic, unseemly, or cacophonous expressions by correct, simpler, current, appropriate, or euphonious readings."[11] Still other substitutions — not to exhaust the functions of the QеRE — reflect "mystic or homiletical" interpretations of the text or "variants found in Talmudic literature."[11] These marginalia are of three varieties: (1) words written in the text but not to be read; (2) words written in the text to be read "with a difference"; (3) words not written in the text, but to be supplied by the reader. Although there are between thirteen hundred and fourteen hundred such indicated substitutions in the Old Testament text — a considerable body of textual criticism — it would be injudicious indeed to conclude that all the corruptions of the Hebrew manuscripts have been thereby eliminated. The suggested readings are merely the most available corrections of those errors which are most readily discerned. In the well over seven hundred instances in which the marginal alternative presents a completely different reading from the traditionally received text (KеTHIВh — כתיב), we may assume that textual corruption had been frankly conceded and that, in all probability, we have pre-Massoretic examples of conjectural emendation,[12] perhaps the vestiges of the earliest Scriptural *apparatus criticus*. That the embryonic critical process was not under ideal control is apparent from those cases in which modern scholars are now compelled to reject the marginal reading as "clearly the inferior," and from others in which neither of the two readings is today acceptable.[13] Even Jewish scholars — who, it must be understood, are obliged to follow the QеRE — feel constrained in their most recent English translation of the Old Testament occasionally to reject the Massoretic emendation and to adopt the consonants of the text (KеTHIВh).[14]

In the medieval period, post-Massoretic Jewish students of the Old Testament recognized the need of further emendation, even to the extent of suggesting deliberate alteration of the received consonantal text. In that rigidly established text, as it had come down to them, there were admittedly no less than eighteen such deliberate alterations, which had achieved uni-

versal sanction, none of which is held to be spurious by competent Biblical scholars of today.[d] Obviously, the question naturally
enough presented itself, if eighteen errors of the text might be
corrected, why not a nineteenth? And if nineteen, why not a
twentieth?

> "He shall deliver thee in six troubles;
> Yea, in seven there shall no evil touch thee." (Job v. 19)

Some Hebrew grammarians of the middle ages, to be sure, did
not hesitate to propose numerous textual improvements in the
Old Testament, some of which, though falling at the time on
barren ground, anticipated the suggestions of scholars of the
nineteenth and twentieth centuries.[15] Medieval scholarship went
as far, no doubt, as it dared or could. The modern scholar,
equipped with a linguistic science unavailable to his predecessors,
and sustained by fairly recent findings of archaeology and history, is justified in moving freely along critical paths which were
naturally closed to the earlier Sopherim and Massoretes, and
which their successors of a later epoch had not learned to tread.
By the year 1886, however, even without archaeological support,

---

[d] Not to be confused with the 18 *Tiqqune Sopherim* (*v. supra*, p. 37) which
belong rather to the field of exegesis than to textual criticism, nor with
the 18 Massoretic insertions and omissions (*v. supra*, p. 37), nor with the
euphemisms and other substitutions mentioned at pp. 37, 51. In the case of
Judg. xviii. 30, it should be noted — where, it is traditionally held, the introduction of a suspended consonant (*nun*) changes the conjecturally earlier reading "Jonathan, the son of Gershom, the son of *Moses*" (משה — MŠH) to the
alternative "son of *Manasseh*" (מנשה — MNŠŠH) — the modern English translations are divided: *Moses* is retained by the Douay Version and the R. V.;
Manasseh is adopted by the A. V. and the A. J. V. Moses, to be sure, is recorded
as having had a son Gershom by his wife Zipporah (Ex. ii. 22), but no grandson
Jonathan. According to the medieval scholar Rashi (*i. e.*, Rabbi Solomon
bar Isaac), the purpose of the interpolated *nun* was for the honor of Moses,
presumably by dissociating him from the backsliding priesthood of later days.
[For transliteration see p. 63.] Similarly, a suspended *ayin* (ע) is introduced
into the text at three places: Ps. lxxx. 14 (M. T. 15), Job xxxviii. 13 and 15.
These suspended letters are very likely instances of unresolved metatheses,
the ancient authorities being unable, in each of these four cases, to determine
which of two variant sequences of the consonants should be relegated to the
QERE. See *Jewish Encyclopedia*, XI, 603. *V. infra*, pp. 62 ff., and pp. 106 ff.

it was possible for a Biblical scholar to assert with conviction that "Hebrew grammar and science are well enough settled to maintain with certainty that the text [of the Old Testament] must in many places be altered."[16] It is none the less still advisable to bear in mind that there are "minutiae and subtleties of syntax whose inadequate treatment in Hebrew grammars has misled many exegetes into emending perfect texts."[17] Caution is certainly to be recommended. In textual criticism a tact which few possess is required, and effectiveness, as Canon Streeter took care to inform us,[18] is contingent upon "the insight, judgement, and common sense of the individual scholar, which are necessarily 'subjective' " and, he adds, "rare."

In addition to insight, judgment, common sense, and tact — qualities which are not without value in all departments of scholarship — the critical editor of the Biblical or any other text must have, in the first place, an understanding of the various ways in which errors arise, and, in the second place, must proceed, in the correction of errors, only in accord with certain acceptable principles. His primary purpose, of course — to which emendation of any kind is secondary — is to preserve exactly as it has been transmitted as much as possible of the text: to retain, if that may be, every word, every letter, every mark of punctuation; to support every questionable reading with every available external witness. In the case of the Old Testament, the readings of the oldest surviving manuscripts of the Massoretic Text may be confirmed or modified in the light of the Talmud, *Targumim* and *Mishna*, and, as will be seen, by rabbinical quotations,[19] the Septuagint and other ancient versions, and latterly certain fragments of papyri. This multifold evidence gives ample indication that the Massoretic Text, since its final crystallization, has been handed down with a scribal fidelity such as to give the textual critic more than ordinary pause. The tradition of textual integrity is stronger in the case of the Massoretic Text than in that of any other medieval documents. Yet errors do appear. In the particularly well-guarded Pentateuch they are found only here and there, but they occur much more frequently in the Prophets and the Hagiographa, the separate Books of which at first no doubt circulated privately, and, long under no synagogal supervision, suffered textual corruption by undisciplined transcribers.[e] Even after all the books which now constitute the Old Testament had been gathered into the canon and were subject to official scrutiny — indeed, throughout the centuries during which the Massoretes were at their extraordinary pains to establish the textual tradition in its every jot and tittle — deviations from the ancestral pattern crept into the text. Textual differences, for instance, between the two authoritative codices of Ben Asher and Ben Naphthali have long been recognized.[f]

Lists of variants which were acknowledged throughout the Middle Ages occur in divers manuscripts, including, among many others, one of the early twelfth century in the Bodleian Library;[g] another in de Rossi's collection[h] dated A. D. 1270;

[e] *Cf.* Margolis, *The Story of Bible Translations*, p. 125; and H. L. Strack, in Hastings' *Dictionary of the Bible*, IV, 726. Even in the Masorah, whose special function was to put a protective "fence" around the Torah, errors occur. One of these appears in connection with the initial verse of Genesis. The Masorah points out that the particular collocation of words of that verse "the heaven and the earth" (את השמים ואת הארץ) are found together three (ג) times only. There are, however, *thirteen* (יג) such occurrences: Gen. i. 1; Ex. xx. 11; xxxi. 17; Deut. iv. 26; xxx. 19; xxxi. 28; II Kgs. xix. 15; II Chr. ii. 12 (M. T. 11); Is. xxxvii. 16; Jer. xxiii. 24; xxxii. 17; Hag. ii. 6; ii. 21. Walton, who remarks that this is "stumbling at the very threshold," fails to note that this error could be scribal rather than rabbinical, the *yodh* (י) of *thirteen* (יג) probably having been overlooked by the copyist. See Benjamin Kennicott, *State of the Printed Hebrew Text of the Old Testament*, Oxford, 1759, p. 275.

[f] At Is. xxx. 23, for example, the Ben Naphthali tradition gives us "rain for *thy earth*" (אַרְצָךְ — 'aʀṣeʀhā); whereas Ben Asher — largely followed by the manuscripts and adopted by all printers of the received Hebrew text — reads "for *thy seed*" (זַרְעֶךְ — zaʀ'aʀhā). At Job xxxiv. 14, as the Massoretes note, some MSS. of the Babylonian school read יָשִׂיב [yāsīʙh], with יָשִׂים [yāsīm] — the Palestinian and traditional reading — in the margin. [For transliteration see p. 63, note t.]

[g] MS. Arch. Seld. A 47 (probably to be dated A. D. 1104), which, on fols. 95[v]-97[r], contains some eleven columns of differing readings in Ben Asher and Ben Naphthali, the total variants recorded being 207. Another Bodleian MS. — formerly Laud Or. 326, now Western MS. 467; No. 179 in Neubauer and Cowley's Catalogue — containing the inscription "Praefiguntur Discrepantiae Hagiographorum, sive variae lectiones in eam Bibliorum partem,

and a third in the Vatican Library,[i] undated but assigned to
the thirteenth century. Early in the sixteenth century these
lists of variant readings found their way for the first time into
print. In the second edition of Bomberg's Rabbinic Bible,[j]
variants to the number of 216 were cited by the editor, Jacob
ben Ḥayyim. Variant readings were a feature of Capell's
excellent study of 1650, previously referred to. But it remained
for Benjamin Kennicott, Fellow of Exeter College and Vicar
of Culham in Oxfordshire, to carry this investigation further.
In his *State of the Printed Hebrew Text of the Old Testament*,
Kennicott discusses the textual variations discovered by him in
an examination of no less than seventy Hebrew manuscripts,
and indicates their value in textual emendation. For his edition
of the Old Testament, published at Oxford in 1776–1780, in
which he attempts to establish the several kinds of alteration
the text had undergone in antiquity, Kennicott and his assistants collected variants in the consonantal text of more than six
hundred manuscripts. Shortly thereafter, the basis of textual
criticism was still further enlarged by de Rossi[20] whose collations of Old Testament manuscripts, added to those examined
by Kennicott, brought the total of manuscripts investigated to
1346. Upon this eighteenth-century foundation later Biblical
scholars have built so well that twentieth-century editions of

---

quae inscribitur כתובים," lists no less than 367 Ben Asher-Ben Naphthali
divergencies (fol. 2ᵛ) and devotes about three hundred lines to variant readings
in Chronicles alone (fol. 1ᵛ–2ᵛ).

[h] Cod. No. 782. *Cf.* Giovanni Bernardo de Rossi, *MSS. codices Hebraici
biblioth. I. B. de Rossi . . . .*, 3 vols., Parmae, 1803.

[i] Assemani, *Bibliothecae Apostolicae Vaticanae Codicum manuscriptorum Catalogus*,
Pars I, tom. 1, p. 7: "Is Codex (MS. No. VII) ad decimum tertium Christi
seculum videtur referendus . . . . A folio 457 . . . habentur variae aliae Lectiones accentuum in multis Sacrae Scripturae dictionibus inter Ben-Ascer, &
Ben-Naphtali, quae . . . in fine Tomi IV Magnorum Bibliorum Rabbinicorum
editionis Venetae, & Basilleensis Leguntur."

[j] Venice, 1524–25. *V. infra*, p. 176. A Latin translation of ben Ḥayyim's
critical Introduction to Bomberg's Rabbinic Bible, found at the Bodleian in
MS. Laud Misc. 404 (dated 1610, and once the property of Archbishop Laud),
was printed by Benjamin Kennicott, *op. cit.*, and an English translation was
published at London, by C. D. Ginsburg, in 1865.

the Bible openly recognize the validity of their text-critical claims.[k]

The ultimate source of textual deviations was, of course, the Scribe. Infallibility is hardly a human characteristic; and those "blind guides," the scribes, who strain out[1] a gnat and swallow a camel, were, from the scholarly point of view, all too human. To understand the various ways in which the scribe's errors arose, it is essential to consider the copyist as a human being while at work at his desk in the scriptorium. It may be recalled that the authorities of the medieval synagogue so considered him, and, knowing his frailties, laid down certain rules under which his work was to be performed.[m] The scribe was no man of learning. Erudition, in fact, would have been an occupational liability. The scribal function was to transcribe, not to edit. Intelligence the scribe had to possess — less, perhaps, than would today be required of a competent stenographer. But it was not for him either to question the text he was set

---

[k] *Cf.* the 1893 Encyclical *Providentissimus Deus*, of Pope Leo XIII, which serves as Introduction to subsequent printings of the Douay Version. His Holiness, though suggesting that the textual question be handled with care, says: "It is true, no doubt, that copyists have made mistakes in the text of the Bible." (Benziger Brothers' edition, 1914, p. xxx). See, also, the Preface, p. v., of A. J. V.

[1] This, undoubtedly the correct reading, at Mt. xxiii. 24, of English versions from Wycliffe through Rheims N. T. [*cf.* Stanley Cook, *An Introduction to the Bible*, Harmondsworth, 1945, p. 41], has yet to find its way into the King James Version. Msgr. Ronald Knox renders this passage "a strainer for the gnat," Goodspeed "straining out the gnat," and Moffatt "filtering away the gnat." For these and other modern translators see Chapter VIII.

[m] *V. supra*, p. 31. In Christian circles the scribe was not so hedged about with sacerdotal solemnities or mechanical checks such as word-counting. By Origen's time, the transcription of manuscripts was no longer dependent upon voluntary and unskilled labor, but was performed by slaves especially trained for the task. Subsequently, the copying of the Scriptures was taken in hand by ascetics as a work of piety. Later still, in some of the monastic foundations, the labor of copying was assigned to the younger men, and often, with no improvement in the performance, it was made a penance. *Cf. Encyclopedia of Religion and Ethics*, II, p. 583. One of the scribes of Codex Sinaiticus was so illiterate that his assignment to work on a manuscript of that distinction passes comprehension. *Cf.* [British Museum], *The Codex Sinaiticus and the Codex Alexandrinus*, printed by order of the trustees, Oxford, 1938, p. 15.

to copy or to interpret it. That is to say, he was a technically *
skilled man at a daily job. Speed and accuracy were the
measures of his success; no doubt the former was sometimes
achieved at the expense of the latter. Whether the transcription were done rapidly or not, however, its accuracy was
dependent upon the scribe's "attention span." However conscientious a member of the scriptorium he may have been, a
scribe's mind would, from time to time, like anyone else's,
involuntarily wander. At such moments inaccuracies in his
copy were likely enough to appear. Such, in any case, is the
scribal record that, according to the late Librarian of the
Bodleian, certainly an excellent and conservative authority,
"all who . . . have studied palaeography will acknowledge that
the probability against two consecutive leaves being really correctly transcribed is about a hundred to one."[21]

Faulty transcription, psychological in its operation, has its
origin, frequently, in what may be called "accidental" characteristics of the ancestral document. Certain casual features
result in additions to the text; others result in omissions. One
such feature now well known to be a source of textual expansion is the gloss or marginal commentary. The incorporation
of annotations into the central text of his transcript is a common failing of an undiscriminating or slavish scribe. These
marginalia, though informative or edifying in themselves, constitute no part of the original document, the coherence of
which is sadly destroyed by their inclusion. Especially is the
result confusing when through careless copying several glosses
are concurrently assimilated by the text, as is held by at least
one scholar to be the case throughout Ecclesiastes[22] and here
and there in the Book of Job.[n] Sometimes it is the rubric or

---

[n] For incorporation of marginalia in the N. T., *v. infra*, pp. 135 ff.; also
B. H. Streeter, *The Four Gospels*, 4th impr. rev., London, 1930, pp. 566–7.
Biblical printers, as well as scribes, mistakenly incorporate marginalia. In a
Cambridge edition of the A. V., published in 1805, Gal. iv. 29 reads — non-
sensically — "Persecuted him that was born after the Spirit to remain even
so it is now," the words *to remain* being originally a proof-reader's notation to
the printer that a comma in the text after *Spirit* was not to be deleted.

the colophon, rather than a marginal annotation, which the scribe incorporates into the central text — witness "The words of Job are ended" at Job xxxi. 40, or "The prayers of David the son of Jesse are ended," Psalm lxxii. 20. Restoration of the text to its pristine state by the segregation of such intrusive passages not only contributes to the artistic effectiveness of Scripture, but sometimes gives logical form to an otherwise inconsistent or unintelligible passage.

Another accidental feature likely, in any manuscript, to result in scribal error is *homoioteleuton;* that is, the occurrence of two identical terminal words (or phrases or groups of letters) within a short distance of each other. This is the origin of both textual expansion and textual abbreviation. The scribe, on the one hand, having copied a passage which ends with the *second* of two such terminal duplicates, may, when he glances again at the text he is transcribing, inadvertently focus upon the *first* of the two identical terminals, from which point he will resume his copying, thus unintentionally retranscribing the intervening words. This is most probably the explanation of the previously noted *compositor's* repetition of three lines of Exodus xiv. 10 in the first edition of the King James Version. An even larger textual duplication of a similar nature, made by a pre-Massoretic scribe and uncorrected to this day, is to be found in the Massoretic Text, in which no less than ten verses of I Chronicles (viii. 29–38) are repeated, with only minor variations, at the following chapter, I Chronicles ix. 35–44. The scribe, on the other hand, having copied a passage ending with the same words as those which terminate a subsequent portion of the text, may, upon continuing his work, carelessly resume his transcription at the *second* of the textual twins, thus entirely omitting the intervening passage. [23] Large scale omissions of this origin can be discovered, of course, only in manuscripts which are seen to be deficient in comparison with others containing the unbroken text. Within the received text itself, though on the analogy of other manuscripts homoioteleuton may be occasionally suspected, there is no longer the likelihood of its detection.

Omissions of different origin, more limited in scope, occurring throughout the Massoretic Text, are likewise attributable to scribal inattentiveness. One of the best known examples is at I Samuel xiii. 1, which, owing to an omission of a word, now tells erroneously that Saul was but one year of age when he ascended the throne of Israel. The American Jewish Version frankly admits the difficulty and reads: "Saul was . . . years old when he began to reign." Early Septuagintal manuscripts omit the entire verse; some later manuscripts insert the word *thirty*. Occasionally, an omission in the text is clearly enough indicated by incompletion of the thought. At Genesis iv. 8 we read: "And Cain said to Abel his brother; and it came to pass, when they were in the field, that Cain rose against Abel his brother and slew him." One would like to know just what Cain said to his brother. Happily, we can find out by going to the Septuagint, which by informing us that Cain said to his brother, "Let us go into the field" (Διέλθωμεν εἰς τὸ πεδίον), not only supplies the want but restores the logical sequence of the thought. The Septuagintal reading is here adopted both by the Douay Version and by the Smith-Goodspeed American Translation. To render the first portion of this verse, with the King James translators, "And Cain talked with [R. V.: *told;* A. J. V.: *spoke unto*] Abel," is a questionable recourse to an intransitive form of the verb employed in order to cover up the anacoluthon. In the preceding chapter of Genesis (iii. 22) there is another sentence the unfinished state of which was sufficient to provoke that scribal indication of something amiss, the note-line. There we read: "And the LORD God said, Behold, the man is become as one of us, to know good and evil; and now, lest he put forth his hand, and take also of the tree of life, and eat, and live forever: therefore the LORD God sent him forth . . ." To this, a conclusion is obviously required. In this case, however, the Septuagint comes not to the rescue. Another indication of omitted text is found in the violation of the acrostic pattern of certain Biblical poems, notably Psalms. Where, as in Psalm cxlv, each succeeding verse begins with a successive letter of the Hebrew alphabet, the absence of a verse beginning with *nun* [נ] at the expected place in the sequence is without question a sign of something missing. In this instance we can corroborate the loss — and in part restore it — with the aid of the Septuagintal reading, which at this point in the poem begins a verse with Πιστὸς κύριος ["Faithful is the LORD"]: words which presuppose a Hebrew original נאמן יהוה [N'MN YHVH] the first letter of which supplies the necessary consonant *nun*.

Of different character is the unintentional omission of a letter or letters, a word or series of words, when those letters or words occur twice in close juxtaposition in the original manuscript; or, to state it differently, the inadvertent transcription of only one of the two occurrences of the repeated letters or words. This type of accidental abbreviation of the text, known as *haplography*, is particularly common when the first of two consecutive words terminates with a consonant with which the following word begins.[o] Contributory to this is the genius of the Hebrew language which in general is unfriendly to the writing of doubled or repeated consonants. Frequently omitted, for example, is the definite article ה in immediate sequence to a word ending in that letter. In Jeremiah xii. 12, to illustrate from the King James Version, we read: "the sword of the LORD shall devour from the *one* end of [the] land even to the *other* end of the land," the bracketed *the* having no counterpart in the Massoretic Text.[p] In Judges xx. 13 occurs a haplographic slip long since recognized by the Massoretes themselves. At that verse, in the Authorized and the American Jewish Versions, we read: "But the children of Benjamin would not hearken . . . ,[q] although there is no justifying equivalent of *children* in the Massoretic Text. For this the

[o] An analogous English example of haplography is *Riding* in "North Riding of Yorkshire," originally *North Thridding*; *i. e.*, North Third.

[p] The M. T., which is translated in the present tense by both R. V. and A. J. V., reads: מקצה ארץ ועד־קצה הארץ. Observe the article ה in the second phrase [הארץ].

[q] M. T.: "Benjamin [they] would not hearken," the verb being in the plural; thus: ולא אבו בנימן. Douay, ignoring *Benjamin* of the text, renders: "But they would not hearken." Smith-Goodspeed: "Benjaminites would not accede to . . ." Moulton: "Benjamites would not . . ."

simple explanation is that, in Hebrew, the three letters (בני)
which spell *children* happen to be the first three letters of Benjamin
(בנימן), with a resultant scribal omission of the first three-letter
group.[r]

Exactly the reverse of haplography is another scribal failing,
dittography — the inadvertent duplication, in the transcription,
of letters, words, or even entire sentences which appear in a
neighboring part of the original. Massoretic recognition of dittographic corruption of the text, though infrequent, does occur.
Marked as "written but not to be read" is the superfluous *five*
(חמש) in the "five five hundred" of Ezekiel xlviii. 16; the duplicated *tread* or *bend* (ידרך) of Jeremiah li. 3; and the carelessly repeated first letter of המדה in the preceding word קוה
(properly קו) at Jeremiah xxxi. 39 (M. T. 38). Dittographs unacknowledged by the Massoretes are numerous. In II Samuel
xxii. 7, by way of illustration, both lines of the verse contain
the verb *I call* (אקרא). In the eighteenth Psalm, however, which,
except for minutiae, is identical with II Samuel xxii, only the
first line of verse 6 (M. T. 7) has *I call*. The second line of the
verse varies the sense with the verb *I cry for help* (אשוע). The
Septuagint at this point in Samuel employs, like the Psalmist,
two distinct verbs: ἐπικαλέσομαι in the first line; βοήσομαι in
the second. It would seem reasonable, accordingly, to attribute
the second *I call* of II Samuel xxii. 7 to a dittographic slip of the
copyist.[24] Even more obviously a case of dittography is the disturbing repetition, in Joshua xxi. 25, of *Gath-rimmon*, one of the
Levitical cities of refuge included, *in the immediately preceding verse*,
among those assigned to the families of the children of Kohath.
In the parallel account of the Chronicler, Gath-rimmon is properly listed but once.[25] Dittography is less immediately apparent
when, as sometimes happens, the duplicated passages are widely
separated. The final words of I Chronicles ix. 34, for example,

---

[r] For additional examples of haplographic omissions from the text where,
as in this instance, the Massoretic injunction is "read though not written,"
see, among other passages, the Hebrew text of II Sam. xviii. 20; Ruth iii. 17;
and Jer. xxxi. 38 (M. T. 37).

are, in their Englished form, "these dwelt in Jerusalem." If, as we may imagine, the scribe who was copying this Book of the Old Testament interrupted his work at this point and returned to it only after an interval — perhaps the day following — he may quite easily have made the careless error of resuming his transcription at another "these dwelt in Jerusalem" occurring not very far away in the same Book as the concluding statement of verse 28 of the adjacent eighth chapter. This, it would seem, is precisely what the scribe did, and he did not discover his dittographic error until he had re-copied ten complete verses which he had previously written in chapter viii. His error, allowed to stand, has been perpetuated to the present day.

Of greater exegetical interest is a scribal error in Genesis ii. 2 which may also be attributed to dittography. There we now read: "And on the seventh day God finished his work which he had made; and he rested on the seventh day from all his work which he had made." Inasmuch as God, according to the preceding verses, had completed his work of creation, and had seen that it was very good, on the *sixth* day, we need feel no surprise to find in the Septuagint — sustained by the Samaritan Version and the Peshitto — the logically anticipated reading: "And on the *sixth* day God finished his work which he had made; and he rested on the seventh day . . . ." Exegetical ingenuity in support of the received but illogical text has here, as elsewhere, secured the preservation of what appears to be an ancient transcriptional error.

The scribe, without adding to the text he is copying, or omitting anything from it, may yet produce textual confusion merely by inadvertent transposition of the letters or words in his original. Such an interchange — known as *metathesis* — is a very common failing of compositors and typists of the twentieth century as well as of ancient workers in the scriptorium. The psychological tendency which in vulgar speech produces "I axed (aksed) him" for "asked him"; and, even in cultivated speech permits "hunderd" for "hundred," is no doubt largely responsible for those unintentional anagrams known to every modern proof-reader and familiar to students of handwritten documents of whatever epoch.⁸ Metathesis, it may well be held, is even more likely to occur in a vowel-less script such as that of Hebrew than in an orthography, like that of English, more rigidly controlled through literal indication of its every vowel. The Hebrew word for *outer garment*, to illustrate this contention, occurs as שלמה [SLMH] eight times, and as שמלה [SMLH] six.

Textual error through consonantal transposition is, in not a few of its many Biblical occurrences, acknowledged by the editors of the received Hebrew text. At Joshua vi. 13, the Massoretes rightly suggest (QERE) the transposition of the two interior letters of the participial form הולך [HÔLKh — *he who goes*] so as to give the infinitive הלוך [HLÔKh — *going on*]; and at Proverbs xiii. 20 they indicate again, quite properly, the exchange of these same two forms, but in the reverse order. At Ezekiel xlii. 16, the Massoretes, with equal propriety, instruct the reader to substitute for the obviously erroneous אמות ['MÔTH — *cubits*] of the text the appropriate word מאות [M'ÔTH — *hundreds*],ᵗ again

---

⁸ Words metathesized in pronunciation, frequently establish themselves in their transposed form as the accepted written norm; witness, in English examples alone, *bird* from *brid*; *what* from *hwaet*; *curl* from *crulle*. In Hebrew, metathesis is a phonetic characteristic of the *Hithpaʿel* of verbs whose initial root letter is a sibilant. This sibilant and the *tav* of the verbal prefix חת [HTH] are regularly transposed. Example: סָתַר [SĀTHAR — *to hide*]; הִסְתַּתֵּר [HISTATTĒR — *to hide oneself*]. Metathesis is responsible for the opinion, long held, that Ibn Ezra, despite the geographical unlikelihood, produced at least some of his work on the Isle of Rhodes. MS. authority for this mistaken belief resides in the transposed transliteration into Hebrew of a place-name: רדוס (RODÔS). Graetz relocated Ibn Ezra on the Continent, but far from the right neighborhood, by interpreting this metathesized spelling as Rodez, Departement of Aveyron, in the south of France. The original reading, from which the corruption arose, must, in the opinion of Wilhelm Bacher [*Revue des études juives*, XVII (Paris, 1888), pp. 301 ff.], have been דרוס (DRUS); *i. e.*, Dreux, a town in the Departement of Eure-et-Loire in that northern part of France whence came the rationalist exegesis not only of Ibn Ezra but of Rashi, the Kimchis, and their associates. *V. infra*, pp. 255 ff.

ᵗ The transliteration here employed — designed to exhibit points which might elude the reader unfamiliar with Hebrew — is as follows: The consonants — except *aleph* [א — '] and *ayin* [ע — ʿ] — and the vowel-letters *vav* [ו — ô, U] and *yodh* [י (ִ, ֵ) — E, I] are represented by their approximate English equivalents in SMALL CAPITALS; *qoph* [ק] is indicated by Q, and an

nothing other than the reversal of the order of two letters, the
first two consonants of the word in question. Less likely to cause
misinterpretation of the text, but none the less evidence of the
scribal tendency to depart from the original order of what lies
before him, is the transposition, not of individual letters, but of
whole words. In Hebrew, where such reversal of word order is
of less syntactical significance than it would be in English, the
scribe's interchange of two words may go entirely unnoticed.
Psalm xxv. 2, the interpretation of which offers no difficulty,
illustrates this point perfectly. The Psalm, being an alphabetical
acrostic, requires that its second verse begin with the second
letter *beth* [ב] of the Hebrew alphabet. As the Massoretic Text
now stands, however, the initial letter of the first word of that
verse (אלהי) is an *aleph* [א]. The word immediately following
(בך) begins with the desired *beth*. An interchange of these first
two words[u] is all that is needed to restore to the Psalm its acrostic integrity. Metathesis as an instrument of textual revision will
be further considered in a subsequent chapter.

Errors arise in two other ways, neither of which necessarily
involves accidental omission of letters from the text or their
insertion. Both originate in the scribal custom, previously referred to, of leaving insufficient space between words, or omitting the point or fine stroke by which words were separated.
One of these ways — which in some instances does result in loss
of a letter — is *fusion*; its antithesis — which often requires the

infra-literal dot distinguishes *ḥeth* [ח — Ḥ], *ṭeth* [ט — Ṭ], and *ṣadhe* [צ — ṣ].
A supra-literal inverted caret differentiates *shin* [שׁ — š] from *sin* [שׂ — s].
The six aspirates ב, ג, ד, כ, פ, ת are characterized by an affixed lower-case
'h.' Final *he* [ה — H] when pointed with *mappiq* is underscored. Consonantal
yodh, when silent, is shown by lower-case 'y.' *Daghesh forte* doubles a consonant.
Thus, *beth* may be transliterated as B, BB, or Bh; *tav* as T, TT, or Th; *vav* as
consonantal v or vv and vocalic ô or U; *yodh* as Y, YY, E, I, or y. The vowel-
points, when transliterated, are in lower case, long vowels being indicated,
when advisable, by a macron [¯]. The indeterminate vowel *sh'va* [ְ] is
indicated by italicized 'e' [*e*]. The transliteration, of course, reverses the
Hebrew order, from right to left, and reads in the English manner.

[u] *I. e.*, בך אלהי ("In Thee, O my God") instead of the received אלהי בך
("O my God, in Thee"). *V. infra*, pp. 106 ff.

addition of a letter — may be known as *fission*. Fusion is the mistaken coalescence of two consecutive words into one. A case in point is found at Song of Songs viii. 6, where the Massoretic Text, retaining the seven-letter combination of Ben Asher which in the Authorized Version is translated "a most vehement flame," is at variance with Ben Naphthali's reading of these seven consonants as *two* separate words which may be rendered, as they are in the Revised and the American Jewish Versions, "a very flame of the LORD."[v] An excellent illustration of fusion is provided by the seventy-third Psalm, the first verse of which, in the received text, gives us the reading:

> "Surely God is good to Israel,
> Even to such as are pure in heart."

"Pure in heart" certainly requires something other than "Israel" as a parallelism.[w] Recovery of the requisite expression calls for nothing more than the assumption, first made by Duhm,[26] that the six-letter word לישראל [LYSR'L — *to Israel*] is an unfortunate union of two words, לישר אל [LYŠR 'L], meaning, with the rest of the verse, "Surely God is good to an upright man." Of the numerous examples of fusion involving loss of a letter, some have been recognized by the Massoretes, as at Isaiah iii. 15 where the combination מלכם [MLLKhM] of the received reading has been erroneously formed by the amalgamation of the two words מה לכם [MH LKhM — *What mean ye*]. Not corrected by the Massoretes, but marked by them with the querying note-line, is Job xxiv. 14, where the murderer is pictured as rising at dawn (A. V.: "with the light") to kill his victims. To the killer is restored some professional competence, and to the poem its customary poetic parallelism,[x] by the assumption that the four-letter word לאור [L'ÔR], translated "with the light," is a careless scribe's fusion of the two words לא אור [L' 'ÔR], pro-

[v] Ben Asher: שַׁלְהֶבֶתְיָה [šaLHeBheThyaH]. Ben Naphthali: שַׁלְהֶבֶת־יָה [šaLHeBheTh yaH]. Note also the difference in vocalization. *V. supra*, p. 39, note z. *Cf.* QeRE: Gen. xxx. 11; Ezek. viii. 6; Jer. vi. 29; *et al.*

[w] For parallelism *v. infra*, p. 82.

[x] *I. e.*, with "in the night" of the second half of the verse.

viding, with the adjacent verb, the suitable reading: "rising (while there is) no light."

Fission — the antithesis of fusion — sometimes called *diatomy*, has been given occasional Massoretic recognition. Their judgment, for instance, of the two words כי טוב [KI ṬÔBh] of Judges xvi. 25 is that they are erroneously formed by the splitting of the four-letter word כטוב [KṬÔBh], and the insertion of a *yodh*.[27] Remarkable is the unjustifiable case of fission, without the addition of a single letter, which is responsible for the introduction into the English language of the now well-known word *scapegoat*. At Leviticus xvi. 8, 10 and 26, but nowhere else in the Old Testament, occurs a rare and still unexplained word of six letters [לעזאזל — L'Z'ZL] which, in the Revised Version and in the American Jewish Version, is merely transliterated as the only way out of the difficulty, giving the reading "for Azazel." The translators of the Septuagint, puzzled by this word, gave to the passage a vague rendition which in no way helps to clarify its meaning. Later non-Jewish scholars, not content with an incomprehensible "for Azazel," found what to them was a more satisfactory interpretation by the simple process of splitting the strange word into two equal parts of three letters each, thus: לעז אזל [L'Z 'ZL]. The first of these two tri-literals means "for a goat"; the second signifies "going about" or "wandering." Thus illegitimately divided, "for Azazel" entered the fourth-century Latin version of Jerome[y] as *Capro emissario* (rendered in the Douay Version as "emissary goat") and into Tyndale's English translation of 1530, the Great Bible of 1539–41, and the King James Version, as *scapegoat*.[z]

<hr />

[y] Before him, both Symmachus and Aquila had supplied the equivalent Greek: εἰς τράγον ἀπερχόμενον (Symmachus); εἰς τράγον ἀπολυόμενον (Aquila).

[z] In non-Biblical Hebrew literature also, it may be incidentally mentioned at this point, textual difficulties have arisen through fission. In *Pirkē Aboth*, for instance, as far back as the twelfth century, Rabbi Israel of Toledo conjecturally emended II. 1 by coalescing the two words לעושה ו [L'ÔSH v] into one, giving "to his Maker" instead of the traditional reading, "to him that does it." And in recent years, it was proposed by the late Chief Rabbi J. H. Hertz of London to amend VI. 3 by combining the two words שני דברים

Yet another source of error in the Hebrew text was the scribal practice of leaving no blank space at the end of a line. For this, the scribe would frequently employ abnormally expanded letters, or, unaware, apparently, of the consequent textual confusion, would sometimes fill up a line which did not happen to conclude with a complete word by inserting one or more letters of the word immediately following. This, in itself, would not have been too disturbing a custom; but coupled with the natural scribal tendency to begin the next line with a whole word — thus repeating the first letters of that word which had been previously used merely to fill up the blank space — the practice rendered the text liable to perversion. Potential textual corruption resulting from this custom was twofold: in the first place, the letters inserted at the end of a line might have been read, occasionally, as a word, and, so taken by a later copyist, introduced into the body of the text; or, in the second place, a perfectly legitimate word of the original text, if written at the end of a line and if repeated, by chance, in the beginning letters of the line following, might have been dropped out by a later copyist who mistakenly considered them mere filler.[28] An example of what is very probably a specimen of the first of these two types of corruption may be found at II Samuel xiii. 33, where, as the Massoretes indicate, the carelessly repeated first two letters of *Amnon*,[aa] which form a word אם ['M] by themselves, are to be rejected. The second of these two types of corruption may well be illustrated by the omission, previously cited, of *children* [בני] from *children of Benjamin* [בני בנימן] at Judges xx. 13.

Of all the foregoing sources of transcriptional error none operates so frequently as one to which reference has already been made in the previous chapter — the scribal confusion of letters

---

[ŠNE DBhRIM — two things] so as to read שנדברים [šaNNiDhBaRIM]; *i. e.*, David did not learn [anything] but was merely *conversing* [*cf.* הנדברים Ezek. xxxiii. 30] with Ahitophel. See *Pirkē Aboth*, ed. R. T. Herford, 3rd ed., rev., New York, 1945, pp. 40 and 153.

[aa] M. T.: כי־אם אמנון לבדו מת; *i. e.*, "For [Am] Amnon only is dead."

similar in form or pronunciation or both. Common among these literal confusions is that between *aleph* [א] and *vav* [ו], especially when used as vocalic consonants. These two letters, resembling each other not in the least in their present form, are, as they appear in the Siloam Inscription, hardly distinguishable.[bb] Their pronunciation, moreover, at a later period, when, as we have seen, vowel-letters were introduced into the text, was, in certain circumstances, identical; and, if used with a common consonant, they formed utterly unrelated words of different meaning but of identical pronunciation. Confusion, in such instances, may have been aural as well as visual. Owing to a slip either in taking dictation or in transcribing, there is frequent erroneous substitution in the Hebrew Old Testament of the negative לא [LO' — *not*] for the pronominal form לו [LÔ — *to him*], and *vice versa*. Both of these words are pronounced as the English *low*. Of the numerous examples of this particular failure to discriminate correctly — a failure repeatedly recognized and recorded by many generations of rabbis — two antithetical instances will suffice. At Isaiah xlix. 5, the reading of the Hebrew *textus receptus*, "Israel be *not* [לא] gathered," is changed by rabbinical marginal notation in the Hebrew manuscripts to "Israel be gathered *unto him*" [לו]; and, conversely, at I Samuel ii. 16, the Massoretic Text, "but to him [לו] thou shalt give (it) now," marked by a note-line, is assumed by rabbinical authority, including the editors of the American Jewish Version, to be a corruption of "Nay [לא], but thou shalt give (it me) now."

Even more common is the confusion of *vav* [ו] with its resemblant *yodh* [י]. In the earliest forms of the alphabet these two letters possessed sufficiently distinct features to obviate their interchange; any substitutions of one of them for the other must have taken place after crystallization of the Hebrew square script. That late possibility — frequently realized in the

[bb] *Cf.* Table of Alphabets; also W. H. Saulez, *The Romance of the Hebrew Language*, London and New York, 1913, pp. 3-4.

'Ain Fashkha rolls[29] — does not, of course, preclude this confusion of *vav* and *yodh* in those manuscripts which underlay the
Alexandrian translation into Greek in the third and second pre-
Christian centuries.[30] To give but two of several instances of
this, the Septuagintal reading of עינם ['INM — *their eye*, retained
by the American Jewish Version] in Zechariah v. 6 must have
been עונם ['VNM — *their iniquity*] in view of the Greek translator's ἡ ἀδικία αὐτῶν [Smith-Goodspeed: "their guilt"]; and
at Hosea xii. 5 (M. T. 6), remarkably enough, יהוה [YHVH —
Yahveh] has been read as יהיה [YHYH] and consequently rendered ἐσται [*will be*]. That *yodh* had been misread as a *vav* is
acknowledged by the Massoretes at Genesis viii. 17, where the
mispointed traditional הַוְצָא [HVṢ'] is corrected to היצא [HYṢ' —
bring forth]; also at Genesis xxxix. 20, in which the word
prisoners, appearing in all English versions, is obtained only by
changing the textual אסורי ['SVRE] to אסירי ['SIRE]; and at six
other places in the Pentateuch alone.[31] At Proverbs xi. 3 — to
cite one of many occurrences outside of the Pentateuch — the
same misreading is admitted by the Massoretes, who at that
point substitute ישדם [YŠDhM — *shall destroy them*] for the
received reading ושדם [VŠDDM — *and destroyed them*]. The converse scribal error of mistaking *vav* for *yodh* is recognized by
the Massoretes at eight places in the Pentateuch, one of them
being Genesis xxv. 23,[32] where the KeTHIBh גיּים [GYOYIM] becomes the QeRE גוים [GÔYIM — *nations*], and at no less than fifteen
places in Job.

At some stage in the development of the Aramaic script —
probably prior to the introduction of vowel-letters — it is
apparent that the consonants *resh* [ר — R] and *nun* [נ — N]
were not markedly differentiated. In II Kings xxiv. 1 and
Jeremiah xxix. 1, for example, the Chaldaean founder of the
new Babylonian kingdom of the sixth century B. C. is referred
to as Nebuchadnezzar [נבכדנאצר], by which name he is still
popularly known. In Jeremiah xxi. 2, Ezekiel xxix. 18, and
elsewhere, however, that monarch is identified as Nebuchad-

rezzar [נבוכדראצר].[cc] This mistaking of *resh* for *nun*, or *vice versa*, is responsible for the variant spelling of another Biblical proper name. At Ezra ii. 2, we find listed among the children of the province who return from the Babylonian captivity a certain Rehum [רחום — REḤUM]; whereas, in the parallel account of Nehemiah vii. 7, this personage is put into the historical record as Nehum [נחום — NEḤUM]. Of these two variant spellings the Massoretes take no notice.

Resh, indeed, has baffled many a scribe, having been mistakenly interchanged, in transcription, with several letters other than *nun*: notably with *daleth* [ד]. These two consonants, in their present form, as throughout the evolution of the Hebrew alphabet, are exceptionally liable to easy confusion.[dd] Here, as in previous illustrations, we cite in evidence certain proper names. In the duplicate genealogical lists of Genesis x. 3–4 and I Chronicles i. 6–7, we may note that the Pentateuchal worthies Riphath [ריפת — RIPHATH] and Dodanim [דדנים — DODHA-NIM] have been transformed under the Chronicler's hand (or perhaps it were better to say under the careless glance of some ancient transcriber of Chronicles) into Diphath and Rodanim,[ee] showing that the scribal interchange of *resh* and *daleth* runs with equal facility in either direction. The proper names not only of minor personages but even of well-known countries suffer from this particular scribal confusion. The difference between ארם ['aRAM — Syria] and אדם ['eDOM] is, chirographically speaking, merely the difference between a square and a rounded shoulder of the second letter. It is not surprising to the palae-

---

[cc] This latter spelling is now known to be preferable, the cuneiform version of the royal name, of which the Hebrew is a transliteration, being Nebu-kudurri-ussur — *i. e.*, "Nebo, protect my crown (boundary ? seed ?)." *Cf.* Fritz Hommel, *The Civilization of the East*, London, 1900, p. 130.

[dd] It may be that the practical identity of these two letters was a contributory factor in the ancient rabbinical decision, previously noted (*v. supra*, p. 37, note t) to edit the text, for sacerdotal reasons, of Isaiah xix. 18.

[ee] Thus the R. V. and the A. J. V. The A. V. and Douay O. T. read Riphath and Dodanim in Chronicles as well as in Genesis. MS. authority for either reading is available. See R. Kittel and P. Kahle, *Biblia Hebraica, etc.*, 3rd ed., Stuttgart, 1937.

ographer, accordingly, to find, in II Samuel viii. 13, the geo-graphically incorrect "Syrians [ארם] in the Valley of Salt," where, as the parallel references of I Chronicles xviii. 12, II Kings xiv. 7, and the title to Psalm lx all indicate, the reading should have been: "Edomites [אדם] in the Valley of Salt." An exact duplicate of this error is discovered by com-paring II Samuel xxii. 11 with its deuterograph, Psalm xviii. 10 (M. T. 11). In the first of these two parallel passages the re-ceived text (A. V.) reads: "and he was seen [וירא — vayyērā'] upon the wings of the wind"; in the second, "Yea, he did fly [וידא — vayyēde'] upon the wings of the wind." That the Massoretes were aware of this source of textual error is suffi-ciently indicated by their willingness, at Jeremiah ii. 20, to substitute for לא אעבוד ['e'eвhôdh] — the "I shall not serve" of the received text — the emendation לא אעבור ['e'eвhôr]; that is, "I shall not transgress."[ff]

The Septuagintal translators, too, confounded *resh* and *daleth*, sometimes misinterpreting the Massoretic Text and sometimes setting it aright. The Greek "gate of the slayers," for instance, instead of the received "fish-gate" of Zephaniah i. 10 is based upon the misreading הרגים [HORеghIM] instead of הדגים [HaddaghIM]. At Joshua ix. 4, to illustrate this point further, where, on the one hand, nearly all manuscripts of the Massoretic Text, followed by the Authorized, Revised and the American Jewish Version, inform us that the inhabitants of Gideon "sent and made as if they had been ambassadors," but, on the other hand, the Septuagint, copied by nearly all the ancient versions and the Douay Bible, declares that these Gideonites merely "took for themselves provisions," the discrepancy is easily accounted for as a *daleth-resh* confusion.[gg] Again, at Isaiah viii. 20, the Alexandrian Version apparently replaced the Hebrew word for

---

[ff] This willingness, shared by A. V. and A. J. V., is not manifested by R. V. or current editions of Douay, both of which, in conformity with modern exegesis, follow the keThiвh. So, too, Smith-Goodspeed and Moffatt.

[gg] Although the M. T. ויצטירו [vayyiṣṭayyaru] is acceptable, the LXX reading ויצטודו [vayyiṣṭavvеdu — *Hithpa'el* of צוד] appears preferable in the light of the context in vv. 5 and 12.

light [שחר — šaḤaR] with its resemblant שחד [šoḤaDh — *gift*], as indicated by the Greek translation.[hh] This unacceptable substitution may be contrasted with the commendable Septuagintal rejection, at Ezekiel xi. 19, of the received אחד ['eḤaDh — *one*] in favor of אחר ['aḤēR — *another*]. The Greek reading at this point has a confirmatory parallel at I Samuel x. 9 and is supported by the immediate context, "a new spirit."[33] The Alexandrian translators, unable to make sense out of Isaiah viii. 9,[ii] provide a final illustration of the *daleth-resh* interchange by reading the unsatisfactory form רעו [RO'u] of the Massoretes as דעו [DĘ'u] — the imperative, as their version plainly shows, of the verb ידע, *to know*.[jj]

The consonants *resh* and *daleth* have both been carelessly interchanged with several other letters, among which may be cited *beth, he, vav, ayin* and *tav*. The *beth-daleth* confusion was recognized at least once by the Massoretes, at Joshua xv. 47, where the traditional הגבול [HGBhôL — *the border*] is properly rejected by them in favor of הגדול [HGDhôL — *the great*]. The received text, in this instance, is a case of homoioteleuton.[kk] What may well be a *beth-resh* inversion is responsible for the various renditions[11] of Exodus xxiii. 5, where the thrice-repeated verb עזב ['āzaBh — *to leave*] would seem to be an error for the more suitable עזר ['āzaR — *to help*].[mm] A Massoretic acknowledgment of the confusion of *resh* with *he* is made at I Kings xxii. 48 (M. T. 49) where the reader is instructed to substitute עשה

[hh] A. V. and A. J. V.: light. Vulg.: matutina lux. Douay: morning light. R. V.: morning. LXX: δῶρα δοῦναι. M. T.: אשר אין דלו שחר. *Cf.* David Daiches, *The King James Version of the English Bible*, Chicago, © 1941, p. 195.

[ii] This crux — variously rendered "Break down" (Kimchi and Bishops' Bible); "Congregamini" (Vulgate, followed by Douay, Coverdale, and Great Bible); "Gather together in heapes" (Geneva Version); "Associate yourselves" (A. V.) — is translated in the R. V. and the A. J. V. "Make an uproar"; *i. e.*, a hypothetical imperative of רוע. *Cf.* Daiches, *op. cit.*, p. 194.

[jj] LXX: γνῶτε ἔθνη καὶ ἡττᾶσθε. This is an acceptable parallel to *give ear* in the following line.

[kk] M. T.: והים הגבול ובול.

[11] Douay: (thou) shalt lift him up with him. A. V. and R. V.: thou shalt surely help with him. A. J. V.: thou shalt surely release it with him.

[mm] M. T.: מעזב לו עזב תעזב עמו. *Cf.* QERE, Ezek. iii. 15.

['āsaʜ — *he made*] for the traditional but obviously inappropriate עשׂר ['āsāʀ — *ten*]. Similarly the converse of this substitution recommends itself to the textual critic at Proverbs xxiii. 5, and also, apparently, though without Massoretic authorization, to the translators of the American Jewish Version, which with the Authorized Version reads "For *riches* certainly make themselves wings."[nn] Practically identical with this substitution is another one offered[34] for Jeremiah xxii. 17, the confusion of *resh* in this instance, however, being not with *he* but with its close resemblant *tav*. The context in this verse ("but for thy covetousness") prompts the replacement of the innocuous and insipid closing verb לעשׂות [ʟ'asôʜ — *to do it*] by the appropriate infinitive לעשׂר [ʟ'ašoʀ — *to grow rich*]. That *resh* and *tav* were susceptible to scribal interchange, is seen in several other passages, one of which is at I Kings i. 11. Here, the Septuagintal version transliterates the name of Solomon's mother[oo] as if the underlying Hebrew were בר-שׁבע [ʙaʀ-šeʙhaʻ] instead of בת-שׁבע [ʙaʜ-šeʙhaʻ]. *Tav* is likewise interchanged with *daleth*, as at II Samuel xvii. 12 [באחת — ʙ'ʜʜ; Q*e*RE באחד — ʙ'ʜᴅh]; and at Isaiah lxvi. 17 [אחד — 'ʜᴅh; Q*e*RE אחת — 'ʜʜ]. A *daleth-vav* blunder recognized and corrected by the Massoretes is to be found at I Kings xii. 33, the unacceptable מלבד [ᴍʟʙᴅh] of the text being reasonably sacrificed for מלבו [ᴍʟʟʙhô — *from his heart*]. That these two letters could be readily mistaken for each other is further demonstrated by the Septuagintal misreading of the perfectly correct בידם [ʙʏᴅhᴍ — *in their hands*], which, in the light of the Greek text, must have been read ביום [ʙʏôᴍ — *in the day*].[pp]

[nn] M. T.: כי עשׂה יעשׂה-לו כנפים.
[oo] LXX, Lucian, Cod. B: βηρσαβεε. Cod. A: βηϑσαβεε.
[pp] I Sam. xxi. 13 (M. T. 14); LXX (xxi. 12): ἐν τῇ ἡμέρᾳ.

CHAPTER IV

Revision of the Old Testament Text—II

"Hillel said: . . . . say not of a word impossible
to understand that it will be understood in the end."
Pirkē Aboth II, 5 (ed. R. T. Herford)

KNOWLEDGE of the nature of transcriptional errors and the processes by which they take shape, at one and the same time reveals the legitimacy of textual emendation and circumscribes its scope. Freedom to amend the text imposes upon the emendator a strict confinement within certain prescribed limits. No correction of a scribal blunder can satisfy the judicious textual critic unless it manifestly reverses the process by which the textual corruption clearly must have arisen. This is fundamental. An emendation must bear the stamp of its origin. An emendation, moreover, must not vary greatly from the *ductus litterarum* of the suspected text; must be in conformity with contemporary linguistic law and literary usage; must be appropriate to the palaeographic history of the manuscript in question and the orthographic characteristics of its prototypes; and, of course, must be consistent with established facts — historical, geographic, archaeological, and other — which are relevant to the subject-matter of the impaired text. Ideally, for every emendation there should be a reasonable precedent. With these basic conditions satisfied, an emendation, to be acceptable, must in addition make good sense — beyond question an improvement on the traditional reading — and must recommend itself to the judgment of qualified scholars as a highly probable restoration of the original meaning demanded by the context.

Reconstruction of incorrectly transcribed texts, in accordance with the foregoing limitations, is by no means always possible. In some portions of the Old Testament, particularly the Prophets, the Massoretes have preserved reading upon reading so corrupt as to preclude the possibility of their restoration.[1] The text in such instances can only be pronounced unintelligible. In numerous cases, however, in which an impaired textual tradition can be rectified, emendation is based either upon external documentary evidence or upon minute analysis of transcriptional error. Documentary evidence in support of an emendation is of two kinds: first, variant readings in kindred passages of the Massoretic Text itself; and, second, variants found in the ancient versions and commentaries. When, as frequently happens, such documentary foundation for textual reconstruction is lacking, a painstaking examination of the faulty transcription may warrant a purely conjectural emendation. Where no variants of a corrupt passage exist, of course, conjectural emendation is the only alternative to the admission, often to be made, that recovery of the correct reading is apparently no longer possible. This type of emendation, the most hazardous but often the most brilliant and convincing, will be considered presently. First, let us examine the restoration of the text by means of the two kinds of documentary evidence.

The Old Testament, in numerous instances, repeats itself. These repetitions, or *deuterographs* as they are frequently called, vary in size from single verses to extensive passages. Genesis xlix. 26 is imitated by Deuteronomy xxxiii. 15. The second, third and fourth verses of the second chapter of Isaiah are the equivalent of two verses [2 and 3] in the fourth chapter of Micah. The entire second chapter of Ezra is paralleled by Nehemiah vii. 6–73. Isaiah xxxvi–xxxix is largely a duplication of II Kings xviii. 13–xx. 19. The Decalogue itself appears twice, the familiar Commandments of Exodus xx being restated, with slight variations, in the fifth chapter of Deuteronomy. Even longer deuterographs occur. The whole of Psalm xviii is incorporated into II Samuel xxii. Psalms xiv and liii are, except for details, identical. Most extensive of these Biblical correspondences is that between portions of both Books of Chronicles on the one hand and, on the other, of sections of I and II Samuel and I and II Kings.

Such deuterographs are very instructive. An unintelligible reading in one of the two kindred texts is sometimes readily enough corrected by its mate. At II Chronicles ii. 10 (M. T. 9), for example, where Solomon offers, among other payments to Hiram's workmen, twenty thousand measures of *beaten* wheat, there is appropriately a note-line of interrogation in the Massoretic Text. The curious translation "*beaten* wheat," as it happens, is obtained only by an exceedingly forced and unique adjectival interpretation of a plural form of a noun מכות [MKKÔTh] which usually means *slaughter, plague, wound*. The translators, rather than thus straining the linguistic possibilities only to secure a very dubious meaning, might well have turned to the kindred passage in I Kings v. 11 (M. T. 25) where it is stated that Solomon's largesse on the same occasion was twenty thousand measures of wheat *for food*: מכלת [MKKLTh]. The only correction necessary to restore the Chronicler's lucidity, and the translator's reputation, at this point, is to replace the copyist's careless *vav* by a *lamedh* [ל]; that is, by adoption of the reading of the corresponding text of I Kings.

In some instances, on the contrary, a comparison of Biblical duplicates throws little, if any, light on the obscurity. At Isaiah xxxvii. 30, and at no other place in the Old Testament, occurs the word שחיס [šḤIs]; in the deuterographic passage at II Kings xix. 29, and at no other place in the Old Testament, occurs the word סחיש [sḤIš]. Both of these unique forms, which are seen to be reciprocal anagrams, are indifferently translated "that which springeth from the same"— which would seem to indicate that the translator was as hard put to it as the scribe.

At II Samuel xxii. 12, to return to the more helpful kind of comparison, we find the awkward plural reading: "And he made darkness *pavilions* [סכות — SKKÔTH] round about him"; whereas, in the correlative verse eleven [M. T. 12] of Psalm xviii, appears the far more suitable singular noun with its enclitic possessive pronoun: "he made darkness . . . *his pavilion*" [סכתו — SKKTHÔ]. This, it will be observed, is plainly a case of metathesis of the two terminal letters. Another case of deuterographic transposition occurs at Judges ii. 9 where the burial place of Joshua is named Timnath-heres [חרס-] although it had been previously twice mentioned in the Book of Joshua as Timnath-serah [סרח-].[a] Deuterographs, like this, of proper names are plentiful. At II Samuel xvii. 25, for example, the father of Amasa is said to be Ithra *the Israelite*; at I Chronicles ii. 17 he becomes Jether *the Ishmaelite*. The first-born son of Samuel, to illustrate further, is clearly named Joel at I Samuel viii. 2; and his second son, Abiah. This reading, undoubtedly correct, reappears at I Chronicles vi. 28 in the Syriac Version alone, and is adopted at that verse by the Revised Version. The Chronicler, however, according to both the Septuagint and the Massoretic Text,[b] followed here by the Douay, Authorized, and American Jewish Versions, unfortunately records the sons of Samuel to be "the first-born Vashni, and Abiah." A glance at the Hebrew text will show that in some ancestral manuscript of the received text Joel must have been inadvertently omitted, never again to be reinstated in this verse, which must once have read: "The sons of Samuel: the first-born Joel, *and the second* Abiah"; and the usurper Vashni [ושני — všNI], otherwise unknown, turns out, upon closer inspection, to be nothing more substantial than an imaginary proper name mistakenly vocalized out of the four letter ושני [všNI] which spell *and the second*

---

[a] Even the serious discrepancies between the lists of the Levitic cities of refuge in Joshua (Chapter xxi) and their counterparts in I Chronicles (vi. 54 ff.), can, in the opinion of Albright, be shown to be no more than orthographic variations from a common ancient prototype. See his *Archaeology and the Religion of Israel*, Baltimore, 1942, pp. 121 and 208.

[b] M. T. vi. 13: הבכר ושני ואביה.

in Hebrew. Restoration of Joel to the passage in question is, accordingly, not only reasonable but practically obligatory.

Again, there is the interesting case of Goliath the Gittite, who — some time after having been felled by David's accurate sling and then decapitated by his own sword in David's prevailing hand (I Sam. xvii. 51) — miraculously reappears to be slain a second time by Elhanan, here said to be a Bethlehemite, an heroic personage whose ghastly exploit is rehearsed to this day by Moffatt, Smith-Goodspeed, the Douay, Revised and American Jewish Versions in orthodox adherence to the corrupted Massoretic reading of II Samuel xxi. 19: "Elhanan . . . the Bethlehemite slew Goliath." All doubt of the complete success of David's famous adventure with the gigantic Philistine should be removed by the deuterographic account (I Chr. xx. 5) of Elhanan's prowess. Here — no longer a Bethlehemite, but simply the son of Jair — Elhanan, encountering no resurrected Goliath, has as his victim the Gittite giant's surviving brother, named Lahmi. The Authorized, alone among the Versions, on the documentary evidence of the Chronicler, judiciously replaces the sign of the accusative את ['th] with the requisite Hebrew word אחי ['ḤI — *(the) brother of*] to restore to the mangled narrative in Samuel[c] the obviously correct reading, "Elhanan . . . (slew) Lahmi, *(the) brother of* Goliath the Gittite."

The second of the two kinds of documentary evidence in support of textual reconstruction is that of the ancient versions and commentaries. Of these, the Septuagint is commonly the most useful; rabbinical literature and the testimony of the Church Fathers are frequently very helpful. Greek translations

---

[c] The confusion of the text at II Sam. xxi. 19, in reality a very simple one, is immediately apparent when the Massoretic deuterographs are placed in juxtaposition as follows:

Sam.: בית הלחמי את גלית . . . ויכהו אלחנן

Chr.: את ־לחמי אחי גלית . . . ויכהו אלחנן

Cp. also I Sam. xxxi. 9: בית, which, as its deuterograph in I Chr. x. 9 proves, should be את. Cp. Judges xvii. 2 for a similar, though converse, shift by the Massoretes from the erroneous ואתי [v'tti] to ואת [v'th].

other than the Alexandrian, and translations into languages other than Greek, also make their contribution. All of these, to be sure, in large measure corroborate the traditional Hebrew text. When, as sometimes happens, they differ from the Massoretic reading, they pre-suppose a Hebrew original at variance with the received text. Occasionally, as in Job, the Septuagintal indication of divergence between a lost ancestral manuscript and its extant Hebrew counterpart is of considerable scope. [2] Textual discrepancies, however, not only in Job, but throughout the Old Testament, are in the main minute; and those which indicate a significant alteration of the meaning are happily not very numerous. Where the translation is paraphrastic rather than literal, as in certain parts of the Septuagint, it may yet clearly indicate either the validity of the traditional reading or the necessity of its revision. Even those passages of a translation which now make only nonsense, can sometimes, if correctly diagnosed, establish the true character of the prototypic manuscript,[d] and justify, as the case may be, either the acceptance or the rejection of the text which has survived. It is, accordingly, quite within the limits — and the duty — of scholarship to bring some order out of the chaos of Books so textually corrupt as Ezekiel, Kings or Samuel[3] through judicious use of the ancient versions. As a matter of fact, nearly all the Books of the Massoretic Text — including those whose textual tradition has suffered little corruption — have already benefited by emendations suggested by the Septuagint and, less frequently, by other documentary sources. [4]

The Septuagint itself, of course, was as liable to accidental corruption — and perhaps to deliberate alteration — as other manuscripts; a natural consequence of which was its revision from time to time by dissatisfied scholars. By the fourth century, Jerome had at his disposal for editorial purposes no less

---

[d] At Judg. vi. 13, 15, and xiii. 8, for example, the LXX absurdly, in this context, renders the precative בִּ [BI — *Oh*] by ἐν ἐμοί, as if it were the inseparable preposition with suffix [בִּי] meaning *in me*. No better evidence could be adduced for the existence of that supplicatory word in the original text. *Jubilees* xliii. 11, Eth. version, exhibits the identical error.

than seven separate Septuagintal recensions.[e] One of these, that of Lucian made at Antioch late in the third century, is of particular value to the textual critic of the Old Testament; for some of its renderings, unique as they are, seem to be derived from a Hebrew text superior to that of the Massoretes. Such passages often make possible the confident restoration of the corresponding but corrupt reading of the received text.[5]

Variant readings of the several Greek versions, superior to their counterparts in the Massoretic Text, are corroborated here and there by another type of documentary evidence, the ancient writings of the scholars of the Synagogue and the Jewish academies. Rabbinical literature of the early centuries of our era is, indeed, an unexhausted mine, insufficiently explored, of textual variants by means of which the pre-Massoretic readings may frequently be recovered. Early rabbinical quotations from the Old Testament, truly at variance with the received Hebrew text, can hardly be rejected as spurious when, as happens time and time again, they receive full confirmation from one or another of the ancient versions. Reciprocally difficult is the rejection of Septuagintal readings, at odds with the traditional Hebrew, when they are well substantiated by earlier rabbinical literature. The Authorized and Revised Versions, for example, following, like the American Jewish Version, the Massoretic reading at I Samuel xiv. 18, inform us that the encamped Saul, wishing to consult the oracle, said to the priest Ahijah, "Bring hither the ark of God."[f] The unusual character of this royal request is sufficiently indicated by the immediately following "For the ark of God was there at that time with the children of Israel." The ark, as Saul must have known, had it been present in his camp, was not the accepted vehicle of

---

[e] Those of Aquila, Theodotion and Symmachus (all used by Origen — c. A. D. 185–253); that of Origen himself (who knew and made use of at least three more Greek versions, of which, however, he merely quotes a few passages without specifying the authors or the dates); and those of Hesychius, Lucian and Eusebius.

[f] This is conceivably a marginal annotation in support of the reading "ark" which has been assimilated into the text.

oracular consultation. For his purposes on that occasion the orthodox instrument would have been the *ephod* with its *urim* and *thummim*. So thought the twelfth-century Jewish scholar Ibn Ezra. So reads the Septuagint. [6] The two words *ark* [ארון — 'RÔN] and *ephod* [אפוד — 'PHÔDH] are quite possibly scribal variants. Doubt, if there be any as to the validity of the Septuagintal reading, moreover, is not likely to survive the threefold corroboration of "Bring hither the ephod" found in the sixth-century *Seder Olam*, in the fourth-century *Jerusalem Talmud*, and in a *Baraita*[g] of so early a period as the second century. [7]

Rabbinical confirmation of the Septuagintal divergence from the Massoretic Text is sometimes provided by liturgical literature. An interesting illustration occurs in the traditional ceremonialism of the Passover service. At a certain point in this time-honored domestic rite, the liturgy is enlivened by questions directed at the father of the celebrating family by children of nicely differentiated types. These questions, as well as the father's answers, are skillfully derived, for homiletic purposes, from passages in the Old Testament. "What," at one point demands the *wicked* son with a certain detachment from the others, "is this service unto *you*?" "What," in his turn asks the *wise* son, adroitly identifying himself with the celebrants, "are the statutes which the Lord our God has commanded *us*?" This commendable shift from the second to the first person would seem to indicate that the wise son's reading had been in the Septuagint, in which version the reading of Deuteronomy vi. 20 (from which the wise son's question is derived) is identical with his "commanded *us*" ($\dot{\eta}\mu\hat{\iota}\nu$). Or perhaps the wise son may have been reading the *Mechilta*[h] or the *Jerusalem Talmud*, [8] from either of which his question, with the telling first personal pronoun, might have been appropriated. Of one thing, however, about the wise son's literary sources there can be no doubt: he had indisputably formulated his effective question on the basis of something other than the Massoretic

[g] A non-Mishnaic, Tannaitic traditional work.
[h] A Tannaitic, non-Mishnaic exegesis (*Midrash*) of Exodus.

Text, which, at the Deuteronomic passage under consideration, preserves the reading "hath commanded *you*" [אתכם — 'ᴛʜκʜᴍ]. It is, accordingly, not in the least inconceivable that the accepted reading is here in need of emendation. Restoration of the first personal pronoun would in no way violate the sense of the passage, and, indeed, might appear to the sensitive reader to be most suitable to the context.

Documentary evidence of textual deterioration is, unfortunately, not always available; nor, when available, does it always indicate the limits within which the critic may safely work. Under such circumstances the controlling factor will necessarily be the context. If the text under consideration be poetry, there are at least two additional technical features within the text itself by which the critic may be guided. Both have been incidentally referred to in the preceding pages. Of these two controls the first, though very useful, is available only in those poems, such as Lamentations and some of the Psalms, which are written in alphabetical acrostics. In poems of this pattern, in which the initial letters of the individual lines, distichs, or other poetic units, taken in succession throughout the work, spell out the Hebrew alphabet, it is obviously incumbent upon the critic to suspect textual corruption wherever the alphabetical order is defective or violated. The only alternative to such suspicion is condemnation of the poet as incompetent. Conjectural emendation of an acrostic will the more readily gain acceptance, if, while meeting basic critical requirements, it also restore the alphabetization.

The second of the two technical controls is available throughout Old Testament poetry, acrostics included. Hebrew poetry, lacking, for the most part, the formal artistic devices of European verse, has as its underlying technical characteristic a principle discovered in the eighteenth century by Robert Lowth, bishop of London, and now known as parallelism. This feature of Hebraic versification is essentially a rhythmic structure, not of the syllables and their quantities or stresses, but of the thought. In its simplest form it consists of a carefully balanced restatement; the poet, moved to ecstatic expression, repeats himself with just enough variation to sustain the interest and prolong the mood.

> "Its ways are ways of pleasantness,
> And all its paths are peace."

The repetitious character of this illustrative couplet is immediately apparent. It is to be noticed that *ways* and *paths* are synonymous, and peace is assuredly one kind of pleasantness. These poetic assertions, although always balanced, need not be purely repetitive couplets. They may be antithetic; they may form triplets, quatrains, sestets, or octets; they may be so arranged that the symmetrical design weaves itself through alternating lines of the verse or in other more complicated patterns. In the most complex forms of parallelism the symmetry of the clauses is frequently elaborated into an extremely intricate structure, strophic and antistrophic. Simple in its manifestation or complex, parallelism remains the basic poetic principle, and its violation immediately suggests corruption of the text. The direction of textual emendation in such instances is indicated by the dictates of this guiding principle. The nature of such emendation, determined not by external documentary evidence, but solely by analysis of peculiarities within the text itself, is, of course, entirely conjectural.

The necessity of conjectural emendation originates from the fact that through the ancient versions and other documentary evidence, generally recognized today as invaluable in textual criticism, it has been possible to correct only a portion of the numerous errors of the Old Testament.[9] Many passages remain quite unintelligible; others, superficially read, give an impression of making sense, but, more attentively examined, cannot fail to excite suspicion. Owing to the circumstances under which the writings of the Old Testament have been transmitted, even the absence of textual variants in extant Hebrew manuscripts is no guarantee, unless we assume the infallibility of generations of scribes, of freedom from transcriptional errors.

Such errors, when discovered, can be corrected, if at all, only by means of conjectural emendation. This, admittedly, is a hazardous undertaking. That it is legitimate, however, is no longer to be doubted. That it is sound, is sometimes established by subsequent documentary confirmation.[i]

Conjectural emendation of the Massoretic Text begins with the vowel-points. These, as previously stated, came into use centuries after the consonantal text had been cast into its present mold, and constitute, indeed, a species of critical commentary upon that consonantal text. There is nothing sacrosanct about this vocalization. Ben Asher's, representing one school, it will be recalled, differs in hundreds of instances from that of Ben Naphthali, his rival; and the American Jewish Version, like the received text underlying it, is in this particular matter eclectic. At Genesis xlix. 6, variant vocalization is responsible on the one hand for the rather unexpected "they digged down (undermined) a wall" of the Authorized Version, and on the other hand for the Revisers' "they houghed an ox."[j]

---

[i] See, for example, Graetz, *Geschichte der Juden*, Leipzig, 1875, Bd. II, Th. 1, p. 99, where for the Massoretic but un-Hebraic קבל־עם [QBL-'M] of II Kgs. xv. 10 (LXX: κεβλααμ; A. V. and A. J. V.: "before the people"; Douay: "publicly") he suggests ביבלעם [BIBL'M]; *i. e.*, in Ibleam (a city of Manasseh; see Josh. xvii. 11; Judg. i. 27; II Kgs. ix. 27; I Chr. vi. 70 [M. T. 55] where it has been metathesized [*cf.* W. F. Albright, *Archaeology and the Religion of Israel*, pp. 121, 208] into *Bileam*) — a reading afterward substantiated when Lucian's Greek version from the Hebrew [. . . Σελλημ . . . ἐπάταξεν αὐτὸν ἐν Ιεβλααμ] was first published by Lagarde, *Librorum Veteris Testamenti Canonicorum pars prior Graece*, Göttingen, 1883. Graetz's suggestion (repeated in his *Emendationes in plerosque Sacrae Scripturae Veteris Testamenti libros*, Breslau, 1894, fasc. III, p. 36) was adopted by Kittel in his edition of the M. T. Parallels to this ב–ק confusion — an interchange of two letters with one — are recognized by the Massoretes at Josh. v. 1; II Sam. xix. 41; Prov. xxvii. 20. Documentary confirmation of a conjectural emendation is provided by the St. Mark's Isaiah scroll which, at xliii. 19, exhibits the reading נתיבות (*paths*) recently proposed by E. J. Kissane (*The Book of Isaiah*, Vol. II, Dublin, 1943, pp. 55 and 57) instead of the M. T. נהרות (*rivers*). *Cf. Bulletin of the American Schools of Oriental Research*, 113 (Feb. 1949), p. 30.

[j] A. V. presupposes עָקְרוּ שׁוּר ['aQRU šUR]. M. T. (followed by LXX and R. V.): עִקְּרוּ־שׁוֹר ['iQQeRU šÔR]. Cp. II Sam. viii. 4; I Chr. xviii. 4. The A. J. V. and Moulton, despite the unquestionably singular form in the M. T. of both

Erroneous vocalization is frequently revealed by a comparison of the Massoretic and the Septuagintal readings. Although there are instances in which the choice between divergent interpretations of these two texts is an indifferent one, and others in which the Alexandrian version is the inferior,[k] there are many more cases in which it is apparent that the Greek translation, based upon a non-Massoretic reading of the yet unpointed text, has preserved the original sense of the passage which the vocalization of a much later Hebrew tradition either obscured or utterly transformed.[10] Adoption of the untraditional pointing in such instances — indicated as desirable in the three following typical passages — would, of course, be emendation on the basis of our second kind of documentary evidence. At Nahum iii. 8, for an initial illustration, the Massoretic "her wall (was) *from the sea*" [מִיָּם — MiYYaM] would appear less suitable as an indication of the strength of No-Amon than the Septuagintal "*water* [מַיִם — MaYiM] was her wall."[1] At Psalm li. 16 (M. T. 18), for a second specimen, where a note-line invites critical attention, the accepted reading is "For thou delightest not [לֹא — LO'] in sacrifice, else [ו] would I give (it)." There is, to be sure, nothing intrinsically wrong with this rendering, and it accords satisfactorily with the remainder of the verse. The Greek translator, however, with a perfectly legitimate alternative vocalization gives to the passage an interpretation not only harmonious with the subsequent statement but possessed of a subtle flavor of its own: "If [לֻא — LU']

---

nouns, render: "For in their anger they slew *men*, And in their self-will they houghed *oxen*." Similarly in the plural Smith-Goodspeed.

[k] *E. g.*, Is. xxvi. 14, where the consonantal text, in the Massoretic version, correctly asserts that "*shades* [רְפָאִים — RePha'IM] rise not," and LXX, inappropriately vocalized, reads "*physicians* [רֹפְאִים — ROPh'IM] do not rise." Also Is. xxiv. 23, where the Greek readings, ἡ πλίνθος and τὸ τεῖχος plainly indicate that the translator ineptly vocalized the poetic Hebrew words for *the moon* [הַלְּבָנָה — HALLeBhanaH] and *the sun* [הַחַמָּה — HaḤaMMaH] into *brick* [הַלְּבֵנָה — HALLeBhēNaH] and *wall* [הַחוֹמָה — HaḤÔMaH].

[1] LXX: ὕδωρ τὰ τείχη αὐτῆς.

Thou hadst delighted in sacrifice, I would have given (it)."ᵐ
Jeremiah xxxi. 13 (M. T. 12) provides our third example. There
the received text reads "Then shall the virgin rejoice in the
dance, both young men and old *together* [יַחְדָּו — yaḤDAV]; for
I will turn their mourning into joy . . ." The Septuagint, more
suitably to the context (observe the preceding *rejoice*), renders
the passage "Young men and old *shall be glad*" (χατήσονται)
by the entirely warranted assumption of the variant vocalization
יַחְדּוּ [yeḤDU].

From such documentary evidence as the foregoing that textual improvement has resulted from alternative pronunciation
of the consonantal text, it is reasonable to surmise that elsewhere
among the many unsatisfactory passages of the Hebrew Old
Testament there are those whose difficulties could be judiciously
eliminated by purely conjectural emendation of the vowel-points.
At Job iii. 22, for instance, the first line of the distich insufficiently satisfies the demands of poetic parallelism with the
second. We read:

"Which rejoice exceedingly [אֱלֵי־גִיל — GIL]
And are glad when they can find the grave."

Rejoice and *are glad* meet the poetic requirement well enough,
but there is nothing in the couplet to balance *the grave* unless,
as has been suggested, the vocalization be altered to אֶל גַּל [GAL],
giving the reading "Who rejoice *in the heap* or (funeral) *mound*,"ⁿ
or, as Moffatt translates it, "who would rejoice to lie covered
with stones." At Isaiah ix. 20, "They shall eat every man the
flesh of his own *arm*" [זְרֹעוֹ — zeRO'ô] can be easily made both
more vigorous and more suitable to the context merely by a

ᵐ LXX: εἰ ἠθέλησας θυολάν ἔδωκα ἄν. The use of [לוּא, לוֹ] לֹא to introduce the protasis in a hypothetical proposition, is not uncommon; see II Sam.
xix. 6 (M. T. 7); I Sam. xiv. 30; Job xvi. 4. See also LXX at Gen. xxxi. 27,
which turns the traditional "didst *not* [לֹא] tell me . . . ." into "If [לֹא] thou
hadst told me . . . ." (εἰ ἀνήγγειλάς μοι).

ⁿ *Cf.* Morris Jastrow, *The Book of Job*, Philadelphia, 1920, p. 209. At
II Sam. iii. 3 and xvii. 25, conversely, the syllable גל is mistakenly written for
גיל. There is, it must be admitted, no known use of the word גַּל [GAL] as *funeral*
mound. A. J. V.: "Who rejoice unto exultation."

modification of the vowel-points to read "the flesh of his own
seed" [זַרְעוֹ — zar'ô]. Again from Isaiah (ii. 4), and also from
its deuterograph, Micah iv. 3, comes a conjectural vocalization.[11] In this celebrated passage, the couplet immediately
preceding the prophesied beating of swords into ploughshares,
reads as follows:

> "And he shall judge between the nations,
> And shall reprove many peoples."

Many peoples, though not objectionable, is less in harmony with
the context ("Neither shall they learn war any more") than
contending peoples would be; and this appropriate participle
[רָבִים — rābhīm] can be obtained, it is at once apparent, by a
slight modification of the punctuation of the adjective *many*
[רַבִּים — rabbīm]. At Job iii. 5, in the English versions the man
of patience curses the day he was born, as follows: "Let darkness
and the shadow of death [צַלְמָוֶת — ṣalmaveth] claim it for
their own." If "shadow of death" be the correct translation,
then its Hebrew equivalent is a compound word — so rare a
phenomenon in Hebrew as to excite suspicion.[12] If, however,
its punctuation be slightly modified to read צַלְמוּת [ṣalmūth],
we arrive at the etymologically sound meaning[13] "deep darkness," found in the margin of the Revised Version, and probably
recover the verse as originally written. The word under consideration occurs frequently to denote darkness quite unassociated
with death, as at Job xxviii. 3 to describe the gloom of a mine.

Job, who is intelligent as well as upright and patient, is yet
made to say [xxi. 24], in both the Authorized and the Revised
Versions:

> "His breasts are full of milk
> And the marrow of his bones is moistened."

(Authorized Version: "And his bones are moistened with marrow"). This reading — something of a biological impropriety
— owes its unfortunate existence solely to the word for *milk*
[חלב — ḥalabh] in the Massoretic Text. The Hebrew word
inappropriately rendered as *breasts* occurs only here; and this

translation, like the parallel ἔγκατα (entrails) of the Septuagint and the *viscera* of the Vulgate (Douay: *bowels*), is nothing more than a desperate guess. "Some vessel," according to the *International Critical Commentary*, had obviously to contain that milk; and, on the basis of New Hebrew and Arabic analogies, renders the unique form by the admirably functional, if anachronistic, *pails*. This is adopted by the American Jewish Version. But even had the Hebrew been Englished more suitably as *pitchers* or *earthen vessels* rather than as *pails*, it would still have been unacceptable. This reading, throwing the baby out with the bath, rids the text of its biological awkwardness only to destroy the required poetic parallelism with *bones* in the adjacent verse. This will never do. Our singular word must remain some part of the human anatomy, and definitely a masculine anatomy. The difficulty, as we have said, lies in the Hebrew word for *milk*. Vocalize it differently, and the word becomes the Hebrew for *fat* [חֵלֶב — ḤĒLEBh], a good parallelism with *marrow*, and not inappropriate for males. If, in lieu of anything better, the troublesome word be rendered conditionally, with Jastrow, as *legs*, we then arrive at a reading which, though not definitive, violates no matter biological or principle prosodic:

> "His legs [?] are full of fat,
> And the marrow of his bones is moistened."

In the Revised Version of Job xxiv. 12, by way of further illustration, we read:

> "From out of the populous city men groan,
> And the soul of the wounded crieth out,
> Yet God imputeth it not for folly."

The Authorized Version reads: "God layeth not folly *to them*." The American Jewish Version, retaining the orthodox pointing of the text, replaces the rendering *folly* with the preferable and semantically more sensitive *unseemliness*.[14] The underlying Hebrew word, as traditionally pointed, is תִּפְלָה [TIPhLAH]. At least two ancient manuscripts, however, corroborated by the Syriac Version, preserve a variant punctuation תְּפִלָּה [TEPhILLAH

—*prayer*]. Together with metathesis of the preceding word,° this vocalization permits the English "But God does not hear the prayer." This reading — concurred in by Graetz, Geiger, Budde, Stikel, Jastrow, Smith-Goodspeed, and adopted by the American Baptist Publication Society — is certainly superior to that of the Authorized and Revised Versions as a sequence to the immediately preceding lines of the verse.

For a final illustration of textual improvement by re-pointing we turn to Job xxvi. 9. There the reading of both the Revised and the American Jewish Versions informs us that God "closeth in the face of his throne [כִּסֵּה — kisēh], And spreadeth his cloud upon it." To this there are three objections. First, the Hebrew word for *throne* is mis-spelled, as the Massoretes have noted in the margin. Secondly, there is nothing in the Massoretic Text corresponding to the supplied pronoun *his*. And, thirdly, the verse as it stands constitutes no parallelism. The mis-spelled word for *throne*, as it chances, is the correct spelling of another word, כֶּסֶה [keseh], requiring only a different pair of vowel-points. Substitute with Ibn Ezra this required punctuation, read with him *moon*, and we not only obviate the necessity of supplying a pronoun which is not in the text but at the same time provide an entirely adequate parallelism with the *cloud* of the line immediately following;¹⁵ that is to read:

> "He closeth in the face of the moon,
> And spreadeth his cloud upon it."

Elimination of Old Testament difficulties by modification of the fairly modern vowel-points in no way disturbs the ancient, purely consonantal, text. The vowel-*letters*, similar in function, though of much earlier invention, may likewise be interchanged without in the least disarranging the original consonants. This substitution of one vowel-letter for another has, indeed, been repeatedly made by the Massoretes themselves. Especially frequent has been the replacement of *he* [ה] by *vav* [ו] — no less

---

° M. T.: וֶאֱלוֹהַּ לֹא־יָשִׂים תִּפְלָה. Emended: יִשְׁמַע תְּפִלָּה. A similar metathesis occurs at Jer. xvii. 23, where the received שׁוֹמֵעַ is corrected to שׁמוע. For metathesis *v. supra*, pp. 62 ff., and *infra*, pp. 106 ff.

than fifteen times in the Hexateuch alone.[16] Sometimes the order of their vocalic exchange is reversed, a *vav* being rejected for a *he*.[17] In view of this ample Massoretic precedent it should be possible, without evoking the charge of irresponsibility, to replace a *vav* by a *he* in the Hebrew text of the twenty-fourth verse of the first chapter of Genesis so as to make its spelling of "beast of the earth" conform to that of a like expression in the verse immediately following. This emendation — וחיתו־ארץ [vḤYTHÔ-'RṢ] into וחית הארץ [vḤYYTH H'RṢ] — requires, in addition to the vowel-shift, a correction of the word-division.

The vocalic consonants *he* and *yodh* are occasionally interchanged by Massoretic authority. At Judges xvi. 18, where the traditional consonants produce "he hath told her [לה — LH] all his heart," the rabbinical notation in the margin fittingly indicates the reading to be "he hath told me [לי — LI] all his heart." Conversely, at Joshua xviii. 24, the Massoretes, shifting from *yodh* to *he*, change the name of one of the cities of the tribe of Benjamin from Chephar-ammonai [עמוני — 'MMÔNY] to Chephar-ammonah [עמונה — 'MMÔNH]. At Genesis xlvii. 3, accordingly, it would appear legitimate to emend the spelling of *shepherds* [רעה צאן — R'H Ṣ'N] to רעי צאן [R'E Ṣ'N], which is the orthography employed by the scribe a few lines previously at Genesis xlvi. 32. In like manner, the hardening of Pharaoh's heart, expressed by the verb-form והכבד [vHKhBDh] at Exodus viii. 15 (M. T. 11), is preferably read as an imperfect ויכבד [vYYKhBDh].[18]

A sufficient number of illustrations of the Massoretic interchange of *vav* and *yodh* have already been given to indicate the multiple justification of the following emendations. At Psalm lix. 9 (M. T. 10), the accepted "*his* strength" [עזו — 'ZZÔ] seems less desirable than "*my* strength" [עזי — 'ZZI], which is also the reading in verse 17 (M. T. 18) of the same Psalm. At Psalm lxxiii. 24, the well-known and theologically crucial rendering of the Authorized Version reads as follows: "Thou shalt guide me with thy counsel, And afterwards receive me *to* glory." The American Jewish Version adheres closely to this interpretation with the notable replacement of "*to* glory" by "*with* glory."[p] Inasmuch as neither of these two prepositions, nor any other, appears at this point in the traditional Hebrew, each, from the textual point of view, is equally acceptable. If, however, as has been suggested,[19] the vowel-letter *vav* of the Hebrew word for *glory* [כבוד — KBhôDh] be changed for a *yodh*, then, with a perfectly legitimate accompanying alteration of the word-division, we may read "Thou wilt take me after Thee by my hand," an interpretation which not only obviates the intrusive concept of immortality but accords harmoniously with the content of the immediately preceding verse.[q] Another *vav-yodh* emendation, again from the Psalms, recommended by Graetz, Cheyne and others, applies to the third verse (M. T. v. 4) of Psalm iv. In this instance, there are two Hebrew words involved, in one of which a *vav* is to be replaced by a *yodh*, and in the other a *yodh* by a *vav* — a double interchange which can be duplicated, and with Massoretic approval.[r] This twofold replacement, accompanied by a simple transposition, yields the pleasant and appropriate reading, "The Lord hath set apart his kindness to me," instead of the received rendering, "set apart him that is Godly for himself."[s]

As common as the careless interchange of the vowel-letters is their inappropriate insertion or their inadvertent omission.[t] The vocalic *yodh* essential to the plural form of certain nouns is

[p] So, too, the Douay Version. The A. J. V. has happily abandoned the practice of the Geneva Version and the A. V. of indicating by italics those words supplied in English although their equivalent is wanting in the Massoretic Text.

[q] Moffatt and Smith-Goodspeed adopt this interpretation. The traditional ואחר כבוד [v'ḤR KBhôDh] could, of course, have arisen from the suggested ואחריך ביד [v'ḤRIkh BYDh] only before the fairly late development of elongated final *kaph*. A *yodh*, it is seen, is restored to the preposition אחרי.

[r] *Cf.* Job xxxi. 11: K*e*ThIbh, הוא זמה והיא [HV' ZMMH VHYY']; Q*e*RE, היא זמה והוא [HI' ZMMH VHU'].

[s] A. J. V.: "set apart the Godly man as His own." M. T.: חסיד לו [ḤSIDh LÔ]. Proposed: חסדו לי [ḤSDhô LI]. This suggestion is concurred in by Moffatt.

[t] Reference is here made to cases other than those of *scriptio plena* and *scriptio defectiva*; *cf.* Gesenius, *Hebrew Grammar*, § 8, 4.

wanting — and so recognized by the Massoretes — in many scores of cases, among which, for illustrative purposes, may be cited Deuteronomy ii. 33 and xxxiii. 9, where the received reading *his son* [בנו — BNÔ] is properly changed in the margin to the plural *his sons* [בניו — BNYV]. In verb forms, also, the *yodh*, either vocalic or purely consonantal, is occasionally missing. The Massoretic margin sanctions its restoration, for instance, at Job xlii. 2 where the traditional text omits the terminal vowel from *I know* [ידעתי — YDḤ'TI]; and at I Samuel xxx. 24 — marked by a note-line — it indicates that into the textual form הורד [HVRDh] should be inserted the *yodh* required to yield the appropriate היורד [HYÔRDh] — "that goeth down to." It would therefore appear quite in order to approve such a non-Massoretic emendation as the like restoration of *yodh* to ראו [R'U] at Job xix. 27 to produce יראו [YR'U] — which is the correct antecedent of the usual translation of the passage "and mine eyes shall see." The loss of this *yodh* is the more likely as the immediately preceding word ends with the same letter — a case of haplography.ᵘ An identical correction of the text is called for at Judges xix. 11.ᵛ That there is a textual difficulty at that point may be seen even from the English translations. The Authorized Version renders this verse "*And* when they *were* by Jebus, the day was far spent; and the servant said . . ." Italics correctly indicate the absence from the beginning of the Hebrew sentence of anything equivalent to the *and*. According to the American Jewish Version this passage, with the slightest modification, is Englished to read: "When they were by Jebus — the day was far spent — the servant said . . ." Correctly, no initial *and* is

---

ᵘ M. T.: ועיני ראו. If this unemended perfect be here translated as a future, it may with equal justification be so treated elsewhere. Indeed, that is the opinion of Gesenius (*Hebrew Grammar*, § 126). At Isaiah ix. 2 (M. T. 1), however, where haplography is not operative, the Douay, A. V., R. V., and A. J. V. render this very verb-form as a perfect: "The people that walked in darkness have seen a great light." This, of course, is correct. The so-called prophetic perfect, perhaps, had best be resorted to sparingly; and altogether avoided in passages where the expected imperfect, missing in the text, may be arrived at through cautious emendation.

ᵛ M. T.: והיום רד מאד.

here supplied. Both of these translations, however, silently omit
that very copulative which appears in the original as the initial
word of the second clause, "the day was far spent." The American Jewish Version, it will be observed, breaks the rhetorical
structure at that point with a dash — hardly a typical construction in so parataxic an idiom as Biblical Hebrew. The
trouble in this passage resides in its verb. Transform it, as in
the preceding cases, from a perfect to an imperfect, merely by
the introduction of a *yodh* [רד — RDh to ירד — YRDh], and
syntactical requirements will be met. The verse, thus adjusted
to customary Biblical usage, may then be legitimately rendered:
"When they were by Jebus, and the day was far spent, . . ." —
a reading with which Moffatt's translation is in harmony.
Another verse in which grammatical considerations suggest the
insertion of a *yodh* is Micah iii. 8, "I am full of power by the spirit
of the Lᴏʀᴅ," in English versions.ʷ The Hebrew text, with
"spirit of the Lord" clearly indicated as a direct object — but
of what verb does not appear — will hardly sustain this interpretation. May it not, then, be reasonably conjectured that a
yodh has dropped out from an original אתי [ʼᴛᴛɪ — *with me*]
leaving the sign of the accusative את [ʼᴛʜ]? If so, and it be
accordingly restored, the Prophet said, and very well said:
"I am full of power; with me *is* the spirit of the Lᴏʀᴅ." ²⁰

Yodh, conversely, appears now and then as an entirely superfluous character. It is deleted, to give but two examples, by
Massoretic prescription, at Ruth iv. 5, where "I have bought"
[קניתי — QNIThi] is to be read "thou hast bought" [קנית —
QNITh]; and at Joshua xxi. 10 where the Hebrew word for
first [ראשנה — R'šNH] is mistakenly written ראישנה [R'YšNH].
There is, manifestly, adequate precedent for an emendation of
identical nature which suggests itself at Lamentations iii. 28,
which, in the Authorized Version reads: "because he hath
borne *it* upon him." This lame ending, "upon him" [עליו —
ʻʟʏᴠ], would, with excision of the *yodh*, give the more felicitous

---

ʷ M. T.: אתירוח יהוה. Douay: "I am filled with the strength of the spirit of
the Lord."

"because he hath borne his yoke" [עלו — 'LÔ], a reading harmonious with — and, of course, arising from — the immediately preceding verse: "*It is* good for a man that he bear the yoke in his youth."

Like *yodh*, both vocalic and consonantal *vav* are unstable in the text, being at times incorrectly inserted, and, again, inadvertently omitted. At Joshua vi. 7, as at I Samuel xv. 16, on the one hand, the Massoretes have had to withdraw an intrusive *vav* from the text to replace the inappropriate plural "and they said" [ויאמרו — VYY'MRU] with the required singular "and he said" [ויאמר — VYY'MR]. At I Samuel xxvii. 4 they have recognized the necessity of removing the *vav* from the traditional יוסף [YÔSPh] to yield the required word יסף [YSPh — *more*]. At Judges xxi. 20, on the other hand — another case of haplography — they have found it necessary to re-insert the missing final *vav* of a verb-form which, thus restored, provides the suitable reading "and they commanded" [ויצוו — VYYṢVU]. Following these patterns, emendations of an identical character, essential to the grammatical context, ought to compel critical acceptance. At Numbers xxxi. 29, to illustrate a dittographic insertion which requires deletion, there is an objectionable *vav* (derived, presumably, from the initial *vav* of the immediately following word)[x] the removal of which would produce the precise verb-form תקח [TQQH — *thou shalt take*] expected in the Hebrew — it appears in the immediately following verse — and underlying all the English translations. And conversely at Zechariah xiii. 9, there is a haplographic omission of a *vav* before the verb אמרתי (owing, it would seem, to the final *vav* of the immediately preceding word)[y] the restoration of which would convert the received "I have said" into "and I will say," a reading demanded by the context and exhibited by all the English versions. Restoration of a carelessly omitted final *vav* would here and there acceptably transform a verb, traditionally singular, to its corresponding plural form — as, for a single

[x] M. T.: תקחו ונתתה [TQQHU VNThTTH].
[y] M. T.: אתו אמרתי ['ThÔ 'MRTI].

example, at Psalm lxxix. 7, in which the obviously plural *they have devoured* [אכלו — 'кнLU] incorrectly appears in the Massoretic Text in its singular form אכל ['кнL].

The letter *he* is often conspicuously missing from the received text, and is so indicated by the Massoretes.²¹ Its omission, at Jeremiah xii. 12, where it is required as the definite article, has previously been cited in exemplification of haplography. Its restoration here, as in other similar instances, would seem reasonable. *He*, on the contrary, is sometimes mistakenly introduced into the Massoretic Text.²² A case in point to which the Massoretes call no attention occurs at Ruth iii. 14: "Let it not be known that a woman came into the floor." The indefinite "a woman" is undoubtedly the intention of the author; it was so understood by the Septuagintal translator, and so appears without apology (as quoted) in the King James Version and in Moffatt's translation. The received Hebrew text, however, can only signify "*the* woman," an intrusive *he* (probably dittographed from the preceding word)ᶻ being responsible for the infelicitous shift to the definite form, retained by the Revised and the American Jewish Versions.

Of the many other literal omissions or inclusions scattered throughout the Massoretic Text which serve as a pattern for emendation, only a few may find space here. *Aleph* is frequently recorded in the Massoretic notes as missing.²³ When, accordingly, a troublesome passage is satisfactorily improved by the insertion of an *aleph*, the precedent is ample. Such an emendation is widely approved²⁴ at Job xxvii. 8 where the difficulty of ישל [yšL] — a unique use here of this verb in the sense *draw out* — is overcome by reading ישאל [yš'L], *requireth*. *Kaph*, which by Massoretic admission has been omitted from a word, *out-of-the-armies*,ᵃᵃ in I Samuel xvii. 23, is, conversely, incorrectly prefixed, at II Samuel vii. 23, to ישראל [ysr'L],ᵇᵇ as the deuterographic text, without *kaph*, at I Chronicles xvii. 21, fully cor-

---

ᶻ M. T.: באה האשה [B'н н'šŠн].
ᵃᵃ M. T.: ממערות; Qᴇʀᴇ, ממערכות.
ᵇᵇ M. T.: מי כעמך כישראל.

roborates. This, like a similarly inserted *kaph* in נגדך [NGDKh — *before thee*] at Psalm lxix. 19 (M. T. 20), appears to be ditto-graphic.[cc] Deletion of this final *kaph*, as in the Syriac Version, would replace the dubious "mine adversaries *are* all before Thee" with the surely more appropriate reading, "my dishonor *is* before all mine adversaries." The omission of *mem*, admitted by the Massoretes, from החצים [HḤṢṢIM — *the arrows*] at I Samuel xx. 38, is paralleled at Psalm lxxviii. 4, where "we shall not hide from their children" [נכחד מבניהם — NKhḥḌh] — marked by a note-line — lacks the pronominal suffix ם [*mem*], lost apparently by haplography, necessary to produce the read-ing of the Authorized and Revised Versions, "we will not hide *them* from their children," [נכחדם — NKhḥḌhM]. The transla-tors of the American Jewish Version, it must be noted, appar-ently finding the note-line of no great significance, skillfully, and legitimately, avoid the restoration of the suffix in question by uniting verses 3 and 4 syntactically as follows: "That which we have heard and known, And our fathers have told us, We will not hide from their children." An instance of intrusive *mem* — creeping into the text, again, by dittography[dd] — is afforded by the opening verse of Isaiah xxxv. Deletion of this unwanted letter provides the verb, otherwise missing, which justifies the established translation, "The wilderness and the solitary place shall rejoice." At Isaiah xliv. 5, only by prefixing a missing *beth* to ידו [YDhô — *his hand*] do we arrive at a text which permits the rendering, "and another shall subscribe *with* his hand [בידו — BYDhô] unto the LORD." At Joshua viii. 16, on the contrary, it is only by dropping a *resh* from בעיר [B'IR — *in the city*] that we arrive at the city's name, בעי [B'Y — *in Ai*]. *Lamedh* [ל] is superfluously written in sundry places — among them, Joshua x. 21, where it should be deleted from לאיש [L'iš] to yield, with the preceding negative, the accepted "*none* [לא ... איש — LO' ... 'iš] moved his tongue against any of the children of Israel"; and Proverbs xxi. 11, where it

---

[cc] M. T.: נגדך כל־צוררי. *V. supra*, p. 91, note q. Cp. QERE II Kgs. xix. 23.
[dd] M. T.: ישׁשׂום מדבר; emend to ישׂישׂו. Note restoration of a lost *yodh*.

should be dropped from לחכם [Lḥkhm] in harmony with the translation, "and when the wise is instructed." Both of these are cases of dittography, the final letter of a preceding word being in each instance *lamedh*.[ee] So strongly articulated a consonant as *ḥeth* [ח] — to conclude this series of illustrations of literal intrusions and omissions — can be negligently dropped in transmission even from an entrenched position within the body of a word. An instance is recorded by the Massoretes in their marginal note[25] to Jeremiah ii. 16. Another instance, overlooked or more probably unsuspected by the Massoretes, may well be the source, it has been suggested,[26] of one of the numerous troublesome passages in that most baffling and textually suspicious of poems, the sixty-eighth Psalm.[ff] At verse 4 (M. T. 5) we read in the Douay Version (Psalm lxvii. 5): "Sing ye to God: sing a psalm to his name: make a way for him who ascendeth upon the west. The Lord is his name. Rejoice ye before him . . . ." The latter portion of this becomes in the Authorized Version: "extol him that rideth upon the heavens, by his name JAH, and rejoice before him." The Revised Version alters this to: "Cast up a high way for him that rideth through the deserts;[gg] his name is JAH; And exult ye before him." The reading of the American Jewish Version varies this a little: "Extol Him that rideth upon the skies, whose name is the LORD; And exult ye before Him." None of these Versions, it should be noted, satisfactorily renders the received ביה שמו [Bᵉyaḥ šemô], literally *in Jah his name*. The inseparable preposition ב [*in* or *by*], in accordance with Biblical usage,[27] must be deleted to warrant the interpretation of the

---

[ee] Josh. x. 21, M. T.: ישראל לאיש. Prov. xxi. 11, M. T.: ובהשכיל לחכם. Cp. Qᵉre, II Sam. xvi. 2.

[ff] In a poem written about the end of the thirteenth century by Immanuel of Rome, the relative merit of all the commentators on the Psalter is to be established, in the judgment of David, by their ability to expound this extremely difficult Psalm.

[gg] So, too, Jerome, *plain* or *desert* being the usual sense of the frequently occurring ערבה [ʿaRaBaH]. *Heavens* is dubious, found, as it is, only here. For further discussion of this word, see Ch. VIII, p. 220.

Revisers, or transferred to the second word שמו [šemô] to justify the translation of the time of King James. If, however, instead of these emendations — suggested by no one — it be assumed that a *ḥeth* [ח] has been inadvertently dropped from an orig nal שמחו [simḥu — *be ye glad*] to result in the traditional, but unintended, שמו [šemô — *his name*], then the passage, restored to the reading "Be ye glad in the Lord; and rejoice before him," acquires both a coherence and a smoothness of thought which otherwise are inexplicably and noticeably lacking.

Of greater frequency than the emendations necessitated by inadvertent omission or faulty insertion of otiose consonants are those required because of consonantal confusion. In support of this assertion, a few illustrations, out of the large number possible, will now be offered. Not mentioned previously in our account of interchanged consonants is the displacement of *resh* by *lamedh*. This not uncommon substitution may be well illustrated by Elihu's challenging question (Job xxxvii. 16) "Dost thou know the balancings [מפלשי — MPhLSI] of the clouds?" Now this, though acceptable enough as a picturesque image, had better be rejected on two counts. In the first place, the key word occurs only here, and, like any other such unique form, must be viewed with suspicion. In the second place, Elihu, in the preceding chapter (verse 29), has already put this rhetorical question in the slightly variant form: "Can any understand the spreadings [מפרשי — MPhRSI] of the clouds?" Underlying *spreadings* is a root of frequent occurrence, employed elsewhere, moreover, in connection with clouds. It was probably used here originally, as Budde suggests,[28] but was carelessly transformed by some ancient scribe into the traditional *hapax legomenon*, a word of single occurrence. Surely it would not seem unreasonable, accordingly, to restore it to its place in Elihu's exhortation.

Resh, as previously recorded, is also confused, either by scribe or translator, with *tav*. The Septuagint, for instance, at Genesis xxxvi. 40, reads the proper name Jetheth [יתת — YThTh] as ᾽Ιεθερ [Yether]. A difficulty in the text at Psalm x. 3 becomes apparent merely by comparison of the variant translations. The

Authorized Version reads: "[the wicked] blesseth the covetous."
For the same Hebrew text[hh] the American Jewish Version,
reversing the syntax, offers: "the covetous vaunteth himself."
Neither reading is wholly satisfactory. Replace the *resh* of ברך
[BRKh — *blesseth*] with a *tav* to form בתך [BTKh — *with deceit*],
and a reading, more acceptable for several reasons, results:
"[the wicked] is greedy with deceit." Another *tav-resh* substitution recommends itself at Psalm xix. 2 (M. T. 3). This superb
passage informs us poetically that

> "Day unto day uttereth speech [אמר — 'MR],
> And night unto night showeth knowledge."

To this well-known couplet there are two possible objections.
In the first place, the parallelism between *speech* and *knowledge*
is certainly questionable; and, in the second place, the verse
immediately following completely repudiates the idea of utterance with "There is no speech nor language"— the American
Jewish Version, more accurately, "there are no words." The
apparent contradiction can, of course, be explained away as a
proclamation that the testimony of the heavens is impressively
silent. This type of interpretation, however, can be avoided, and
the parallelism with *knowledge* can at the same time be secured,
by substituting for the *resh* of אמר ['MR] a *tav* which will yield
אמת ['MTh — *truth*]. It in no way impairs the beauty of this
Psalm to read "Day unto day utters truth."

Resh, as we have seen, sufficiently to obviate further illustration,[29] is often mistakenly interchanged, also, with *daleth*.
Accordingly, whenever a substitution of one of these two letters
for the other will improve the text, such emendation is in
order. At Isaiah v. 17, for our first example, we read, in the
Authorized Version:

> "Then shall the lambs feed after their manner,
> And the waste places of the fat ones shall strangers eat."

[hh] M. T.: ובצע ברך. The reflexive use of ברך elsewhere always requires the
Hithpaʻel. For בצע used, as suggested here, participially, *cf.* Prov. i. 19 and
xv. 27.

This passage in the American Jewish Version is rendered:

> "Then shall the lambs feed as in their pasture,
> And the waste places of the fat ones shall wanderers eat."

This, being a poetical distich, requires something as a parallelism to *lambs*, and that something is assuredly not supplied either by *strangers* or by the improbable alternative *wanderers*. Substitution of *daleth* for the *resh* in *strangers* [גרים — GRIM] produces *kids* [גדיים — GDhYIM] — a reading confirmed by the Septuagint, and most probably therefore the word which was originally written. If such were the case, then the usual allegorical interpretations of this passage — including Jerome's as well as Rashi's "the poor will now come to sojourn in the houses of the rich who had oppressed them, and will devour their portion"— convey a meaning exactly opposed to that which the Prophet himself intended. [30] At Proverbs xv. 33, for a second example, the English versions announce "the fear of the LORD is the instruction (Douay: lesson) of wisdom." *Instruction* can hardly recommend itself, in this collocation, to the judgment of a logical reader. Replace the *resh* of the word so translated [מוסר — MUSR] with a *daleth*, as first advocated by Perles, [31] and the proverbial statement is transformed, most acceptably, to "The fear of the LORD is the *foundation* [מוסד — MUSDh] of wisdom." For a third and final illustration of a thoroughly warranted *resh-daleth* emendation, attention may be called to the strangers [זרים — ZRIM] in Psalm liv. 3 (M. T. 5) — marked by a note-line — who are risen up against the Psalmist. This reading, though in itself exciting no serious suspicion, is rendered inferior by its deuterograph — also marked by a note-line — at Psalm lxxxvi. 14. There, instead of *insurgent aliens*, the Psalmist confronts, or is confronted by, presumably local *proud ones* [זדים — ZDhIM] — a suitable parallelism for the *violent* (*men*) of the same couplet.

Daleth, the supplanting letter in the foregoing emendations, is sometimes confused with *beth*, by which it should itself be replaced. At Jeremiah ii. 12, where the American Jewish

Version reads "be ye exceeding amazed," the received "be ye very desolate" [חרבו — ḤRBhU] is less suitable as a sequence to the preceding injunction "be horribly afraid" than a hypothetical "tremble ye exceedingly" [חרדו — ḤRDhU]. Among medieval commentators the *beth-daleth* substitution was recognized by Rashi, who proposed, beside other emendations, that the inappropriate "*stones* [אבני — 'BhNE] of the field" in Job v. 23 be presumed to be an erroneous transcription of an original אדני ['DhNE — *gnomes*].[ii] Among critics of the modern school, Graetz suggested[32] the alteration of ידעון [YDh'UN — *they know*] to יביעון [YBhI'UN — *pour forth*] in Proverbs x. 32 (M. T. 31).

The similarity to *ayin* [ע] of both *beth* and *daleth* — mistaken as they were for each other — was apparently sufficient, particularly in the Palmyrene script, to cause occasional corruption of the text. A note-line in the Massoretic Text calls attention, for example, to a difficulty at Psalm xvii. 1. At that point, the phrase which, in the received text, should constitute a poetic parallelism with "attend unto *my cry*" and "give ear unto *my prayer*" is the inapposite "Hear the *right*" [צדק — ṢDhQ]. Substitution of an *ayin* for the *daleth* of this word produces צעק [Ṣ'Q] which, with the restoration of the feminine ending and the pronominal enclitic which occurs in the two other clauses in this verse, gives us "hear *my outcry*" [צעקתי — Ṣ'QThI] and completely satisfies the poetic requirement. Graetz has suggested[33] the converse of this for Judges x. 12, where, by replacing the *ayin* of ומעון [UM'ÔN — *and Maon*] with a *daleth*, he secures ומדין [UMDhYN — *and Midian*]. At Job xxviii. 13 another *ayin-daleth* interchange seems to have taken place. "Where," at that point asks the poet, "shall wisdom be found?"

> "And where is the place of understanding?
> Man knoweth not the price thereof;
> Neither is it found in the land of the living."

[ii] In this suggestion Rashi has been followed by two modern critics, Kohler and Beer. *Cf.* QeRE, Josh. xv. 47. Alternatively proposed is deletion of *aleph*, giving בני [BNE — *sons of* the field]. *Cf.* Job (*I. C. C.*), p. 57.

The expected poetic parallelism disappears here between *price* and *land of the living*; nor does the idea of price seem in the least appropriate in this context. The Septuagint provides the key to the solution of the ineptitude. In the Greek version we find "Man knoweth not *its way*" [ὁδὸν αὐτῆς]. This, translated back into Hebrew, gives דרכה [DRKhH]; this, in turn, can be, and apparently was, converted into the Hebrew word *price* [ערכה — ʻRKhH] through a careless replacing of its *daleth* with an *ayin*. Reversing the process, we obtain a reading, now recommended, which, as well as meeting the requirement of parallelism, fits suitably into the thought pattern of the poet: "Man knoweth not the way thereof." The confusion of *ayin* with *beth*, though less common, also occurs. It has probably taken place at Psalm lxxvi. 12 (M. T. 13), the opening word of which [יבצר — YBhṢR] appears in the Authorized Version as *He shall cut off* — the sole recorded instance of this meaning — and in the American Jewish Version as *He minisheth* (the spirit of princes), which is a more suitable sentiment, but not easy to derive from the received text. A substitution of *ayin* for the *beth* of the opening word produces יעצר [YʻṢR], *to retain, restrain, reign over* — any of which meanings is sufficiently appropriate in the context.

Beth is very often erroneously interchanged with *kaph*, their resemblance, obvious enough in the square script, extending to their ancient forms in Aramaic and Palmyrene. The Septuagintal translators more than once stumbled over this similarity.[jj] The Massoretes, while acknowledging in many places[34] that a textual *beth* should have been *kaph*, overlook such an interesting instance as that found in II Samuel i. 21. There David laments over the death of Saul upon Mount Gilboa where, he complains, according to the Authorized Version, "the shield of the mighty is vilely cast away, the shield of Saul, *as though he had not been* anointed with oil." The American Jewish Version and Smith-Goodspeed, faithfully translating, like the Revisers, ex-

---

[jj] Cp. Is. lxvi. 15: M. T., באש — *with fire*; LXX, ὡς πῦρ — *like fire* [=כאש].

actly what appears in the Hebrew[kk]— and no more — give, for
the concluding portion of the passage under consideration, "the
shield of Saul, not anointed with oil"— a remarkable version,
certainly, inasmuch as Saul was indubitably, in David's own
words, "the LORD's anointed!" That the shield itself was not
anointed — the English construction is responsible for this interpretation — is obviously not the meaning; nor can it have been
the translators' intention. They can, moreover, have been no less
aware than was David that Saul, as king over Israel, had been
duly anointed. So too, of course, were the scholars of the time
of King James, who, consequently, found it necessary to supply
in italics those five extraneous words of reconciliation: *as though
he had* [not] *been* [anointed]. This procedure, although it in-
geniously eliminates a contradiction in the text, is, from an
editorial point of view, highly questionable. The American
Jewish editors are entirely justified in rejecting it. Their own
handling of the passage, however, indifferent as it seems to be
to at least one ancient ceremonial custom, is likewise unsatisfactory. Under these circumstances, it would appear legitimate
to explore the possibilities of emendation. Erasure of a single
tittle, in this case, instantly provides a solution. Replace the
beth of בלי [BLI — *not*] with its resemblant *kaph*, to yield the
common word כלי [KLI — *armor, instrument, weapon*], and the
resultant text, freed of its dubious negative, may be put into
the English of Moffatt: "Saul's shield, the armour of the
anointed."

Beth and *kaph*, practically indistinguishable at times from each
other, are both frequently confused with *mem* [מ]. Similarity of
these letters is characteristic of the majority of Semitic scripts.
Septuagintal misreadings of these letters are common, and
Massoretic acknowledgment of this confusion is easily found.[35]
Suggested improvement of the sense of the traditional text
through interchange of these consonants, is, accordingly,
nothing other than an imitation of the critical achievements of

[kk] M. T.: מגן שאול בלי משיח בשמן.

the scholars of the medieval Synagogue. At Isaiah i. 25, then, the accepted reading, "And I will turn my hand upon thee," [ואשיבה — v'šɪʙhh] can be changed, by replacing the *beth* with a *mem*, into the more natural "And I will lay my hand upon thee" [ואשימה — v'sɪмн]. This is the usual expression.[11] This substitution of *mem* for *beth* appears equally desirable at Job iii. 14. The Authorized Version here speaks of kings "which built desolate places for themselves," an absurdity not greatly helped by the American Jewish Version's "built up" — even with the interpretation, as in Isaiah lviii. 12, "re-built." This is not after the manner of kings. What *is* after the manner, assuredly, is the erection of monumental memorials to themselves: mausoleums, pyramids — the "solitary piles" of the Revised Version. Scriptural confirmation of this royal custom may be readily achieved in this passage by replacing the *beth* of the traditional חרבות [ḥɪʀʙhôth — *waste places*] with a *mem*, to produce חרמות [ḥʀмôth]; that is, *pyramids*.[36] Conversely, at Isaiah xi. 15, where the Prophet announces that the Lord will cause men to pass over the tongue of the Egyptian sea dryshod, it would appear more in consonance to proclaim that the Lord *will dry up* [והחריב — vhḥʀɪʙh] rather than, as we now read, *utterly destroy* [והחרים — vhḥʀɪм] that body of water. The more appropriate of the two verbs — obtained by changing the final consonant from *mem* to *beth* — is employed with reference to water five times in the Old Testament, two of these being in Isaiah.[37] Again, at Job vii. 15, a like replacement of *mem* with *beth* would improve Job's preference for "death rather than these *my bones*" [מעצמותי — м'ṣмôthɪ], to "death rather than *my pains*" [מעצבותי — м'ṣṣʙhôthɪ] — which in the American Jewish Version is Job's very expression a few verses later, at ix. 28; Authorized Version, *sorrows*.

The *kaph-mem* confusion, and its correction, may be illus-

[11] *Cf.* Judg. xviii. 19; Job xxi. 5; xl. 4; xli. 8 (M. T. xl. 32); *et al.* "Turn thy hand upon" occurs only twice elsewhere in the A. V. — at Ezek. xxxviii. 12, where the A. J. V. properly renders "turn thy hand against"; and at Zech. xiii. 7, where the A. J. V. might well have changed from "upon" to "against" but did not. The prepositional form, in all these cases, is על ['ʟ].

trated by Psalm lxxxi. 16 (M. T. 17), the last word of which [אשביעך — 'sbi'ᴋ] means, as in the English versions, "I should have satisfied *thee*." The reading obviously required by the context demands that this form have its final consonant changed to a *mem*, to yield the desired plural "satisfied *them*" [אשביעם — 'sbi'ᴍ]. Both the Peshitto and the Septuagint confirm this emendation.ᵐᵐ The converse of this interchange has apparently taken place at I Samuel xv. 18, where, not only the context but also the Septuagint, Peshitto, and Targum indicate clearly that the final *mem* suffixed to the *Pi'el* infinitive construct כלותם [ᴋʟʟôᴛʜᴍ — *to consume them*] must originally have been a *kaph* to provide the verb with its appropriate pronominal subject *thou*; that is to say, Saul.

The three consonants last considered — *beth*, *kaph*, and *mem* — have generally been unrecorded by the Massoretes when, as frequently happens, both through their labial similarity and through their resemblance in form, they have been mistakenly interchanged with *pe* [פ]. At Isaiah lxv. 4, however, a *mem-pe* substitution is noted in the margin. An unnoted faulty substitution of *kaph* for *pe* seems to have been made at Job xxi. 20, where the unchallenged *hapax legomenon* כידו [ᴋɪᴅʜô — *destruction*] is very likely a scribal perversion of the resemblant פידו [ᴘɪᴅʜô] which is employed elsewhere for *destruction* — twice in Job, at xxx. 24 and xxxi. 29. The absence of Massoretic notation is especially remarkable where deuterographic witness fully attests to confusion of *beth* and *pe*. A certain Aramaean captain, named Shobach [שובך — šôʙʜᴋʜ] at II Samuel x. 16, reappears in the parallel account at I Chronicles xix. 16 as Shophach [שופך — šôᴘʜᴋʜ]; and, for a second illustration, the same Chronicler (xvii. 6) writes *judges* [שפטי — šᴘʜṭɪ] in the passage corresponding to II Samuel vii. 7, where the word in question is transformed to *tribes* [שבטי — šʙʜṭɪ]. There is, accordingly, ample textual precedent for the alteration at Job

---

ᵐᵐ So also Douay. Although the first hemistich of this verse has its pronominal object in the 3rd sg. [וַיַּאֲכִילֵהוּ], the English versions, in conformity with the context of the preceding verses, render it in the plural [*them*].

xxxi. 39 — silently made in the American Jewish Version — of *owners thereof* [בעליה — Bʻlih] to *tillers thereof* [פעליה — Pʻlih], a reading more suitable to the context, and long since adopted by the Vulgate.

In a few instances *pe* is inexplicably replaced by a consonant of quite dissimilar character. At Job iv. 18, for one example, the verse as originally written was presumably designed to convey the idea, preserved in all English versions, "And his angels he charges with folly" [תפלה — Tphlh]. Scribal carelessness, it appears, produced at this point in the received text an otherwise unknown form תהלה [Thlh], which can only be rendered, if it be rendered at all, by something like "error." The retention of this *hapax legomenon*, and its strained derivation from a root הלל [Hll], are both questionable. The restoration of the word תפלה [Tphlh — *folly*] to the text is supported by several scholars including Graetz. For another illustration of inexplicable scribal misreading of a *pe*, Job xiv. 10 may be cited. There, in the English versions, Job complains: "man dieth and wasteth away." Yet *wasteth away*, rejected by the American Jewish Version, is altogether out of the question as the meaning of the Hebrew form ויחלש [vyyḥlš];[38] nor is its *lieth low* an acceptable substitute. The basic meaning of the word in question is *to become weak*; but "man dieth and becometh weak" is assuredly not the natural order of events. A change, however, of the final *shin* [ש] of our crucial form to a *pe*, as suggested by Graetz and others, yields a word ויחלף [vyyḥlph] found elsewhere in Job (ix. 26) which warrants the satisfactory translation, "a man dieth and passeth away."[nn]

Improvement of the Massoretic Text through deletion, insertion, or substitution of letters — such as has here been exemplified — may be further accomplished through their transposition. A common transcriptional error, as we have previously seen,[39] is to copy the letters of a document in the wrong order.

[nn] An alternative emendation, perhaps of equal merit, is suggested by the LXX ᾤχετο, which indicates an underlying ויהלך [vyyhlkh — *and is gone*]. Cp. Job xiv. 20.

Most common of all is the simple reversal of the sequence of
two adjacent letters; less often the inadvertent interchange
produces more complicated anagrams. Emendation, in such
cases, consists of nothing other than rearrangement of the
letters in the desired order. Emendation of this character is
frequently called for throughout the received Hebrew text;
indeed, in no less than sixty-two instances it has been indicated
as necessary by the Massoretes. [40] It is hardly to be disputed, of
course, that if ancient rabbinical authority discovered sixty-two
instances of metathesis and recommended their correction, it is
not only likely that there be a sixty-third and a sixty-fourth,
but that scholars of a later period will find them and suggest
their correction.

At Isaiah xxi. 4, to select for a first illustration of uncorrected
metathesis one that has the benefit of Septuagintal corroboration, we read, in the prose of the Revised Version, "My heart
panteth, horror hath affrighted me: the twilight [נשף — nšph]
that I desired hath been turned into trembling unto me." The
American Jewish Version, retaining, with insignificant verbal
changes, this inept sentiment, rightly prints it, with the surrounding verses, as poetry. The required parallelism with
heart, unfortunately missing here, is recoverable from the
Alexandrian translation, which, at this point, reads ψυχή, the
standard Greek equivalent of the Hebrew נפש [nphš — *soul*],
which is apparently the original from which the traditional
Hebrew reading has been metathesized. *Twilight*, it may be
noted, occurs nowhere else — as might be expected — in conjunction with *heart*. Soul [נפש], on the other hand, is more than
once associated with *heart*, and like that organ it even *panteth*. [41]
The evidence here points persuasively to the rejection of *twilight*, and the reinstatement of *soul*.

A second example of metathesis in which the Septuagintal
translation and the Massoretic Text are transposed is found at
Isaiah xxii. 8. In this case it is so difficult to determine the
priority of either of the two readings that the traditional Hebrew
must be allowed to stand. "Documentary" evidence, indeed,

largely supports this opinion, although sustaining argument is not lacking for the contrary conclusion. This is a particularly interesting case of metathesis inasmuch as it involves a simultaneous transposition of letters within two consecutive words. In the English versions we read "thou didst look in that day to the armour in *the house of the forest*" [בית היער — BETh HYY'R]; in the Septuagint this becomes *the houses of the city* [οἴκους τῆς πόλεως], of which the underlying Hebrew could have been read only as בתי העיר [BTTE (BTE) H'IR]. In the context, the Alexandrian reading appears the more suitable. *Houses of the city* makes very good and appropriate sense; *house of the forest* does not — until it is recalled that the armoury built of cedars by Solomon in Jerusalem was known as *the house of the forest of Lebanon*.[42] Only here, however, is Solomon's armoury referred to as the house of the forest, without the distinctive addition *of Lebanon*. Perhaps this distinction was considered superfluous by the Prophet. Perhaps it was originally uttered by him and subsequently dropped from the text in the course of its transmission. One may be reasonably certain that it did not appear in the document from which the Greek version was made. It is entirely conceivable, although not demonstrable, that the Septuagint preserves the original reading, and that the double metathesis occurred at the hands of a Jewish scribe under the influence of the five Pentateuchal passages in which the armoury is given its full poetic name.

Metathesis, of course, may be inferred from the context without Septuagintal assistance, in which case proposed rearrangement of the letters of the text will be dependent upon subjective, if critical, judgment. For the first of such conjectural transpositions attention is directed to Psalm xxii. 25 (M. T. 26). Here the Psalmist sings:

"Of thee (cometh) my praise in the great congregation;
I will pay my vows before them that fear him."

Whether the supplied verb be *cometh* as in the Revised and American Jewish Versions, or *shall be* as in the King James, or

simply *is* as in the Douay Version, the statement, because of
its ineptitude, is not above editorial suspicion. The initial words
of the Douay Version are *With thee* — an effort, hardly justified
by the Hebrew, to make something intelligible of the verse.
These two words, in the American Jewish Version, become
From Thee — a true rendering of the Massoretic Text [מאתך —
M'TTKh], but no improvement on the Revised Version. A reversal of the initial letters of this form, first suggested by
Graetz, [43] produces the recurring Hebrew *thy truth* [אמתך —
'MTTKh], permitting the translation, consonant with the adjoin-
ing verses, "thy truth (shall be) my praise."

A second example of conjectural transposition may be taken
from the eighty-second Psalm. In verse 7 we read:

> "Nevertheless ye shall die like men
> And fall like one of the princes." [השרים — HSRIM]

The Psalm is in all conscience obscure enough without this
illogical threat. The order of things from men to princes is
ascending; whereas the order obviously intended by the Psalmist
was from men to something equal, if not inferior. This intention
may be recovered by the reversal of the second and third consonants of השרים [HSRIM — *princes*], to yield הרשים [HRŠIM] —
the poor, who, be it noted, are the subject of verses 3 and 4.

Job viii. 13 provides a third instance in which an apparent
metathesis may well be corrected. In both the Revised and
the American Jewish Versions it reads as follows:

> "So are the paths of all that forget God;
> And the hope of the godless man shall perish."

Instead of *paths*, which is not acceptable as a poetic parallelism
with *hope*, the Septuagint presents *end* — the equivalent of the
Hebrew אחרית ['HRITh] which, with the transposition of two
letters, and a *yodh-vav* substitution, has presumably become the
paths [ארחות — 'RḤÔTh] of the received text. This conjunctive
use of *end* and *hope* is paralleled at Jeremiah xxxi. 17. Earlier
in Jeremiah, at xii. 4, it is quite likely from the context, this
particular case of metathesis has been reversed, the traditional

reading, *latter end* [אחריתנו — 'ḤRIThNU], having been originally *paths*.

For a fourth and final illustration of a reading which may be improved on the assumption that transposition of letters has occurred, we cite the difficult passage at Job xiii. 15, the first line of which in the Authorized and the American Jewish Versions is Job's familiar and superb proclamation:

"Though he slay me, yet will I trust in him."

The Douay Version, with insignificant variations, says the same thing.[44] The Revised Version offers a different interpretation:

"Though he slay me, yet will I wait for him";

beside which it adds in the margin an alternative rendering of the second clause: "yet I have no hope." The editors of the American Baptist Publication Society, more courageous than their predecessors, incorporate the Revisers' margin into their text:

"Behold, he will slay me, I may not hope";

and, finally, the *International Critical Commentary* supports with its grave authority the harassed Job's flat assertion (adopted by Smith-Goodspeed):

"Behold, he will slay me; I have no hope."

A progression has thus been achieved from trusting in the Lord even under extreme provocation to what is surely its opposite — hopeless resignation to the inevitable and the cruel. None of these interpretations, however, can have been the author's original intention. The *International Critical Commentary* sacrifices the magnificence of the earlier versions not only to achieve nothing more than a slavish adherence to the letter of the traditional Hebrew such as even the Massoretes could not impose upon themselves, but to alienate itself, with a lamentable lack of sympathetic understanding, from the dramatic culmination of Job's intrepid and impassioned challenge. The earlier translations depart, with Massoretic approval, from the received

text, only to convey a sentiment entirely out of keeping with
the remainder of Job's outburst. Surely when the most patient
of men, no longer able to endure his undeserved misery in
unprotesting silence, finally determines, at all hazards ("let
come on me what will") to speak out, even if in so doing he
take his flesh in his teeth and his life in his hand, he does not
utter anything so inconsistent and so lame as we have heretofore been asked to accept. Job's is here a defiant attitude. He
is about to say something he knows to be a heavy, perhaps a
fatal, risk. Like any other human being thus driven through
exacerbation of the spirit to reckless utterance, he piles defiance
upon defiance: "Though he slay me," and, belligerently,
"nevertheless I will maintain my ways before him." The alert
reader of the long speech in which these blustering, if not
impious, assertions occur will observe that the "ways" which
Job is busy "maintaining" are certainly not his own, but, just
as certainly, God's. Therein, of course, lies the hazard; for Job,
who, if consistency and logic are not to be denied him, must
have concluded his defiance with "nevertheless I will maintain
his ways before him" (literally, as in xxi. 31, *to his face*). This,
it would seem, exceeded exegetical tolerance.[oo] *His ways*
[דרכיו — DRKhyv] could readily enough have become *my ways*
[דרכי — DRKhi] through an accidental or even a deliberate
deletion of the *vav* — of which type of omission there are, as we
have seen, numerous precedent-creating instances acknowledged
by the Massoretes. A frequently occurring vocalic interchange
is partly responsible for the variants of the preceding line:
"I will trust in him" contrasted with "I have no hope." The
latter of these two readings, with its definite negative *no*, is an
accurate representation of the traditional text[pp] with its indis-
putable לא [LO' — *no, not*]. Circumvention of this apparently
unacceptable statement on the part of Job was achieved by the
Massoretic replacement [QᴇRE] of this לא by its vocal resemblant

---

[oo] A phenomenon encountered elsewhere in the O. T. For examples in
Job, see i. 11 and ii. 5.

[pp] M. T.: הֵן יִקְטְלֵנִי לֹא אֲיַחֵל אַךְ־דְּרָכַי אֶל־פָּנָיו אוֹכִיחַ.

לוֹ [LÔ — *in him*].[45] This easy emendation, consonant with orthodoxy, disguises the established pattern of Job's eloquent impiety, and must, accordingly, give way to a textual modification, if one can be found, more suitable to the context. A transposition of two adjacent letters, suggested by Ehrlich and adopted by Jastrow,[46] seems to be all the change required, and a metathesis, deliberate or accidental, is certainly no more unlikely than a substitution. Reversal of the second and third letters of the verb איחל ['YḤL — *I will trust* or *hope*] yields אחיל ['ḤIL], *I will fear* or *tremble*. With this transposition, and retaining the textual negative, Job's address to his comforters, disconcerting perhaps to the pious, acquires an effective consistency:

> "Hold your peace, let me alone, that I may speak,
> And let come on me what will.
> At all adventures I will take my flesh in my teeth,
> And put my life in my hand.
> Though he slay me, yet will I tremble not;
> Nevertheless I will maintain his ways before him" —

which is precisely what Job, to the exasperation of his three self-righteous friends, has persistently been doing; and exactly what, as not only their vexed rejoinders of disapprobation and accusation but also the thundering rebuke of the Lord make abundantly clear, he consistently continues to do in the subsequent verses of the chapter.

*   *   *

From consideration of the manner in which, as the preceding illustrations demonstrate, restoration of the impaired Old Testament text — through rectification of mispunctuations, literal substitutions, consonantal transpositions, inadvertent insertions or omissions, and other scribal lapses — may be legitimately accomplished, attention is now invited to critical procedures through which it has been possible to approximate, if not to recapture, the original form of numerous corrupted readings of the Greek text of the New Testament.

CHAPTER V

The Greek Text of the New Testament

"These are the generations of . . ."

THE New Testament, creation though it be of a varied cultural heritage, is, from a textual point of view, primarily a Greek document. Some of the writings which constitute this unique collection, may, indeed, have been composed originally in another tongue. The four Gospels, and portions of the Acts of the Apostles, exhibit linguistic features which, it is held, can best be explained as reflections of an underlying Aramaic. [1] Recent discoveries make it increasingly probable that that Semitic dialect had become the official language of diplomacy as early as the seventh century B. C. [2] In any case, it is certain that Aramaic — cropping out occasionally in each of the three main divisions of the Old Testament [3] — eventually superseded Hebrew as the vernacular of the Jewish people throughout the Diaspora until the era of Arab ascendancy beginning in the seventh century. Aramaic was the language in which Josephus composed his celebrated *History of the Jews*, and, as we learn from Acts xxi. 40 and xxii. 2, it was employed by Paul in his own defense before the multitude at Jerusalem. For Jesus of Nazareth and the Evangelists it was the customary medium of communication. There is, accordingly, nothing historically improbable in the contention that several books of the Greek New Testament, as

we now possess them, may be descended from an Aramaic ancestry — just as the Greek text of Ecclesiasticus is now known
to be a translation, however corrupt, of a long-lost but recently
discovered Hebrew original, [4] and the Book of Enoch is seen
to have sprung from an ancestor either Aramaic or Hebrew. [5]
This assumption of an underlying Aramaic is the more likely to
overcome a natural critical resistance as, through its instrumentality, an increasing number of obscurities — glossed over
in the English versions — are eliminated from the Greek text.
The Gospels, in particular, are frequently rendered less than
completely intelligible by grammatical constructions or idioms
which are essentially Semitic, and are sprinkled with forms of
expression which — like the thoroughly Anglicized *Amen, sabbath, hosanna, Mammon, Messiah, cherub,* and *hallelujah* — are
derived from Hebrew[a] or — like the words spoken on the
cross[a] — from the vernacular Aramaic. No such ancestral Aramaic text of any book of the New Testament, however, has
thus far come to light. For immediate purposes, accordingly,

---

[a] Mk. xv. 34: "Eloi, Eloi, lama sabachthani?" (אלהי אלהי למה שבקתני). See
Mk. xiv. 36, *et al., Abba* (Aram. אבא — *father*); Mk. vii. 34, *Ephphatha* (Aram.
את־פתח — *be opened*); I Cor. xvi. 22, *Maranatha* (Aram. מרן אתה — *our Lord,
come*); Acts ix. 36, 40, *Tabitha* (Aram. טביתא — *gazelle,* used here as proper
name); Mk. v. 41, *Talitha, cumi* (Aram. טליתא קומי — *maiden, arise*). [קומי is
also Heb.].

For Heb. origins see Mk. v. 41, κοῦμι, *i. e.,* קומי [QUMI — *Arise*]; or Mk.
vii. 11, κορβᾶν, *i. e.,* קרבן [QORBAN — *dedicated as a gift*]; or Lk. i. 15, σίκερα,
i. e., שכר [šēкhaʀ — *strong drink*]; or Heb. ix. 19, ὕσσωπος, *i. e.,* אזוב ['ēzôʙh —
hyssop]; or Mt. viii. 29, Lk. viii. 28, "What have we to do with thee?" — a
literal adaptation of מה לי ולך, as at Judg. xi. 12. The N. T. use of πᾶς with a
negative, instead of οὐδείς or μηδείς, is a Hebraism [Gen. xi. 6: כל ... לא,
nothing; Prov. xiii. 7: כל ואין (hath) *nothing*]. Cp. Lk. i. 37, οὐκ ... πᾶν ῥῆμα,
nothing will be impossible, with Eccl. i. 9, כל־חדש אין, *there is nothing new;* also
Eph. iv. 29, πᾶς λόγος ... μή, *no evil talk,* with Prov. xii. 21, כל־און ... לא,
no evil; also I Cor. i. 29, μή ... πᾶσα σάρξ, *no human being,* with II Chr.
xxxii. 15, כי־לא יוכל כל־אלוה כל־גוי, for *no God of any nation was able.* Again, the
intrusion of the word *servant* [οἰκέτης; *i. e.,* bondslave; *cf.* Ecclus. xxiii. 10] at
Lk. xvi. 13 into the familiar "no man can serve two masters" of Mt. vi. 24,
can be best explained by the assumption of an underlying לא יעבד which may
have been dittographed, either in a Hebrew source used by Luke or in the mind
of its translator into Greek, to read לא יעבר עבד. *Cf.* T. H. Weir, ... *The
variants in the Gospel reports,* Paisley, 1920, pp. 80–81.

no exception need be taken to the usual practice of treating the Greek text of the New Testament, in each of its twenty-seven Books, as if it were "original."

This Greek, it should be constantly borne in mind, was by no means the "classical" idiom of Plato or Aristotle. The Greek spoken and written by Paul — κοινή, or *vulgar tongue* as it is now called — was that later phase of the language popularly current at cosmopolitan centers of the Empire such as Rome itself and Alexandria during the first century. In pronunciation, construction and meaning it differed from the language of Homer or Socrates to about the same extent as the English of Chaucer from that of Dryden. This linguistic modification, unappreciated by the classically educated translators of the English versions of the New Testament — as Dryden in the seventeenth century failed to comprehend the archaic features of the *Canterbury Tales* of the fourteenth — is only of recent years sufficiently recognized to reflect itself in independent Biblical translations such as those of Weymouth, Moffatt, Goodspeed and Msgr. Ronald Knox. It is to this classical approach to Apostolic Greek that certain stylistic qualities of the English versions, and some of their unintelligibilities, may at times be attributed.

The Greek of the New Testament, however interpreted, presents a textual problem which, though in one aspect distinctly simpler than that of the Old, is, in another way, vastly more complicated. The complication arises from the extraordinary proliferation of Scriptural manuscripts which accompanied the rapid spread of Christianity. Each newly-created center of the Pauline Faith required a copy of the sacred book as its own. Throughout the Mediterranean region — at Antioch in Syria, at Caesarea in Palestine, at Alexandria in Egypt, in Italy at Rome — the precious writings, particularly the Gospels, were copied and re-copied until their numbers exceeded anything previously or subsequently known to scriptorium or scribe.

Multiplication of scrolls or codices, made in response to an immediate and insistent demand, with only the propagation of the faith in mind, inevitably resulted, before many years had passed, in variations of one type or another within the Greek text. Such divergent readings were, it would appear, sometimes deliberate: editorial revisions of the text either in the interest of style;[b] or — as at Matthew xxiv. 36, where three words are deleted,[6] or at Colossians ii. 18, where one word is inserted,[7] or at John i. 18, where one word is substituted for another[8] — in the interest of doctrine.[c] Intentional or not, important textual variants, slavishly reproduced in succeeding generations of copies, became the distinguishing features by which the genealogical history of New Testament manuscript-families may in part be traced. In the case of the Hebrew Old Testament, where every effort was made, as we have seen, to assimilate all copies to a standard form — the Massoretic Text — whatever problems of manuscript genealogy may once have existed were practically eliminated prior to the tenth century.[9] The Old Testament, as we now possess it, is, in this respect, unique. In the case of the Greek manuscripts of the New Testament, genealogical problems — still only partially solved — are a universal claim upon critical attention. Owing to the unrecorded but indubitable disappearance in the course of many centuries of manuscript rolls or codices in the line of textual transmission, the surviving manuscripts of the New Testament can exhibit their ancestral annals in only a fragmentary way. Of fifty vellum Bibles, for instance, ordered through Eusebius in A. D. 332 by Constantine[d] — for which ample material provision was made

---

[b] Substitution, for instance, of a participle in place of the conjunction καί [*and*] followed by a finite verb; or replacement of a word by its synonym, or of one preposition by another; or rearrangement of the word order. *V. infra,* p. 136.

[c] Tischendorf [*Codex Sinaiticus,* 8th ed., 1934, p. 18] found it "difficult . . . to understand, how writers could allow themselves to bring in here and there changes, not verbal only, but such as materially affect the meaning, and . . . did not shrink from cutting out a passage or inserting one."

[d] Constantine to Eusebius, *De conficiendis sacris codicibus* [Migne, *Patrologiæ Cursus Completus, Ser. Lat.,* Vol. VIII, col. 553]: ". . . Accipe igitur libenti animo quod facere decrevi. Visum est enim id significare prudentiæ tuæ, ut quinquaginta codices divinarum Scripturarum, quarum apparatum et

— not one is known to have survived. For the only two extant Bibles of the fourth century, Vaticanus and Sinaiticus, there is no satisfactory evidence that either was made to the order of the first Christian Emperor.[10] Genealogical study of such manuscripts as have been preserved reveals important documentary relationships. No manuscript, it may be safely asserted, is without its peculiar variant readings. These transcriptional stigmata frequently not only reappear in immediate descendants but — dominant characteristics so to speak — perpetuate themselves through many generations of daughter transcriptions. Such discriminating features of a manuscript establish its membership in a group or family, the individual documents of which, similarly distinguished, are obviously descended from a common progenitor which, if no longer extant, may legitimately be inferred.

An important inference of this nature, now accorded general acceptance, has been made with respect to two groups of New Testament minuscules. The first of these two families, as originally recognized, consisted of four manuscripts,[11] dating from the eleventh to the fifteenth centuries, three of which appear to have been derived from a common ancestor of Calabrian provenance. With these, eight other manuscripts[11] have been subsequently associated. In recognition of the scholar who first published their texts, they are customarily referred to as the Ferrar Group, or, with reference to the manuscript at Paris which heads their list, as Family 13. Conspicuous among the features peculiar to this group of minuscules is the transfer of

---

usum maxime necessarium Ecclesiæ esse intelligis, in membranis probe apparatis, ab artificibus antiquariis venuste scribendi peritissimis describi facias; qui et legi facile, et ad omnem usum circumferri possint. Litteræ porro a nostra clementia missæ sunt ad rationalem diœcesis, ut cuncta ad eorum codicum confectionem necessaria præberi curet. Tuæ erit diligentiæ, ut scripti codices quantocius apparentur. Cæterum duorum publicorum vehiculorum usum auctoritate hujus epistolæ accipies. Sic enim quæ eleganter descripta sunt, ad conspectum nostrum commodissime perferentur: uno scilicet ex ecclesiæ tuæ diaconis id ministerium obeunte. Qui quidem ubi ad nos pervenerit, humanitatis nostræ experimentum capiet."

the story of the Woman taken in Adultery from its usual position in John to the preceding Gospel of Luke.[12] Family 1, the second of the two minuscule groups, is comprised of four codices,[13] at the head of which stands a twelfth-century manuscript (No. 1) at Basle, which, it may be noted in passing, was among those employed by Erasmus in the editing of his Greek New Testament. Remarkable peculiarities of these two families will be quoted in following pages. Further genealogical information concerning these manuscripts became known with the publication of the text of the Gospels from the monastery at Koridethi,[e] from which source it is evident that the Ferrar Group and Family 1 are themselves interrelated, being collateral branches of a prolific family at the head of which, so far as conclusions may at present be drawn, stands Codex Koridethianus. It is in this greater group that the principal evidence for the "Caesarean" text,[14] the most significant textual discovery of contemporary Biblical scholarship, is embedded.

Whatever is ultimately accomplished in straightening out the intra-familial textual difficulties of these relatively few consanguineous manuscripts, the profusion of Greek copies of the New Testament books which have survived to the present day is so great,[f] and the divergencies of those documents — the vast majority — which lie outside the family-groups are so intricate, that the complexity of their textual problems will still be approached, as it is now, by that of no other literary monument of antiquity. Attestation of the New Testament text is overwhelming in its abundance, and its infinite variety such as no scholarly custom is ever likely to stale. Reconstruction of the text — ideally the recapture of the identical words originally

---

[e] Koridethi is situated near the eastern end of the Black Sea. The codex, however, when discovered, had been removed to a community in the Caucasus. It is now, presumably, at Tiflis. *Cf.* Gustav Beermann and C. R. Gregory, *Die Koridethi Evangelien*, Leipzig, 1913.

[f] More than 1800 N. T. Greek MSS. are known, including 167 complete Testaments, 278 Acts and Epistles, 43 Apocalypses, and some fifty-odd miscellaneous Epistles.

set down by the hand of Apostle or Evangelist — is, for considerations such as these, of an unusually complicated nature.

Another circumstance, however, as we have indicated, makes the textual study of the New Testament much simpler than that of the Old. To some extent compensatory for the bewildering multiplicity of New Testament manuscripts is the fact that, in the initial phase, they were written — according to our assumption — in Greek. In that language — far better known to Christian scholars than Hebrew had ever been[15] — the obligatory use of written vowels precluded the possibility of such orthographic ambiguities as those which have been observed in the consonantal text of the Hebrew Old Testament. It is, of course, not necessary, in reading Greek manuscripts, either to accept the superimposed vocalization of tradition or to supply one's own. Nor are individual letters of the Greek alphabet liable, after the manner of the Hebrew, to be mistaken one for another. In the Greek uncials, particularly, there is no scribal uncertainty comparable to a *daleth-resh* or a *beth-kaph* confusion. New Testament Greek, insofar as it is unsusceptible to errors arising from these two orthographic features, is less complex, palaeographically speaking, than the Hebrew of the Old Testament.

The Greek manuscripts of the New Testament, none the less susceptible, like all others, to the universal sources of textual error, are more than ordinarily involved through their accumulation of diverse and even inconsistent readings, the correction or reconciliation of which provides ample opportunity for the exercise of critical judgment. Editorial or scribal in origin, variations in the Greek text of the New Testament are, like the devils whom Jesus exorcised, legion,[g] even in manuscripts of greatest antiquity.

[g] Out of an estimated 150,000 recorded variants [see *New Schaff-Herzog Encyclopedia*, II, 112], about 30,000 were considered significant enough for inclusion in Young's *Analytical Concordance to the Bible* (21st American ed., n. d.). Of these, perhaps less than five per cent. really modified the sense of the text, and fewer than 500 did so seriously.

The Biblical story of the exorcism of devils — from which, of course, comes the now proverbial "their name is legion" — unintentionally provides a conspicuous illustration of the variant tendencies of the New Testament scribes. This miracle, recorded, but not consistently, in each of the three synoptic Gospels, is said to have occurred, according to Mark and Luke in the King James Version, in the country of the *Gadarenes*; and is commonly referred to, in consequence, as "the story of the Gadarene swine." For this reading the Jacobean scholars who produced the Version of 1611 could have found support in both Mark and Luke of the Codex Alexandrinus,[16] when, some sixteen years after their translation was published, that splendid manuscript was sent from Constantinople as a gift to the English king. For the same reading in Matthew (viii. 28), they might have cited the authority, had they but known, of the Vaticanus.[17] In Mark (v. 1) and Luke (viii. 26, 37), however, they would have discovered that the Vatican manuscript locates the swine of whom the devils had taken disastrous possession in the land of a different folk, the *Gerasenes*,[18] the reading adopted by all three Gospels in the Vulgate, and in its Rheims translation. *Gerasenes*, the reading in Mark and Luke of the Revisers, occurs, furthermore, in Codex Sinaiticus, but in Mark alone. In Luke, Sinaiticus presents still another people, the *Gergesenes*,[19] among whom dwelt the obsessed man who said his name was Legion; and in Matthew and Mark one of the correctors of that codex has brought the text into conformity with this third but universally rejected reading.[h]

Other variants which, like *Gergesenes*, fail for one or another reason to gain acceptance, are readily found in the Greek manuscripts of the New Testament. Unlike *Gergesenes*, some of these carry dogmatic implications, and have their modern advocates.

[h] Gadara was the name of the capital of Peraea, several miles distant, unfortunately for the King James reading, from the Sea of Galilee into which the herd of swine was stampeded. Gerasa is presumably to be identified with the ruins of Gersa or Kersa on the eastern shores of the Lake. For "Gergesa" there is no known origin other than a scribal confusion of the two preceding place-names.

The Voice from heaven at the baptism of Jesus, in illustration of this observation, is reported by Luke (iii. 22) to have said: "Thou art my beloved Son; in thee I am well pleased." The words of the Voice, as reported by Matthew (iii. 17; xvii. 5) and Mark (i. 11), differ in no significant way: "This is my beloved Son, in whom I am well pleased." These readings in Matthew and Mark have the universal support of the Greek uncials, and in Luke the support of all but one; they are, accordingly, included without question in English versions of whatever sectarian origin and use. The single non-concurring uncial is Codex Bezae, which, in Luke only, exhibits the striking variation: "Thou art my beloved Son, this day have I begotten thee."[1] Unique as this Lucan reading is among the Greek manuscripts, it is duplicated in several copies of the Old Latin version, and finds support in writings of certain important Church Fathers.[20] Though this Bezan variant, rejected by all English versions other than that of Moffatt, is in all likelihood nothing other than a pious echo of Psalm ii. 7, at least one modern and very competent scholar, "on grounds of internal probability," finds it "clearly to be preferred."[21]

Another variant which is admitted to the text of only one modern version occurs in the opening chapter of the Gospel according to Matthew. The Evangelist, it will be recalled, dedicates the initial portion of his narrative to a detailed statement of the genealogy of Jesus culminating with verse 16: "And Jacob begat Joseph, the husband of Mary, of whom was born Jesus, who is called Christ." This reading — obviously of fundamental significance for Christian dogma — is found in numerous manuscripts, including not only the two earliest uncials, Vaticanus and Sinaiticus, but also in an even earlier papyrus fragment now in the library of the University of Pennsylvania.[22] It is further substantiated by the Peshitto and the Egyptian Versions, and enjoys the corroboration of Tertullian. Jerome,

---

[1] ἐγὼ σήμερον γεγέννηκά σε. (Moffatt: "Today have I become thy Father,") — a reading which, favoring the heresy that Jesus became the Son of God only at his baptism, was inevitably rejected.

in an exhaustive discussion,[23] made it the reading of all Latin manuscripts since his day. Prior to his time, however, the Old Latin manuscripts[24] gave this crucial verse an entirely different construction which, being interpreted, reads as follows: "And Jacob begat Joseph, to whom was betrothed the virgin Mary. He begat Jesus who is called Christ." Moffatt, alone among English translators, respects this naturalistic tradition: "Joseph (to whom the virgin Mary was betrothed) [was] the father of Jesus, who is called 'Christ'." This unorthodox genealogy is recorded, furthermore, in the Curetonian Old Syriac and in the fifth-century Armenian version,[j] and is testified to by 'Ambrosiaster' and others. Although it appears in no early Greek uncial, it comes to light in the Koridethi Gospels, and in four Greek minuscules of the Ferrar Family.[j]

At Luke ix. 10, to return to non-controversial illustration of scribal variants, the available documents offer a selection from eight different word-combinations within a single phrase. There in the Revised Version we read: "And he took them, and withdrew apart to a city called Bethsaida."[k1] Support for *city called Bethsaida* is found in Codex Vaticanus and other manuscripts.[k2] In Sinaiticus and elsewhere, instead of the specific word *city*

---

[j] Nos. 346, 543, 826, 828: Ἰωσὴφ ᾧ μνηστευθεῖσα παρθένος Μαριὰμ ἐγέννησεν Ἰησοῦν τὸν λεγόμενον Χριστόν. In the Armenian version the two readings are combined to produce the conflate: "Joseph, the husband of Mary to whom was betrothed Mary the virgin, from whom was born Jesus." In the corresponding passage in Luke (ii. 5), observes Streeter (*The Four Gospels*, London, 1930, p. 267), if, with Syr. S., and O. Lat. MSS. a, b, c, ff², we read γυναικί instead of μεμνηστευμένη, the idea of virginity is clearly expressed only at Luke i. 34, which verse, omitted in MS. b, is replaced by "And Mary said, Behold, the handmaid of the Lord; be it unto me according to thy word" — possibly, as Streeter intimates, the original form of the Lucan text.

[k1] Rheims: ". . . he went aside into a desert place, apart, which belongeth to Bethsaida." A. V.: ". . . went aside privately into a desert place belonging to the city called Bethsaida." Goodspeed: ". . . and quietly retired to a town called Bethsaida." Moffatt: ". . . and retired in private to a town called Bethsaida." R. S. V.: ". . . and withdrew apart to a city called Bethsaida."

[k2] B, L, X, Ξ, first corrector of ℵ, 33: πόλιν καλουμένον βηθσαιδά.

[πόλιν] we have only an indefinite *place* [τόπον],[k3] the vagueness of which can hardly be said to be dissipated by the attached descriptive *desert* [ἔρημον]. To this *desert place* there is added in three of the versions[k4] — but in no Greek manuscript — *which is* [belongs to] *Bethsaida*. In Codex Laurensis alone, the *place*, no longer desert, is simply *named* [καλούμενον] *Bethsaida*;[k5] whereas in several manuscripts the scribes give a good example of conflation with a *place urban named Bethsaida.*[k6] This, again by conflation, is extended, in codices Alexandrinus and Washingtonianus I, to a *desert urban place named Bethsaida.*[k7] In Codex Bezae both *city* and *place* have been abandoned in favor of *village;*[k8] and in Codex Koridethianus this has been combined with a previously recorded variation to produce a *village named Bethsaida in a desert place.*[k9] Unable, out of this rich variety, to make his own selection, the scribe of minuscule 579 omitted the clause entirely.

An even greater variety of readings occasionally confronts the Biblical editor. From the dozen variants in the Greek manuscripts at Colossians ii. 2 the Revisers selected for their Version that one which justifies their translation: "... that they may know the mystery of God, even Christ." This rendering, except for the interpolated *even*, may claim the authority of the Vaticanus and Washingtonianus I, as well as the sanction of Hilary. The wording of the King James Version is based upon a Greek text appearing in none of the uncials but frequently found in the cursives: "to the acknowledgement of the mystery of God, and of the Father, and of Christ." The Vulgate, from which comes directly the reading of Rheims — "the mystery of God the

---

[k3] ℵ, and its second corrector, Fam. 13, 157, Syr. C.: τόπον ἔρημον; 69: ἔρημον τόπον.

[k4] O. Lat., Vulg., Psh.: τόπον ἔρημον ὅς ἐστιν βηθσαιδά.

[k5] Ψ: τόπον καλούμενον βηθσαιδά.

[k6] Fam. 1, 700, Syr. S.: τόπον πόλεως καλουμένης βηθσαιδά(ν).

[k7] A, W, Byzantine MSS.: τόπον ἔρημον πόλεως καλουμένης βηθσαιδά(ν).

[k8] D: κώμην λεγομένην βηθσαιδά. Note replacement of καλουμένην by λεγομένην.

[k9] Θ: κώμην καλουμένην βηθσαιδάν· εἰς τόπον ἔρημον.

Father and of Christ Jesus" — is derived from a Greek text
which (with insertion of *Jesus* erratic) is approximately that of
Sinaiticus, Alexandrinus, Ephraemi, and a few minuscules.
Moffatt's translation, on good manuscript authority, offers "of
God, the father of Christ"; Goodspeed's is an unusually free
paraphrase; and the Revised (American) Standard Version
supplies "God's mystery, of Christ." In the original hand of
Codex Bezae, as in the Latin portion of Codex Claromontanus,
the mystery is "of God, which is Christ." Our oldest authority,
Chester Beatty Papyrus II [P 46] reads: "the mystery of God
Christ." The simplest of these variations, from which the others
have apparently grown by accretion, concludes the clause briefly
either with "the mystery of God," as in uncials Coislinianus,
Porphyrianus, Bezae (according to a corrector), and a few cursives, or with "the mystery of Christ," as in the fifth-century
uncial fragment 048 at Rome.

Textual discrepancies such as these inevitably repeated themselves in the early translations — Latin, Syriac, Egyptian, and
Ethiopic; so that Jerome, when requested by Pope Damasus to
bring order out of this recognized confusion, felt called upon,
after diplomatic preliminaries, to inform his Holiness that he
knew no two copies of the Latin version which were alike, and
that the Greek texts of Lucian and Hesychius current in the
fourth century were so unreliable as to compel him, for correction of the Latin, to make use only of Greek documents which
were, as he saw them, really old.[1] There is unfortunately no

[1] Preface to Gospels [*Opera*, ed. Vallarsi, Tom. X, pars 3, 559 ff.]: "Novum
opus facere me cogis ex veteri, ut post exemplaria Scripturarum toto orbe
dispersa, quasi quidam arbiter sedeam: & quia inter se variant, quae sint illa
quae cum Graeca consentiant veritate, decernam. Pius labor, sed periculosa
praesumptio, judicare de caeteris, ipsum ab omnibus judicandum: senis mutare
linguam, & canescentum jam mundum ad initia retrahere parvulorum . . . .
Si enim Latinis exemplaribus fides est adhibenda, respondeant, quibus: tot
enim sunt exemplaria pene quot codices. Sin autem veritas est quaerenda de
pluribus; cur non ad Graecam originem revertentes, ea quae vel a vitiosis
interpretibus male edita, vel a praesumtoribus [*sic*] imperitis emendata per-
versius, vel a librariis dormitantibus addita sunt, aut mutata, corrigimus?
Neque ego de Veteri disputo Testamento . . . . De Novo nunc loquor Testa-

means of identifying these unspecified manuscripts, which are most probably no longer extant.[25] For more than a thousand years after Jerome's became the established Latin version of the Roman Church, little, if anything, was done to sift the Greek manuscripts of the New Testament until in the early sixteenth century the editions of Erasmus and the Polyglot of Cardinal Ximines gave fresh impetus to such investigation. By the beginning of the eighteenth century the diligent collation of numerous codices had resulted in critical editions of the New Testament in Greek which placed beyond scholarly doubt the fact that its textual tradition, as far back in time as it could then be traced, was a variant one. By the mid-nineteenth century, Tischendorf — whose Greek New Testament was the first (in its eighth edition, 1869–1872) to include readings from the Codex Sinaiticus — could publish his conviction not only that textual variations had been in existence even since the second century but that "the original text of the Apostles' writings, copied, recopied, and multiplied during fifteen centuries, . . . had in many passages undergone such serious modification of meaning as to leave us in painful uncertainty as to what the Apostles had actually written."[26] With arrival of the twentieth century, Biblical scholarship has so well established its position that an edition of the New Testament, designed for popular consumption, can be issued with explicit acknowledgment of the fact of unsolvable textual corruption.[27] In support of this conclusion, the evidence of the oldest extant Greek uncials — which could not have been considered "old" by Jerome — appears increasingly to be of less

---

mento: quod Graecum esse non dubium est . . . . [The omitted portion of this quotation will be found on page 325, footnote 1] Hoc certe quum in nostro sermone discordat, & diversos rivulorum tramites ducit; uno de fonte quaerendum est. Praetermitto eos codices, quos a Luciano et Hesychio nuncupatos, paucorum hominum asserit perversa contentio: quibus utique nec in Veteri Instrumento post Septuaginta Interpretes emendare quid licuit, nec in Novo profuit emendasse: quum multarum gentium linguis Scriptura ante translata, doceat falsa esse quae addita sunt. Igitur haec praesens Praefatiuncula pollicetur quattuor tantum Evangelia, quorum ordo [*i. e.*, Greek *vs.* O. Lat. order] est iste, Matthaeus, Marcus, Lucas, Joannes, codicum Graecorum emendata collatione, sed Veterum."

importance than that of quotations of Biblical passages by writers living in the third or second centuries, or the testimony of the earliest translations, which undoubtedly reflect Greek readings at variance with those preserved in the fourth-century codices Sinaiticus and Vaticanus or the somewhat earlier papyri fragments.

Although the New Testament — under no such scrutiny of transcription as was accorded the Hebrew texts by the Massoretes — is seen to be characterized by a multitude of scribal inaccuracies, it provides, owing to the nature of the Greek script, far less opportunity than does the Old Testament for restoration of its corrupt text by purely conjectural emendation. In the majority of instances of textual difficulty within the New Testament the multiplicity of variants suggests that solution of the problem should be attempted through determination of the most suitable of the available readings rather than through use of critical conjecture. It would nevertheless be undesirable, in clarifying obscurities of the New Testament, altogether to rule out the possibility of textual reconstruction by an intelligent and judicious exercise (within controls previously suggested [28]) of the creative faculty. That would eliminate not only pioneer contributions such as were made by Erasmus; [m] but recent emendations such as, for example, those offered at Colossians ii. 18 by Bishop Lightfoot and at I Peter iii. 19 by Rendel Harris. [m] In the main, however, textual criticism of the New Testament, having established itself as firmly as possible upon the conflicting evidence of Greek manuscripts, is coming more and more to rely upon the earlier testimony supplied by the ancient versions and quotations from the Fathers.

For this modern approach to the Greek New Testament it is obviously essential that the scholarly world be provided with

[m] At Jas. iv. 2, Erasmus replaces φονεύετε [ye murder] of the MSS. with the certainly preferable φθονεῖτε [ye envy]. At Col. ii. 18, Lightfoot [*Commentary on Colossians*] emends ἅ ἑόρακεν ἐμβατεύων [R. V.: "dwelling in the things that he hath seen"] to ἑώρᾳ [or αἰώρᾳ] κενεμβατεύων [to tread on air, to indulge in vain speculation]. Knox: "his is the ill-founded confidence that comes of human speculation." For Harris' emendation *v. infra*, pp. 131 ff.

readily accessible editions of the Old Latin, Syriac, Ethiopic and other versions, in their oldest forms, and with equally accessible editions of the early ecclesiastical authors. Great progress in this direction has been made within the past half-century; and, although evidence from these sources can, in the nature of the situation, never be complete, it has already necessitated modification of the textual position arrived at by scholars such as Westcott and Hort,[29] in the latter part of the nineteenth century. In illustrating the textual variations of the New Testament, accordingly, it is obligatory, in the following presentation of the subject, to exhibit readings from representative authors such as the second-century Irenaeus, Justin, Marcion, Polycarp, and others; the slightly later Tertullian, Hippolytus, Clement of Alexandria; the still later third-century Origen, Cyprian, Eusebius, Julius Africanus. A register of such writers would include approximately one hundred and fifty names.

Of these ecclesiastical authors, one whose study may serve to illustrate the complexity of the modern approach is Tatian, a Syrian disciple of Justin Martyr. Late in the second century (c. 170–180) Tatian, in his *Diatessaron*, so successfully welded the substance of the four Gospels into a single continuous narrative that it apparently displaced the separate Gospels among Syriac-speaking Christians. This Harmony of the Gospels, which may, in its original form, have been a selective rearrangement in Greek[30] of the very words of the Evangelists, was adopted for public reading in the Syrian churches, and was the subject of commentary by Syrian theologians. Although ecclesiastical use of this *Diatessaron* became so general in Syria in the middle of the fifth century that Theodoret, bishop of Cyrrhus, located more than two hundred copies in his district, not one of these Syriac manuscripts has escaped an apparently systematic destruction. As a consequence, it is now known only through translations (Arabic, Latin, Old Dutch, none of which is of text-critical value); through quotations by the Syrian Bishop Aphraates; and through a fourth-century Armenian commentary on it by Ephraem of Edessa. Yet, even thus removed from its pristine state, the *Diatessaron* makes valuable contribution to our knowledge of the earlier phase of New Testament textual tradition. [31]

The ultimate purpose of the indirect approach through early translators and commentators is, then, like direct inspection of Biblical manuscripts, to establish, so far as is possible, the archetypal New Testament text of which the surviving documents are imperfect descendants. In the final analysis, textual study is concerned with the extant Greek codices themselves, and the elimination of their imperfections. In this process, recognition that corruption of the text of the New Testament is frequently merely the result of faulty transcription, is fundamental. Scribal error of every type is as characteristic of the New Testament as it is of the Old. *Homoioteleuton* is a transcriptional feature from which, according to one authority, [32] "probably no Greek MS. of the New Testament is free." Of this common error forty-eight instances have been recorded in Codex Sinaiticus within the four Gospels alone. Omissions and additions, whether through haplography, dittography, assimilation, conflation, incorporation of marginalia, or other cause, occur again and again. Such errors are often minor in scope, involving a single word or two; frequently, however, they embrace a phrase, a clause, a whole verse, and even large sequences of verses.

Of the many minor slips of the scribes one type is peculiarly surprising inasmuch as it involves, in one way or another, the sacred names. Scribes of the Old Testament, though without exception in surviving Scriptural scrolls writing out the Tetragrammaton [יהוה — Y H V H] in full, at a much earlier date, in Hebrew texts designed for purposes other than synagogal, adopted, out of piety, the practice of indicating their respect for its sacrosanct nature — from the close of the Babylonian exile it had been deemed too sacred to utter — by transcribing the Divine Name only in abbreviated form. [33] These same scribes of Israel, when employed in pre-Christian times in copying out the Greek text of the Scriptural translation, naturally continued their pious custom, writing *God* [ϑέος; Θ Ε Ο C in the uncial script] as $\overline{\Theta\,C}$, and *Lord* [κύριος — K Y P I O C] as $\overline{K\,C}$. Suitable modifications of these abbreviations were employed for the oblique cases.³⁴ It was only natural that this practice should have perpetuated itself, as it did, in the composition, some centuries later, of the New Testament in Greek. That there could be scribal confusion between forms so similar as the contracted substantive $\overline{\Theta\,C}$ (*God*) and the relative pronoun O C (ὅς — *who, which*), may be seen in the manuscripts at I Timothy iii. 16, where the pronominal form O C originally written in Codex Sinaiticus,³⁵ and followed by the Rheims Version ["which was manifested in the flesh" — gracefully transformed by Msgr. Knox to "Revelation made in human nature"] has been "corrected" by a subsequent scribe to *God* ($\overline{\Theta\,C}$),³⁶ the reading adopted by the Authorized Version ["*God* was manifest in the flesh"]. In Codex Bezae, at this verse, neither of these two resemblants was originally written, the scribe contenting himself with the definite article ὁ (*he*).³⁷ Conflation of two of these three variants makes possible the reading of the Revised Version, followed here by Moffatt: "*he who* was manifested in the flesh."

Abbreviation of the words for *God* and *Lord* became, by an obvious extension of the idea, the practice of the New Testament scribes with respect to other words peculiarly sacred to the Christian community.³⁸ Among these *Nomina Sacra* so abbreviated, in addition to the two already cited, the most frequently encountered in the early uncials are *Father* (πατήρ — $\overline{\pi\rho}$), *Son* (υἱός — $\overline{\upsilon s}$), *Ghost* or *Spirit* (πνεῦμα — $\overline{\pi\nu a}$), *Christ* (χρίστος — $\overline{\chi\rho s}$, $\overline{\chi s}$), and *Jesus* ('Ιησοῦς — $\overline{I\eta s}$, $\overline{I\eta}$). For the inflected forms of these words appropriate variations were devised. In majuscule letters, the nominative of *Jesus* ('Ιησοῦς), if fully written, would have appeared as I H C O Y C; in scribal usage, however, it was customarily abbreviated to $\overline{I H C}$ or $\overline{I H}$. The accusative 'Ιησοῦν (I H C O Y N) was usually contracted to $\overline{I H N}$ or, as in Codex Sinaiticus for example, to the even shorter form $\overline{I N}$.

This practice gave rise in certain manuscripts to a most

striking departure from the text of Matthew xxvii. 17, at which, in its familiar version, Pilate asks the multitude: "Whom will ye that I release unto you? Barabbas, or Jesus which is called Christ?" In Codex Koridethianus, and elsewhere, Pilate's second question is given the unexpected turn: "Jesus Barabbas, or Jesus which is called Christ?"[n] It may well be that this rhetorically effective opposition of the one Jesus with the Other was originally included by "Matthew"— traditional name of the unknown author — in his Gospel. Indeed, on purely palaeographic evidence, it is a highly probable conjecture. Had there been such a Jesus Barabbas in Matthew's narrative, his name, in the accusative, would have been written — as, indeed, it *was* written in Codex Koridethianus — $\overline{\text{IN}}$ B A P A B B A N. These two words are immediately preceded by Y M I N ($\hat{\upsilon}\mu\hat{\iota}\nu$ — *unto you*), with which the first of Pilate's two questions terminates. No space being employed by the scribe to separate words from each other, the combination " . . . unto you? Jesus . . . " takes the uncial form, clearly preserved in the Koridethianus, Y M I N $\overline{\text{I N}}$. In this grouping of six letters in which the scribe finds himself repeating one $I\,N$ immediately after another, nothing would be easier for him than a haplographic slip resulting in the omission of the final $\overline{I\,N}$; that is, in the loss of the name *Jesus* before *Barabbas*. That omission, if accidental, would probably have been welcomed as providential by the faithful, to whom it was naturally repugnant that the sacred name of the Saviour had been shared by any criminal, and particularly by that one whose liberation led to the Crucifixion. Among those who felt this repugnance was Origen, who, encountering the reading *Jesus Barabbas* in unspecified manuscripts examined by him, very probably at Caesarea,[39] rejected it on precisely this ground. The authoritative opinion of Origen, nourished by the especially reverential attitude toward this *Nomen Sacrum*, may well have sufficed to insure that the name *Jesus*, once it had been dropped before

---

[n] Θ: $\tau \acute{\iota}\nu\alpha$ $\vartheta \acute{\epsilon}\lambda\epsilon\tau\epsilon$ $\tau\hat{\omega}\nu$ $\delta\acute{\upsilon}o$ $\dot{\alpha}\pi o\lambda\acute{\upsilon}\sigma\omega$ $\hat{\upsilon}\mu\hat{\iota}\nu$ $\overline{\text{Ἰν}}$ $\beta\alpha\rho\rho\alpha\beta\beta\hat{\alpha}\nu$ $\mathring{\eta}$ $\overline{\text{Ἰν}}$ $\tau\grave{o}\nu$ $\lambda\epsilon\gamma\acute{o}\mu\epsilon\nu o\nu$ $\overline{\text{Χν}}$. Similarly Fam. 1 and Syr. S., Arm. Note $\tau\hat{\omega}\nu$ $\delta\acute{\upsilon}o$, not found elsewhere.

Barabbas, would never again be reinstated. Its retention in Codex Koridethianus alone among the known uncials, and in Family 1 among the cursives,[40] would appear, accordingly, to be the vestigial remains, so to speak, of an earlier, not quite extinct, manuscript tradition.°

Another Biblical name, Enoch, has apparently been lost through haplography at I Peter iii. 18–19: "Because Christ also suffered . . . being put to death in the flesh — but quickened in the spirit: in which also he went and preached unto the spirits in prison, which aforetime were disobedient, when the longsuffering of God waited in the days of Noah, . . ." The obscurity of this passage is not noticeably diminished in the Revised Standard Version by its substitutions of "made alive" for "quickened," and "God's patience" for "the longsuffering of God." By restoration to the text of the lost *Enoch,* however, Peter's thought at this point is relieved of its apparent incoherence and, in Moffatt's translation, resumes its original comprehensibility: "Christ himself died . . . ; in the flesh he was put to death but he came to life in the Spirit. (It was in the Spirit that Enoch also went and preached . . . at the time when God's patience held out . . . in the days of Noah . . .)." Goodspeed's translation is in like vein: "For Christ himself died . . . and was physically put to death, but he was made alive in the Spirit. In it Enoch went and preached . . . when in Noah's time God in his patience waited, . . ." Whence comes this *Enoch*; and on what basis do these two independent translators incorporate it into their versions? Attention is invited to the first three words of the Greek text of verse 19 [ἐν ᾧ καί . . . ἐκήρυξεν — "*in which also . . . he preached*"], which in the first place were written in unspaced uncials, thus: ΕΝΩΧΑΙ. . . . Of this six-letter combination, ΕΝΩΧ, the first four letters, happen to spell *Enoch.* Had Peter originally put into his Epistle "*in which also Enoch . . . preached*" [ἐν ᾧ καί Ἐνώχ . . . ἐκήρυξεν], the sequence of the capital letters — ΕΝΩΧΑΙΕΝΩΧ. . . , with ΕΝΩΧ appearing twice in close proximity —

° It still lives in Moffatt's translation.

would have provided an unexcelled textual foundation for a haplographic error: the omission of the second of the two identical groups of four letters. This, it has been conjectured,[41] is exactly what took place; and upon this assumption independent scholars have markedly improved the lucidity of the Epistle of Peter by developing a suggestion implicit in the text. Their emendation, however reasonable as a reversal of a scribal error, cannot be held to justify itself on palaeographic grounds alone. Such justification is indispensable; but it is secondary. Inspiration for the insertion of *Enoch* in verse 19 comes in the first instance from *Noah* in the verse immediately following. From Genesis [v. 21–29] we learn that Enoch was the great-grandfather of Noah and that he lived 365 years; but from another source — the pseudapocryphal *First Book of Enoch* — we can enlarge our knowledge of Enoch considerably. This book which, well known to the Biblical writers of the first century, "had more influence on the New Testament than has any other apocryphal or pseudepigraphic work,"[42] was to all intents canonical in the eyes of the early Fathers, and enjoyed that favorable status until nearly the end of the third century. One of the prophecies of its hero is specifically referred to in the Epistle of Jude, and its influence may be discovered elsewhere in the New Testament.[42] Among the many activities of Enoch recorded in the Book bearing his name is his preaching to the disobedient Spirits at the time when Noah was building his Ark — a portion of the Enochian legend which, with the restoration of Enoch to its place in the text, is now reflected in Peter's Epistle.

More readily detected than loss of a single word is the disappearance of phrases or clauses. A relatively simple and obvious instance of the accidental failure to transcribe a group of words occurs in both Codex Vaticanus and Codex Sinaiticus at Mark x. 7, which, in the Revised Version, reads: "For this cause shall a man leave his father and mother, and shall cleave to his wife." This, of course, is borrowed directly from Genesis ii. 24 — if not at second hand from Matthew xix. 5 — and was, consequently, a text with which every Biblical scribe must have been familiar. For some unknown reason the latter portion of this verse, "and shall cleave to his wife," was dropped out not only in the two fourth-century uncials but also in the nearly contemporary palimpsest Syriac Sinaiticus and the later Codex Laurensis. This circumstance, it will be noted, points to a possible common ancestor for these four documents stigmatized by this particular error. It is remarkable that this transcriptional slip was allowed to stand by the several diligent correctors of the Sinaiticus and the Vatican Codex. Goodspeed, presumably on the authority of these two codices, omits the words in question from his translation. An omission of like character, in which an allusion to the *flesh* and *bone* of Genesis ii. 23 has been dropped out, occurs at Ephesians v. 30 in Vaticanus, Sinaiticus, and Alexandrinus. [43]

Omissions are by no means always accidental. Deliberate excision of a clause which will escape the observation of those who read the Rheims New Testament or the King James or the Revised Versions, occurs in the parable of the Prodigal Son in chapter xv of Luke. At verses 18–19, in entire conformity with the Greek, these three English Versions report the Prodigal Son as resolving to return to his father and to say: "I have sinned against heaven, and in thy sight: I am no more worthy to be called thy son; make me as one of thy hired servants." When, however, the Prodigal had returned to his home, and was being compassionately received by his father, a portion of his prepared speech of confession and humiliation seems to have slipped from his memory; for all that he says [v. 21] to his rejoicing father, if we rely upon the three English Versions just mentioned, is: "I have sinned against heaven, and in thy sight: I am no more worthy to be called thy son." In this abridgment by the Prodigal Son of what he had previously determined to say, there is nothing, it will be observed, about making him as one of the hired servants. A subtle touch, this, it will no doubt be thought by many readers, revealing the Prodigal's sensitivity to his father's emotional state and his instant realization of the limited extent to which he need go in self-abasement! Unfortunately for this or other possible interpretations, there is no curtailment by the Prodigal of his resolved-upon speech to his father as it is recorded in the earliest authorities. Every word of that rehearsed confession is repeated in codices Sinaiticus, Vaticanus, and Bezae.[44] In Codex Alexandrinus alone among the early uncials[45] is the hired-servant clause omitted. Before that manuscript had been produced, however, Jerome had dropped the clause from his Vulgate, a deletion which, though concurred in by his contemporary Augustine, perpetuated, as has been noted, into the nineteenth century, and sustained in our times by both Moffatt and the Revised Standard Version, has been restored by Goodspeed.

Intentional, also, is the dropping of three important words — *nor the son* [οὐδὲ ὁ υἱός] — from Matthew xxiv. 36: "But of that day and hour knoweth no one, not even the angels of heaven, neither the Son, but the Father only." Preservation of this reading in the early uncials Vaticanus, Sinaiticus and Bezae — as well as in Koridethianus and Beratinus, and the minuscules of the Ferrar Group[46]— indicates that it is probably original. The same reading is likewise found in the Old Latin, in some copies of the Vulgate, and in other Versions.[47] It is further corroborated by Origen, Chrysostom, Hilary, and other Fathers, including Jerome, who, while rejecting it, locates it in unspecified Greek and Latin manuscripts. It is retained in full by the Revised Version (with a marginal note) and the Revised Standard Version. Deletion of *nor the Son* — to avoid, it would appear, doctrinal misunderstanding — by Washingtonianus I, Regius, and one of the correctors of Sinaiticus [another corrector restored the reading]; by Family 1 and other minuscules; by the Vulgate, Peshitto, Harkleian, and Egyptian Versions; secures the approval of Basil and Didymus and others among the ancients, and of Moffatt ánd Goodspeed among the moderns. The Rheims and the King James Versions concur in the deletion.

Addition of a word or a clause to the primary text is as

remarkable as an omission. In some instances it is hardly to be questioned that augmentation of the text is the result of careless incorporation of marginalia. Of this common scribal error, a few illustrations, all from the Gospel according to Mark, may illuminate the process. At chapter vii, verse 16, the celebrated injunction, "If any man have ears to hear, let him hear," is not to be found in either of the two earliest codices, the Sinaiticus and the Vaticanus;[48] and, although it occurs in the later manuscripts and versions, on the authority of which it is included in the Rheims and the King James Versions — as also in Moffatt's translation — it has been sufficiently suspected by modern scholars of being a marginal annotation — a *nota bene*, so to speak — to have been dropped by the Revisers from their Version, by Goodspeed from his, and by the scholarly editors of the Revised Standard Version.

Again, at chapter xi, the evidence of the codices appears to indicate that verse 26 — Rheims and Authorized Version: "But if ye do not forgive, neither will your Father which is in heaven forgive your trespasses"— is a pious commentator's cross-reference to Matthew vi. 15 which has crept from the margin, where it was first copied, into the body of the text. Like the previous illustration, this passage is wanting in both Sinaiticus and Vaticanus,[49] coming to light only in the later Alexandrinus, Ephraemi, and Bezae.[50] Its retention, accordingly, was deemed inadvisable by the editors of the Revised Version, as also by Moffatt, Goodspeed, and the Revised Standard Version.

Once more, for a final Marcan example of marginal absorption, at chapter xv the annotative character of verse 28 — "And the scripture was fulfilled, which saith, And he was numbered with the transgressors" [Rheims: "And with the wicked he was reputed"] — reveals itself to him who runs if only he can read. This verse — possibly transferred from Luke xxii. 37, which itself is borrowed, in part, from Isaiah liii. 12 — is found in two late uncials, Regius and Koridethianus, and in them alone; it appears in the still later minuscules of Family 1 and some others; it finds support in the Vulgate and additional versions.[51] The passage, however, cannot be located in codices Sinaiticus, Vaticanus, Alexandrinus, Ephraemi (first hand), or Bezae;[52] it is missing from several versions,[53] and it is marked for deletion by Eusebius. The Revisers have rejected the verse in its entirety, and in this they are followed by Moffatt, Goodspeed, and (with a cautionary footnote) by the Revised Standard Version.

Infiltration of the fundamental New Testament text by secondary contributions is frequently accomplished through avenues other than the margin. In such instances, of course, the procedure can never have been unintentional. Motives for deliberate amplification of the original subject-matter, so far as they may now be inferred, were various. In the case of Mark ix. 44 and 46 — "where their worm dieth not, and the fire is not quenched"— motivation for the textual expansion appears to have been purely stylistic, nothing more questionable than a desire to increase the emphasis by repetition. These twin verses — borrowed with fidelity from the final verse of Isaiah — have not intruded themselves into Mark's characterization of hell in codices Sinaiticus, Vaticanus, Ephraemi, Washingtonianus I or Regius;[54] but in those manuscripts into which they have been inserted — Alexandrinus, Bezae, Koridethianus and others[55]— they would seem to be merely rhetorical anticipations of verse 48, with which they are identical. Thus repetitiously emphasized in some manuscripts, the verse is thrice rendered in the Rheims and the King James Versions. In the Revised Version, on the other hand, in the translations of Moffatt and of Goodspeed, and in the Revised Standard Version, the passage is retained only in verse 48, for which the manuscript authority is universal.

Stylistic considerations, be it noted, have little if anything to do with the majority of textual increments. At Colossians ii. 18, for example, an early attempt was made to ameliorate the perplexing nature of that passage[56] by insertion of the negative *not* [μὴ or οὐκ]. This insertion was adopted in codices Ephraemi, Boernerianus, Coislinianus, and many others; it was inserted by correctors into the primary text of codices Sinaiticus and Claromontanus; it is preserved in the Vulgate and several other versions (Armenian, Gothic, Harkleian); and it is recognized by Ambrose, Theodore of Mopsuestia (Lat.), Chrysostom, among others. The intrusive negative, however, is not to be found in codices Vaticanus, Alexandrinus, and Washingtonianus II; nor in Chester Beatty Papyrus II [P 46]; nor in the original scribe's hand in codices Sinaiticus and Claromontanus; it is acknowledged to be missing from some manuscripts by both Jerome and Augustine; it is wanting in several versions — Old Latin (G³), Ethiopic and Bohairic; and it is unrecognized by 'Ambrosiaster,' Lucifer of Cagliari, Marcion, Origen, Tertullian and others. Questionable though this negative be, it is to this day retained in translation in the Version of Rheims ["walking in the things which he hath not seen"], in that of King James ["intruding into those things which he hath not seen"], and, by implication, in that of Msgr. Knox ["takes his stand upon false visions"]; but, in conformity with current critical opinion, has been rejected as an editorial interpolation by the Revised Version, by Goodspeed ["being absorbed in the visions he has seen"], by Moffatt ["presuming on his visions"], and the Revised Standard Version ["taking his stand on visions"].

Stylistic considerations obviously have nothing to do with expansion of the text at Matthew xvii. 21, where, in the Authorized Version, it is explained that the devil which the disciples could not cast out "goeth not out [Rheims: "is not cast out"] but by prayer and fasting." This explanatory verse may conceivably have been in the first place a marginal comment, although that would appear less likely here than elsewhere. In any case, the verse was not included in codices Vaticanus and Sinaiticus — into which it was later inserted by a corrector — nor in Koridethianus; and it is marked for deletion by Eusebius.[57] Codices Ephraemi and Bezae, and some later manuscripts, contain this supplementary verse, which appears also in the Vulgate[58] and receives the sanction of several of the

Church Fathers, among whom may be cited Origen, Chrysostom, Hilary and Augustine. Rejected from the Greek text of Westcott and Hort, and omitted from the Revised Version, this verse has been discarded by both Moffatt and Goodspeed, and, with marginal notation, by the Revised Standard Version.

Of the numerous conscious additions of an entire clause a second illustration may be cited from Luke xxiv. 51: "And it came to pass, while he blessed them, he parted from them, and was carried up into heaven." Virtual identity of phraseology in the English versions of this passage results from the concurrence of readings in many Greek codices — including Vaticanus, Alexandrinus, Washingtonianus I, and Koridethianus. The final clause, however — "(he) was carried up into heaven" — is wanting in codices Sinaiticus (into which it has been inserted by a corrector) and Bezae, in the Old Latin and Old Syriac (Sinaitic) versions, and in some readings of Augustine. It is possible, to be sure, that the clause has been transferred to Luke by some well-intentioned scribe from the corresponding statement, near the close [xvi. 19] of the so-called "appendix" to Mark's Gospel.[59] In view of these considerations, both the Revised Standard Version and Goodspeed's translation omit the clause in their rendering of Luke.

Luke ix. 55b–56a offers an even more conclusive illustration. There, in the Authorized Version, we read: "And he said, Ye know not what manner of spirit ye are of. For the Son of man is not come to destroy men's lives, but to save *them*." These two complete sentences which are included in none of the five early codices, Vaticanus, Sinaiticus, Alexandrinus, Washingtonianus I, and Ephraemi,[60] make their appearance in the later uncials Laurensis and Koridethianus; in Family 1, and many other Greek manuscripts; in the Vulgate and other versions;[61] and are sanctioned by several of the early writers of the Church.[62] They are rejected as later additions — possibly reflecting John iii. 17 or John xii. 47 — by the Revised Version, and by Goodspeed, Moffatt, and, with footnote, the Revised Standard Version.

It has not always been possible for modern editors of the Greek New Testament, nor for their beneficiaries, the Revisers,[p] to persuade themselves to abandon certain passages which, on the evidence of the manuscripts, appear to be additions to the original text. Noteworthy among such passages is that in Luke xxii. 43–44 which records the bloody sweat of Jesus as he prayed upon the mount of Olives while his disciples slept from sorrow: "And there appeared unto him an angel from heaven, strengthening him. And being in an agony he prayed more earnestly: and his sweat became as it were great drops of blood falling down upon the ground." That these vivid verses were of dubious authenticity is apparent from Codex Sinaiticus, in which they were included by the original scribe, then marked for deletion by a second hand, and finally restored by a subsequent corrector. Apart from this wavering acceptance of the passage by Sinaiticus, it appears in three other uncials — Bezae, and the later Regius and Koridethianus — and in numerous minuscules including those of Family 1. The two verses, however, are not to be found in the early codices Vaticanus, Alexandrinus, Washingtonianus I, nor in later uncials and minuscules. [63] Jerome, while retaining the episode of the bloody sweat in his Vulgate, notes its absence from many Greek and Old Latin manuscripts, as do also Epiphanius, Hilary and others, who none the less advocate its retention. The evidence of the Versions is, as usual, conflicting. [64] Although Cyril and Ambrose among the Fathers are not alone in their rejection of the passage, admission of the two verses into the text obtains the preponderant sanction of Justin, Irenaeus, Hippolytus, Tatian, Eusebius, Didymus, Augustine and numerous others. Goodspeed, alone among the modern editors, rejects the verses as spurious and excludes them from his translation.

An addition even more striking in character occurs at Luke xxiii. 34, where the celebrated words of Jesus upon Calvary,

[p] Westcott and Hort, both of whom were on the committee of revision, issued their *New Testament in the original Greek* in 1881 within a few days of publication of the English Revised Version.

"Father forgive them, for they know not what they do"—
although found in the Greek codices Alexandrinus, Ephraemi,
Regius, Purpureus Petropolitanus, and many others; in the
Vulgate and other versions;[65] and in many of the Fathers[66]
— have been deleted by a corrector from Codex Sinaiticus; are
completely omitted from codices Vaticanus, Washingtonianus I
and Koridethianus; were originally wanting in Codex Bezae —
into which they were subsequently inserted by a corrector; are
lacking in a few minuscules and some of the Versions;[67] and
were regarded as spurious by Cyril. These words, which Goodspeed thought it necessary to reject, were retained in the nineteenth-century Revision, are adopted with slight modification
by Moffatt, and find place, with a cautionary footnote, in the
Revised Standard Version.

Conspicuous among additions to the original text is the doxology — peculiar, in post-Elizabethan English translations, to
the Authorized Version — at the close of Matthew's form of the
Lord's Prayer: "For thine is the kingdom, the power, and the
glory forever. Amen." The Greek original of these words occurring at Matthew vi. 13b in codices Washingtonianus I, Koridethianus, Regius, and others,[68] will be sought for in vain in
codices Sinaiticus, Vaticanus, Bezae, Dublinensis; in Family 1
and other minuscules; in the Vulgate and Bohairic versions;
and, among other Fathers, in Origen, Tertullian, Gregory of
Nyssa, Cyril of Jerusalem, Hilary and Augustine. It should not
be surprising therefore, except to those whose liturgical expe-
rience embraces this doxology, that it is excluded from both the
Rheims and the Revised Versions. It is included only as a footnote in the Revised Standard New Testament.

An addition to the Greek text of a whole sentence, over which
controversy was prolonged and bitter,[69] may be found in both
the Rheims and the King James Versions in the First Epistle
of John (v. 7): "For there are three that bear record in heaven
[Rheims: " . . . three who give testimony"], the Father, the
Word, and the Holy Ghost: and these three are one." This
verse on the Three Witnesses — held by some authorities to have

been originally a marginal comment — occurs, with slight variations, in manuscripts both of the Old Latin and the Vulgate. It can, however, be found in none of the Greek uncials nor in any extant Greek manuscript written prior to the fourteenth-fifteenth century. No reference to it is made by the Fathers before Priscillian in the late fourth century. In its Greek form it first appeared, so far as is known, in the *Complutensian Polyglot* published by Cardinal Ximenes in 1522. Erasmus, having previously issued two editions of his own Greek New Testament without this verse, was obligated by his own rashness to insert it, against his inclination, in the third edition, 1522. Not having found this verse in any of the Greek codices used by him, and having ascertained that it is likewise wanting in Codex Vaticanus, Erasmus, when challenged on this point, imprudently offered to incorporate the verse in his forthcoming edition if any Greek manuscript containing it were discovered. Not long thereafter the necessary evidence was produced at Trinity College, Dublin — the fifteenth-sixteenth-century minuscule Codex Montfortianus.[q] Erasmus, though suspecting a pious fraud, lived up to his offer, and, to avoid calumny as he says,[70] inserted the disputed verse in his third and subsequent editions. In this, Luther refused to follow him, but the verse, after Luther's death, found its way into the Lutheran Bible. The Latin interpolation, thus dubiously established in both the Greek and the German texts, was carried over into English, to be retained in Anglican editions until the passage, finally recognized as spurious, was unceremoniously abandoned, without so much as a marginal comment, by the nineteenth-century Revisers.[r]

A much larger expansion of the primary Greek than that of the Three Witnesses is the account of the Woman taken in Adultery

[q] The Three Witnesses are included also in MS. 629 of the XIV–XV century in the Vatican library. The *Complutensian* N. T. (*v. infra*, p. 177) was probably translated into Greek from the Vulgate.

[r] Followed by Moffatt, Goodspeed, R. S. V. The verse, retained in the Rheims and A. V., and by Msgr. Knox, is still used by some Protestant sects as a proof-text; and, in the Roman Church, any question of its authenticity is forbidden by the Congregation of the Index.

[John vii. 53–viii. 11]. In Codex Campianus and several other late Greek manuscripts which preserve this familiar story, doubt of its authenticity is indicated by asterisk or obelus. Among the early uncials it is found only in Codex Bezae. Neither the Vaticanus nor the Sinaiticus contains it; nor was it ever included in the Alexandrinus.[71] In Codex Regius, immediately following John vii. 52, a blank space has been left in the manuscript large enough to contain all the twelve verses of this narrative; but the blank was never filled. In one of the minuscules, 209, it is inserted in the customary place, but only upon the scribe's second thought, as is indicated by his erasure of the first words of John viii. 12 which he had written immediately following vii. 52. The *Pericope Adulterae* is sometimes shifted to the end of the Gospel according to John,[72] and sometimes transferred to Luke, either at the close of that Gospel or following xxi. 38.[73] This latter transfer is one of the more conspicuous variations by which the "Caesarean Text"[74] is distinguished. Although cited in *Constitutiones 'Apostolicae'* and known to Jerome, Augustine, Ambrose and 'Ambrosiaster,' the story of the Woman taken in Adultery was one with which, it would appear *ex silentio*, Origen, Clement, Theodore of Mopsuestia, Chrysostom, Cyril and other Fathers were not concerned. The story, missing from certain ancient translations and present in others,[75] nevertheless retains its established place in the Vulgate. According to the guarded statement of Moffatt, who keeps the *Pericope* in his translation but encloses it within square brackets, "It is uncertain to which, if any, of the canonical gospels this fragment of primitive tradition originally belonged." It is, to be sure, possible that the story, seemingly of wide circulation, records an historical incident; but the instability of its location in the text, and its obvious interruption of the thought in its customary position, have contributed to the critical judgment that it was not originally a part of John's Gospel.[s] It has, accordingly, been removed from

---

[s] Additional considerations responsible for this opinion include the numerous expressions uncharacteristic of the Fourth Gospel and the suspiciously large number of its variant readings. *Cf.*, however, Rendel Harris, *New*

the Revised Version, is rejected by Goodspeed, and appears in the Revised Standard New Testament only in fine print at the foot of the page.

Another lengthy passage which is apparently an addition to the original text occurs at the close of the Gospel according to Mark [xvi. 9–20]. These twelve verses — a compendium of the post-resurrection appearances of Jesus — are altogether wanting in the fourth-century codices Vaticanus and Sinaiticus, and in the Old Syriac (Sinaitic) Version. They are found, however, in the somewhat later codices Alexandrinus, Ephraemi, Washingtonianus I, Bezae; and in the still later Regius, Laurensis, Koridethianus and many others. They are retained by the minuscules of Families 1 and 13. Manuscripts 1 and 1582 of Family Θ exclude these verses, in each case with a *scholion* in the hand of the original scribe to indicate that the exclusion is deliberate.[76] Some manuscripts exhibit a variant, and greatly abbreviated, conclusion of the Gospel: "But they reported briefly to Peter and his companions all they had been told. And afterwards Jesus himself sent out by them from the east to the west the sacred and incorruptible message of eternal salvation." The scribes of codices Regius and Laurensis[77] resolve their doubts by giving both this shorter form and, immediately following, the familiar longer ending. The extended conclusion regularly appears in the Vulgate and in many of the versions;[78] and is referred to by several of the early Church writers.[79] Eusebius is of opinion that the passage is not to be found in the best manuscripts. A notable variant in Codex Washingtonianus I is a unique insertion[t] following ἐπίστευσιν in verse fourteen, the first portion

---

Testament Autographs, Suppl. No. 12 to *American Journal of Philology*, [1882], pp. 10 ff.

[t] And they replied saying, This generation of lawlessness and lack of faith is under Satan who does not suffer the foul things ruled by spirits to comprehend the true power of God. Therefore, said they, speaking to Christ, manifest now thy justice. And Christ said to them, The term of the years of Satan's dominion is finished, but other terrible things are at hand for the sinners for whom I was delivered up to death in order that they might return to truth and sin no more, that they might inherit the spiritual splendor, and incorruptible, of that justice which is in heaven. (Author's translation)

of which was familiar, in unspecified manuscripts, to Jerome.[80] In none of its variations, be it remarked, is the passage in question a suitable continuation of the preceding subject-matter. The reader naturally anticipates an account, which is not forthcoming, of the appearance of the risen Jesus in Galilee. The opinion of some scholars that the Gospel originally terminated with verse eight has to contend with the unwanted abruptness which would then have marred the presentation.[u] It is perhaps less objectionable to hold, with others, that these twelve verses, intended to round out the interrupted narrative, are a substitution for the original conclusion, which, being on the outside sheet of the codex or at the end of a roll, may well have become detached from that copy of the separately circulating Gospel which served as archetype of the extant text. The passage, printed as an "Appendix" in the Revised Version, and by Moffatt and Goodspeed, has been relegated to the notes in the Revised Standard New Testament.

Additions of shorter length than the *Pericope Adulterae* or the spurious conclusion to the Gospel according to Mark, frequently are best explained as instances of assimilation: the transfer of a passage from one part of the Biblical text to another. This is an error to which the transcribers of the Gospels were peculiarly liable owing to the similarity of the basic subject-matter of the several narratives. Assimilation, according to Jerome, in his preface to his Latin translation of the Gospels,[81] is one of the chief sources of corruption of the text. It is, also, as he was certainly aware, one which can not always be easily detected. Its origin being in the scribe's memory, assimilation was the more likely the oftener the scribe copied a text. With repeated copying he must have had the Biblical material well in mind, if, indeed, he did not know it perfectly by heart. It was inevitable, under the circumstances, that passages of a like nature would, in the course of transcription, tend to acquire each others' characteristic phrasing.

---

[u] Not noticeable in English translation. Greek text: ἐφοβοῦντο γάρ.

This tendency may be illustrated by a simple parallel from the English versions. At Matthew xvi. 3, in the Authorized Version only, we read: "O *ye* hypocrites, ye can discern the face of the sky; but can ye not *discern* the signs of the times?"[82] The Rheims and Revised Versions, *correctly following the Greek text*, make no mention at this point of hypocrites, who have here been plainly assimilated into the Authorized Version, without documentary justification, from the similar statement at Luke xii. 56, where use of the word *hypocrites* enjoys universal textual sanction.

An instance of this assimilative tendency, not apparent in the English versions, occurs in the Greek text at the end of Matthew xxvii. 49. At that point, in codices Sinaiticus, Vaticanus, Ephraemi and Regius,[83] there has been inserted a sentence from John xix. 34. The sentiment of this borrowed verse — which, in the Revised Version, is translated: "howbeit one of the soldiers with a spear pierced his side, and straightway there came out blood and water" — is appropriate, as some earlier editor noted, to the circumstances of the narrative of Matthew into which it was inserted; but it is excluded from the First Gospel by numerous ancient authorities,[84] and is retained only by Moffatt's translation among the English versions.

A more notable instance of assimilation is the Lord's Prayer as it is now read at Luke xi. 2–4. The evidence of the manuscripts points unmistakably to a considerably shorter form of this prayer in the original Lucan version. Codex Vaticanus contents itself with the relatively brief: "Father, Hallowed be thy name. Thy kingdom come. Give us day by day our daily bread. And forgive us our sins, for [Sinaiticus: ὡς καί, *as*] we ourselves also forgive everyone that is indebted to us. And lead us not into temptation."[85] Codex Sinaiticus duplicates this abbreviated reading except for the insertion (after "Thy kingdom come.") of the sentence: "Thy will be done, as in heaven, so upon earth."[86] The familiar "But deliver us from evil," wanting in the fourth-century uncials after "lead us not into temptation," finds place in codices Alexandrinus, Ephraemi,

Bezae, Washingtonianus I, Koridethianus and many others of later date.[87] Of the scribes who were assigned the copying of Luke none is likely to have been unfamiliar with Matthew; the probability, moreover, is great that they had transcribed "Matthew's" Gospel more than once before, and one or another of them, remembering its expanded and more satisfying form of the Lord's Prayer, consciously or unwittingly assimilated a part of its wording to his transcription of Luke. That this actually occurred is the judgment of the editors of the Rheims, the Revised, and Revised Standard Versions, by all of whom only the unelaborated form of the prayer is considered the authentic work of Luke.[88]

Variant readings such as the foregoing occasionally resist definite classification as additions or deletions. Apparent expansion of the text in one set of manuscripts may in reality be only an omission, deliberate or unintentional, which should be supplied in another set. Abridgment of the text, on the contrary, far from being an accidental abbreviation, may be the result of careful editing. This is especially to be borne in mind with reference to the early codices Vaticanus and Sinaiticus, both of which benefited by extensive correction. Some idea of the thoroughness of manuscript revision may be gleaned from Tischendorf's edition of that portion of the Sinaiticus which is now lodged in the British Museum, in which he records nearly fifteen thousand editorial alterations.

Revision of the text may consist not only of additions or deletions, but of substitutions as well. It is entirely possible that the variant readings at I Timothy iii. 16 — previously presented in illustration of scribal confusion[89] — may have arisen through deliberate replacement of one word by another under the influence of doctrinal tendencies. Editorial substitution in support of doctrine is unmistakable in the codices at John i. 18, which, in the Revised Version, is rendered: "No man hath seen God at any time; the only begotten Son . . . hath declared him." With this reading, so far at least as the word *Son* is concerned, English translations are in universal agreement. The Greek words for *the Son* [ὁ υἱός] do not occur at this verse in codices Vaticanus, Sinaiticus, Ephraemi or Regius, but in their place appear the words for *the God* [ὁ θεός]. This reading, found also in the Peshitto and Egyptian versions, has the sanction of Origen and many other Fathers.[90] To them, it would seem, "the . . . God" was both intelligible and acceptable, whatever the meaning they assigned to the adjective [μονογενής] which the Revisers and others have erroneously translated as *only begotten*.[91] *Son*, had it been originally written, would presumably have been coupled — as Msgr. Knox realizes[v] — not with the article *the* [ὁ], but with the possessive pronoun *his* [αὐτοῦ], as at John iii. 16 and I John iv. 9. In only two early uncials, the Alexandrinus and Washingtonianus I, was the replacement of *the . . . God* by *the . . . Son* made in the hand of the original scribe. In only one other early uncial, Codex Ephraemi, was it effected by a later reviser. It appears, however, in Koridethianus and the codices of Family I and in numerous other minuscules, and enjoys the confirmation of several Versions and of numerous Fathers.[92] Both *God* and *Son* are omitted in one manuscript of the Vulgate, in the *Diatessaron*, and in several Fathers.[93] It is scarcely conceivable that *Son*, attractive as it is on doctrinal grounds, once written in this Johannine passage, would be replaced by any editor with any other word, even with *God*. The reading *God*, however it be regretted in Vaticanus and its associates, must, accordingly, be considered original; and *Son*, although in conformity with dogmatic predilections, can only be deemed an editorial substitution.

[v] Knox, alone among English translators, adopting "*his* only-begotten Son," knowingly departs from the original text, as is shown by his marginal note: "Some of the best manuscripts here read 'God, *the* only-begotten' instead of '*the* only-begotten Son' " [italics supplied]. Elsewhere Knox retains the article *the* of the original even though he senses the desirability of an alternative. See his marginal note to Mt. i. 18: "Isaias vii. 14. '*The* virgin' is a literal translation of the Hebrew; '*a* virgin' would equally express the sense of the original prophecy." [Italics supplied. This, if intended, as apparently it was, to refer to the article alone, is correct; on *virgin* as "a literal translation of the Hebrew" see *infra*, pp. 245 ff.].

Comparison of the numerous variant readings of which the preceding examples are but a representative fraction, has led to the classification of New Testament manuscripts into several major categories, the number and the designation of which have varied with the progress of Biblical criticism. At the present time these categories are four: the Received Text or *Textus Receptus*, the Neutral Text, the Western Text and, the most recently established of all, the Caesarean. The first of these, the *Textus Receptus*,[w] is, in all essentials, the Greek text put forth first by Erasmus at Basle in 1516 and in four later editions. The relatively few manuscripts consulted by Erasmus were all of late date and of a type which, because it was that used by Chrysostom,[x] was ultimately named Antiochene or Syrian by Hort. The lateness of the Received Text, as shown by its notable conflate readings constructed out of earlier sources,[94] was recognized neither by Erasmus — and his successors, Étienne and Beza — nor by the Jacobean scholars who depended upon its authority throughout the New Testament portion of the King James Version. Today, it is completely discredited, one eminent scholar referring to it as "the degenerate descendant" of Lucian's text.[95] Investigation has demonstrated beyond question that the *Textus Receptus*, consecrated though it be through some fifteen centuries of theological service, must be denied its pretension to primacy as the faithful custodian of the original text.[y]

[w] This universally employed designation originated with the brothers Elzivir of Leyden, who, in promoting the sale of the second edition (1633) of their Greek N. T., based upon the text of Theodore Beza (*v. infra*, p. 178, note h), advertised it as "textum . . . nunc ab omnibus receptum."

[x] Chrysostom, before his long term of asceticism and his elevation to the Archbishopric of Constantinople, lived at Antioch in Syria, where he was born c. 347.

[y] The first important step in this investigation was taken by John Mill of Queen's College, Oxford, who, with the 1550 text of Stephanus as a foundation, issued his edition (1707) of the Greek New Testament, in which, from a collation of 78 MSS., the Peshitto, such O. Lat. as was at hand, and the Vulgate, he recorded some 30,000 variants. This disclosure of the unreliability of the *Textus Receptus* led to the search for textual-groups by several scholars, first among whom was J. A. Bengel of Tübingen who, in 1734, proposed two classifications, the African, represented by a few old MSS., and the Asiatic,

The second of the four major categories into which contemporary scholarship divides the Greek manuscripts of the New Testament is the Neutral. This designation, first employed by Westcott and Hort, was intended to convey the idea that the codices so classified, having evaded editorial revision or scribal deterioration, closely approximate the very words originally set down by the Biblical writers. This optimistic idea of practically uncorrupted transmission can no longer be entertained, but the label *Neutral* is apparently with us to stay. The excellence of the codices in this category — Vaticanus, Sinaiticus, and, in Acts alone, Alexandrinus — is the result, we now know, not of scrupulous scribal fidelity but rather of thoroughgoing editorial revision. Most vigorous pruning of the text, to clear it of accretions and errors, is seen in Vaticanus. Sinaiticus, a close second, still retains some of the traits peculiar to manuscripts of the third category, the Western. These manuscripts of the Neutral class associate themselves, through common features, most closely with Egyptian documents of the second century, and particularly with those written in Sahidic, the Coptic dialect of the Nile Valley. Conspicuous among such Egyptian stigmata, for example, is an unorthodox order of the Pauline Epistles — an arrangement which from the evidence of Vaticanus must have been characteristic of the prototype of that splendid codex. [96] More than a century older than Vaticanus, the Chester Beatty Papyrus of the Pauline Epistles [P 46], certainly Egyptian in origin, is markedly more Neutral than Western. Egypt, it is tempting to conjecture, may well have been the home of the

---

found in the later copies. These two categories were modified and expanded by J. J. Griesbach [Halle, 1774–5] to three: the Alexandrian or Origenic, preserved in codices B, A, C, L; the Byzantine (Bengel's Asiatic); and the Western, exhibited by Latin MSS. and D. Westcott and Hort, *op. cit.*, refining the analysis, distinguished a Syrian or Antiochene group which, being of later date, and attributable to Lucian, was, they maintained, a revision derived from three earlier sources: the Western (as in Griesbach, plus Syr. C.), the Alexandrian (Griesbach's C and L, plus Δ, Ξ, Ψ, 33), and, of prime importance, the Neutral, as they called it, found throughout codices B and ℵ, in Acts alone in A, and in quotations by Origen.

Neutral codices, and the place in which they were subjected to editorial revision. Of this supposition, however, there is no proof; and, especially in the case of Sinaiticus, there are indications of an origin in Caesarea rather than in Alexandria.[z] Whatever the provenance of these magnificent codices of the Neutral type, and however they may survive the scrutiny of critics who examine them in the light of the ancient Versions and the early Fathers, their imprint is now permanently marked upon the English Bible; for Hort, their chief sponsor, convinced that he was championing the next thing to Evangelical holographs, exercised an influence so great upon his fellow Revisers that their Version of the New Testament, published in the same year (1881) as was his — and Westcott's — Greek edition, is to a large degree a reflection of the Neutral text.

Third among our presently-held categories of New Testament manuscripts is the Western, the representatives of which are the earliest Old Latin translations and Codex Bezae, supplemented — geographically Eastern though it be — by the Old Syriac (Sinaitic) Version, and by quotations chiefly by Clement of Alexandria. Distinguishing aspects of Western manuscripts include an unorthodox order of the Gospels — Matthew, John, Luke, Mark; notable divergencies both of language and of factual detail in Acts; inclusion of the story of the Woman taken in Adultery and other additions; and omissions of numerous passages such as that at John iv. 9: "For the Jews have no dealings with the Samaritans," or at Luke xxiv. 51: "and he was carried up into heaven." This Western Text, about which there is great diversity of scholarly opinion, circulated not only throughout the western portion of the Roman Empire, but as far east as Syria. It was apparently widely in use in the second century.

The fourth classification of New Testament manuscripts — the Caesarean — though of recent discovery, already appears

---

[z] Such as the scribal error at Acts viii. 5 where Philip is reported as having gone down not to Samaria, as in other MSS., but to Caesarea. *Cf.* also Rendel Harris, *Stichometry*, Cambridge, 1893, p. 75.

to belie its name. Evidence is accumulating, as will be seen, that it would have been more appropriately called the Alexandrian. Creation of this fourth category awaited the recognition that manuscript-groups 1 and 13, and some other scattered minuscules, were members of a larger unit which, because at its head stands Codex Koridethianus, is designated by the symbol for that manuscript as Family Θ. That this Family has an historical association with Origen, and therefore with Caesarea where that distinguished and influential scholar did some of his later work, is the critically momentous discovery of Canon Streeter.[97] Origen, at odds with the local ecclesiastical authorities, voluntarily removed himself about A. D. 232 from Alexandria, where he had been a prolific writer of theological works for more than a quarter of a century, and established a school, which was to become famous, at Caesarea. At that center of Christian learning in Palestine, where he had at his disposal the library built up by his disciple Pamphilus, Origen resumed his *Commentary on John*, the writing of which had been interrupted, at the end of the fifth book, by his flight from Alexandria, and subsequently produced, among other books, his *Commentary on Matthew* and his *Exhortation to Martyrdom*. In these three works Origen quotes copiously from the Gospels. Examination of these quotations — at least so far as they are taken from Mark — reveals that Origen, while at Alexandria, made use of a manuscript or manuscripts with Neutral characteristics; but that, not long after his arrival at Caesarea, he began to utilize a text of the Family Θ type as a source of his quotations in the latter part of the *Commentary on John*, and that he continued this reliance upon the Family Θ prototype in the two other works just mentioned. This would appear to indicate that Origen, having left his Neutral-type sources behind him in Alexandria, was dependent upon manuscripts such as were at hand in Caesarea, and that these were of the Family Θ type; hence the identification of Koridethanius and its kindred manuscripts as Caesarean.

Unfortunately for this natural inference, at least two pieces of evidence to the contrary can be produced, one of them from

Origen himself. The first five books of his *Commentary on John*, written, as has been noted, in Egypt, contain quotations practically identical with those of the great Neutrals, Vaticanus and Sinaiticus. This happens surprisingly also to be the case in the immediately ensuing books of the *Commentary* written *at Caesarea*. Quotations of the Family Θ type do not appear in this work until the middle of the twelfth book. It is difficult to explain Origen's use of a Neutral source in preparing books six to twelve of this *Commentary on John* at Caesarea if only the Koridethian brand of text were available to him in the library of Pamphilus. The suspicion is inevitable that Origen may have carried with him his own manuscript of the Gospels — Neutral in character — from Alexandria to Caesarea. If so, why does he abandon his private and authoritative source when he arrives at the middle of the twelfth book of his *Commentary on John*? Assumption that this was Origen's procedure would appear to be less valid than the conjecture that his own manuscript, brought with him from Egypt, and continuously used by him at Caesarea, was Neutral only in part, and that those of its features which we now associate with the Koridethi Gospels were embedded in the "Origenian" codex before it had been transported to Palestine.

Support for this conjecture is provided by the Chester Beatty Papyrus of the Gospels [P 45], the second of our two pieces of anti-Caesarean evidence. This text, undoubtedly of Egyptian provenance, was produced in the third century, probably in the first half, and if not in the lifetime of Origen then certainly within a short interval after his death. It is characterized, at least in Mark, by readings distinctly at variance with those predominant in Vaticanus, and establishes beyond doubt the fact that the text of the Gospels circulating in Egypt in the third century was by no means exclusively Neutral. Some of the readings of this Papyrus are Western. In Mark, if not elsewhere, it exhibits a text closely akin to the "Caesarean" — an indication not to be ignored that that variety of text was in existence in Egypt approximately at the time when Origen migrated to Palestine. This, of course, increases the probability that the type of text which marks the Koridethi Gospels is not indigenous to Palestine, and that it may have been Origen himself who, in the third century, introduced it into Caesarea. If that be the case, the term *Caesarean* is a misnomer, and, like *Western*, is misleading. It would seem, therefore, that, with analysis of the exceedingly intricate interrelationship of Biblical manuscript-groups at its current stage of evolution, it might be judicious to suspend the practice of assigning to manuscript-groups a definite place of origin. The wide dissemination of early variants from the Neutral Text demands, it may well be, historical rather than geographical explanation.

CHAPTER VI

Translation of the Text: Early Versions

"Into every province according to the writing thereof,
and to every people after their language."
Esther i. 22

TRANSLATION of the Scriptures, now a major concern of the publishing industry, began with something of a flourish under Ptolemy Philadelphus, King of Egypt, in the third pre-Christian century. So at least tradition runs. The letter of "Aristeas" to Philocrates through which this tradition has been transmitted, though recently adjudged worthy of partial credence, has long been recognized, despite its attestation by Josephus, as a forgery by an Alexandrian Jew of a later Ptolemaic period, presumably possessed of little, if any, historical authority. [1] From Aristeas, whether the letter to Philocrates be spurious or not, it is apparent, from his silence as to Prophets and Hagiographa, that the earliest of Scriptural versions, from Hebrew into Greek, was initially a translation of the Pentateuch — and of the Pentateuch alone; and from Aristeas comes the tradition that Ptolemy, desirous of enriching the regal collection of books at Alexandria, persuaded Eleazar the high priest — persuaded with lavish gifts for the Temple at Jerusalem and with freedom for a hundred thousand Jewish captives — to send him seventy-two elders, "six in number out of every tribe . . . skillful in the laws, and of abilities to make an accurate interpretation of them," who, royally entertained upon their arrival at Alexandria with presents for the king and a sacred scroll written in letters of gold, effected a translation of the Torah for Ptolemy in precisely seventy-two days. This remarkable performance, as recounted by Aristeas and repeated by Josephus, was a co-operative undertaking, the seventy-two elders being provided by Ptolemy with a suitable retreat on the island of Pharos for "discoursing together" while engaged on their scholarly work. Legend, however, not content with this sufficiently embroidered account of the Version, soon magnified the achievement of the Jewish elders, first extending the translation to include not only the Law but also the rest of the Hebrew Scriptures, then promoting it to the realm of the miraculous by assigning to each of the elders a separate cell from which, at the end of seventy-two days, he emerged, having produced independently a version identical in every respect with those of his seventy-one associates. In lasting tribute to this traditional record the Alexandrian Version is universally known as the Septuagint, that being an abbreviated form of *septuaginta et duo*, Latin for *seventy-two*.

Tradition is sufficiently well-founded only with respect to time and place of Septuagintal origin; certain it is that only the first five Books of the Old Testament were made available to the Greek-speaking Jews of the Ptolemaic period. Less certain, but not out of the question, is the possibility that expansion of the Septuagint was initiated with translation of Joshua, or a portion of that Book, before the end of the third pre-Christian century. Favorable acceptance of the Pentateuchal Version by the Alexandrian Jewish community resulted not only in immediate multiplication of copies, but ultimately, and especially during the century following, in "publication" of additional Books of Hebrew Scripture in Hellenistic form. By the middle of the second century B. C. the work begun by "the Seventy" had been enlarged to include Joshua, I Samuel, and the Major and Minor Prophets. By the year 132 B. C., as we learn from the Prologue to Ecclesiasticus, [2] at least some of "the Writings" had been added to the translation. Probably not until the first pre-Christian century were Judges, II Samuel, the two Books of

Kings, and the remainder of the Hagiographa[a] set forth in
Greek, by which time the Septuagint, universally accepted by
Christians as the sacred Scriptures of Israel, and freely quoted
as such by the writers of the New Testament, had been re-
pudiated as unauthoritative and corrupt by scholars of the
Synagogue.[b]

The first installment of the Septuagint — the Pentateuch —
was in all probability less a creation of Ptolemaic origin than a
product of cultural miscegenation. The Jews of Alexandria, like
Jews of other and later metropolitan centers, though preserving
their religious tradition and observing its ceremonies, rapidly
lost command of the language in which that tradition and its
ceremonies had been written by their forefathers. Hellenized to
the degree at which Greek had replaced Aramaic as their vernacular, the large and influential community of Alexandrian
Jews required for synagogal and ceremonial purposes a version
of the *Book of the Law* which they and their children could
understand. In the preparation of such a Greek version of the

[a] Except Daniel (included among "the Writings" in the Hebrew Scriptures)
and Ecclesiastes, the Septuagintal form of which dates from the second century
of the Christian era. *V. infra*, p. 331, note 11.

[b] Later Talmudic tradition regards several passages as instances of faulty
word-division, and claims thirteen deliberate alterations of the original by
"the Seventy," one of which was the substitution of "rough-foot" for *hare*
(Lev. xi. 6), to avoid possible royal displeasure had the word λαγῶς (*hare*),
closely resembling the ancestral Ptolemaic name, Lagus, been employed in
this context of things "unclean" (Margolis, *The Story of Bible Translations*,
p. 35). Larger variations, both interpolations and omissions, are frequent,
especially in Jeremiah, Job, Esther and Daniel. Of even greater concern to
the rabbis was the incorporation in the LXX of the Apocryphal Writings —
I and II Esdras, Wisdom, Ecclesiasticus, Baruch, Tobit, Judith, I and II
Maccabees, and additions to Esther and Daniel — some of which, apparently,
had been originally composed not in Hebrew or Aramaic but in Alexandrian
Greek. To this comprehensive character of the LXX may be attributed the
preservation of portions of Hebrew literature which, excluded by the rabbis
from the canonical writings, would otherwise have perished. Jews the world
over, celebrating their Feast of Dedication (Ḥannukkah) in languages as
varied as the lands in which they dwell, may rejoice over the heroic deeds of
Judas Maccabeus only because they were recorded, and thus saved from
oblivion, in the Hellenistic vernacular — long obsolete — of the Israelites
of ancient Alexandria.

Pentateuch it is not at all unlikely that the Jewish subjects of Philadelphus profited by the assistance of Palestinian scholars — although not to the extent related by Aristeas and Josephus. Undoubtedly the work of Alexandrian Jews, as its occasional departure from Palestinian Hebrew indicates, the Septuagintal Pentateuch reflects something other than the traditional pattern subsequently stabilized by the Massoretic Text.[c] In the preparation, during later centuries, of the post-Pentateuchal portions of the Greek translation, no aid whatsoever, if the text itself be any indication, came to the Alexandrian Jews from Jerusalem. "The translators," as Driver puts it,[3] "stand remarkably aloof from the Palestinian tradition — often . . . not only missing the general sense of a passage, but showing themselves to be unacquainted with the meaning of common Hebrew words." Particularly in the Prophets and Hagiographa, the Septuagint — based upon a textual prototype which varied greatly, in places,

[c] Although details both of the text and of its interpretation must have been occasionally blurred in Jewish memory as the People of Israel accommodated themselves to their shifting historical position, the traditional meaning of their sacred Scriptures — especially the Pentateuch — was, on the whole, apparently well preserved. Prime witness to the fidelity of the tradition is the Torah of the Samaritans. This Jewish sect, alienating itself, in the fifth century B. C., from the body of Israel, refused to adopt the "square" writing attributed to Ezra [*v. supra*, p. 29], and, employing only the archaic Phoenician script, has transmitted a Hebrew Pentateuch (the Prophets and Hagiographa being rejected as of insufficient authority) which, beneath consideration by the orthodox Massoretes, escaped such stabilization as might have been effected through vowel-points. Surprisingly close to the Massoretic Text despite this freedom, the Samaritan Pentateuch provides independent evidence of the extraordinary consistency of the Hebrew Scriptural tradition [*cf*. John Skinner, *The Divine Names in Genesis*, London, 1914]. Occasional textual discrepancies between the Samaritan and the received Hebrew readings, though originating, as some think, with the Massoretes [*cf*. Benjamin Kennicott, *The State of the Printed Hebrew Text of the Old Testament*, Oxford, 1759], are naturally held in conservative circles to be deliberate alterations by the Samaritans in questionable support of contentions peculiar to their heresy. Conspicuous among these textual deviations is that in Deut. xxvii. 4, where the received Mt. Ebal is replaced, in the Samaritan text, by the geographically more convenient Mt. Gerizim, upon which, to this day, the nearly extinct Samaritan community (perhaps 200 souls) of the neighboring Nablus [ancient Shechem] assembles annually for the celebration of Passover. Many of the Samaritan variants are concurred in by the LXX.

from the text of the Masorah — is an unimpeachable witness to the translators' unsatisfied need of instruction, such as no scholar from Jerusalem would require, in the semantic refinements of Biblical Hebrew.[d]

Septuagintal deviations from the received Hebrew Scriptures are also due, in some instances, to the Alexandrian translators' misunderstanding of a text written, as most of the Books of the Old Testament were, without vowel-letters;[4] other textual discrepancies owe their existence, without doubt, to the translators' failure to supply correct vocalization to the unpointed original. At Baruch iii. 4, for example, the Septuagint (followed by the Vulgate and the Douay Version) requests the Lord to hear the prayer of *the dead of* Israel. This inept translation is literally correct if the two consonants and single vowel-letter of the underlying Hebrew word [מתי — MThy][5] are pointed one way [מֵתֵי — MēThE]; these three letters, however, differently pointed, yield *men of* [מְתֵי — MeThE] Israel — a reading exactly duplicated at Isaiah xli. 14, and approximated in a dozen other passages, and doubtless here intended by the original Jewish author in whose mind the prayer was presumably to be uttered by men of Israel who were still alive. At Jeremiah xxxii. 36, to give a second illustration, the assumed vocalization דָּבָר [DaBhaR — *message, mission*] underlying the Septuagintal ἀποστολή is erroneously employed instead of דֶּבֶר [DeBheR — *pestilence*], the correct pronunciation, which is reflected in all English versions including the Douay. To the translators, imperfect in their mastery of the underlying language, may be attributed, no doubt, some of the numerous obscurities of the Septuagintal Version, which, though in the main a readable specimen of Alexandrian Greek, suggests now and then the alien syntax of

---

[d] At Jer. xxiv. 1, and elsewhere, the Hebrew for *smith* [מסגר — MASGēR] is incorrectly translated *prisoner* [δεσμώτης]; *outside of* [ἔξωθεν] is made to do service for the explicit *in the streets* of Jerusalem (Jer. xi. 6 and xxxiii. 10); *multitude* [המון — HAMÔN], at Baruch ii. 29, is rendered by *noise* [βόμβησις], one of its meanings, to be certain, but inappropriate at this passage, as the Douay Version recognizes; *to serve* [עבד — 'BHDh] is repeatedly misinterpreted (Jer. xxx. 8 and elsewhere) as *to work* [ἐργάζεσθαι].

the original tongue; destroys, frequently, through a rendition too literal, any flavor of literary quality; and, at least as it has survived the vicissitudes of repeated transcription, becomes here and there entirely unintelligible.

The Septuagint is none the less an indispensable document for Biblical studies. Obviously the uneven performance of many individual translators, varying from slavish literalness in Samuel and Kings to extremely free treatment in the Book of Job, the Alexandrian translation of the sacred literature of the Jewish people is yet, with all its inadequacies and errors, a substantially correct rendering of the sense of those portions of the Hebrew original — the bulk of the Old Testament — which are not in themselves impaired beyond comprehension. The Septuagint, accordingly, despite its imperfections, may be frequently invoked in the clarification of Old Testament difficulties. Used with critical judgment, it is an invaluable instrument of textual emendation. Errors which occur in the Massoretic Text of nearly every Book of the Old Testament — particularly in Samuel, Kings and Ezekiel, the prototypic manuscripts of which seem to have been especially corrupt — may in instance after instance be confidently corrected, as previously indicated,[6] with the assistance of the Septuagintal reading.[e]

The Alexandrian was not the only Jewish community of ancient times which, having forgotten its mother tongue, required a translation of the Sacred Books into the language which had become its vernacular. This need was felt by the Syriac-speaking Jews whose fortune had carried them far north of Jerusalem, north of Damascus, to Edessa, which at the dawn of the Common Era, had become their cultural center. Approximately at the time when the last of the Septuagintal translations

[e] For this purpose a definitive critical edition of the LXX, recording the variant readings of many codices, would have been invaluable, had one been available in the nineteenth century, to the editors of the R. V. A useful edition published by Alfred Rahlfs, 2 vols., Stuttgart, 1935, will ultimately be superseded by the edition in preparation at Cambridge, begun in 1906 by A. E. Brooke and Norman McLean, continued by H. St. J. Thackeray, several parts of which — Genesis-Esther — have been issued.

were being made at Alexandria, a Syriac version of the Pentateuch, written, it appears, in Hebrew characters, was provided by Jewish scholars at Edessa for synagogal purposes.[7] From its earliest appearance, this Jewish version was adopted by the Syrian Church. Like the Septuagint a product of many hands, this Syriac translation — the Peshitto[f] — was ultimately enlarged to include all the canonical Books of the Old Testament. Its very literal rendition presupposes a Hebrew prototype closer to the Massoretic Text than that which underlies the Septuagint. Translated directly from the Hebrew, it was later revised under Christian influence to conform more closely with the Alexandrian Version. The origin of the Peshitto, though less wrapped up in legend than that of the Septuagint, is equally obscure. Fourth-century Christian writers — Augustine, Chrysostom, Ephraem of Edessa — refer to it; and Theodore of Mopsuestia, of the same century, asserts that its translator is unknown. The Syriac Version of which mention is made by Melito of Sardis in the latter half of the second century, can hardly be anything other than the Peshitto, which is generally thought to date from the early part of that century. Josephus, however, in his *Antiquities of the Jews* (XX. ii. 4), gives a tantalizing inkling of an even earlier possible date for the Pentateuchal portion of the Syriac translation. Izates, King of Adiabene, having been converted to Judaism, is persuaded to circumcision, as Josephus tells the story, while reading the Law of Moses. In what language this Torah was written is not revealed by the historian. The enthusiasm of the newly converted monarch, which Josephus does report, was such that he domiciled all his five sons at Jerusalem for their proper education. Furthermore, if the later tradition of Bar Hebraeus[8] be respected, he had, for his own edification, caused a Syriac translation to be made by scholars sent expressly for that purpose

---

[f] *I. e.*, the *Simple* Version; so labeled by a Syrian theologian, Moses bar Kepha, in the ninth century, presumably to distinguish it from Origen's *Hexapla*; *v. infra*, p. 163. *Cf.* F. C. Burkitt, *Early Eastern Christianity*, London, 1904, pp. 41 ff.

from his Parthian realm beyond the Tigris to the Temple on Mt. Zion. The conversion of Izates had been effected early in the first century — not later, in any case, than A. D. 35.[9] The temptation, consequently, arises to identify the Law which Izates was reading as the Syriac translation which, according to Bar Hebraeus, the King had commanded, and to equate it with the first installment of the Peshitto, the origin of that version being thus set back a century earlier than the commonly accepted date.

Jewish and Christian acceptance of the Peshitto in Syria developed simultaneously with increasing Jewish disparagement of the Septuagint as it permeated the Mediterranean world. This dissatisfaction was responsible for the appearance, during the second century, of three separate revisions of the Septuagint, all of them by men who had been converted to Judaism. Jews of the Roman Empire, accustomed to the translation of "the Seventy," could repudiate the Septuagintal Version of their Scriptures only if provided with an alternative likewise in Greek, the language of their adoption. The first of such substitutes was produced by Aquila, who had gone to Palestine from Sinope on the Black Sea to sit at the feet of the famous Rabbi Akiba, and, in accordance with the Pharisaic orthodoxy of his great teacher, had issued, possibly before the middle of the second century, an entirely independent translation of his own.[g] Indifferent in its word-for-word rendering to the requirements of Greek idiom, scrupulous in its fidelity to traditional interpretation of Jewish law and custom, and freed from the mass of uncanonical material which had been incorporated into the Septuagint, this version of Aquila's successfully displaced the Septuagint in Jewish circles, and acquired an authority, long maintained, as the one Greek translation sanctioned within the

[g] Of Aquila's Version, known chiefly from Hexaplar citations, no MSS. have survived. Included in Schechter's discoveries in 1897 at the Cairo *Genizah*, however, were fragments of two MSS. (I Kgs. xx. 7-17; II Kgs. xxiii. 12-17; Ps. xc. 6-13; Ps. xci. 4-10; parts of Ps. xxiii) exhibiting the pedantic features typical of Aquila's translation. Akiba (c. A. D. 50-132) was the leading spirit of a rabbinical school at Bene Berak near Jaffa.

Synagogue. Origen, as will be seen, knew this version well; and Justinian, four centuries after the appearance of Aquila's version, recommended it as an alternative to the Septuagint for the Jews of Byzantium who worshipped in Greek.[10]

Another version of the second century, rather a revision of the Septuagint than a new translation from the Hebrew, is the work of Theodotion — an Ebionite,[h] according to Irenaeus, from Ephesus. Theodotion, despite a weakness for transliteration, is far more readable than the pedantic Aquila. His redaction revives certain passages of the Hebrew text which were not included in the Alexandrian Version, but at the same time preserves Septuagintal readings for which there is no Hebrew authority. His translation of Daniel has the unique distinction of adoption by the Church in place of the Daniel of the Septuagint.[11] Customary assignment of Theodotion's work to the latter half of the century, and therefore subsequent to the version of Aquila, is to be accepted with reserve. There would seem to be little, if any, reason for presenting to the Jewish community a translation such as Theodotion's once it had come into possession of the satisfying work of Aquila. It may be, in view of this consideration, that the date of Aquila's version should be advanced.

Of Symmachus, whose version was probably made toward the close of the second century, possibly with copies of Aquila and Theodotion before him, we know very little. Epiphanius records the unlikely tale that Symmachus was a Samaritan who deserted to the Jews. Both Eusebius and Jerome designate him an Ebionite. His translation, commended by Jerome for conveying, as Aquila's does not, the sense of the underlying Hebrew, was the chief Greek basis for the Vulgate.

In addition to these three recensions by Aquila, Theodotion and Symmachus, at least three other Greek versions of the

[h] Ebionites, "the poor" [אביונים — 'EBHYÔNIM], were Judaeo-Christians whose Messianic acceptance of Jesus excluded his divinity. Their sole gospel, attributed to Matthew, was in Aramaic (*v. infra*, p. 324, n. 1). Their ritual, Jewish throughout, included circumcision. *Cf.* Irenaeus, *Adversus Hæreses*, I. 262, and Origen, *Contra Celsum*, II. 1.

Septuagint, by unknown authors, were available in the first half of the third century to Origen. Pioneer in textual criticism of the Bible, that distinguished scholar of the Church devoted twenty years to the study of variant manuscripts in the hope of establishing the original Septuagintal text. The *Hexapla*, as Origen's monumental contribution to that textual problem is called, was completed about A. D. 245. For convenience of comparative study, Origen assembled variant Septuagintal material in parallel columns — for the most part six,[i] whence *Hexapla* — three of which (the third, fourth and sixth) presented the versions of Aquila, Symmachus and Theodotion, and the first two of which contained the contemporary pre-Massoretic Hebrew text by the side of its transliteration into letters of the Greek alphabet. The fifth column, between Symmachus and Theodotion, was reserved by Origen for his own edition — theoretically the recaptured original — of the Septuagint. Origen's unfortunate assumption of identity between the Hebrew Biblical text current in his day and that which had served, five centuries earlier, as the basis of the Hellenistic Pentateuch, not only defeated his own attempt to recover the original text of the Septugint but has impeded its attainment by later generations of scholars. Although Origen failed in his difficult — and still to be accomplished — undertaking, his *Hexapla* is none the less outstanding as initial milestone on the long trail of the "lower criticism."

Jerome, we learn from his Commentary on Titus,[12] examined Origen's *magnum opus*, late in the fourth century, in the library of Pamphilus at Caesarea; and evidence is available of its existence there at the beginning of the seventh century. Not long afterwards, the Hexaplaric manuscript seems to have perished, probably one of the casualties of Arab vandalism at the destruction of Caesarea in A. D. 653. Of the *Hexapla* only two fragments

---

[i] Inclusion of additional readings from unknown translators increases the columns, in some of the Books, to eight, and even, occasionally, to nine. An *editio minor*, the last four columns only, is known as the *Tetrapla*. *Cf.* F. Field, *Origenis Hexaplorum quae supersunt*, 2 vols., Oxford, 1867–1874.

are known: a palimpsest leaf, containing part of Psalm xlv, at Milan; and at Cambridge a portion of Psalm xxii which was found at the Cairo *Genizah*. Indirectly, however, Origen's own recension may be fairly well recovered, owing to the extremely literal character of the Syriac translation of the entire fifth Hexaplaric column produced by Paul, bishop of Tella, in A. D. 617.[13] The voluminous nature of the *Hexapla* sufficiently accounts for the fact that it was, presumably, never duplicated in its entirety. Origen's own version — column five — was singled out for separate circulation as the essential portion of his text-critical edition. A manageable manuscript thus limited in scope must have been available eventually at Alexandria; for in that city lived Bishop Paul while at work on his Syriac translation.

At Caesarea, three hundred years prior to Paul's Syro-Hexaplar redaction, Eusebius, disciple of Origen, isolating the text of his master from its textual neighbors, had issued it, with the aid of Pamphilus, in an edition of his own. This Eusebian recension, produced early in the fourth century, was adopted, as Jerome later reported, by the churches throughout Palestine. Concurrently, two other Septuagintal versions, again according to Jerome,[j] had established themselves: one, in general use in the churches of Egypt, prepared by Hesychius,[k] of whom little can be said except that he was a bishop in that country; the other by Lucian, a priest from Antioch who suffered martyrdom at Nicomedia in Asia Minor, A. D. 311 or 312. Lucian's revision,[14] accepted as the received text in eastern churches from Constantinople to Antioch, is distinguished from its rivals by several

[j] Jerome, *Praefatio in Libros Paralipomenon, Opera omnia*, ed. Vallarsi, IX, 1405: "Alexandria & Aegyptus in Septuaginta suis Hesychium laudat auctorem: Constantinopolis usque Antiochiam, Luciani Martyris exemplaria probat. Mediae inter has Provinciae Palaestinos codices legunt; quos ab Origene elaboratos Eusebius & Pamphilus vulgaverunt; totusque orbis has inter se trifaria varietate compugnat."

[k] Known, chiefly, through quotations from his version by Cyril of Alexandria, and through traces of his text in Codex Marchalianus and other Egyptian MSS.

marked peculiarities, notably the frequent replacement of words originally employed by their synonyms, and conspicuous expansion of the text by twofold renderings. Lucian, like Origen before him, attempted to eliminate, by comparison with what he thought was the Hebrew original, the many corruptions in the Septuagintal text; but the principles of criticism by which he was guided were those prevalent at Antioch rather than at Caesarea. In many passages this Antiochene recension, in agreement with the Peshitto, departs from the Massoretic Text, the deviations, as previously noted, [15] frequently indicating the correction inevitably required for restoration of the impaired Hebrew. Attention to the readings of the Lucianic version is, accordingly, essential in the textual criticism of the Septuagint.

Further light is thrown upon the Septuagint, of which, after the middle of the fourth century, no new redactions were made, [1] by the translations into other languages than Greek of the entire Bible — the Alexandrian Version together with the New Testament — which accompanied the spread of Christianity. The need of versions, as the Church established itself in regions northeast of the Mediterranean, was first felt, and met, in Syria, where, as we have seen, the Septuagintal Peshitto is thought to have existed from the early second century. There too, but toward the end of the second century, appeared a translation in Old Syriac of the New Testament — the Gospels certainly, and probably, to judge by quotations by Ephraem and Aphraates, also Acts and the Pauline Epistles. This Old Syriac New Testament is known through two manuscripts, both of the fifth

---

[1] A translation of the canonical Books of the LXX into Attic Greek, with the Aramaic portion of Daniel in Doric, was made about the beginning of the fifteenth century, by a Jewish scholar — possibly Eliseus, of the Court of Murad I (*cf.* Swete, *Introduction to the Old Testament in Greek*, Cambridge, 1900, p. 56) — who followed Kimchi's interpretation of the M. T. Of this work, eleven Books (the Pentateuch, Ruth, Prov., S. of S., Eccl., Lam. and Dan.) which have survived in MS. Gr. VII of St. Mark's Library, Venice, have been edited by Oscar von Gebhardt, *Graecus Venetus*, Leipzig, 1875. Translations into modern Greek began in 1543 with a rendering of the Septuagintal version of Psalms by Agapiou, a monk from Crete.

century: the older (the Sinaitic Syriac)[m], a palimpsest discovered in 1892 at the monastery of St. Catherine on Mt. Sinai, where half a century earlier, Tischendorf had rescued Codex Sinaiticus from utter destruction; the other (the Curetonian Syriac)[m], fragmentary and divided between the British Museum and Berlin, presenting the Gospels in the unusual order, Matthew, Mark, John, Luke. This Old Syriac Version failed to diminish the popularity of the *Diatessaron* of Tatian[16] among Syrian Christians. Early in the fifth century, presumably to effect dislodgment of Tatian, a new translation of the Gospels — based, like the Curetonian, of which it is apparently a revision, upon Antiochene Greek sources of the second century — was prepared by Rabbula, bishop of Edessa.[17] The remaining Books of the New Testament — except four of the Catholic Epistles (II Peter, Jude, II and III John) and Revelation[n] — whether translated by Rabbula himself or not, were added to the Gospels to constitute the New Testament Peshitto. This Version, together with the entirely distinct, second-century Septuagintal translation whose name it shares, established itself, apparently "for all time," as the Bible of Syriac-speaking Christians.

Expansion of the Church still further to the northeast than Syria, created a demand for an Armenian Bible which was satisfied, early in the fifth century, by Armenian versions of both the Septuagint and the New Testament. The Armenian New Testament is of text-critical value; for, reflecting as it does an Old Syriac foundation, it supplies some evidence for the

[m] The Sinaitic Syriac is cited as Syr. S.; and the Curetonian Syriac, so named in recognition of its editor, William Cureton, as Syr. C.

[n] These five Books — all that survive from an idiomatic Syriac translation made by Polycarpus, in A. D. 508 for Philoxenus, bishop of Hierapolis in E. Syria — are often bound as a part of the Peshitto. This Philoxenian version is supplemented, as witness for the Syriac N. T. text, by two additional sources: the freely-rendered sixth-century Antiochene lectionary once thought to have come from Jerusalem and still called the Palestinian Version [cited as Syr. H(ier.).]; and the early seventh-century translation, as literal as that of Aquila, prepared by Thomas of Heraclea (Harkel), bishop of Hierapolis, the very year (616) in which Paul, bishop of Tella, was working at Alexandria upon his Syro-Hexaplar LXX, finished in 617. [The Harkleian text is cited as Hkl.].

character of that text, being especially useful in Acts and the Epistles in which the surviving portions of both the Sinaitic and Curetonian manuscripts are deficient.

First among Biblical versions to be provided for Christian communities as they established themselves, one after another, along the southern shores of the Mediterranean, was the Old Latin of the second century. Although of this version, as both Augustine and Jerome testify,[18] there were extant in the fourth century many variant copies, it is now available only in fragmentary form[19] or in quotations[20] chiefly by Cyprian (*ob*. A. D. 258), bishop of Carthage during the first portion of the third century. This, the African Version, designed originally for the Latin-speaking provinces of Rome — the language of that capital city still being Greek — gives evidence of having been produced, not, as formerly supposed, at Carthage, but at Antioch. In its Septuagintal portion it translates a pre-Hexaplaric Greek text closely resembling that from which Lucian, at Antioch, some time later, must have assimilated some of those renderings formerly thought to be peculiarly his own.

This Old Latin Version — the African — appropriate for the Church in the neighborhood of Carthage, was, of course, linguistically unsuitable at Memphis or Thebes. Coptic translations of the Bible — first into the Sahidic [Thebaic] dialect for use in churches of the Nile valley; later, into Bohairic [Memphitic] for churches of the Nile delta — were accordingly produced in the third century. That Biblical translations into other Egyptian dialects were made is evidenced by surviving but inconsiderable fragments. Most completely preserved is the Bohairic. The Greek manuscript tradition upon which that Version apparently rests is excellent, being close to that of the codices Vaticanus and Sinaiticus. Officially adopted by the early Coptic Church, and still employed in its service, Bohairic, like other ancient languages in other modern churches, is no longer "understood of" its worshipers. Early African versions include, in addition to the Old Latin and Coptic, the fourth-century Ethiopic translation [of some text-critical value] prepared for the churches of Abyssinia, west of the Red Sea; and, several centuries later, an Arabic Version.

Across the Mediterranean from Africa, in districts removed from Rome, an Old Latin Version, different at many points from its African sister, was available before the close of the second century. This European branch of the Old Latin Version is of undetermined origin. Its distinctive features which differentiate it from the African text are counterbalanced by similarities sufficient to establish some interrelationship between the two versions. Both, it is possible, derive from a common ancestor. If, as is more probable, one is a revision of the other, the African Version, contrary to the expected order of things Roman, appears to be the original. In Italy, progressive revision of the European Version had produced, by the fourth century, a third Old Latin recension,[21] commonly, but mistakenly, called the *Italic*.

The variety of text exhibited by these Old Latin versions, intolerable to the Church of Rome in the fourth century as divergencies in the Greek texts had been to Origen in the third, prompted Pope Damasus, in A. D. 382, to invite the scholar Eusebius Hieronymus, familiarly known as Jerome, to undertake the preparation of a new and authentic revision of the Old Latin text of the entire Bible. Jerome, devoting himself immediately to his pontifical assignment, was able to complete his revision of the Gospels — the best part of his work — and to present it to Damasus with the dedicatory epistle from which we have previously quoted,[22] before his papal sponsor died in A. D. 384. He completed his version of the Pauline Epistles the year following. His revised New Testament, though benefiting by his collation of early Greek recensions, some of which differed from those now known, is essentially an improved edition of the "Italic," the contemporary form of the European variety of the Old Latin Version. With the death of Damasus, Jerome found it advisable to remove himself from Rome, and, after considerable travel, to settle down, in 386, in Bethlehem. In this new environment, he rejected the original instructions to base his revision, the Old Testament as well as the New, upon the "Italic" foundation. In accordance with that design of Damasus he had, indeed, already completed, under Hexaplaric correction, a portion of the poetical Books of the Hagiographa.° At Bethlehem, abandoning this partially executed plan, he determined to translate the Old Testament directly from the Hebrew.

Jerome's knowledge of Hebrew was doubtless more than adequate for giving instruction in that language, as he did, to ladies at Rome; but at no time, though excelling all the Fathers in Hebrew, was he possessed of Hebrew learning sufficient unto itself for Biblical translation. He accordingly obtained, as he informs us, the assistance of several Jewish scholars, one of whom, Bar Anina [בר חנינה], is said to have worked with him secretly, in fear of his fellows, by night. Neither Jerome nor his rabbinical collaborators could have realized the relative modernity of the Hebrew text current in Bethlehem in comparison with that upon which the Septuagint and, at second remove the Old Latin, had been based. Of the various Greek versions, however, Jerome made considerable use, the redaction most noticeably reflected in his Latin being that of Symmachus. For the accuracy of his Old Testament he frankly relied in the final analysis upon his rabbinical consultants, to whom indeed he referred his critics — and he had many of them — for the trustworthiness of his renderings.ᴾ No attempt at translation of the Apocryphal Books was made by Jerome, except for a rendering of Judith and Tobit from the Aramaic. Reluctant to offend the sensibilities of those accustomed to the current textual pattern, he had, at the outset, indicated to Damasus that he would

---

° His Job, based on the Hexaplar text, is extant; and his Psalms have survived in two forms: the *Roman* — the earlier revision (A. D. 383) of the "Italic" text — still used at St. Peter's in Rome; and the *Gallican* — the second revision (A. D. 392), Hexaplaric in tone — introduced into Gaul by St. Gregory of Tours in the sixth century, and universally adopted for Catholic ritual outside of Rome.

ᴾ Many of these have been rejected by modern scholars, as, for example, that at Ex. xxxiv. 29, on the authority of which Michaelangelo portrayed Moses with horns protruding from his forehead.

"restrain his pen" from modification of the Old Latin text except as the sense required.[q] When his work was made public, Jerome had none the less to defend it — which he did with a forthright vigor[r] — from the attacks of critics who, themselves incapable of his performance, resented, as he had anticipated, the alteration of passages familiar to them in the "Italic" rendering. Jerome's version of the Bible — the Vulgate, or commonly accepted Version, as it has been known ever since it was so labeled in the thirteenth century by Roger Bacon — was brought to its conclusion about A. D. 405, becoming, after a protracted struggle for acceptance, not only the officially recognized version of the Roman Church, but the only Bible known for a thousand years in western Europe.

Well over a century elapsed after Jerome's Version appeared before it completely supplanted the Old Latin. Transcription of the Hieronymean text during this period suffered not only from usual scribal deterioration but from contamination with its "Italic" rival. Although in the tremendous multiplication of Vulgate manuscripts — approximately eight thousand are still extant — corruption of the text became more and more apparent, no successful effort by the Church to restore the original readings of Jerome was made until the thirteenth century.[s] In A. D. 1236 an official attempt was made by the Dominican Cardinal Hugh of St. Cher to re-establish the text, not through a completely revised "edition" such as the printing-press was later to make possible,[23] but through provision of a list of

---

[q] *Praefatio in Quattuor Evangelia, Opera,* ed. Vallarsi, X. iii. 661: "Quae ne multum a lectionis Latinae consuetine discreparent, ita calamo temperavimus, ut his tantum quae sensum videbantur mutare, correctis reliqua menere pateremur ut fuerant."

[r] Not to say vilification, as, *e. g.,* when, in one of his letters to the Lady Marcella, he refers to those who differ with him as *two-legged asses* — "Verum . . . revertimur ad nostros bipedes asellos; & illorum in aure . . . concrepamus." *Cf. Opera,* ed. Vallarsi, I, col. 132–133.

[s] Earlier unsuccessful attempts included, most notably, that of Alcuin, renowned English churchman, who, at the close of the eighth century, upon invitation of Charlemagne, led a body of scholars at Tours in revising the Latin Bible.

correct readings — a *correctorium*. This list, severely criticized by Roger Bacon, was revised from time to time, serving as model for the *Correctoria* of the Sorbonne and the Vatican. Further improvement of the Vulgate awaited the invention of printing.

Meanwhile, in England, side by side with the Vulgate, manuscript Bibles in the vernacular were increasingly available. Since the eighth century, when the Venerable Bede first made a beginning by putting into English prose a portion of the Gospel according to John, the people of Britain, unlike those of the Continent, had been in position to enjoy at least some of the Scriptures in their native tongue. Both the Gallican and the Roman Psalters of Jerome, magnificent manuscripts of which were available in England from the days of Bede, were neatly provided, during the ninth century, with interlinear glosses in various dialects of Old English.[t] About the middle of the tenth century the Lindisfarne Gospels — a superbly executed Latin codex [Cotton Nero D 4] of the late seventh century — was made more useful to English churchmen, if less beautiful, by a Northumbrian interlineation; and not long thereafter a gloss, in the Mercian dialect, was supplied for the Latin text of Mark, Luke and John in the Bodleian Library manuscript [Auct. D ii. 9] known as the Rushworth Gospels. For Matthew, in this codex, instead of a word-for-word gloss, an independent version in Mercian was inserted between the lines. Toward the close of the tenth century, all four Gospels were translated for the first time into West-Saxon, a dialect peculiar to the south of England. Large portions of the Old Testament, including the Apocrypha, had been put into idiomatic Anglo-Saxon by the eminent scholar Ælfric[24] before the close of the first decade of the eleventh

---

[t] The earliest of these — a Mercian gloss — is the Vespasian Psalter now in the British Museum [the name of which inappositely derives from its shelf-mark — Cotton Vespasian A 1 — indicating the Roman Emperor under whose bust it originally stood in the library of Sir Robert Cotton]. This, like five other contemporary MSS., glosses the Psalterium Romanum. From this period also six glossed Gallican Psalters have survived, two of which — Vitellius E 18, and Tiberius C 16 — though formerly part of the Cottonian collection, have escaped popular identification through adventitious imperial association.

century. It was, accordingly, a people familiar with many of
the Scriptural Books in one or another of their Old English
dialects, who yielded in 1066 to William the Conqueror.

Old English, however, undergoing profound modification
under the influence of Norman-French, the language of the
invaders, soon became obsolete. Vernacular versions of Scripture designed for use in England during the three centuries
following the Conquest were, as a result, in Anglo-Norman. By
the mid-fourteenth century, the English of Alfred and Bede had
given way to the language of Wycliffe and Chaucer, a supple
and delicate instrument which, supplanting the alien French,
established itself as a suitable medium alike for *Canterbury Tales*
and Scriptural translation.

Manuscript copies of the Vulgate, though costly, were sufficiently available in fourteenth-century England to have come
generally into possession of the cathedral clergy. That the
Scriptures should circulate widely among people humbler in
social position than the churchmen and lacking their Latin
learning, was the determination of those religious reformers —
the Lollards — of whom John Wycliffe was leader. The version
produced by the Wycliffites in furtherance of their democratic
aim was a scholarly translation, accurate as the learning of
the times permitted. It was entirely unaffected — sectarianism
having yet to develop in England — by doctrinal contention,
and consequently unmarred by questionable readings such as
appear in later English Bibles. In its original state, the Wycliffite
Bible follows the letter of the Vulgate so faithfully as to be hardly
better, in some of its pages, than a Midland-dialect gloss. A co-
operative undertaking, the Lollard Bible was produced, between
1380 and 1384, by a group of scholars at Oxford. Whether or
not Wycliffe himself translated the New Testament — a probable but unestablished circumstance — or any part of it, his was
the controlling spirit. More certain than the contribution of
Wycliffe is that of his associate, Nicholas of Hereford, of Queen's
College, Oxford, leader of the Lollards after Wycliffe's death
in 1384. From his hand, as we are informed by a contemporary

copy of the text in the Bodleian Library,[25] comes the translation of the Septuagintal Books as far as Baruch iii. 20. Unknown scholars of the Wycliffite community brought the work to its completion. A dozen years later this literal rendering was superseded by a completely revised idiomatic edition in the Oxford dialect, the work of John Purvey, Wycliffe's devoted secretary and literary executor. Of these, the only complete English Bibles to appear in manuscript form, the industrious Lollards issued an astonishing number. In addition to the one hundred and seventy copies recorded a century ago,[26] others have been subsequently discovered. These bulky and not easily concealed codices have survived despite their interdiction in 1408 by Archbishop Arundel[u] — a vitality surpassing that of earliest English editions of Scripture which, in an abundance which would have surprised and gratified Wycliffe and Purvey, issued, as we shall see, more than a century later, from the newly-invented printing-press.

[u] At Arundel's instigation, the provincial council of Oxford decreed and ordained "that no one shall in future translate on his own authority any text of holy scripture into the English tongue or into any other tongue, by way of book, booklet, or treaties. Nor shall any man read this kind of book, booklet, or treaties, now recently composed in the time of the said John Wycliffe, or later, or any that shall be composed in future, in whole or part, publicly or secretly, under penalty of the greater excommunication, until that translation shall be recognized and approved by the diocesan of the place, or if the matter demand it, by a provincial council." [Deanesly's translation (*The Lollard Bible and other mediaeval Biblical versions*, Cambridge, 1920, p. 296) of Latin text from Wilkins' *Concilia*, III. 317]. In Wycliffe's lifetime, the Lollard insistence upon the vernacular Scriptures — entirely in accord with English tradition — was not considered heretical. Wycliffe enjoyed the support not only of the University of Oxford, where he was made Master of Balliol in 1361, but also of John of Gaunt, the most influential political personage during the reign of Richard II. It was the socially disturbing activities of the Lollards which brought their Bible into official disfavor, and made possible the introduction into England of the Papal policy (originating with Pope Gregory VII, 1072–1085) of condemnation of vernacular versions of Holy Writ. Wycliffe's remains, after forty-four years of decent burial, were, for his posthumous heresy, "taken up and cast out" in 1428.

CHAPTER VII

The Printed Bible

"Though an angel should write, still 't is devils must print."

Thomas Moore

INVENTION of printing in Holland, about the middle of the fifteenth century, greatly accelerated on the Continent the program of Biblical vulgarization which Wycliffe and his followers had initiated in England. Although Latin was the language of the first major work — the "Gutenberg" Bible[a] — to

[a] The Vulgate, in a handsome edition, two volumes folio, printed and published at the German city of Mainz, not later than August 15, 1456. Our terminal date for this notable incunabulum — the "Mazarine" Bible or, in the language of bibliopoly, the "42-line" Bible — derives from its inscription by the rubricator in a copy (included in the Mazarine collection of the Bibliothèque Nationale) which, on that date, he had completed. To Henne Gensfleisch, printer, better known by his assumed name Johann Gutenberg, should be credited neither the printing of the "42-line" Bible — the work, it is now believed, of Peter Schoeffer von Gernssheym — nor the invention of printing. That momentous discovery was made, probably before 1446 (aside from the fact that block printing and movable type were employed in the Orient perhaps a millennium earlier), by Lourens Janszoon Coster of Haarlem, printer, among other items, of several editions of the Latin Grammar of Aelius Donatus, teacher of St. Jerome. *Cf.* Jan Henrik Hessels, *Gutenberg: was he the inventor of printing? an Historical Investigation*, London, 1882. Also, J. H. Hessels, *The Gutenberg fiction*, London, 1912. Two rival editions of the Vulgate appeared soon after the "Gutenberg" Bible: the "Bamberg" or "36-line" Bible, two vols., fol., printed by Albrecht Pfister, c. 1460, at Bamberg; and, the same year, a Vulgate printed at Strassburg by Johann Mentelin.

issue from a European press, within a few years translations of Jerome's Bible were printed in half a dozen European vernaculars. Beginning with a German version published at Strassburg in 1466, printed Bibles included, well before the close of the fifteenth century, translations of the Vulgate into Italian, French, Dutch, Spanish and Bohemian.[b] Demand for these earliest vernacular Bibles was undiminished by their artistic shortcomings, the German version alone exhausting eighteen editions within half a century. These pioneer translations, possessed of insufficient stylistic grace to insure survival, were one and all superseded, as the Reformation gathered momentum, by versions superior in scholarship and literary elegance.

Concurrently with this proliferation of vernacular Bibles, fifteenth-century printers were busy issuing books in the two primary Biblical languages, Hebrew and Greek. Four presses in Italy competed with each other in the production of Biblical incunabula in Hebrew.[c] At Bologna, after some preliminary efforts with Hebrew fonts, the first printed Hebrew Pentateuch was published in 1482. The Soncino press, having issued the Prophets in Hebrew in 1485 and 1486, presented to the world in 1488 its first complete Hebrew Old Testament.[d] At Naples, from 1486 to 1491, various portions of the Hebrew Bible were printed; and in 1494, at Brescia, there was published a second complete Hebrew Old Testament which, about a quarter of a

[b] Venice, 1471; Lyons, c. 1474; Delft, 1477; Valencia, 1488; Prague, 1488.

[c] Biblical Hebrew incunabula issued also from four presses of the Iberian peninsula: in Portugal, a Hebrew Pentateuch was printed at Faro in 1487; at Lisbon another edition in 1491. The first Hebrew Pentateuch printed in Spain came from a press at Hijar in 1490. In 1492 a Hebrew press at Leiria, Portugal, published the Book of Proverbs, and two years later an edition of the Former Prophets. Non-Biblical Hebrew incunabula issued from Italian presses at Mantua, Reggio, Piove di Sacco, Ferrara, Casal Maggiore, Barco and possibly Rome; from Guadalajara and Zamora in Spain.

[d] No more than 15 copies of this work — peculiar in its regular substitution of ד for the ה of אלהים (God) and the final ה of יהוה (Lord) — are known, of which only one, at the Pierpont Morgan Library, is in America. The rarity of this book is probably due to biblioclasm, its pictures of animals — even of "unclean" rabbits like those in its ornamental heading to Genesis — being contrary to "Mosaic Law."

century later, served as the basis of the German translation by Martin Luther. Although the Biblical text of some of these fifteenth-century Hebrew publications was accompanied by the commentary of Kimchi, Rashi or Ibn Ezra, the accumulated learning of Jewish exegetes was not disclosed in all its amplitude to the world of scholars until the early sixteenth century when Daniel Bomberg, Christian printer of Hebrew books, issued from his celebrated press at Venice volume after superb volume of Jewish lore. Bomberg's long list of publications, including not only four editions of the Hebrew Old Testament, but the *editio princeps* of both the *Babylonian* and the *Jerusalem Talmud*, begins with a Rabbinic Old Testament,[e] four volumes, dated 1516–1517. Dedicated to Pope Leo X, this first printed *Biblia Rabbinica*, edited by Felix Pratensis, a Jewish convert to Christianity, was superseded, in 1524–1525, by the most influential of Bomberg's productions, an enlarged second edition, greatly improved under the editorship of a Tunisian Jew, Jacob ben Ḥayyim Ibn Adonijah, who not only supplied Massoretic notes and lists of variant readings from the manuscripts he employed but, in a notable *Preface*,[1] revealed textual and exegetical inconsistencies many of which, having arisen since the time of Jerome, were unfamiliar to scholars of the Church. Bomberg, accordingly, in publishing this Rabbinic Old Testament, contributed in no minor degree to that revival of Hebrew learning among Christian scholars which, rather than their knowledge of the Vulgate, henceforth determined the quality of their vernacular versions of the Old Testament.

Printers of the fifteenth century, equipped, though sparingly, with Greek fonts, produced no New Testaments, in whole or in part, in the original language. The only Biblical Greek incunabula known are Psalters from Milan and Venice. Early in the

[e] Frequently referred to as "the first Bomberg Rabbinic Bible," this *Biblia Rabbinica*, like its successors, consists of the standard pointed Hebrew text of the O. T. accompanied, however, both by the Targums and — printed in a modification of the "square" type known as "Rashi" type or "Rabbinic" — by the commentaries of medieval Jewish scholars.

sixteenth century, however, the Renaissance gave added impetus to the emerging Reformation through the publication at Basle in 1516 of the first New Testament to be published in Greek, the work of the renowned humanist Desiderius Erasmus, and, in 1522, at Alcalá de Henares, Spain, of the *Complutensian Polyglot,*[f] sponsored by Cardinal Ximenes — the first printed edition of the entire Bible in the original tongues. The New Testament volume of the Complutensian Bible prints the Greek and Latin texts side by side, with a Greek-Latin glossary following. In the four volumes containing the Old Testament and the Apocrypha, arrangement of the texts is in three adjacent columns: first, the Massoretic Hebrew; second, the Latin of the Vulgate; third, the Septuagintal Greek.[g]

[f] The N. T. portion of this first printed Biblical polyglot — the identification of which derives from *Complutum*, the Latin name of Alcalá — issued from the press [if its colophon, at the end of Revelation, has not been ante-dated; *cf.* John Nichols, *Literary Anecdotes of the Eighteenth Century, etc.*, London, 1812, Vol. IV, pp. 15 ff.] in 1514; as actual publication, not only of the N. T. but also of the O. T. — completed, according to the colophon at end of III Maccabees, some three years later — was postponed, for undisclosed reasons, until 1522, the distinction of being the first to publish the N. T. in Greek is enjoyed by Froben, the printer of Basle, who, in anticipation of the Alcalá production, had invited Erasmus to prepare his edition. The Ximenes polyglot [*Vetus Testamentum multiplici lingua nunc primum* (Vol. I, *primo*) *impressum. Necnon Testamentum Novum cum Vocabulario Hebraico et Chaldaico, et Grammatica Hebraica, etc.*], with some slight revision, was republished in eight folio volumes by Plantin at Antwerp, 1569–1572. This was superseded by two greatly expanded Biblical polyglots: that of Le Jay, Paris, 1645; and, most ambitious typographical undertaking of the seventeenth century, that of Brian Walton, in nine languages: *Biblia Polyglotta, Complecentia Textus Originales, Hebraicos cum Pentateucho Samaritano, Chaldaicum, Graecum; versionumque antiquarum, Samaritanae, Graecae, Chaldaicae, Syriacae, Arabicae, Aethiopicae, Persicae, Vulg. Lat. quicquid comparari poterat.* 6 vols., fol., London, 1655–1657.

[g] This sequence of the texts, the Complutensian *Preface* is at pains to make clear, represents the position of the Church of Rome between Synagogue and Greek Church — "Christ crucified between two thieves!" [*Prologus*, iii[v]: ". . . tres praecipuas columnas . . . ex quibus ea quae ad marginem exteriorem sita est: Hebraicam continet veritatem. Quae vero interiori margini adhaeret: Graeca est septuaginta interpretum editio: . . . Mediam autem inter has latinam beati Hieronymi translationem velut inter Synagogam & Orientalem Ecclesiam posuimus: tanquamque duos hinc & inde latrones medium autem Iesum hoc est Romanam siue latinam Ecclesiam collocantes."]. The Greek

The New Testament of Erasmus was, like that of Ximenes, bilingual; but the Greek text of the Basle production was paralleled by an independent and annotated Latin version with which Erasmus, deviating freely and effectively from the Vulgate, established the secondary and sometimes erroneous nature of the Hieronymean text, and initiated emancipation of Biblical scholars from the linguistic authority of Jerome. The Greek of the Erasmian edition, much as it contributed to Biblical progress, is not a work of profound scholarship nor is it possessed of critical value. Owing, it seems most likely, to the commercial urgency of his friend and publisher Froben, Erasmus based his Greek text upon a few late manuscripts immediately available at Basle, one of which, by no means the best, he put without alteration through the press, editing the proofs in the light of other Basle codices and with collations of manuscripts supplied by the Oxford scholar Colet. Erasmus' New Testament, thus hastily produced, and inevitably destined to early eclipse,[h] was none the less epochal. Successors merely developed the exegetical science it had inaugurated, and none of them contributed so momentously to the liberation of the western world from clerical dominion.

Publication of Erasmus' New Testament, the Complutensian Polyglot and the Hebrew Old Testaments of Soncino and Brescia, stimulated vernacular Biblical translation, without ben-

---

of the third column is interlineated with Latin, and at the foot of each page is printed the Aramaic version and its Latin translation. For the Apocrypha, of course, there is no Hebrew column. The Prayer of Manasses is in the Vulgate only, and III Maccabees is given only in the Greek of the LXX with Latin interlineation. A sixth volume contains a Hebrew-Latin Dictionary, dated March 17, 1515; a Latin index to the entire work; Interpretations of names in both Testaments; variant readings of names; and a Hebrew Grammar, dated May 31, 1515. The order of the volumes varies in different copies.

[h] After going through five editions in which the Greek text was modified in no essentials, Erasmus' work was superseded first by the Greek N. T. of Robert Étienne (Stephanus) of Paris, whose third edition, 1550, was probably most influential of early editions, and subsequently by the Greek New Testaments of Theodore Beza, ten editions of which were issued between 1565 and 1611.

efit of the Vulgate, directly from the original languages. First
to avail himself of these new Biblical sources was Martin Luther,
who was sufficiently accomplished in Greek to produce, with
Erasmus' edition before him, a German New Testament, in
1522; and, in the year following, a German Pentateuch based
upon the Hebrew Old Testament published at Brescia in 1494.
Luther, less proficient in Hebrew than in Greek, found the Old
Testament portion no easy task. At times he had to fall back
upon the Vulgate; at times he made use of Nicholas de Lyra,
whose exegetical interpretations, originating with Rashi, had
been the theological staple of his student days at the University
of Erfurt; at times he turned, pragmatically, to the very men
of the marketplace for whom he was writing — the local butcher,
for instance, who, with a slaughtered sheep for the lesson, gave
instruction in anatomical nomenclature required in translating
Leviticus. Even a twentieth-century translator, linguistically
equipped as a sixteenth-century scholar could never have been,
will sympathize with Luther's admission of difficulty in didactic,
philosophic or sententious portions of Scripture, and will comprehend his laborious output, in Books as baffling as Job, of
only a handful of verses a day. Not until 1534, after more than a
decade of labor upon the Old Testament, was Luther able to
publish his *complete* German Bible, the popularity of which demanded ten editions during his lifetime. Whatever his deficiencies in Hebrew and Greek, in his Biblical translation into
his native tongue Luther was a master. Aiming to reach the
hearts of the humblest citizen, Luther, like Tyndale in England,
whom he influenced, so phrased the Scriptural message as to
make his translation the possession of the German people, the
foundation of their linguistic idiom and literary attainments.

French vernacular Bibles of the Reformation followed a
more conservative pattern than the German. Jacques Lefèvre
d'Étaples [Jacobus Faber], though a leader in the Protestant
movement, reflects nothing of the newer Greek and Hebrew
learning in his French translation of the New Testament, Paris,
1523, contemporary with Luther's; and his complete Bible,

published at Antwerp in 1530, is based in orthodox fashion upon the Vulgate. The earliest example of a French Bible truly Protestant in character is that of Pierre Robert Olivétan, a folio edition, issued, according to its colophon, in 1535, from the press of Pierre de Wingle at Neuchâtel, principal city of the Swiss canton of Vaud. Circumspection with respect to the authorship of vernacular Bibles was apparently advisable at this time even in Switzerland; for the translator's name, placed inconspicuously on the *verso* of the title-page — easily excised should occasion require that precaution — and undisclosed in the colophon, is discreetly concealed at the seventh preliminary leaf, in some Latin distichs, the initial letters of each line of which will be seen by the *cognoscenti* to comprise the acrostic, Petrus Robertus Olivetanus. Responsibility for publication of this first Olivétan Bible, cryptically embedded at the end of the New Testmanent in ten lines of mediocre French verse, is attributed, safely enough, to the Protestant citizens of Vaud.[i] In the second edition of this version, a quarto printed at Geneva

---

[i] On the recto of sheet SS vj [fol. (CVʳ)], below the *Registre des cayers*, the printer's device, and the title *Au Lecteur de la Bible*, occur the rhyming lines:

> Lecteur entendz si Verite addresse
> Viens donc ouyr instamment sa promesse
> et vif parler: lequel en excellence
> veult asseurer nostre grelle esperance.
> lesprit Jesus qui visite et ordonne
> noz tendres meurs icy sans cry estonne
> tout hault raillart escumant son ordure
> remercions eternelle nature
> prenons vouloir bienfaire librement
> Jesus querons veoir Eternellement.

The *initial* letters of all the words of these verses ["i" being interchangeable with "j," and "v" with "u," as customary in cryptography], taken in the order in which they occur, compose, as the reader may verify, the sentence: "Les Vaudois, peuple evangelique, ont mis ce thresor en publique." Attention of the initiated is directed to this concealed statement by a quotation from Ezekiel i. 16, printed immediately after the verses, the significance of which will be apparent to any experienced cryptographer: "Et leur ouurage estoit comme si une roue eust este au millieu de lautre roue." (R. V.: "and their work was as it were a wheel within a wheel.")

by Jehan Michel in 1538, the translator's identity is no longer disclosed even by cryptic devices, and the colophon attributes the translation, at least for bilingual readers, to the Nameless One from Nowhere.[j]

In Britain no English translation of the Bible or of any of its parts could find a printer until 1536 when Thomas Berthelet, king's printer, issued the first Scriptural text to be printed in England — an unauthorized reprint, in folio, of William Tyndale's revised English New Testament, previously published at Antwerp.[2] Tyndale, an ordained priest, distinguished among the distinguished sons of Hertford College, Oxford, was the first English scholar to set the Interdiction of 1408[3] at naught. Early in life, according to a well-known passage in John Foxe's *Book of Martyrs*,[k] Tyndale had determined to produce a vernacular version, but finding it impossible to translate and publish the Scriptures in his own country, had exiled himself in 1524 to the free city of Hamburg. The year following he was at Cologne, supervising, as it was passing through Peter Quentel's press, a quarto edition of his English New Testament, translated, as befitted a disciple of Erasmus, directly from the Greek. Enemies of the Reformation, having discovered what Tyndale was doing, not only persuaded the Senate of Cologne to interrupt the printing of his New Testament but contrived to have its importation into England prohibited and its use proscribed by royal proclamation. Tyndale thereupon fled to the Lutheran stronghold of Worms, salvaging the first ten sheets of his book — all that had been printed. Evidence that printing of the quarto edition was resumed at Worms resides, precariously, in

[j] The colophon, at end of Revelation, p. 711, reads: "translate par Belisem de Belimakom"; *i. e.*, by שֵׁם בְּלִי [BeLI šēM — *without name*] from מָקוֹם בְּלִי [BeLI MAQÔM — *without place*].

[k] *Actes and Monuments of these latter and perillous dayes, touching matters of the Church*, etc., London, 1563, p. 514: "Maister Tyndall . . . disputing with [a learned man], droue him to that issue that the learned manne sayde, we were better be without Gods law then the Popes: Maister Tyndall hearing that, answered hym, I defie the Pope and all his laws, and sayde, if God spare my lyfe ere many yeares, I wyl cause a boye that dryueth y[e] plough, shall knowe more of the scripture then thou doest."

a single fragment[1] which escaped the hands of a very efficient common hangman, who, upon orders from Cuthbert Tunstall, bishop of London — destined to participate ten years later in authorization of the Tyndale text in the Great Bible[4] — conducted the spectacular burning of Tyndale's books before St. Paul's Cathedral in 1530. Not quite so complete was the destruction of another edition — an octavo — of Tyndale's New Testament issued at Worms early, it seems, in 1526, *two* copies out of the original three thousand having survived their attempted extirpation, one perfect except for the loss of its title-page.[m] Tyndale followed his New Testament some years later with English translations from the printed Hebrew Bible, the first portion to be published being a Pentateuch especially interesting for the controversial quality of his marginal notes. Of this volume, printed, despite its deliberately deceptive colophon, in 1531 at Antwerp,[n] but one perfect copy is known, that of the Grenville collection in the British Museum.[o] Unique also is the British Museum copy of Tyndale's next work, an English translation of the Book of Jonah, considerately provided "with an introduccion before teachinge to understonde him," issued from an undisclosed Continental press presumably in 1531. A translation of post-Pentateuchal Books — Joshua through II Chronicles — concluding, so it appears,[p] Tyndale's Old Testament work,

[1] Mt. i–xxii. 12; now in the Grenville collection at the British Museum.

[m] Preserved at the Baptist College of Bristol. The second copy, imperfect, is at St. Paul's Cathedral. This octavo edition may have been published late in 1525.

[n] M. E. Kronenberg holds, on typographical grounds, that the colophon — Emprented at Malborow [Marburg] in the land of Hesse, by me Hans Luft, the yere of oure Lorde . M. ccccc. xxx. the xvij. dayes of Ianuarij — is a protective blind for Hoochstraten, printer at Antwerp. *Cf. The Library*, Series 4, vol. 9, p. 139, London, 1928.

[o] This Pentateuch, with a slightly revised text of Genesis, was reissued by Tyndale in 1534.

[p] *Cf.* Edward Halle, *The Union of the two noble and illustre famelies of Lancastre and Yorke, etc.*, London, 1548, fol. CCxxvii[r]: "This man [Tyndale] translated the New Testament into Englishe and fyrst put it in Prynt, and likewise he translated the v. bookes of Moses, Iosua, Iudicum, Ruth, the bookes of the Kynges and the bookes of Paralipomenon, Nehemias or the fyrst of Esdras, the Prophet Ionas, & nomore of y[e] holy scripture."

though never printed during his lifetime, is preserved through its incorporation in the Bible attributed to Thomas Matthew,[5] published in 1537.

Unauthorized reprints of Tyndale's New Testament, issued, without his sanction or supervision, to meet an insistent demand, culminated in a surreptitious edition in August 1534 by a fellow English expatriate in Antwerp, George Joye. This "some tyme felowe of Peter College in Camebridge," having begun his own acknowledged additions to the Bible in English, some three years earlier, with the first translation of Isaiah[6] to appear in print, had augmented his contribution, by 1534, with original versions both of Jeremiah and of Psalms,[7] and, by 1535, with selections ["Epistles"] from the Old Testament included in his second New Testament. Joye's unscrupulous reprinting of Tyndale's New Testament, commendable for its revision of errors tolerated in previous pirated editions, but reprehensible both for its introduction of renderings alien to the original and for the non-committal nature of its title-page,[q] seems to have moved Tyndale to an indignation the fury of which could be quieted only by a complete revision of his own. This, the first of Tyndale's two revisions of the New Testament, issued at Antwerp, from the press of Martin de Keyser,[r] November 1534, is supplied with marginal glosses, selections from the Old Testament ["Epistles"], and three general prologues, the last of which — *Willyam Tindale yet once more to the christen reader* — rebukes George Joye "that he dyd not put his awne name" to his pirated edition "and call it rather his awne translacion." Joye, undeterred by this public reprimand, within a few months brought out still

[q] The title-page of the sole surviving copy of Joye's N. T., now in the British Museum, presents neither his name nor Tyndale's, but contains the following evasive identification: "The New Testament as it was written and caused to be written by them which herde yt Whom also oure saueoure Christ Iesus commaunded that they shulde preach it vnto al creatures."

[r] "Imprinted at Anwerp [*sic*] by Marten Emperowr." A copy, printed on vellum for Anne Boleyn, is at the British Museum. It is this edition a folio reprint of which in 1536 by Thomas Berthelet [if not, as sometimes claimed, by Thomas Godfray] was the first Scriptural text printed in England. *V. supra*, p. 181.

another New Testament reprint, slightly improved, with an address "Vnto the Reader" retorting to Tyndale's "vncharitable pistle agenst me." Tyndale, pursuing this unseemly controversy no further, busied himself with what proved to be his final revision: *The newe Testament yet once agayne corrected by Willyam Tindale*, an octavo published at Antwerp, presumably from the press of Godfrid van der Haghen,[8] 1535.

Tyndale, more than any other single translator, is responsible for the literary excellence of the English Bible. Basing his version — as Wycliffe and Purvey in their time could not — upon the traditional Hebrew and Greek, Tyndale, though occasionally adopting the precise phraseology of the Lollard Bible, faithfully translated the Scriptures — the New Testament and part of the Old — into a homely but dignified English unquestionably his own.[s] With respect at least to the New Testament, his statement, addressed to the reader of the Worms octavo edition of 1526, is an unequivocal assertion that he had neither imitated any man nor been helped "with englysshe of eny that had interpreted . . . the scripture beforetyme." Although errors of interpretation and inadequacies of style inevitable in a work of this pioneering nature — "a thynge begunne rather then fynnesshed" — were gradually corrected or eliminated by later translators in subsequent versions, none succeeded in replacing Tyndale's translation as the foundation upon which, in the next century, the editors of the King James Version were willing to build.[t] When, in the late nineteenth century, the

---

[8] Tyndale, defending himself against the charge of infidelity of translation, wrote to his friend, John Frith: "I call God to record against the day we shall appear before our Lord Jesus, to give a reckoninge of our doings, that I never altered one syllable of Gods Word against my Conscience . . ." *Cf.* John Foxe, *op. cit.*, p. 522.

[t] The degree to which the text of Tyndale survives in the A. V. may be gauged by the following excerpt from his rendering of the Sermon on the Mount (Mt. vi. 24–29): No man can serve two masters. For ether he shall hate the one & love the other: or els he shall lene to y*e* one & despise y*e* other: ye can not serve God & mammon. Therfore I saye vnto you be not carefull for your lyfe what ye shall eate or what ye shall drincke nor yet for youre body what ye shall put on. ys not y*e* lyfe more worth then meate & the body more of

Authorized Version — that "noblest monument of English prose" — underwent what many thought a drastic revision, its scholarly editors, attempting to establish their conservatism, announced that, according to their own estimate, four-fifths of the words in their revision of the New Testament were still those written by Tyndale four and a half centuries earlier.

Tyndale's impress upon the Old Testament, however marked, extends no further than the Books of Chronicles, and is rivalled, in the Latter Prophets and the Hagiographa, by that of his fellow-reformer, the Augustinian friar, Miles Coverdale. In 1535, while Tyndale, "*homo doctus, pius et bonus*,"[u] was awaiting his martyrdom in a Belgian prison, Coverdale distinguished himself by producing, for the first time since the invention of printing, an English version of the Scriptures complete from Genesis through Revelation. For this huge undertaking Coverdale borrowed liberally from his predecessors, translating, as he freely admits in his dedication to King Henry, "with a clere conscience purely & faithfully ... out of fyue sundry interpreters" — probably Jerome, Luther, Pagninus (Latin version, 1528), Zwingli (who, with Leo Juda, produced a Swiss-German Bible at Zurich in 1531), and Tyndale.[9] To these should be added George Joye. Although both his Pentateuch and his New Testament were patterned after Tyndale, and his Psalter reflects the translation of Joye,[v] Coverdale's delicate appreciation of

---

value then rayment? Beholde the foules of ye ayer: for they sowe not nether reepe nor yet cary in to ye barnes: & yet youre hevenly father fedeth them. Are ye not moche better then they? Which of you (though he toke thought therfore) coulde put one cubit vnto his stature? And why care ye then for rayment? Considre ye lylies of ye felde how they growe. They labour not nether spynne. And yet for all yt I saye vnto you yt euen Salomon in all his royalte was not arayed lyke vnto one of these.

[u] So characterized, according to Halle [*op. cit.*, fol. CCxxvii^v], by the Procureur Général at Vilvorde Castle, near Brussels, where Tyndale, betrayed by one Henry Phillips, "not without the helpe and procurement of some bishoppes of this realme" [*loc. cit.*], and condemned as a heretic by the Inquisition, was strangled to death and his body publicly burned, October 6, 1536. For a full account, with an illustration, see Foxe, *op. cit.*, pp. 516 ff.

[v] Coverdale apparently made no use of Tyndale's unprinted translation

graceful expression frequently prompted him to depart from his models, improving the text unto this generation in memorable fashion. Coverdale it was, to illustrate from a single Psalm, who introduced into the texture of literary English "The Lorde is my shepherde," "Thou preparest a table before me," "thou anoyntest my heade with oyle," and "the valley of the shadowe of death." Coverdale too it was, pioneering even as Tyndale, who first made available in print an English version — some of whose felicities of phrasing are retained to this day[w] — of Esther, Job and Song of Songs, the Apocryphal Books, and all the Prophets (Jonah excepted) from Ezekiel through Malachi.

Coverdale, having printed his Bible of necessity on the Continent,[10] was situated, as was no one else in 1535, to take advantage of the English monarch's changing attitude toward vernacular versions of Holy Writ. Henry VIII, by whose proclamation Tyndale's New Testaments had been publicly burned in 1530, having, in defiance of the Pope, married Anne Boleyn, and, with the consent of a complacent Parliament, become the recognized head of the Church of England, had by December 1534 so modified his orthodox position as to permit the synod of the province of Canterbury to petition his Majesty, without fear of incurring displeasure, that he nominate learned men to provide a translation of Sacred Scriptures into the vulgar tongue to be offered to the people in accordance with their learning ["*populo pro eorum eruditione*"].[11] Coverdale, just off the press with his translation, struck while his iron was hot. Relying, no doubt, upon the protection of his friend Thomas Cromwell, newly-appointed King Henry's Vicar-General, Coverdale shipped the unbound sheets of his version to England, where, early in 1536, at the hands of James Nicolson of Southwark, his

---

of the Former Prophets, and very little, if any, use of Joye's *Isaiah* and *Jeremiah.* *Cf.* Charles C. Butterworth, *The Literary Lineage of the King James Bible,* Philadelphia, 1941, pp. 68–79.

  [w] Wisd. vii. 26: "for she [Wisdom] is y*e* bryghtnes of y*e* euerlastinge light, : . . & y*e* ymage of his goodnesse." Is. xxxv. 6: "Then shal the lame man leape as an herte."

Complete Bible, "faithfully and truly translated out of Douche [German] and Latyn in to Englishe," was published with a fulsome dedication addressed not only to the king but, with an opportune tact, to "his dearest just wyfe, and most vertuous Pryncesse, Queen Anne." Coverdale's Bible, [12] meeting with royal approval, postponed beyond Henry's reign the nomination of the Biblical commission for which the synod of Canterbury had petitioned. Translation of the Bible into English by a commission of learned men was not to be realized for another third of a century.

Publication, in the meantime, of Biblical versions by individual translators became a flourishing business. In 1537, Nicolson brought out two new editions of Coverdale's Bible, "Imprynted in Sowthwarke," of which the earlier, a folio, "newly ouersene & corrected," has the distinction of being the first *complete* Scriptures to be printed in England, and the later, a quarto, the more momentous distinction of displaying on its title-page, as no previous edition had done, the significant words "Set foorth with the Kynges moost gracious licence." These same words, indicative of the changing political sentiment in England, appear on the title-page of a rival Bible, a handsome folio, "truely and purely translated in English by Thomas Matthew," which, printed like Coverdale's somewhere on the Continent, was published in London in the same year (1537) by Richard Grafton and Edward Whitchurch. Thus "authorized," Matthew's Bible competes with Coverdale's for the honor of having established the custom of Biblical "authorization" which three years later placed on the title-page of Cranmer's Bible, however unofficially, that comforting and apparently irrevocable fiction, "apoynted to the vse of the churches." Whatever the contribution of Matthew to the Bible which bears his name, it certainly was not, despite the assertion on its title-page, that of translator. [13] Sponsored by Tyndale's friend and literary executor, John Rogers, who supplied the marginal commentary, this Bible consisted of little more than an amalgamation of Tyndale's printed translations of the Pentateuch and the New Testament, his unprinted version of Joshua through II Chronicles, Coverdale's Old Testament (Ezra through Malachi) and Coverdale's Apocrypha. To Rogers, presumably, is due the only new material in the "Matthew" Bible: the apocryphal Prayer of Manasses and a Preface to the Apocrypha, both of which, like his marginalia, were based upon the Olivétan Bible of 1535. Those portions of the Bible which Tyndale had translated — most of which had been officially destroyed by fire, and for all of which Tyndale had just suffered martyrdom — came thus, through the intervention of John Rogers, masquerading as Thomas Matthew,[x] into the possession of the English people. The necessary preparation for a favorable reception of this Bible, in which Tyndale's text could not escape detection, had been so carefully attended to — first by Archbishop Cranmer, who had recommended it as a "new translacion," and next by Thomas Cromwell, now Lord Privy Seal, who secured the royal sanction[14] — that the publisher Grafton was emboldened to petition the king, through Cromwell, for the exclusive privilege of printing and vending this "Matthew" version,[y] which was

[x] *Cf.* Foxe, *op. cit.*, p. 1022: "It chaunced him [J. Rogers] ther to fal in company with that worthy martir of God Wylliam Tindal, & with Miles Couerdale ... & ioyned him self with them two in ... translating yͤ bible into the English tongue, which is intituled, **The translation of Thomas Mathew**." In his second edition, London, 1570, in which the Tyndale material is amplified, Foxe says: "it was thought good [after Tyndale's arrest] to them that had the doing thereof [printing of Matthew's Bible] to change the name of William Tyndale, because that name then was odious, and to father it by a strange name of Thomas Matthew." Rogers' apprehension, evidenced by his self-effacement, though natural, was premature; he was to live yet eighteen years to become the first martyr burned by Queen Mary. Thomas Matthew, far from being, as is frequently held, merely a pseudonym of John Rogers, was a reputable citizen of Colchester known to have interested himself in the proscribed first edition of Tyndale's N. T. The use of his name, not only on the title-page but also at the close of the dedication to the king, may indicate a more substantial participation in the publication of this Bible of 1537 than has hitherto been accorded to Matthew. *Cf.* W. T. Whitley, *Thomas Matthew of Colchester and Matthew's Bible of 1537: A Study of Editing and Publishing*, London, 1935.

[y] Grafton to Cromwell: "But now moost gracyous lorde, ... by reason that of many this worke is commended, there are that wil and dothe go aboute the pryntynge of thesame worke againe in a lesser letter, ... and so to make that

destined to become, without benefit of ecclesiastical formalities, the ancestral issue from which generation upon generation of the Scriptures in English are descended.

The year 1539 marks the next advance in Scriptural publication with two new English versions,[z] one of which, hastily prepared in anticipation of the other, is little more than a revision of the Matthew Bible, issued primarily in the commercial interest of the London publisher Thomas Berthelet. This revision,[15] "newly recognised" with excellent literary taste by Richard Taverner — a Greek scholar who gives to this edition its name — though commendable both for its idiomatic quality and for its exploitation of the Anglo-Saxon components of the English vocabulary, seems to have contributed relatively little to the literary flavor of subsequent translations. Eclipse of Taverner's Version may be attributed in part to its over-shadowing by the second English Bible of 1539, sometimes referred to as Cromwell's Bible, but, because of the magnificence of its folio format, commonly known as the Great Bible.[16] According to its title-page, this version was "truly translated after the veryte of the Hebrue and Greke textes by y*e* dylygent studye of dyuerse excellent learned men, expert in the forsayde tonges"; but if Coverdale, who had been placed in charge of the project by Cromwell, had any such assistants as these words indicate, their identity has yet to be established. This first edition of the Great Bible —

I shall sell none at all, or elles verye fewe, to the vtter vndoynge of me your orator . . . Therfore by your moost godly fauor if I maye obtayne the kynges moost gracyous priuiledge that none shall prynt them tyll these be solde, . . . your lordship shall not fynde me vnthankfull . . ." With what success Grafton's anticipation of "copyright" was promoted does not appear. Grafton's letter to Cromwell — written after August 28, 1537, and preserved in MS. Cotton Cleopatra E v, 325 — is reproduced in full in A. W. Pollard, *Records of the English Bible*, London and New York, 1911, p. 219. *Cf.* also *Letters and Papers of the Reign of Henry VIII* arranged and catalogued by James Gairdner, London, 1891, Vol. 12, pt. 2, Appendix, p. 489, item 35.

   [z] In 1538, a N. T., the English text paralleled by the Latin of the Vulgate, was published twice by Coverdale; first, from the press of Nicolson at Southwark, "Set forth wyth the Kynges moost gracious licence," and, second, from the press of François Regnault at Paris.

the printing of which, started at Paris, had, after political inter-
ferences, been transferred, press, fonts, sheets, printers and all,
to London [17] — was, in fact, the Matthew Bible of 1537 com-
petently revised by Coverdale with the help of Sebastian
Münster's Hebrew and Latin diglot [18] of 1534–1535 for the Old
Testament, and of Erasmus' Greek text for the New. In anticipation of its publication — according to the colophon, in April
1539 — Cromwell, who had given the venture considerable
financial support, issued, late in 1538, certain Injunctions to the
clergy, one of which was intended to insure that no church in
England would be without its own copy of this superb volume.[aa]
Within two years demand for the Great Bible had exhausted
eight editions, the second of which, [19] revised and published
sumptuously as the first, in April 1540, is distinctive in having
a lengthy Preface by Archbishop Cranmer,[bb] and on its title-
page the earliest "authorization" to state explicitly "this is the
Byble apoynted to the vse of the churches."

[aa] "Item, that ye shall provide on thysside the feast of all sainct*es* [altered
from *Christmas*] next commyng, one boke of the hole bible of the largest volume
in englys*he*, and the same sett vpp in sum convenient place wi*th*in the said
churche that ye have cure of, where as yo*ur* parishners may most commodiouslye
resorte to the same and reade yt." This item, dated 5 Sept., 1538 [Public
Record Office, London, *State Papers, Henry VIII, Theological Tracts* (S. P. 6),
Vol. 3, pp. 1–5; summarized by Gairdner, *op. cit.*, Vol. XIII, pt. 2, No. 281],
is cited, with insignificant variants, by Foxe, *op. cit.*, p. 526.

[bb] The Archbishop's Preface gives to this and subsequent editions of the
Great Bible the designation "Cranmer's Bible." The fifth [Tunstall and Heath]
edition of the Great Bible, issued at London, by Richard Grafton, in 1541,
merits special attention as the one which most liberally contributes textual
support to the common but inaccurate assertion that Coverdale's Psalter in the
Great Bible survives, without alteration, in the Anglican *Book of Common
Prayer* (*cf.* Butterworth, *op. cit.*, p. 154). This fifth edition, furthermore, is
noteworthy for the length and explicit character of its title-page, which, *inter
alia*, announces that the volume had been sanctioned ("Ouersene and perused")
on behalf of the king by two "ryghte reuerende fathers in God," one of whom,
by the irony of history, was "Cuthbert bysshop of Duresme [Durham]"; that
is, Cuthbert Tunstall, who, as Bishop of London, had rejected, in 1523, Tyndale's appeal for assistance in translating the New Testament from Greek into
English, and, in 1530, had ordered the public burning of the version which
Tyndale had produced on the Continent.

The Great Bible, the eighth edition of which appeared in
1541, was the last English version to be printed during Henry's
reign. Possession or use of Tyndale's works was declared illegal,
by a Parliament subservient to the conservative clergy, in 1543;
Coverdale's Bible was proscribed in 1546. Protestants, as it
happened, did not have long to wait until, with the death of
Henry, January 28, 1547, they were again at liberty, for the
six years of the youthful Edward's reign, to resume their interrupted production of Biblical translations. Full advantage was
taken of this interlude. Before the accession of Mary Tudor
in 1553, which stopped the Biblical presses of England for
another five years, printers of London had supplied English
booksellers with several Biblical editions, including four of
Tyndale's New Testament[20] and two of Cranmer's Bible. No
new English translation of Scripture appeared during Edward's
reign, and when Mary came to the throne not even those English
Bibles in use by the clergy were allowed to remain in the
churches.

The Marian persecution, though making martyrs of conspicuous Protestants who, like Rogers and Cranmer, continued
within the country, was unable to reach those who had taken
refuge in Geneva. Prominent among these were Coverdale,
John Knox the Scottish reformer, and his follower William
Whittingham. Associating themselves with the Genevan Protestants, chief of whom were the scholars Theodore Beza and John
Calvin, the English refugees devoted themselves to Biblical
revision, the first result of which was the publication, in 1557,
from the press of Conrad Badius at Geneva, of an English New
Testament edited, it would seem, by Whittingham, with marginal annotations and a prefatory epistle by Calvin.[21] Printed,
as none of its forerunners had been, in roman type, this readable
quarto, convenient for private devotion, was enthusiastically
received upon its surreptitious arrival in Mary's ruthless realm.
Whittingham, with the collaboration of others[22] at Geneva,
followed up his New Testament, in 1560, with a complete
English Bible,[23] destined to serve for half a century as the house-

hold Scriptures of the English people, to be virtually accepted as the authorized version of the Church of Scotland, and to fortify the spirit of those pioneering Puritans who crossed the Atlantic to settle Massachusetts and Virginia. This, the Genevan Bible,[cc] passing through one hundred and sixty editions, has left its unmistakable impress upon the Scriptures in English. To this day, unfortunately, some Bibles continue the pedantry initiated by Whittingham, owing presumably to an exaggerated sense of integrity, of printing in italics those words, supplied by the translator as essential to English idiom, which are lacking in the original Hebrew or Greek. To this day, also, Biblical editors find it obligatory to break up the text, regardless of literary requirements, into irrelevant verses, a practice first taken over into English by Whittingham from Étienne's Greek New Testament. These purely technical features, though regrettable, have nothing to do with the quality of the translation itself, which, more accurate than that of previous versions, frequently achieves a stylistic excellence deemed worthy of perpetuation by the editors of the King James Version.[dd] In the New Testament, the Genevan Version now and again supplies the Bible of 1611 with a turn of expression superior in cadence or diction to the parallel passage in Tyndale; and in the poetical Books of the Old Testament it approaches Coverdale in anticipating the precise phrasing of the Authorized Version. Particularly felicitous was the Genevan translation of the Major and Minor Prophets, numerous passages of which were assimilated word for word, as the ultimate in translation, into the text of

[cc] Known among bibliophiles as the *Breeches Bible*, its translation of Gen. iii. 7 being, "They sewed fig leaves together and made themselves breeches [so, too, Wycliffe]." Two subsequent editions are known to have been published at Geneva: a folio in 1562 and a quarto in 1570.

[dd] From the Geneva Bible, by way of limited illustration, at Mt. vi. 29 the Jacobean translators adopted, without modification, "even Solomon in all his glory" (Tyndale 1525–6: "in all his royalte"); at I Cor. xiii. 12, "For now we see through a glass darkly" (Tyndale: "in a glasse even in a darke speakynge"); and at Prov. xxx. 19, "the way of a ship in the midst of the sea; and the way of a man with a maid."

the Bible produced for King James.[24] Dedicated to "the most vertuous and noble quene Elizabet," who had succeeded to the throne during its preparation in 1558, the Genevan Bible, despite its popular acclaim in England, found no publisher in that country until after the death of Elizabeth's Archbishop Matthew Parker in 1575;[25] nor, owing largely to the controversial flavor of its marginal annotations, was it ever able to dislodge the Great Bible, which Elizabeth, upon her accession had immediately restored "to the vse of the churches" of England.

Replacement of the Great Bible, inferior as it was in scholarship to its Genevan rival, was obviously now incumbent upon the authorities of the Church of England. The outcome of the first official effort to provide a suitable substitute, made by Archbishop Parker, was the publication, at London, in 1568, of a pretentious folio Bible,[26] in size exceeding all preceding editions, which, ten or eleven bishops having participated in its preparation, came to be known as the Bishops' Bible.[ee] This is the first of English versions to be produced by a Biblical commission such as the synod of Canterbury had vainly requested of Henry VIII. Although this commission formulated a set of "observacions" by which its members were to be guided — especially, with the Genevan Version in mind, "to make no bitter notis vppon any text" — the final result of their combined but not co-ordinated labors was a lamentably uneven performance in which the inequalities of the dignitaries' learning and the varieties of their prejudices were plain for all to see. Least acceptable of their translations was that of the Book of Psalms, which, meeting with nearly universal disapprobation, was replaced, beginning

[ee] Archbishop Parker had commissioned, in addition to the bishops, several other church scholars, the total involved being, so far as can now be determined, seventeen. The third edition of the Bishops' Bible, 1572, owing to the printer's scarcely appropriate use, at the beginning of the Epistle to the Hebrews, of an ornamental initial capital letter, featuring Leda and the swan, designed for an edition of Ovid's *Metamorphoses*, is known among bibliophiles as the Leda Bible.

with the undated fourth edition, [27] by the Psalter of the *Book of Common Prayer*. [ff] To the Bishops' Bible we owe such a pedantry of Hellenism as the rejection of *love* — followed by the Rheims and King James Versions but not by the Revised Version — in favor of *charity* at verse 13 of the thirteenth chapter of I Corinthians; and so ideologically motivated an inaccuracy as the substitution, throughout the New Testament, of *church* instead of *congregation* as the rendering of ἐκκλησία. [28] Repeated ecclesiastical enactments following John Whitgift's elevation (1583) to the archbishopric of Canterbury failed, it appears, to secure that universal adoption of the Bishops' Bible which Elizabeth desired for the churches of England.

Religious persecution which, under Mary Tudor, had sent English Protestants into exile at Geneva, subsequently, under Elizabeth, caused English Catholics to make for themselves cities of refuge at Douai and Rheims. Prominent among Catholics fleeing the wrath of the Virgin Queen was William Allen, principal of St. Mary's Hall (Oriel College), Oxford, through whose efforts there was established at Douai, in 1568, a Catholic seminary for the training of English priests. Not only for this particular purpose, but for private devotional use by Catholics in exile, the Douai scholars undertook, for the first time in the history of the Roman Church, to replace the available Anglican and Genevan Bibles — unacceptable from their point of view — with an English version of their own. This project, under the leadership of the Jesuit scholar Gregory Martin, another Oxonian exile, was completed in 1582 at Rheims, to which city the college had transferred itself four years earlier to escape the consequences of Allen's political activities. Political difficulties, it seems, could be avoided more readily than financial; for, owing to "lacke of good meanes to publishe the whole," only the New Testament portion, "the principal, most profitable & comfortable peece of holy writte," was put through the press at

[ff] In the third edition [2nd fol. ed., 1572], the Bishops' and the Prayer Book versions of the Psalms were printed in parallel. In only one later edition, that of 1585, did the Bishops' Version reappear.

Rheims[29] although the entire Bible, "out of the authentical Latin, according to the best corrected copies of the same," had been translated. No more critical edition having been published, among the "best corrected" editions of the Vulgate, than the early ventures of Robert Étienne in 1528 and 1530–40, the scholars at Rheims, as their title-page reassures us, had "diligently conferred" the available Latin text "vvith the Greeke and other editions in diuers languages."

The Hieronymean text from which the Rheims New Testament was translated had unfortunately, through repeated reprintings, so far deteriorated that, in 1586, its revision was entrusted to a papal commission, one of whose members was the afore-mentioned scholar William Allen, presently head of the College at Rheims, about to be elevated to a cardinalship, and to be appointed, in 1591, Librarian of the Vatican. The revision, ordered by Pope Sixtus V, appeared in 1590, the last year of his reign, with his name upon the title-page, and the threat of excommunication upon him who should alter it. In spite of this deterrent feature of the Sixtine Vulgate, the succeeding pope, Gregory XIV, conscious of its multitude of errors, commanded the expeditious preparation of a new revision, which, rushed to completion, and with more than two thousand textual corrections, was published under the auspices of Pope Clement VIII — Gregory having reigned less than a year — in 1592.[gg] The Rheims New Testament, published, it will be remembered, ten years earlier, is thus seen to have been translated from a

---

[gg] This, the Clementine Vulgate, diplomatically retaining the name of Sixtus on its title-page, and with its own anathema upon any person presumptuous enough to modify its text, became the authoritative edition of the Roman Church. No definitive critical edition of the Vulgate had been published prior to that now in progress, which, in preparation by a Biblical Commission created by Pius X in 1907, has advanced as far as II Chronicles: *Biblia Sacra iuxta latinam vulgatam versionem ad codicum fidem, . . . cura et studio monachorum Sancti Benedicti Commissionis pontificiae a Pio pp. x institutae sodalium praeside Aidano Gasquet S. R. E. cardinale edita . . . recensuerunt* † *Reverendissimus abbas Henricus Quentin et monachi Sancti Hieronymi*, Romae, 1926–1948. Convenient, meanwhile, is *Novum Testamentum . . . Latine secundum editionem S. Hieronymi . . .* recensuit J. Wordsworth . . . adsumto H. J. White, Oxford, 1889 *et seq.*

Vulgate the inferiority of which was recognized by scholars of the Roman Church. Its Septuagintal companion,[30] however, printing of which was, for financial reasons, deferred a quarter of a century, though originally based upon the same vitiated text of Jerome, was revised before publication at Douai in 1609–1610 by Gregory Martin's successors, to conform with the text of the Clementine Version. This translation — the Rheims-Douay Bible — is, to the present day, with some accommodation to the phraseology of the Authorized Version and with a few slight modernizations, the recognized English version of the Roman Catholic Church.[hh]

Publication of the Douay Old Testament and Apocrypha anticipated the most remarkable of all Biblical versions by less than two years. The King James — or "Authorized" — Version, appearing in 1611, is the culmination of two centuries of devotion to the difficult problem of putting the Scriptures accurately into idiomatic and effective English. Unrivalled in literary excellence by any of its predecessors, and superior to all of them in scholarly accuracy, this version, unlike all but one of its forerunners (the Bishops' Bible), is the product of the labor of a large group of men. Of the fifty-four members of the commis-

[hh] The further revision which the Rheims-Douay Version required was first undertaken in the middle of the eighteenth century by Bishop Richard Challoner. The N. T. portion has been recently twice revised: (1) *The Westminster Version of the Sacred Scriptures: a new translation from the original Greek and Hebrew Texts* [N. T. only published], ed. by Cuthbert Lattey, S. J. and Joseph Keating, S. J., London, New York and Toronto, 1928–1931; and (2) *The New Testament of our Lord and Savior Jesus Christ. Translated from the Latin Vulgate. A Revision of the Challoner-Rheims version. Edited by Catholic scholars under the patronage of the Episcopal committee of the Confraternity of Christian Doctrine*, Paterson, New Jersey, 1941. A N. T. translation, not from the Vulgate but from the original Greek, is announced by the Confraternity as in preparation. The improved readability of an entirely new Catholic version of the O. T., in "a twentieth-century vocabulary," undertaken in 1943 by the Episcopal committee of the Confraternity of Christian Doctrine, may be gathered from two volumes recently published at Paterson: Genesis, 1948, and Psalms, 1950. Of this, the first Catholic O. T. translation into English direct from the original Hebrew, the complete Pentateuch is scheduled to appear in 1951, and the whole O. T. in 1955. For Knox's recent version — not a revision of the Vulgate but a new translation — *v. infra*, p. 232, note ff, *et al.*

sion originally approved by King James in 1604 for the task of
revising the English translation of the Bible again, forty-seven
can still be identified as distinguished scholars either within the
Anglican Church itself or from the two universities of Oxford
and Cambridge. Dr. John Reynolds, president of Corpus
Christi College, Oxford, who had first proposed the new version
to the king, was only one of several Puritans among the revisers,
who, it seems, had been wisely selected with respect rather for
their erudition than for their doctrinal views. This impressive
commission, when in 1607 it finally settled down to its work,
divided itself into six companies, to each of which was appor-
tioned an appropriate section of the Bishops' Bible, the text of
which, according to the first of the fifteen rules[31] by which the
revisers proposed to guide themselves, was to be preserved as
far as possible and "as little altered as the truth of the original
will permit." The "original," in the case of the Old Testament,
was nothing more authoritative than the Complutensian Polyglot
or the earlier Hebrew Bibles from Soncino and Brescia; and,
in the case of the New Testament, nothing more satisfactory
than the imperfect Greek text of Étienne (1550) which had
previously served both William Whittingham and his associates
at Geneva, and Archbishop Parker and his Episcopal collaborators at London. Codex Alexandrinus, the very existence of
which was unsuspected by the royal commission, was not to
arrive in England for a score of years; Codex Vaticanus, though
reported in the Vatican catalogue of 1481, was long to remain
inaccessible to non-conformist scholars; and Codex Sinaiticus,
its value unrecognized, lay undisturbed at St. Catherine's
monastery awaiting rescue from flames and oblivion by Tischendorf in the middle of the nineteenth century. Such "original"
texts, however, as were available to the revisers, were to be
translated (rule 14), wherever the rendering of the Bishops'
Bible was inadequate, after the pattern considered by them to be
most accurate in the versions of Tyndale, "Matthew," and
Coverdale, in the Great Bible, and even, with a commendable
freedom from sectarian bias, in the Calvinist Bible of Geneva.

Although doctrinal considerations or political discretion precluded its inclusion in the list of acceptable translational models, the revisers undoubtedly, and to their profit, consulted the Rheims New Testament, the Latinity of which, reflected particularly in the Epistles in the King James Version, enriched its vocabulary and heightened the effectiveness of its style.[32] The Douay Old Testament, unavailable in its entirety until 1610, exercised little influence upon the Authorized Version. The Clementine Vulgate, no doubt, was taken into account; and among the "Translators and Commentators" whom the revisers, according to their celebrated Preface, did not hesitate ["thinke much"] to consult were the foremost Jewish exegetes,[ii] and the Spanish, French, Italian and German [Dutch] vernacular versions. The initial revisions, thus broadly based, were submitted for further refinement and harmonization to a revisory committee of twelve members, two from each of the six companies, from whom the revised manuscript passed, for final preparation for the press, into the hands of Thomas Bilson, bishop of Winchester, and Miles Smith, of Brasenose College, Oxford, who supplied the Authorized Version with its splendid Preface. Thus, concluding approximately three years of painstaking endeavor, the King James Version, a revision of many previous revisions, was brought into being. Robert Barker, "Printer to the Kings most excellent Maiestie," issuing this Bible from his press at London in a handsome folio of 1611, placed upon both of its title-pages,[jj] without any known legal justification, the universally accepted and still living fiction, "Appointed to be read in Churches." This printer's announce-

---

[ii] "Kimchi alone," according to D. Daiches, *The King James Version of the English Bible*, Chicago, © 1941, p. 158, "was quoted directly by non-Jewish scholars of the sixteenth and early seventeenth centuries." Biblical scholars of the Jacobean period, in Professor Daiches' opinion [*loc. cit.*], took their references to Jewish commentators other than Kimchi, at second remove, out of Jean Mercier's אוצר לשון הקדש *hoc est*, *Thesaurus linguae sanctae, sive Lexicon hebraicum*, . . . Lyons, 1577.

[jj] In addition to the regular title-page — an ornate woodcut — there is another preceding the New Testament: an engraving, entirely different in design and variant in typography.

ment, in the absence of any record of official sanction by Privy
Council or King, is the sole and precarious foundation upon
which has been erected the undying tradition that the Version
of 1611 was "authorized."

The King James Version, contending with the extraordinary
popularity of the Geneva Bible, made way but slowly toward
its present pre-eminence — first in the hearts of Englishmen.
From its initial appearance, as previously observed,[kk] it suffered
from a minor plague of printer's errors; and not even the
deliberate alterations of its text, "introduced silently and without
authority"[33] into subsequent editions, could conceal from
scholars of a later generation its major deficiency — an inaccuracy and even at times an unintelligibility of rendering which,
with the advance of learning, would ultimately have to be
eliminated. As early as 1659, more than two centuries before

[kk] *V. supra*, pp. 47–48 and 56. Two impressions of the 1611 edition
differed at Ruth iii. 15: one, faithful to the Hebrew [וַיָּבֹא — vayyaвho'],
reading "and he [Boaz] went into the city"; the other, usually followed today,
reading "and she [Ruth] went into the city." A 1637 quarto edition, issued at
Cambridge, omitted *rise*, at Mt. xii. 42, from "shall rise up in the judgement."
Another Cambridge edition, a folio of the year following, not only substituted
ram for *lamb* at Num. vi. 14, but, at Acts vi. 3, replaced "whom we may
appoint" with "whom ye may appoint" — an alteration for which Oliver
Cromwell is frequently alleged to have paid £1,000 to secure Biblical precedent
for the appointment of officers by the people. In 1653, the London printer
John Field issued a N. T. in which, among other errors, *not* was omitted, at
I Cor. vi. 9, from "the unrighteous shall not inherit the kingdom of God";
God was omitted, at Mt. vi. 24, from "ye cannot serve God and Mammon";
and, at Jn. ix. 21, "or who hath opened his eyes" was dropped out of the text.
In 1656 this same Field published a Bible so full of errors that he was fined and
the edition recalled. At Oxford, in 1717, the press produced a bibliophile's
prize by printing *vinegar* instead of *vineyard* in the headline for Lk. xx; also
from Oxford, in 1804, comes the edition which, owing to its reading "the
murderer shall surely be put together," at Num. xxxv. 18, instead of "put to
death," is known as the "Murderer's Bible," and, in 1801, an octavo in which,
at Jude 16, *murmurers* are turned into *murderers*. Cotton Mather, complaining, at the end of his *Magnalia Christi Americana* (London 1702), of "Scandalous
Errors of the Press-work" through which "The Holy Bible it self : : : hath
been affronted," refers to an unidentified edition of Scripture in which verse
161[a] of Ps. cxix, "Princes have persecuted me without cause," appears, by the
most apposite of printers' errors, as "Printers have persecuted me . . ."

revision of the King James Bible was undertaken, two studies of the Authorized Version by Christians, published contemporaneously at London, [34] courageously anticipated the vigorous criticism by which, in the nineteenth century, bishop and archbishop established the inadequacy of the Jacobean translation. [35] In the first half of that century, Jewish scholars in England, previously silent as to the deficiencies of the Old Testament portion of the Authorized Version, issued call upon call for its revision. [36] Eighteenth-century response to criticism of the 1611 translation resulted in at least one semi-official English version of the New Testament — that of Bishop Lloyd in 1701, [37] the first English Bible known to center its chronology about the birth of Jesus — followed by several which were entirely without ecclesiastical authorization, [38] including one by the Presbyterian minister Edward Harwood, who — certainly a pioneer — attempted, according to the title-page, "to translate the Sacred Writings with the same freedom, spirit, and elegance with which other English translations from the Greek classics have lately been executed." Late in the century, and early in the nineteenth, there appeared a number of equally independent English versions of portions of the Old Testament. [39] Thus alive to the mistranslations of "the former age," the eighteenth and nineteenth centuries, it is seen, abundantly offered both Christian and Jewish preliminaries to that revision of the entire Bible of 1611 — admirable, but yet insufficient — known as the Revised Version.

For an official attempt to remove inaccuracies from the King James Version and to restore intelligibility wherever necessary and possible to its text, the world had to wait nearly three centuries. Although an authoritative revision of the Jacobean Biblical translation had been suggested in England as early as 1810, and, in America, an independent revision of the entire Bible "with Amendments of the language" had been issued by Noah Webster [40] in 1833, it was not until 1870 that the Convocation of Canterbury officially sanctioned such an undertaking by nominating a committee of its own members[11] who, instructed to invite the co-operation of Christian scholars irrespective of denomination, were entrusted with the preparation of a new version, based upon that of King James, but to be revised in conformity with requirements of nineteenth-century learning. Scholars of the Roman Catholic Church, content with such amelioration of the Rheims-Douay text as had been made by Bishop Challoner in the middle of the preceding century, declined to participate in the projected revision. Protestant scholars in the United States, through an American Revision Committee, joined in the venture of their English colleagues.[11]

Revision of the Old Testament, completed, after fourteen years of labor, in 1885, was confined for the most part to such alteration of the King James Version as seemed justified by the available Massoretic Text. Although study of the Hebrew language had sufficiently progressed since the Jacobean period to illuminate numerous obscure passages in the received Hebrew Scriptures, no critical edition of the Hebrew *textus receptus*, based upon the best manuscripts, had been attempted prior to 1861 when Seligman Baer and Franz Delitzsch published at Leipzig the first portion of their conservative and never-completed Massoretic Text.[41] A rare knowledge of the traditional text, however, fortunately possessed by one[42] of the invited members of the company of Old Testament revisers, compensated to some extent for the want of a complete critical edition. The Hebrew text upon which the revisers of the nineteenth century had to rely was essentially that which had been consulted early in the

[11] Nine members of the Convocation of Canterbury, selected for revision of the Old Testament, sought the assistance of just twice their number of English scholars; seven members, assigned to work on the New Testament, and, subsequently, on the Apocrypha, invited the co-operation of twenty-two English men of learning. Of the eighteen invited to serve on the O. T. committee, two declined, and ten died before the work was finished. Two of the original nine also died while the work was in progress. Of the twenty-two asked to participate in translating the N. T. two (John Henry Newman and William H. Thompson) declined the invitation, and four died prior to completion of the work.

seventeenth century by the authors of the King James Version. The revisers, no doubt, found helpful suggestions in the earlier attempts, Christian and Jewish, to improve upon the English of the Authorized Version. Between a new rendering of the Pentateuch and historical Books of the Old Testament by Julius Bate in 1773, and an original version of Zechariah by Benjamin Blayney in 1797, the last quarter of the eighteenth century saw the production of numerous translations of selected Books of the Old Testament;[43] and in the nineteenth century, early enough for the use of the revisers, translations of the entire Hebrew Scriptures into English were published by scholars on both sides of the Atlantic Ocean.[44] Particularly influential, it would seem, was Isaac Leeser's version[44] — the generally accepted standard in those synagogues of England and America which conduct their religious services in English — which, though patterned after the Bible of 1611, renders with especial freedom and originality the Books of Job, Psalms and the Prophets. In the Old Testament portion of the Revised Version, Job and the Prophets, more than any other Books (except Ecclesiastes), exhibit the independence of the revisers from their Jacobean predecessors.

The revisers of the New Testament, able, in the main, like those of the Old, to follow the King James Version in matters of style, were compelled by the progress of scholarship to abandon the underlying Greek text upon which the Jacobean readings had been based. For the New Testament no textual foundation comparable in stability to the Massoretic Text was available. Neither the Greek New Testament of Robert Étienne nor that of Theodore Beza,[45] both obsolete from the moment in 1627 when Codex Alexandrinus arrived in London, had been replaced with an adequate critical edition. Reconstruction of the Greek text, accordingly, was the initial task of the revisers, and a principal cause for the prolongation of their labors for ten years. In this exacting work the company of New Testament revisers was advantaged by the inclusion among its members of the eminent scholars B. F. Westcott and F. J. A. Hort who, concurrently occupied with the preparation of their own *New Testament in the original Greek*,[mm] no doubt exercised considerable influence upon their colleagues. The reconstructed Greek New Testament finally adopted by the revisers — and published, within a week of the Revised English New Testament, in 1881 — deviated from the *textus receptus* in nearly six thousand instances, of which approximately fifteen hundred noticeably affect the sense. Translated from this improved Greek original, the Revised Version of the New Testament, received at first with denunciation as bitter as that which the Romans had accorded the work of Jerome, has established itself, with respect at least to its accuracy of interpretation, as generally the superior of its celebrated Jacobean forerunner.

Revision of the Apocrypha, completed in 1895 by the company which had translated the New Testament, finally brought the Revised Version to its conclusion.

The procedure of the two English companies, as recorded in their Preface to the Revised Version, differed from that of the scholars who produced the Bible of 1611. Their revision was accomplished in three stages. In the initial stage, proposals to modify the reading of the King James Version were adopted by majority vote. These modifications, if challenged during subsequent deliberations, were retained only if favored by two-thirds of the company present and voting. Proposed changes in the reading of the Authorized Version for which a two-thirds vote could not be obtained, but for which a majority expressed a preference, were recorded in the margin. This, the second step in the revisory process, was followed by a third in which, always by a vote of two-thirds, the company came to a final decision as to "reserved points," harmonized inconsistencies, smoothed down roughnesses, removed unnecessary changes, and, in general, gave "finish and completeness" to the revision. Throughout their work both British companies of revisers exchanged views

---

[mm] Westcott and Hort's Greek New Testament — for one generation the authoritative text — has been superseded by Hermann Freiherr von Soden's *Griechisches Neues Testament*, Göttingen, 1913.

with the American Committee of Revision,[46] many of whose renderings were either incorporated into the British text or, like the substitution of *spirit* for *ghost*, included in an appendix. Suggestions of the American revisers to which the scholars of England could not be reconciled, found their place in the American Standard Version which, from its initial appearance in 1901, included its own appendix to which the rejected readings of the English revisers were in their turn duly relegated. Outstanding among such peculiarly American innovations is translation of the Tetragrammaton not by LORD, customary in the British version, but by the popular, though linguistically indefensible, *Jehovah*.

Neither in England nor America was the new revision, however adjusted to regional differences, received with general acclamation, readers on both sides of the Atlantic naturally resenting the necessary emotional accommodation to unexpected variations in familiar textual rhythms. The revisers, as is manifest, were not insensitive to considerations of style. Their careful attention to niceties of diction wherever they abandoned the Jacobean readings, was none the less but partial atonement for their infelicitous decision consistently to employ throughout the New Testament an invariable English equivalent for any recurrent Greek word. This deliberate renunciation of the richness of the vocabulary, made in the interest of translational fidelity, deprived the Revised New Testament of some of that wealth of connotative overtone through which the King James Version frequently preserves precious subtleties which vanish before verbal inflexibility. In the Old Testament, however, where this rule of verbal invariability was not invoked, the revisers — according to that sensitive critic, Quiller-Couch [47] — not only "performed their task delicately, scrupulously, on the whole with great good judgement," but "clarified the sense of the Authorized Version while respecting its consecrated rhythms ..." Although from the strictly literary point of view certain portions of the new version may have left something to be desired,[48] other revised passages — assuredly the majority — once their unfamiliarity had worn away, were felt to be as much the Queen's English as the verses they replaced had been the King's. The Revised Version, demonstrating more than one of the virtues of modern scholarship, often illuminated what was previously obscure or quite unintelligible through a literary medium which, though vigorously assailed upon its appearance, and still rejected by those who prefer aesthetic comfort to scholarly integrity, has gradually achieved generous critical approval.

The Revised Version, and its companion, the American Standard Version, were undertaken, as can now be seen, prematurely, just before new discoveries and searching critical studies of the twentieth century. Discovery of Biblical manuscripts, especially those of the Freer collection and the Chester Beatty papyri, has expanded the palaeographic base upon which the revisers had erected their text; and recovery of non-Biblical Greek documents of early Christian date — such as the Oxyrhynchus papyri [49] — has necessitated an approach other than classical to the grammar, lexicography and idiom of the original language of the New Testament. [50] Had scholarship, moreover, been at a standstill, and discovery brought nothing new to light, the obsolescence of numerous words and phrases of the Jacobean and even the Victorian Biblical versions would of itself induce further Scriptural accommodation to a tongue which no longer employs expressions such as *the Lord do so to me, and more also* or *my reins are consumed within me*. The Revised Version, though eliminating many archaisms currently unintelligible or misleading, is still sufficiently Jacobean "caviar" to the twentieth-century "general" to hamper, if not to defeat, its easy comprehension by the common reader today. Attempted amelioration not only of this stylistic conservatism of the version, but also of its linguistic and textual deficiencies which recent Biblical learning reveals, has resulted in some twenty-odd unofficial Biblical translations — chiefly of the New Testament — in modern English. [51] Four of these — those of Moffatt, Smith-Goodspeed and Knox, and the Basic English — embrace the entire Bible; all are private undertakings, no church having yet authorized for its formal use a Biblical translation in that "simple, straightforward English of everyday expression" which Goodspeed considered most appropriate, or in that "effective, intelligible English" through which Moffatt offered the unlearned "a transcript of . . . Biblical literature as it lies in the light thrown upon it by modern research."

Officially sponsored Scriptural translations issued subsequent to the Revised Version are but two in number, and one of these — the American Jewish Version[52] — relinquishes nothing of its precursor's essentially Jacobean English. Although the group of seven Jewish scholars who were entrusted with the preparation of this American Old Testament, "from the Jewish traditional point of view," naturally rejected the Messianic interpretations of the Massoretic Text[nn] found in Christian versions of Scripture, they not only gratefully declare their obligation to all previous English translations but manifest their especial indebtedness to the Authorized and Revised Versions by retaining, for the most part, their very words and rhythms. Occasionally, the American Jewish Version makes original and skillful contribution to the phrasing of the Jacobean text;[53] but, preserving as it does the stylistic pattern of its predecessors — archaisms and even obsolete terms included — it is rather a Synagogal adaptation of the Anglican Old Testament than a fresh and independent translation.

Greater independence characterizes the second post-Victorian, officially-sponsored American translation of Scripture: *The New Covenant Commonly Called the New Testament of Our Lord and Savior Jesus Christ.*[oo] This volume — the Revised Standard New

[nn] Deviations from the Massoretic texts of Baer and of Ginsburg, upon which the A. J. V. was based, are acknowledged at Ezek. ix. 9 and Ps. lxii. 4; examples of silent alteration of the text occur at Job xiii. 28, Job xxxi. 39, Prov. xxiii. 5, S. of S. viii. 6. Disputed readings were adopted by majority vote, the chairman voting in case of a tie.

[oo] Copyrighted in 1946, this N. T., authorized by the International Council of Religious Education, representing forty Protestant denominations of the United States and Canada, is to be followed by *The Old Covenant Commonly Called the Old Testament* (now in preparation), the two works to be known as the Revised Standard Version.

Testament — is the initial installment of "a comprehensive revision," now in progress, of the American Standard Version of half a century ago. The thirty-one scholars charged with this undertaking, being of opinion that "all of the reasons which led to the demand for revision of the King James Version . . . are still valid," have· prepared a New Testament which, though attempting little of the "ease, boldness, and unpretending vigor" of style advocated by Goodspeed, and less of the freshness of translation achieved by Moffatt,[pp] is nevertheless considerably closer to contemporary usage, particularly in syntax and diction, than is the Revised Version.[54] In this most recent rendering, by way of random example from the Gospel according to Matthew, the birth of Jesus was not "on this wise" but "took place in this way"; Joseph was not "minded to put her [Mary] away privily," but "resolved to divorce her quietly"; "take no thought for" becomes "do not be anxious about"; *publicans* are *tax collectors; suffered him, consented; mocked of, tricked by*; and *the uttermost farthing, the last penny*. Modifications of the earlier text such as these were adopted by the revisory committee — in accordance with a provision of its charter more conservative than any previous rule of Biblical revision — only if they received a two-thirds vote, not merely of those present at a meeting but of the entire membership of the committee. The text thus co-operatively produced, however disturbing it be to readers brought up on and enchanted by the King James Bible, is designed primarily to appeal to the multitude of twentieth-century readers whose first need with respect to Scripture is to comprehend, the better to enjoy and be comforted by, what they read. For the abundant textual rephrasing through which such popular comprehension is presumably facilitated, the Revised Standard New Testament, like its predecessors, has, in its turn, been roundly condemned.[55] Understanding of the Sermon on the Mount is no doubt made easier for Tom, Dick and Harry

[pp] Professors Goodspeed and Moffatt were both members of the subcommittee of nine scholars who prepared the N. T. for submission to the full committee of revision.

by replacement, for instance, of *tittle* by *dot*, or of *mote* by *speck*; but it may well be questioned that ready comprehension of the passages in which these words occur[56] is promoted by the substitution of *an iota* for *one jot* and *log* for *beam*. The unfriendly critic, however he accumulate such instances of translational infelicity, will prevent no judicious reader from concluding that the Revised Standard New Testament has, in the main, approached its goal of contemporary intelligibility. This, moreover, it has accomplished through a modernization of the text radical only as a translation; with respect to matters of doctrine, as is elsewhere indicated,[57] it is an essentially orthodox version.

Evolution of the printed Bible, in English translation, is, as we now see, a persistent, if intermittent, process, and there is no sound reason for thinking that evolution at an end. In the more than four centuries since Tyndale defiantly issued his English translations from an alien press, the unceasing development of language and the cumulative discoveries of scholarship have conspired to produce, as presumably they will continue to conspire, versions of Scripture suitable to the period of their production. The twentieth century, richer than preceding ages in discoveries relating to the historical, linguistic and cultural backgrounds of the Bible, has produced, as a culmination of modern scholarship, the Revised Standard Version; but, whatever the ultimate critical evaluation of that work, no more than any of its numerous excellent predecessors can that version be thought the final and definitive edition of the Book of thirty centuries.

CHAPTER VIII

Translation of the Text—Modern English

"... with another tongue will he speak to this people."
                                        Isaiah xxviii. 11

TRANSLATION of the Bible, under ideal circumstances, would have awaited establishment of a perfect text. Translation, however, began long before the involved problems of textual criticism had been recognized; indeed, in certain cases, before some of those problems were magnified by the multiplication of widely circulating manuscripts. Inasmuch as recovery of a perfect text is an unattainable ideal, and the discovery of a Biblical holograph highly improbable, it is not to be seriously regretted that from early days and "to every people after their language" the Old Testament was made available, however crudely, to those who understood no Hebrew, and the New Testament to those who read no Greek. From every point of view, no doubt, except the scholarly, this was all to the good. In the realm of scholarship, approximation to the Scriptural text as originally written is still the goal; and translation, to meet with acceptance, must accurately reflect such progress in that direction as has been achieved.

Translation, if it be something other and better than a slavish reproduction, word for word, of the original document, is, at its least, an "abbreviated commentary," and, at its best, an art.

Maimonides considered it "a species of original composition."
Ælfric, archbishop of Canterbury (A. D. 969–1006), venturing
"to translate . . . out of the Latin . . . the 'Holy Scriptures' into
our common language," without being "studious to render
word for word," described his performance as "an attempt of
some rashness and presumption."[a] The Franciscan commentator,
Nicholas de Lyra, on the contrary, finding that, in his "modern
times," [1] the literal sense of the Bible, the very foundation, had
been obscured "through our manner of translation," proposed
to re-establish that literal basis through the evidence not only
of his fellow Catholic scholars "but also of Jewish ones, especially
of the Rabbi Solomon [Rashi], who has spoken most reasonably
of all the Hebrew doctors." Rashi himself, whose exegetical
position was intermediate between the traditional interpretation
of the rabbis and that of the more rationalistic school of the
eleventh century, confessed that his own commentary, a basis for
translation, would have to be revised in accordance with the
newer interpretations coming to light day by day. [2] The authors
of the Geneva Bible, dissatisfied, according to their Preface, with
their predecessors' "imperfect knollege of the tongues," and
secure "in respect of this ripe age [1557–1560] and cleare light
which God hath now reveiled," naturally came to the conclusion
that all previous "translations required greatly to be perused
and reformed." Luther, whose genius in this field was so great
as to leave a permanent impress upon the German language,
thought it impossible adequately to reproduce the idiom of
Biblical Hebrew and Greek in his mother tongue. [3] Some sixteen
centuries earlier, the grandson of Ben Sirach, translating his
grandfather's wisdom into Greek, prefaced that apocryphal
Book — Ecclesiasticus — with an apology for any apparent
failure to render some of the phrases correctly; "for," said he,
"things originally spoken in Hebrew have not the same force in

---

[a] *Cf.* F. S. Merryweather, *Bibliomania in the Middle Ages*, London, 1849,
pp. 45–46. Ælfric was sufficiently sure of himself to write the ultimate challenge: "Now, if anyone find fault with one translation, let him compose a book
of his own."

them when they are translated into another tongue; and . . .
the law itself, and the prophecies, and the rest of the books,
have no small difference when they are spoken in their original
language."[b] The eminent tenth-century scholar, Gaon Saadya,
turning the Old Testament from Hebrew even into so closely
allied a cognate tongue as Arabic, discovered the need of
clarifying the sense by the insertion of an explanatory word here
and there, and manifested a tendency, found in succeeding
generations of translators,[4] to make his version intelligible by
skillful circumvention of the obscurities and difficulties of the
Hebrew text as it was known to him.[5]

A modern translator of the Old Testament will likewise feel
impelled to avail himself of "deft manipulation" or "the addition of a few words" if by so doing he can surmount "a textual
difficulty of the lighter order."[6] In Hebrew, as in other languages,
intelligent understanding of an elliptical construction frequently
requires imaginative provision of words which, though not
expressed, are grammatically essential. Although in such cases
the meaning is usually sufficiently established by the context,
there is "a temptation . . . to a translator to facilitate the comprehension of the reader, or to preclude some misapprehension
which he contemplated as possible,"[7] by inserting in his version
the equivalent of the omitted but syntactically necessary word or
words. That the translator's "principal function," in the words
of the American Jewish Version, "is to make the Hebrew
intelligible," will probably be accorded universal approbation;
and only those who have never attempted the exacting labor of
transferring the subtleties and beauties of one language into

[b] The discovery by Dr. Solomon Schechter and others, in 1896, of portions
of a Hebrew text of Ecclesiasticus reveals the extent to which the original was
misinterpreted by the grandson. *Cf.* Schechter and Taylor, *The Wisdom of
Ben Sira*, Cambridge, 1899; also, *Ecclesiasticus: The Fragments Hitherto Recovered
of the Hebrew Text in Facsimile*, Cambridge and Oxford, 1901. *Cf.* also S. R.
Driver, *An Introduction to the Literature of the Old Testament*, New York, 1914,
p. 514; *Cf. Jewish Quarterly Review*, Vols. ix–xiii, *passim*. Observe, further, the
indication in the Preface to Ecclesiasticus, that the threefold canonical division
of the Old Testament had been established by the "thirty-eighth year of
Euergetes the king" of Egypt [Ptolemy VII]; *i. e.*, 132 B. C. *V. infra*, p. 303.

another can be unsympathetic with the contention, again in
the words of the American Jewish Version, that the translator,
"faithful though he must be to the Hebrew idiom, . . . will nevertheless be forced by the genius of the English [or, of course, of
any other] language to use circumlocution, to add a word or
two, to alter the sequence of words, and the like."[c] A translation
which succeeds in achieving Luther's aim of rendering the spirit
rather than the mere letter of the Hebrew or Greek with their
peculiar nuances and characteristic literary flavor, into a modern
idiom like our own,[8] is inevitably at times periphrastic. No
matter how competent and effective a version may be, however,
its readers, if like the translator they are also acquainted with
the underlying languages, will be inclined to complain either
that "the spirit of the original has been sacrificed" or that the
translation is "full of inaccuracies."[9] In view of the apparent
impossibility of achieving a completely satisfactory translation of
certain incomparable passages of our own literature into languages so nearly related to English as German or French,[d]
there need be no undue surprise at the outspoken opinion that
"exact rendering from or into such utterly dissimilar languages
as English and Hebrew . . . is practically impossible."[10] Exactness of translation is frequently unrealized partly because of
the syntactical character of Biblical Hebrew which, to the
western mind, leaves much to be desired. For one thing, it is
noticeably reluctant to employ even those few particles which it
possesses to express the more subtle interrelationships of thought.

[c] *Preface*, p. x: "In general, our rule has been that, where the word or words
added are implied in the Hebrew construction, no device is used to mark the
addition; where, on the other hand, the addition is not at once to be inferred
from the original wording and yet seems necessary for the understanding, it
has been enclosed in brackets [*e. g.*, Is. lxvi. 18; xxvii. 12; xlvi. 3] . . . sparingly
it is true, but nevertheless as often as the occasion required."

[d] See, for example, what happens to Iago's "Not poppy nor mandragora,
Nor all the drowsy syrups of the world" in French, German and other versions,
conveniently assembled in the Variorum *Othello*, Philadelphia, [1886], pp.
453 ff. Or, conversely, examine Longfellow's or any translation ever made of
Goethe's *Ueber allen Gipfeln ist Ruh*. "In every language there is a magic of
words," wrote Southey, "as untranslatable as the *Sesame* in the Arabian tale, —
you may retain the meaning, but if the words be changed the spell is lost."

Conspicuous are "the loose and indefinite connections" made by the more commonly used copulatives such as ו [*and*] or אשר [*which*].[e] For another, its fairly elaborate verbal system includes no inflections equivalent to those with which a language such as English so nicely differentiates distinctions of time. Tenses, in the usual meaning of the term, it does not possess. Temporal niceties are indicated through verbal "aspect," a feature which operates largely with the assistance of the imagination.[11] Temporal and aspectual functions are distinct enough and meaningful in Semitic languages; in translation, however, the shift required by idiom from the one to the other is not easily accomplished and exactness is not always possible.[f] Hebraists, as Driver points out, are sufficiently aware that even the Revised Version, superior though it be to the Authorized Version both in clearness and in accuracy, "does not always, either in the text or in the margin, express the sense of the original as exactly as is desirable."[12] If it be maintained, as it usually is, that the Authorized Version is "probably the best translation in English," but yet acknowledged of this Version and its Revision that "each brings out certain shades of the original according to its own genius; each fails in certain others"; and again that neither "exactly reproduces the full connotation of its Hebrew or even of its Greek original"[13] — surely no previous or subsequent version so far produced is likely to render anachronistic Cheyne's well-considered and authoritative phrase, "the still unsolved problem of Bible translation."[14]

[e] At Job v. 7, for a single illustration, where, in English versions, we have "Man is born unto trouble, *as* the sparks fly upwards," the two clauses of this statement are connected in the M. T. by nothing more cohesive than an indeterminate *and* [ו] — ובני רשף. *Cf.* further, Gesenius, *Hebrew Grammar*, § 155, *passim*.

[f] L. H. Gray, *Foundations of Language*, New York, 1939, pp. 204–5: "The difference between aspect and tense comes out very clearly in translations from Semitic into Indo-European. Thus, for instance, the Hebrew telic YHVH mālaχ of Psalms xciii. 1, *et al.* is translated by a perfect in the Latin Vulgate ('Dominus Regnavit'), and by an aorist in the Greek Septuagint ('κύριος ἐβασίλευσεν'), but, much more accurately, by a present in the English version ('the Lord reigneth')."

Basic to any translation is obviously a comprehensive knowledge of the vocabulary of the primary language. Such knowledge was possessed in greater measure by the Jacobean scholars — to say nothing of their predecessors — who translated the New Testament anew for their king, than by their colleagues who dealt with the Old. Even at the present time — when through recent archaeological discoveries, through the advance of epigraphy of the Middle East, and through the increased mastery of the ancient languages of the Mesopotamian regions, our command of the Hebrew vocabulary is far superior to that which was available, some seventy years ago, to the authors of the Revised Version — even today, it may safely be asserted, our knowledge of the words employed by Scriptural authors is less certain in the case of Prophet or Psalmist than in that of Apostle or Evangelist. Translation of the New Testament is assuredly not without its lexicographical obstacles; but for the Older Covenant, with the inevitable variations of a language continuously spoken throughout many centuries, inadequacies of the dictionary are more abundant. The literature of the Old Testament is not great in bulk, and what there is of it is still further reduced, from a linguistic point of view, by its multifold repetitions.

In all probability there were many words in the language which, for one reason or another, never found their way into the writings which now constitute the Old Testament. Literally hundreds of words appear but once. The meaning of such *hapax legomena* is often dubiously guessed at in the light of the context; sometimes it is arrived at by way of the Versions or through the testimony of cognate tongues; in many instances the meaning cannot be ascertained at all. Saadya, the father of Biblical lexicography, listed from the Old Testament some ninety rare words of undetermined meaning, many of them of unique appearance, and then, with the evidence of Arabic and late Hebrew, indicated how their significance could be conjectured if not definitely established. [15] Helpful in this direction as was the

work of Saadya, and his followers,[g] there yet remain more than
four hundred words in the Hebrew Old Testament the meaning
of which is unknown.[16] The *ladder*, for example, upon which, as
Jacob dreamed [Genesis xxviii. 12], the angels of God were
ascending and descending, is the best the English translators
have been able to do with the Hebrew word סֻלָּם [SULLAM],
which is known only here. The *white of an egg*, in Job vi. 6, is
but one interpretation[h] of the *hapax* חַלָּמוּת [ḤALLAMUTH] to
which Rashi assigned the meaning *saliva*, the American Jewish
Version *juice of mallows*, and the Douay Version *that which when
tasted bringeth death*. At Isaiah xxviii. 25, by way of further illustration, the inept *principal* wheat and barley of the Authorized
Version is but a rash and unwarranted deduction of the meaning
of the unique שׂוֹרָה [SÔRAH] from its resemblance to the well-
known word for *chief* or *prince*, שַׂר [SAR]. This word SÔRAH,
believed from the evidence of the Zingirli inscriptions to mean
a kind of grain, probably millet,[17] is now so interpreted in
current editions of the Douay Version, but has yet to acquire
this meaning in the Revised or the American Jewish Versions.
In this same verse of Isaiah, it may be added, there is another
expression of single occurrence: the verbal form נִסְמָן [NISMAN],
rendered *appointed* in the Authorized, Revised, and American
Jewish Versions, and apparently glossed over in the Douay.
Of such words as these which appear but a single time throughout the entire Old Testament, the total, according to the count
of I. M. Casanowicz, is 414, of which sixty instances are found
in Isaiah and sixty-one in Job.[18] In addition to these absolute
hapax legomena, there occur within the Books of the Old Testament
more than fifteen hundred unduplicated inflectional forms of

[k] Such as Ibn Janaḥ [*V. infra*, p. 321, note 15] — flourished first half of
the eleventh century — greatest of medieval Hebrew philologists, first to recognize the phenomena of literal substitution and metathesis; and in the nineteenth
century Samuel David Luzzatto (1800–1865), first among Jews to permit
himself to emend the Massoretic Text.

[h] That of the A. V. and R. V. which follow Saadya, whose reading is based
upon a Talmudic analogy. So, too, Moffatt.

words, the greatest number, 201, being in Isaiah. Many of these, however, may be readily interpreted by reference to recognized roots from which they are no doubt derived. The various translations of the Bible which appear in English give no indication, of course, of the baffling nature of these unique words in the original. They read smoothly enough. But the translators were unavoidably alive to the problem — witness the *Preface* to the King James Version, which, on this point reads in part as follows: "It hath pleased God in his divine Providence, here and there to scatter words and sentences of that difficulty and doubtfulness . . . that fearfulness would better beseem us than confidence . . . . There be many words in the Scriptures, which be never found there but once (having neither brother nor neighbor, as the Hebrews speak), so that we cannot be holpen by conference of places. Again, there be many rare names of certain birds, beasts, and precious stones . . . concerning which the Hebrews themselves are so divided among themselves for judgement, that they may seem to have defined this or that, rather because they would say something, than because they were sure of that which they said."

A translational problem of an opposite character arises when the interpretation of the original, rather than being entirely in doubt, is embarrassingly ambiguous. Not infrequently a Scriptural passage may be legitimately rendered in several ways. The clarification of such ambiguity — the existence of which is admitted in the Encyclical, *Providentissimus Deus*, prefixed to current editions of the Douay Version[19] — may be greatly assisted, to quote that authoritative communication, by "good hermeneutical methods." To the scholars of the ancient Synagogue not only was the multiple sense of the Biblical text a recognized fact but it was also a source of instruction and pleasure. Although rabbinical emphasis was naturally placed upon those exegetical dichotomies which were ethical in character, the rabbis cannot have failed to observe that the interpretations upon which scholars were at variance were frequently concerned with nothing higher than the primary meaning of the text. Every Book of the Old Testament contains its share of statements the basic sense of which, though apparently simple and straightforward in English translation, has long perplexed the commentator and tried the ingenuity of the translator. The Book of Job, for a conspicuous example, is burdened with passage upon passage whose fundamental import is still controversial among Biblical authorities, but whose multiple interpretative possibilities are never suggested to the reader who knows his Bible in one of its English versions alone. In the thirty-sixth chapter of Job, to cite an extreme instance, no less than thirty different explanations have been offered by the commentators for the two concluding verses. Attention has been previously called to the sixty-eighth Psalm, the exegesis of which, because of its multiple textual interpretations, is said to be "staggering." According to one of the ablest modern Old Testament scholars, "Any reader of the Bible in Hebrew knows only too well how many passages there are that have been from time immemorial the despair of the commentators and have defied all their attempts at elucidation, and yet read smoothly enough in our versions."[20]

Multiplicity of readings of the primary text imposes upon the translator the responsibility of critical selection. One interpretation or another he must finally choose as that which is to be incorporated in his version. This is by no means always an easy decision. Even for the Jewish translator of the Old Testament, who, if orthodox, is obligated normally to follow the QᴇRE, there are troublesome decisions to make; for, as the most competent of authorities[1] avers, "there are cases in which the marginal reading is clearly the inferior, and sometimes both [margin and text] are unacceptable." Frequently there are several consid-

---

[1] *Cf.* Margolis, *The Story of Bible Translations*, Philadelphia, 1917, p. 127: *V. supra*, p. 51. A. J. V. *Preface*, pp. ix, x: "While as a rule the margin (kere) was followed, we have occasionally adopted the consonants of the text (ketib), as for instance in Psalm cxxxix. 16, and II Chronicles xxiv. 27; xxxiv. 9."

erations which point to the validity of the reading which the
conservative translator has ultimately decided to reject; and
often there are good and sufficient arguments available against
the inclusion of his chosen interpretation. In such instances he
may have recourse to marginal annotations, such as are found
in many versions of the Bible in English, either to indicate to
potential critics his knowledge of the textual alternative or to
invite the reader to participate in his dilemma. When the differences of interpretation involve doctrinal questions the margin
may become a field of controversy. Such it was in the Geneva
Bible of 1560, the polemical margin of which, though of great
appeal to the Puritans, appeared to King James as "very partial,
untrue, seditious, and savouring too much of dangerous and
traiterous conceits." Of the five rules laid down for the authors
of the Bishops' Bible, just eight years later, the third, with the
Geneva Bible of course in mind, was "To make no bitter notis
vppon any text, or yet to set down any determination [of meaning]
in places of controversy." The margin of the Authorized Version,
although meeting the expressed desire of King James by ex-
cluding all contentious comment, contains numerous alternate
readings. "Some peradventure," say the translators in their de-
lightful *Preface*, "would have no variety of sense to be set in the
margin, lest the authority of the Scriptures for deciding the controversies by that show of uncertainty should somewhat be
shaken. But we hold their judgement not to be so sound in this
point." In addition the Authorized margin, in accordance with
the sixth of its fifteen rules of procedure,[21] supplies the literal
meaning of Hebrew and Greek words or phrases rendered out
of deference to English idiom with some degree of freedom;
explains certain passages the meaning of which, sufficiently
clear in the original, is clouded in translation; and records instances in which the "ancient authorities" exhibit textual variations. The margin of the Revised Version, following a similar
pattern, calls attention to "some few instances of extreme difficulty" in the Old Testament portions in which, departing like
the Authorized Version[22] from the Massoretic Text, it adopts

a reading "on the authority of the Ancient Versions."[j] Such marginalia, however, are in the nature of the case anything but exhaustive. Besides, once again to employ the superb phraseology of the King James Version — and to repeat a doctrine which the editors of the American Jewish Version apparently took even more earnestly to heart — Biblical scholars "must not weary the unlearned, who need not know so much; and trouble the learned, who know it already."

For the translator of the Bible, who must without question be a very learned man, there is, inescapably, a full measure of trouble. In Hebrew and in Greek, as in any other tongue, the translator will encounter words or phrases which, for various reasons, are to all intents and purposes untranslatable. What can be done, for example, successfully to convey in French, say, or German, the exact shades of meaning in a language whose genius finds expression in locutions such us *putting one over*, *a square deal*, *up against it*, or even the simple *club* or *home*? German has its *Gemütlichkeit*; French its *enfant terrible*; Italian its *dolce far niente*. These cannot, with entire satisfaction, be rendered into English. Of such flavorful but elusive expressions Hebrew and Greek has each its share. They can but be approximated in English. In some instances the difficulty is not merely one of semantic elusiveness but rather one of complete unintelligibility. Words not understood reduce the conscientious translator to transliteration. The *azazel* of Leviticus xvi, previously mentioned in another connection,[23] is a case in point. Another is the frequently occurring אשרה ['ašēRAH], which, erroneously

---

[j] Revisers' *Preface*, p. ix. At Is. lix. 19, for example, the R. V., reading "which the breath of the LORD driveth," follows Douay in rejecting the traditional pointing of the M. T., but records it ("the LORD shall lift up a standard against him") in the margin. The A. J. V. at this text silently follows the lead of the R. V. (cp. Is. xl. 7). This passage can be further improved, according to Graetz, by emending the immediately preceding clause so that what the breath of the Lord driveth is not *the enemy* (A. V.), nor *a rushing stream* (R. V.), nor yet *distress* (A. J. V.), but *a ship* (צי) *on the river*: בנהר צי [BNHR ṣI followed by RUḤ] in place of M. T. כנהר צר [KANNaHAR ṣAR (RUAḤ)], the *resh* of צר abandoned as a dittograph from the adjacent רוח, and the *kaph* replaced by its resemblant *beth* (Graetz, *Emendationes*, etc., I. 34).

rendered as *grove* in both the Douay Version and that of King James, is, for want of understanding, transliterated as *Asherah* in the Revised and American Jewish Versions.[24] Still another illustration is the word *Arabah* [ערבה — 'aRABHaH],[k] taken generally by the Authorized Version and the Douay Bible to mean *plain, desert, wilderness,* but in nearly half of its occurrences, held by the authors of the Revised and American Jewish Versions to be best represented by transliteration.

Technical terms also are not easy to deal with. Shall they be given their nearest English equivalent, or are they one and all to be transcribed letter for letter? Should the translator aim at accuracy, and achieve an unwanted flavor of modernity, by designating a certain Hebrew unit of liquid measure [בת] as so many gallons or risk the unfortunate phonetic coincidence involved in its transliteration as *bath*?[1] And if the decision be for *bath,* and *ephah,* and *homer* [חמר], why not likewise for *qaneh* (reed), *ammah* (cubit), and *kor* (measure)? At Isaiah v. 10, it may be observed, within the limits of a single sentence, inconsistency is the rule in this matter; for there the Prophet woefully proclaims, in the English wording, that "ten *acres* [צמדי — ṢIMDE] of vineyard shall yield [only] one *bath*"; and equally at odds is the method at II Chronicles ii. 10 (M. T. 9), where Hiram's munificence is vaguely rendered as "twenty thousand *measures* [כרים — KORIM] of barley, and twenty thousand *baths* of wine." *Measure,* moreover, has not only been transliterated as *cor,* at Ezekiel xlv. 14, but has there been relieved of its indefinite quality, being clearly defined as "ten *baths,* even an *homer.*" As with units of capacity and length, so is it with units of weight and money. *Shekel* [שקל — šeQEL] is always transliterated in the Old Testament and has become virtually an English term; the

---

[k] *V. supra,* p. 97. Although in 27 of this word's 59 occurrences the R. V. and A. J. V. duplicate the translation *plain* or *desert* of the A. V., they fall back in 26 instances upon transliteration. In this they are followed, with an occasional departure of their own [*cf.* Jer. xxxix. 4], by both Moffatt and Smith-Goodspeed. A. V. once only [Josh. xviii. 18]: *Arabah.*

[1] According to Josephus the *bath* was eight gallons. Rabbinical opinion cuts this estimate in half.

larger monetary unit, KIKKAR [כבר], however, even in immediate association with *shekel*,[25] is never rendered in the English
versions by anything other than the transliterated Greek word
talent,[m] borrowed, of course, from the Greek of Matthew [xviii.
24] where it is appropriately and most effectively employed. At
passages such as Ezra ii. 69 or Nehemiah vii. 70–72, in which the
word *drams*, employed by the Douay[26] and Authorized Versions
to render the Hebrew DARKᴇMONIM [דרכמנים — a word of Persian origin], is rejected by the Revised Version and the American
Jewish Version in favor of the transliteration *darics*, neither of
these two last-named versions departs from its predecessors in
putting the Hebrew MANIM [מנים] into English with the historically unjustifiable *pound*[s]. These two versions, furthermore,
agree in placing *darics* in the same verse with *talents*.[27]

Problems of a similar nature arise for the translator in his
handling of proper names. Readers of the Jewish historian
Josephus in the original are aware of the curious effect of
transforming Hebrew names into Hellenized forms with Greek
endings — such as Libanus for Lebanon. Readers unacquainted
with the Bible of the Roman Catholic Church will be surprised
to find the familiar prophets Isaiah, Hosea, Obadiah, Micah
and Haggai appearing in the Douay Version as Isaias, Osee,
Abdias, Micheas and Aggeus. These, however, are but superficial disturbances to which an adjustment can readily be made.
Deeper, and beyond a translator's power of reproduction, is the
relation of the external form of a Hebrew name to its internal
significance. Proper names of persons as well as of places are
likely, in the earlier phases of a developing culture, to exhibit
a reflection of its language. The meaning of a name is trans-
parent through its form; the form, indeed, is a derivative of the
meaning. A name may reveal some fact of history, some myth,
or the circumstances under which it was acquired and to which
it seemed appropriate. Even under modern and sophisticated conditions, when personal names have lost nearly all recognizable

---

[m] To this there is but one exception: at Zech. v. 7, where the A. J. V.,
rendering *ephah* by *measure*, rejects the familiar *talent* and substitutes *a round piece*.

associations other than with ancestral residence or occupation, it is not impossible for a sufficiently learned and incon-
siderate parent to weigh his child down for life with a name
whose origin is semantic.[n] Such distinction as was achieved by
that celebrated New Englander, Increase Mather, obscures the
affliction of his given name, a direct translation of the Hebrew
verb יסף [yāsaᴘh] meaning *to add, to increase*, from which — as
his father, Richard Mather, remembering Genesis xxx. 24, well
knew — Rachel had hopefully derived the name Joseph.[o] Although Isaac was born so late in the life of Abraham and Sarah
as to cause them *to laugh* with scorn at the very idea, and was
accordingly named from the Hebrew *he laughed* [יצחק —
yiṣḤaǫ];[28] and although Jacob, because at birth he clung to his
twin brother Esau's heel, was so called in perpetual reminder
of the Hebrew word for· *heel* [עקב — ‘aǫēʙh][29] — there is no
way, alas, for a translator to convey these integral linguistic
features of the narrative other than through the non-literary
medium of footnotes. And when, as recorded in the fourth
chapter of the first Book of Samuel, the army of Israel had fled
before the Philistines, and the two sons of Eli, Hophni and
Phineas, had been slain in the battle, and the aged priest Eli
had collapsed in death at the news, what was more fitting —
and more baffling to a future translator — than that the wife
of the late Phineas, dying in childbirth, should bestow upon

[n] That Increase Mather preferred to distinguish his eldest son from himself
not by the commonplace *junior* of Latin derivation but rather by its more
recondite Hebrew equivalent ǫaṭon [קטן] which naturally transmogrified
itself into the more comfortable English homonym, *Cotton*, is a suggestion
[see Abraham I. Katsh, "Hebrew Culture in Secular Institutions of Higher
Learning," in *Jewish Education*, Vol. 18, No. 1, New York, Nov. 1946, pp. 32 ff.]
which, though tempting, can hardly be sustained in view of the fact that
Increase Mather's first wife, Marie, bore the well-known English surname
Cotton.

[o] This, according to the Yahvist text (*v. infra*, pp. 261 ff.). The Elohist, in the
preceding verse, derives Joseph's name from another verb, *to take away* (אסף —
’asaᴘh); for Rachel, relieved of barrenness, ·said, "God *hath taken away* my
reproach." See also the play on the name *Jacob* at Gen. xxvii. 36: "Is he not
rightly named *Jacob*? for he *hath supplanted me* these two times [יעקב ויעקבני]."
V. infra, p. 340 note 29.

her helpless infant the memorable name Ichabod [אִי כָבוֹד —
'ı ĸнaвнôɒн], meaning *inglorious*; for, as she said [verse 22] —
and the translator will be grateful for her explanation — "The
glory is departed from Israel; for the ark of God is taken"?

Noah, and Eve, and Ishmael, and Zebulun, and Benjamin,
and Moses, and Samuel, and a host of other Biblical characters,
have meaningful names immediately apparent in Hebrew which
lose their significance as soon as translated. Naomi, greeted by
friends upon her return with Ruth from the land of Moab,
advises them no longer to call her by her rightful name but to
address her by a new one, Marah. That there is a play upon
the two names in this passage [Ruth i. 20] — obvious at once to
the reader of Hebrew — is intimated to the reader of the English
version by Naomi's ensuing words: "for the Almighty hath
dealt very *bitterly* with me"; but it assuredly is outside the reach
of the most skillful of translators to embody in his text the idea
that *Naomi* conveys the thought of something *pleasant* and the
name she suggests for herself means *bitter*.

Paronomasia such as this is common and is found in the New
Testament as well as in the Old. The Septuagint is exceptionally
successful in preserving the flavor of such word-play at Judges
x. 4.ᴾ Notable among verbal quibbles of this kind which defy
imitation is that of Jesus, addressed to his disciple Simon: "And
I say also unto thee that thou art Peter, and upon this rock I will
build my church." ³⁰ *Rock* and *Peter* being practically identical
forms of the same word in Greek, but entirely different in English translation, it is a matter of some mystification for one who
cannot read the original — or the French, which preserves the
flavor perfectly: Et moi je te dis aussi que tu es le Pierre, et sur
cette pierre je battîrai mon église — to come across Bernard
Shaw's characteristic but unassailable assertion with reference
to this passage that Christianity was "gaily founded with a pun."

ᴾ LXX: καὶ δύο υἱοὶ ἐπιβεβηκότες ἐπὶ τριάκοντα καὶ δύο πώλους [M. T.:
עֲיָרִים — ʿayarim; *ass colts*] καὶ τριάκοντα καὶ δύο πόλεις [M. T.: עָרִים —
cities (apparently a deliberate departure from the customary plural עָרִים)]
αὐτοῖς. The Vulgate, at Acts viii. 30, captures the verbal spirit of γενώσκεις
ἃ ἀναγινώσκεις with *Intellegis quae legis?*

The similarity in the sound of words which, if they be of dissimilar meaning, makes puns possible, is the determining characteristic of another rhetorical device, alliteration. The repetition of similar sounds in stressed syllables in close sequence is a feature of emotional expression in all languages. It is a frequent ornament of the Biblical text. It can seldom, however, if ever, be carried over successfully in translation; a version inevitably loses something of the phonetic flavor. "Dust and ashes," though acceptable enough in our ears, does not reproduce the pleasing repetition of sounds in the original Hebrew of that expression in Genesis and Job.[q] A translator could, in this instance, preserve the alliterative quality by some such combination of words as "dust and debris," but, of course, in so doing he would sacrifice the fine flavor which the English, by happy circumstance, achieves. In the familiar lines of Judges xv. 16 — "With the jawbone of an ass, heaps upon heaps, with the jawbone of an ass have I smitten a thousand men" — Samson's exultation, despite the excellence of its rhythm and the repetition of *heaps*, loses the gratifying feeling of inextricable union of sense and sound which makes the original Hebrew memorable.[r] At Zephaniah ii. 4, by way of final illustration, no one would suspect from the English versions that this verse — "For Gaza shall be forsaken . . . and Ekron shall be rooted up" — contains, in its ancestral form, an alliterative quality both at its beginning and at its end.[s]

Translation is again confronted with technical difficulty whenever in the original something other than the superficial meaning of the text is implicit in the exact arrangement of the letters. Acrostics, mentioned previously in another connection,[31] are a special case in point. A sufficiently ingenious scholar might find it possible to put into English the first stanza of Psalm cxix

---

[q] עפר ואפר — 'apʰaʀ va'ēpʰeʀ: Gen. xviii. 27; Job xxx. 19; xlii. 6. From this and the following illustrations it will be seen that, in contrast to English practice, in Hebrew the syllables which are normally stressed, and which may therefore be used "alliteratively," are not initial.

[r] בלחי החמור חמור חמרתים — BiLḤi HaḤaMÔR ḤaMÔR ḤaMoRaTHaYiM, *etc.*

[s] כי עזה עזובה . . . ועקרון תעקר — Ki 'azzaH 'azuBHaH . . . ve'eQRÔN Tē'aQēR.

in eight couplets each of which begins with the letter "A"; and commence each of the eight couplets of the second stanza with its appropriate letter "B"; and so on in alphabetical sequence throughout the twenty-two stanzas of the poem; but ingenuity of this order, whatever its value in the original Hebrew, would probably be dwarfed by the consequent mutilation of such beauty as the English versions have been able to capture. Lamentations would certainly be less effectively rendered were its acrostic patterns to be slavishly reproduced.

Technical too, but so difficult as to exclude the attempt, is the representation in one language of an anagram or a cipher in another. Fortunately this is a matter of no great moment in the field of Biblical interpretation. When we read in Isaiah lxi. 3 "to give unto them a garland [t] for ashes," we have no way of knowing from the English that in Hebrew the words for *garland* and *ashes* are reciprocal anagrams, and probably so chosen by the Prophet for that reason. Esau's well-known complaint against his brother Jacob: "he took away my birthright; and, behold, now he hath taken away my blessing," reveals nothing in English of the anagrammatic relationship in Hebrew between the words for *blessing* and *birthright*.[u] In English versions at Jeremiah xxv. 26 we are presented with a strange land, Sheshach;[v] and at Jeremiah li. 1, where in the Authorized Version the Lord says he will raise up against "them that dwell *in the midst of them that rise up against me*," in both the Revised and the American Jewish Versions the Yahvistic threat is directed against "them that dwell in Leb-kamai,"[v] an otherwise unheard-

---

[t] A. V., *beauty*; Douay, *crown*. *For*, of course, here means *instead of*. M. T. פאר תחת אפר [pe'ēr ... 'ēpher].

[u] Gen. xxvii. 36, M. T.: בכרתי [bekhorathī — *my birthright*]; ברכתי [birekhathī — *my blessing*].

[v] Douay, *Sesac*, thus utterly concealing the cipher. This, and the cipher of Jer. li. 1, both in the category of systematic substitution, are known in Hebrew as *atbash*. It consists of the interchange of letters occupying positions in the alphabet equally distant from the initial or the terminal letter. Thus, in English, an "A" of a word to be enciphered would be replaced with "Z"; a "B" with "Y"; a "C" with "X"; and so on. The second letter in the Hebrew alphabet is *beth*; the twelfth letter, *lamedh*. The second letter from the *end* of

of country. Leb-kamai, though seen to be a transliteration from the Hebrew, is understood only by the initiated to be a cipher for Chaldeans; no translation without benefit of footnotes can make this clear.

What a translation can at its best succeed in doing is to awaken in the reader a pleasurable reaction in response to its literary qualities. The translator who achieves this must be himself something of a creative artist, alive to the connotative overtones of words, aware of their musical values, and sensitive to the cadences created by their juxtaposition. Such a translator is rare. An Edward Fitzgerald will be found but once in many generations to put the Persian quatrains of Omar the tentmaker into English verses — however at variance with the spirit of the original — supreme in their kind. A group of translators such as those who produced the literary miracle of the King James Version can scarcely be expected to walk this earth again. Now that we possess this Version, all others are inevitably judged by its peculiar literary grandeur; and revisions of its text necessitated by the increase of knowledge are the more likely to gain acceptance as they echo its phraseology, reproduce its rhythms, and are patterned, in general, upon its style.

Unfortunately, from the esthetic point of view, language which is living undergoes continual modification, in consequence of which words become archaic and ultimately obsolete, and memorable phrases, though retaining their stylistic quality, lose in the course of time their original meaning. Shakespeare's greatest plays, written within a few years of the Authorized

---

the alphabet is *shin* ; the twelfth, *kaph*. Substitution of these letters — *shin* for *beth*; *kaph* for *lamedh* — changes *Babylon* [$\underset{12}{ל}\,\underset{2}{ב}\,\underset{2}{ב}$ — BĀBheL] into *Sheshach* [$\underset{12}{ר}\,\underset{2}{שׁ}\,\underset{2}{שׁ}$ — šēšaᴋh]. In an identical manner, in Jer. li. 1, $\underset{10}{'}\,\underset{13}{מ}\,\underset{19}{ק}\,\underset{2}{ב}\,\underset{12}{ל}$. [Lēbh Qāmay] is a concealed spelling of $\underset{10}{ם}\,\underset{13}{'}\,\underset{19}{ד}\,\underset{2}{שׂ}\,\underset{12}{כ}$ [casdim]; *i. e.*, Chaldeans. An analogous, though not identical, cipher of this very simple kind occurs in *Twelfth Night* (Act II, Sc. v) where Malvolio's name is, to his mystification, enciphered by Maria, who wrote it down in the following order: M (first letter); O (last letter); A (second letter); I (second from last). That is as far as Maria went; had she proceeded in this fashion to the conclusion, the cryptic spelling would have continued: L; L; V; O.

Version, are replete with such troublesome archaisms, and are often quoted today by people whose delight in the passage quoted is not paralleled by a recognition of its Elizabethan significance.[w] The verb *to tell*, for an example of archaic usage, frequently employed by Shakespeare in the sense of *to count*, is found with that meaning in both the Authorized and Revised Versions at Psalm cxlvii. 4 and at Jeremiah xxxiii. 13;[x] and in its participial form *told* at II Kings xii. 10.[y] *Sod*, the obsolete past tense of the verb *to seethe*, found in the Authorized Version at Genesis xxv. 29, is retained not only by the Revised Version but, surprisingly, by the American Jewish Version. The American Standard Version and current editions of the Douay Bible considerately substitute the modern equivalent *boiled*. The verb *to ear*, for a third example, used in the Authorized Version in the sense of *to plough* or *till* land, has been sensibly supplanted at four places [Genesis xlv. 6; Exodus xxxiv. 21; Deuteronomy xxi. 4; I Samuel viii. 12] in the Revised Version and American Jewish Version by *plough*, and has been changed to *till* at one [Isaiah xxx. 24]. These substitutions, advisable for a modern reader, in no way injure the prose rhythm. For the modern reader, again, the Psalmist, in one of his ecstatic moments, apparently rivals in supernatural power his predecessor Joshua for whom "the sun stood still, and the moon stayed," with his startling assertion "I prevented the dawning of the morning."[z]

[w] The hackneyed "a foregone conclusion" — used currently to mean "an inevitable result" — is quoted from *Othello* (Act III, Sc. iii, 429) where its meaning is "that which has been previously concluded." "More honoured in the breach than the observance" — Hamlet's way of saying more honorable to violate a custom than to practice it [*Hamlet*, Act I, Sc. iv, 16] — is today frequently employed with reference to insufficient performance of some desirable action.

[x] Douay, Ps. cxlvi. 4: *telleth*; Jer. xxxiii. 13: *numbereth*; A. J. V., in both cases: *counteth*.

[y] Douay and A. J. V.: *counted*. This usage survives in bank *teller*, to *tell* one's beads, and the common expression *all told*.

[z] Ps. cxix. 147, 148. A. V.: "I prevented the dawning of the morning, and cried: I hoped in thy word. Mine eyes prevent the night watches, that I might meditate in thy word." The R. V. is identical except that the second *prevent* is changed to *prevented*. Douay, similar in phraseology, employs *prevented* in

This use of the verb *to prevent* in the obsolete sense of *anticipate* or *forestall*, has been happily abandoned by the American Jewish Version which, without injuring the cadences, restores intelligibility by reading:

> "I rose early at dawn, and cried;
> I hoped in Thy word.
> Mine eyes forestalled the nightwatches,
> That I might meditate in Thy word."

Translational difficulty of this nature is further illustrated by the Biblical use of the word *virtuous*. This word, though in origin associated with qualities masculine, has come in current usage to refer principally to chastity in woman. In Jacobean times its employment was not nearly so confined,[aa] and in three of its four Biblical occurrences it requires more generous interpretation. It is, however, with less assurance that one can insist on the broader meaning of the word in the remaining Biblical instance at Proverbs xii. 4: "A virtuous woman is a crown to her husband; But she that maketh ashamed[bb] is as rottenness in his bones." This is a matter of some delicacy. It may be appropriate in this connection to record that the word *chaste*, known though it was in the language as early as the thirteenth

---

both verses. *Prevent*, thus used, is clear enough to the linguistically prepared reader of *Hamlet* [Act II, Sc. ii: "So shall my anticipation prevent your discovery"; *i. e.*, forestall your disclosure], and was certainly understood by Rosencrantz and Guildenstern in addressing whom the Prince of Denmark uses this verb. At Job iii. 12 and at Is. xxi. 14, where *prevent* is the verb in the A. V., the R. V. and the A. J. V. advisedly replace it with *receive* and *meet* respectively. At Ps. lxxxviii. 13 [M. T. 14] it is replaced by *come before* and *come to meet*.

[aa] Othello, speaking of his wife's accomplishments, could say, "Where virtue is, these are more virtuous." The customary Shakespearean term for *chaste* was *honest*, as Desdemona was made well enough aware by Othello's infuriated iteration of that word once his conviction of his wife's infidelity had been established. Shakespeare does, however, employ *virtuous* in the sense in question [*Merry Wives of Windsor* (IV. ii. 136)]. An identical usage occurs in Chaucer's *Man of Law's Tale*, line 526.

[bb] Thus A. V. and R. V. A. J. V.: "she that doeth shamefully." Douay: "A diligent woman is a crown . . . and she that doeth things worthy of confusion is a rottenness in his bones."

century, occurs not once in the English Bible. The Old Testament *virtuous* is always a translation of the Hebrew חיל [ḤAYIL], which, in its numerous appearances, conveys among other meanings those as varied as *army, forces, strength, wealth, valor.* Applied to a man, this word may equally suggest either one of wealth or one of valor. Boaz, appropriately characterized in the Authorized and Revised Versions of Ruth [ii. 1] as "a mighty man of *wealth*" [Douay: "a powerful man, and very rich"], is designated by the American Jewish Version, for no ascertainable implication within the Biblical narrative, "a mighty man of *valour*." Applied to a particular woman, as it is by Boaz to Ruth [iii. 11], ḤAYIL may be understood to be a term of general commendation — "a woman of worth" according to Moffatt and Smith-Goodspeed — for which the English versions (including the American Jewish Version) find *virtuous* a satisfactory equivalent. Applied to an ideal woman, as in the alphabetical acrostic with which Proverbs closes, ḤAYIL would seem to indicate, rather than *a good wife* [Smith-Goodspeed] or *an able wife* [Moffatt], a paragon of womankind, whose price — in view of her fidelity (verse 11), her strength, her wisdom, her kindness, her fear of the Lord, and (emphasized in several of the verses) her industry — is, like that of wisdom, set far above rubies. And by what encompassing epithet of grateful admiration shall we designate such a woman? Shall we not, admitting the deficiency of the English language and insisting upon the broader use of our inadequate term, abide by the *virtuous* woman who hath done *virtuously* of the Authorized and Revised Versions; or shall we, over-sensitive to but one implication of our troublesome term, disregard the very substance of the acrostic poem, and, with the American Jewish Version, extol to a world of incredulous men a woman who, in her husband's climactic phrase, excelleth all others in having done *valiantly*?[cc]

[cc] Verse 29. The Douay O. T., which like the A. J. V. ("woman of valour"), adopts *valiant woman* at the beginning (v. 10) of this acrostic, concludes the poem (v. 29) with praise of one who excelleth all other daughters in having "gathered together riches."

"Balm in Gilead," appearing for the first time at Jeremiah
viii. 22 in the Geneva Bible of 1560 and adopted by the King
James and subsequent Versions, has become so integral a part
of our literary idiom that it is a little difficult to imagine any
substitute for this mellifluous phrasing.dd Yet two years prior
to publication of the Authorized Version it appeared in the
Douay Old Testament as *rosin* in Gilaad, and, earlier still, in
both Coverdale's and the Bishops' Bible, as *treacle*. Justifiable
translations these two — *balm* (or its linguistic alter ego *balsam*)
being an aromatic and resinous gum, and *treacle* being used in
its now obsolete sense of sovereign remedy — but hardly acceptable to the sensitive ear attuned to the cadence of the Authorized Version! Although current printings of the Douay Bible,
influenced, no doubt, by the Anglican versions, replace the
earlier *rosin* of this verse in Jeremiah with *balm*, they continue
at Ezekiel xxvii. 17 to render the underlying Hebrew word
צרי [ṢORI], common to both of these passages, by *rosin*. The
Authorized and Revised Versions at this point, unwilling to do
more than transliterate the *hapax legomenon* פנג [PANNAG], inform
us that "Judah, and the land of Israel," alas, no longer trade
"wheat of Minnith, and Pannag, and honey, and oil, and balm"
with fallen Tyre. Moffatt and Smith-Goodspeed read "wheat
of Minnith, wax, honey, oil, and balsam." Douay, currently
translating PANNAG by *balm*, is driven back upon the *rosin* of the
Septuagint and the Vulgate for a rendering of ṢORI. The American Jewish Version, unafraid like Douay of the *hapax*, and with

dd *Balm* has been known in English from Anglo-Saxon times. Before its
appearance at Jer. viii. 22 it had been used (baulme) by Tyndale at Gen.
xxxvii. 25 in his Pentateuch of 1530, and had thence entered the English Bible
in Coverdale's Version (1535), had been copied by the Great Bible (1539),
but had reverted to *rosen* at this verse in the Geneva Bible (1560). In the 1568
Bishops' Bible (bawlme), however, and in Parker's 1577 folio edition of the
Geneva Version, *balme* was restored to the verse under consideration, and has
been retained with variant spellings by subsequent English versions. Parker
accompanied his *balme* with the marginal alternatives *rosen*, *triacle*, and *turpen-
tine* — which latter commodity, like *balm*, is an oleoresinous exudation, the
one from the balsam tree, the other (whence, by way of Greek and Old French,
its name) from the terebinth.

apparent indifference to the identity of meaning in English of *balsam* and *balm*, relates that the Tyrian traffic lamented by Ezekiel was in "wheat of Minnith, and balsam, and honey, and oil, and balm." Surely, it must now be seen, the way of the translator is hard.

Stylistic difficulties such as these may be traced in part to the ancestral documents. The authors of the King James Version had several previous editions before them. They reflect at times the Rheims-Douay translation, from which, indeed, they occasionally took over a felicitous expression not available in any preceding versions.[ee] They are influenced by the Geneva Bible, which supplied for the first time — to cite but a few out of many possible illustrations — "even Solomon in all his glory" [Matthew vi. 29]; "For now we see through a glass darkly" [I Corinthians xiii. 12]; and, in the twenty-third Psalm, "He restoreth my soul" and "I shall not want." In the main, of course, they consult the previous Anglican versions, and benefit most of all, stylistically, from Tyndale.

The scholars of Rheims and of Douai, religiously following, as their *Preface* states, their "copie, the old vulgar approued Latin," had a tendency at times to overlook the homely and therefore effective qualities in the Anglo-Saxon linguistic heritage, and to intersperse their generally readable translation with alien and even barbarous words and phrases directly traceable to St. Jerome. This tendency was fortunately counterbalanced by the influence of the earlier English versions — chiefly the Genevan — which were undoubtedly consulted. Latinity none the less asserts itself sufficiently to offend — the Douay Bible would have said *scandalize* — the literary sensibilities. One can hardly be expected to be well pleased — Douay, again, would have said [Hebrews xiii. 16] *promerited* — to discover, at the return of the Prodigal Son to his home, that his brother, instead of being just

---

[ee] Gen. xxxvii. 26: "if we *conceal* his blood"; Prov. xxx. 23: "*odious* woman"; Lk. xv. 25: "he heard *musicke* and *dauncing*"; Rev. xxi. 2: "as a bride *adorned* for her husband." Infelicitous borrowing also occurs, as at Mt. xxvi. 66: "He is *guilty of death*," for "he is *worthy to die*."

plain angry as in the Authorized Version, "had indignation."
Nor is it easy for one unaccustomed to it to refer to the *fruit* of
the vine as its *generation* [Luke xxii. 18], or to pray to the Lord to
"give us this day our supersubstantial bread" [Matthew vi. 11].
Verily, verily — Douay: Amen, amen — it is a strange thing to
find in the twenty-third [22nd] Psalm in the Douay Old Testament of 1609 that "beside the still waters" is "Upon the water of
refection," that "my cup runneth over" is "my chalice inebriat-
ing," and that the length of time I may dwell in the house of
the Lord is not "for ever" but rather "in longitude of dayes."
Recent impressions of the Rheims-Douay Bible have in part
tempered the Latinity of its style by such substitutions as
hallowed for *sanctified* [Matthew vi. 9] and *humbled* for the pre-
posterous *exinanited* of Philippians ii. 8; but to this day they
retain *contumeliously* rather than *spitefully* (R. V. *shamefully*), propose that a man walk *solicitous* instead of *humbly* with his God
[Micah vi. 8], employ *Paralipomenon* as the title of Chronicles,
and insist upon *pasch* and *Azymes* for *Passover* and *unleavened
bread* [Mark xiv. 1].[ff]

Important as the proper choice of words must be to the
translator, his ultimate effectiveness will be dependent upon the
subtler aspects of style. It is only too true that a sufficiently sooth-
ing combination of sounds and rhythm will often conceal
obscurity of thought. Of the Authorized Version it has been
reverently asserted that "even where the translation is wrong . . .
*the splendid stateliness of the English version makes us blind to the
deficiency of the sense.*"[32] Certainly this is the lamentable truth
with respect to passage after passage in the Scriptures. Where,

---

[ff] The passages cited above from Ps. xxiii [Douay xxii] are revised, in current Rheims-Douay editions, to "water of refreshment," "my chalice which
inebriateth me," and "unto length of days." This Psalm, as published in 1950
by the Confraternity of Christian Doctrine [*v. supra*, p. 196, note hh], not only
joins the Authorized Version in adopting the Genevan opening, "The LORD
is my shepherd, I shall not want," but judiciously conforms to modern usage
with "restful waters," "my cup overflows," and "for years to come." Msgr.
Knox, admirably, in his modern translation of the Vulgate, recently issued
under the *imprimatur* of the Church, has skillfully eliminated Latinisms such
as those here noticed.

however, as is usually the case, the sense of a Biblical translation is both accurately given and lucidly conveyed, it may be heightened in impressiveness and strengthened in vitality by a rendering responsive to the music of a language and the cadence of a phrase. This is an elusive matter — for literary supremacy a *sine qua non*. Emotions of a reader inevitably accord with the singing quality of whatever he reads. The eye of the reader conveys what it sees on the printed page not only to the brain but also to the heart. To myriads of English-speaking Christians, for instance, the injunction at Deuteronomy vi. 4, as it appears in the Douay, Authorized, and Revised Versions, "Hear, O Israel: the LORD our God is one LORD," is a sufficiently acceptable statement of the monotheistic principle; but to millions of English-speaking Jews this commandment (to the dying Jew what extreme unction is to the Catholic), recited twice daily by every pious member of the Synagogue, is an inspiriting battle cry or a heart-warming consolation only in that rendering adopted by the American Jewish Version: "HEAR, O ISRAEL: THE LORD OUR GOD, THE LORD IS ONE." That sings!

Or, to make use of an illustration in which no values other than the purely literary are in question, turn for a moment to the concluding sentence of the first episode in the story of Joseph and his brethren [Genesis xxxvii. 36]. Joseph's alleged destruction by a wild beast has just been reported to his father, who, refusing to be comforted, says that he will go down to the grave mourning. In the Douay text this episode concludes with: "And whilst he continued weeping, The Madianites sold Joseph in Egypt to Putiphar, an eunuch of Pharao, captain of the soldiers." And here, in contrast, is the narrative of the Revised and the American Jewish Versions: "And his father wept for him." [Note at this point the change in rhythm, and the sweep of the cadences to their satisfying end.] "And the Midianites sold him into Egypt unto Potiphar, an officer of Pharaoh's, the captain of the guard." That is stylistic perfection.

Differences in phonetic texture not nearly so obvious as those in the preceding example distinguish between even a high degree of competence in translation and its elevation to something creative in itself. We read in Isaiah xl. 31, according to the Douay Old Testament:

> "But they that hope in the Lord shall renew their strength. They shall take wings as eagles; they shall run and not be weary; they shall walk and not faint."

This, be it said, is certainly superior work, of high literary quality. The authors of the King James Version found practically nothing with which it could be improved. The change they make in the first sentence is a matter of Hebrew and does not concern us here. In the second sentence, however, they modify the Douay reading twice, expanding the initial clause one syllable too much but still greatly improving its cadence, and inserting, before the third clause, an entirely superfluous *and*, which, besides being absent from the Hebrew, is destructive of the rhythmic pattern to which the reader is prepared to respond. The Authorized Version reads: "But they that wait upon the Lord shall renew their strength; they shall mount up with wings as eagles; they shall run, and not be weary; and they shall walk, and not faint." This reading is followed by the Revised and the American Jewish Versions except for deletion — a more than gratifying touch — of the intrusive *and* previously mentioned. This is the highest literary level achieved so far in any Biblical rendering of this singing passage, and it is high indeed: "they shall mount up with wings as eagles; they shall run and not be weary; they shall walk and not faint." Superb! Yet even to this majestic measure an added grace has been anonymously given in the liturgy of the American Reformed Jewish Service: [33]

> "They shall mount up with wings as eagles;
> They shall run, and not be weary;
> They shall walk, and not be faint."

There remains only elimination of superfluous punctuation and excision of that rhythmically disturbing and tautological "up" to complete the gratification of at least one reader's literary sensibilities, thus:

> They shall mount with wings as eagles
> They shall run and not be weary;
> They shall walk and not be faint.

In final illustration of the magic touch with which a translator, like a creating poet, can, if art be his, transform the ordinary into the sublime, we subjoin without running comment several versions, in chronological sequence, of the enchanting words of Ruth the Moabitess to her mother-in-law Naomi at Ruth i. 16ͻ

Coverdale: "Ruth answered: Speake not to me therof, that I shulde forsake the, and turne backe from the: whither so euer thou goest, thither wil I go also: and loke where thou abydest, there wil I abide also: Thy people is my people, & thy God is my God. Loke where thou diest, there wil [I] dye, and euen there wil I also be buried. The Lorde do this and that vnto me, death onely shal departe vs."

Geneva: "Ruth answered, Intreat me not to leaue thee, nor to departe from thee: for whither thou goest, I wil go: and where thou dwellest, I wil dwel: thy people *shalbe* my people, and thy God my God. Where y*u* dyest, wil I dye, and there wil I be buryed. the Lord do so to me & more also, if *oght* but death departe thee & me."

Douay: "Who answered: Be not against me, to the end that I should leaue thee and depart: for whither soeuer thou shalt goe, I wil goe: and where thou shalt abide, I also wil abide. Thy people my people, and thy God my God. The land that shal receiue thee dying, in the same wil I die: and there wil I take a place for my burial. These thinges doe God to me, & these thinges adde he, if death onlie shal not separate me and thee."

Authorized Version: "Ruth said, Intreate mee not to leaue thee, *or* to returne from following after thee: for whither thou goest, I will goe; and where thou lodgest, I will lodge: thy people shall be my people, and thy God my God: Where thou diest, wil I die, and there will I bee buried: the Lord doe so to me, and more also, if *ought* but death part thee and me."

In addition to the preceding translational difficulties of a relatively superficial nature, there are those, more fundamental in character, arising either from inadequate scholarship or from limited literary perception. Many of these, in the course of centuries, have one by one been noted and partly eliminated.

Other basic textual misinterpretations were due, as we shall see, to deliberate infidelity of rendering, in devoted, if misguided, support of doctrinal orthodoxy. Typical of errors having their origin in insufficient knowledge is the mistranslation which, it seems, popularized the word *paradise* in our language. The verse [Genesis ii. 8] familiar to us in the Authorized Version, "And the LORD God planted a garden eastward in Eden," is a literal rendering directly from the Hebrew,gg and cannot conceivably be improved upon. The Douay Old Testament, in accordance with Roman practice, translates this verse not from the Hebrew but from the Vulgate, St. Jerome's reading,³⁴ in its turn, being at this point derived not from the Hebrew but from the Greek of the Septuagintal version. Instead of κῆπος, the customary Greek equivalent of the Hebrew גן [GAN — *garden*], the Septuagint here employs παράδεισον [paradeison — *a park*].hh In the Latin of the Vulgate this eastern word is simply transliterated as *paradisum*. So far there has been no mistranslation. The error occurs in the rendering of the accompanying word עדן ['ēDheN], which, though undoubtedly in this passage, as elsewhere, the name of a country,ii serves also to express the idea of pleasure or delight. Apparently indifferent to the geographical implications of the verse, the Vulgate seized upon the attributive interpretation of 'ēDheN to obtain *Paradisum voluptatis*, which, in its English form *paradise of pleasure* is incorrectly perpetuated in the Douay Version to this day. Furthermore, by allegorically straining the Hebrew *eastward* [מקדם — MiQQeDheM — *from the east*] to mean *from the beginning*, the Douay Old Testament produces the English reading, still current, "And the Lord God had planted a paradise of pleasure from the beginning."

Among translational errors which, like the preceding, are of no doctrinal significance, are some whose origin is the perceptive limitation of the translator rather than his grammatical, idio-

---

gg גן־בעדן מקדם [GAN BeʿēDheN MiQQeDheM].

hh A word of Persian origin thrice used in the New Testament, and found three times also in the late Hebrew form פרדס [PARDēs — *orchard, park*]. See Neh. ii. 8; Eccl. ii. 5; S. of S. iv. 13.

ii Gen. iv. 16: "the land of Nod, to the east of Eden."

matic or lexicographical inadequacy. A rendering may be above criticism as to syntax and vocabulary and still miss the precise shade of meaning originally intended. Distinctions which in speech can be delicately achieved by gesture, modulation of the voice, subtlety of emphasis, can be but faintly indicated, as every actor knows, in script. There are, of course, technical devices for just this purpose: italics, for example, or punctuation marks in general. In the Massoretic Text an effort in this direction has been made through the use of an intricate and subtle system of extra-linear marks known as accents. Insufficient attention to these accents has at times caused a translator to overlook that nuance of the original text without a rendering of which his version is a distortion. Probably best known of such mistranslations is that of the Authorized Version at Isaiah xl. 3: "The voice of him that crieth in the wilderness, Prepare ye the way of the LORD." It is not easy to relinquish this faulty interpretation of the Hebrew, the useful expression "a voice crying in the wilderness" having established for itself a proverbial flavor. But this voice, as the Revised Version by implication acknowledges, is of unspecified location; and, as the parallel clause of the verse clearly indicates, is properly that of someone crying, as the Revisers phrase it, "Prepare ye in the wilderness the way of the LORD, Make straight in the desert a high way for our God."[jj]

Another kind of subtle mistranslation is one in which, paradoxically enough, there is no flaw. The perfect fidelity, for

[jj] See C. K. Ogden and I. A. Richards, *The Meaning of Meaning*, 5th ed., New York, 1938, p. 224, note; also *Jewish Encyclopedia*, Vol. I, p. 158. The A. J. V. follows, with unimportant variants, the R. V. Its substitution, however, of "Hark! one calleth" for "A voice of him that cryeth," and a similar change at verse 6, are, in view of the M. T., highly questionable. Douay and A. V. are here practically identical. This faulty rendering is of ancient date, being found in the Greek of the four Gospels, each of which [Mt. iii. 3; Mk. i. 3; Lk. iii. 4; Jn. i. 23], presumably quoting from the Septuagint, perpetuates that Version's mistranslation of the Hebrew as φωνὴ βοῶντος ἐν τῇ ἐρήμῳ. The R. V., quite properly correcting the previous English rendering of the Hebrew of Isaiah, does not presume to correct this error of the Evangelists, whose adoption of the Septuagintal misreading is, accordingly, reflected in the Version of the Revisers, from which to this day one may still offer Biblical authority for "The voice of one crying in the wilderness." So, too, R. S. V.

instance, of the English versions to the Hebrew of Habakkuk
ii. 2 is their sole fault! At that verse we read in the Authorized
Version: "Write the vision, and make *it* plain upon tables, that
he may run that readeth it." Now that is exactly what the
Massoretic Text says.kk The Revisers, accordingly, finding
nothing wrong with it, let the previous reading stand. The
Douay Old Testament, a little more sensitive to the intention of
the original, renders the final clause: "that he that readeth it
may run over it." The American Jewish Version, likewise alert
to the essence of the writer's thought, but capturing it only at
the expense of the Hebrew, concludes the verse: "That a man
may read it swiftly." This is varied in Moffatt's Old Testament:
"that one may read it at a glance." None of these translations
hits the mark. It remained for two English poets, using the
substance of the verse under consideration entirely apart from
things Biblical, to discover just the turn of expression required
to make it a possession of the people. First Cowper in the eighteenth century, then Tennyson in the next,[11] gave to those words
of Habakkuk their ultimate English utterance: "he that runs
may read." Thus quoted from the poets, the statement so effectively conveys what is obviously the Prophet's meaning that it
has usurped the place, in popular idiom, of any translation of the
passage so far adopted in the English versions.

Of no doctrinal moment, again, is a nuance which, it has been
suggested,[35] escaped the translators at Genesis iii. 22. At that
verse, the Lord God, displeased that Adam should have dis-
obeyed his command not to eat of the tree of the knowledge of
good and evil, says in all English versions: "Behold the man is
become as one of us to know good and evil." This, in view of its
traditional vitality, is not likely to be modified; alternative
accentuation of this passage in the Massoretic reading, however,

kk M. T.: ‫למען ירוץ קורא בו‬.
[11] Cowper, *Tirocinium*, 79:   "Shine by the side of every path we tread
                                 With such a lustre, he that runs may read."
    Tennyson, *The Flower*, 17: "Read my little fable:
                                 He that runs may read."
Smith-Goodspeed approximates this with "That one may read it on the run."

permits a shift in the emphasis of the thought to produce the interesting variation: "Behold the man who hath been like one of us, is come to know good through evil."

Even so superb and universally accepted a translation as that of Micah's magnificent summation of man's duty [vi. 8] may have added to it an unexpected illumination by a subtle redirection of the emphasis. The Revisers, content — as who would not be? — with the rendering of the Authorized Version, change not a single jot or tittle of the threefold injunction: "He hath shewed thee, O man, what is good; and what doth the LORD require of thee, but to do justly, and to love mercy, and to walk humbly with thy God?" Unrivalled this; and perhaps it were well not to alter it! But once at least this phrasing has been tampered with — to its disadvantage; and it can, it would seem, be revised — to its improvement. The alteration, in the American Jewish Version, though superficially slight, is essentially unfortunate:

> "It hath been told thee, O man, what is good,
> And what the LORD doth require of thee:
> Only to do justly, and to love mercy, and to walk
> humbly with thy God."

This reading, it will be observed, differs considerably from its predecessors: in a punctuation and a transposition of words which transform a rhetorically effective interrogation into a declarative statement; in a substitution of the dissyllabic *only* for the rhythmically more satisfying monosyllable *but*; and in the questionable elimination of "He hath shewed" — an active form of the verb with a personal subject — in favor of an impersonal and passive construction, "It hath been told."[mm] These modifications of the English interpretation, even if the foregoing objections be waived, produce a reading which, like that of the Authorized Version, takes insufficiently into account

---

[mm] M. T.: הגיד לך אדם. The inexact rendering of the *Hiph'il* here employed of נגד as if it were a *Hoph'al* with passive significance is the less acceptable because of the availability of אדם [*man*] as a subject of the clause. Note its use as such in the suggested reading which follows.

the relation of our passage to that which precedes it. The context here, if the reading is to be improved, must not for a moment be forgotten. The Prophet, in the preceding lines, has been leading up to his main thrust by the typical device of heaping question upon question: "Wherewith shall I come before the Lord . . .? Shall I come before him with burnt offerings . . .? Shall I give my firstborn for my transgression, the fruit of my body for the sin of my soul?" Burnt-offerings, of course, of "calves of a year old," of "thousands of rams," were only less subject to prophetic denunciation than the sacrifice, such as Abraham himself had been ready to perform, of the fruit of the body, one's first-born child. These practices Micah, if no one else in his time, deemed evil. They were institutions, as he well knew, not of God but of men. These things were said to be good *by men,* even by priests who knew not the requirements of the Lord. These things were surely evil in His sight. With what, then, shall man worship his God? Micah, accordingly, putting himself in the place of all men, asks and then answers their question: "Wherewith shall I come before the LORD . . .? Shall I give my firstborn for my transgression, the fruit of my body for the sin of my soul?

> *Man* hath told thee that this is good;
> But what doth *the LORD* require of thee
> But to do justly, and to love mercy, **and to walk** humbly with thy God?" [3] [6]

In like manner, the twenty-eighth chapter of Job, misleading as it is in the King James Version, can be relieved of its obscurity and endowed with an unmistakable and superb meaning by reading *man* rather than the vague pronoun *he* as the unexpressed subject of the verb in verse three: "Man setteth an end to darkness." This rendering, first adopted by the Revised Version, is paralleled by the American Jewish Version. In the Micah passage just examined, a word for *man* is immediately available in the Massoretic Text, and the translator need merely abandon its previous use as a vocative and employ it as a subject; here, however, no explicit mention of *man* occurs in the Hebrew until verse thirteen: "Man [אנוש] knoweth not the price thereof."

But the idea of man's industry is implicit throughout this part of the poem.[nn] It is man — not God — who (in his mining operations) breaketh open a shaft, who hangs afar from men and swings to and fro, who knows a path unseen by falcon and untrod by the fierce lion, who putteth forth his hand upon the flinty rock, who seeth every precious thing and bringeth it forth to light. These things can man do. But *wisdom* — can man by overturning mountains discover her abode; and by cutting out what channels among the rocks shall man come upon the place of understanding? Thus interpreted, this magnificent poem comes vividly to life. Wisdom? God — not man — knoweth the place thereof; and unto man God saith: "Behold, the fear of the LORD, that is wisdom; And to depart from evil is understanding." [37]

Unacceptable readings in the Bible, resulting from no insufficiency of scholarship or of literary perceptiveness but from purposeful infidelity of translation, silently testify to the questionable devotion with which orthodoxies are sometimes sustained. Luther, for an early example, in his translation of Romans iii. 28 — "... a man is justified by faith apart from the works of the law" — emphasized the idea of justification by faith by inserting an extraneous word, *alone*, for which, as he well knew and freely admitted, there was no equivalent in the original Greek.[oo] This he defended as a necessary device to bring out clearly the exact meaning which he, if none other, read into the Apostle Paul's words. [38] In this, of course, he was not followed by the Douay Bible or the King James Version.

The Authorized Version, in its turn, at Hebrews x. 23, sanctioned the deliberate mistranslation "Let us hold fast the

[nn] Current editions of the Douay Version, though recognizing this point by the insertion of a Chapter summary ("Man's industry searcheth out many things. True wisdom is taught by God alone."), retain in this Chapter the equivocal, and poetically inferior, readings of the seventeenth century. *V. supra*, p. 101.

[oo] Luther: "So halten wir es nun, dass der Mensch gerecht werde ohne des Gesetzes Werke, *allein* durch den Glauben." Greek: λογιζόμεθα οὖν δικαιοῦσθαι πίστει ἄνθρωπον χωρὶς ἔργων νόμου.

profession of our faith," the rendering of which, in the Rheims New Testament, the Revised Version, and the Revised Standard Version, is correctly given as ". . . confession of our hope."[pp] The scholars appointed by King James to revise the earlier versions were, as a matter of fact, not entirely free. The King, it appears, had certain orthodoxies of his own which he enjoined upon his translators. To his way of thinking, the word *congregation*, properly employed by both Tyndale and Coverdale to render ἐκκλησία, reveals too clearly the democratic tone of the assemblies of the early Christians. James, accordingly, insisted that the less accurate translation *church*, previously adopted by the Bishops for their version of 1568, be adhered to.[qq] This royal preference, respected even in the Revised Version, is the more firmly established because of its association with many Biblical passages whose cadences gratify the ear.

Intentional departure from the Greek or Hebrew text is likewise found in the Rheims-Douay Bible. This Version, produced, as the Rheims *Preface* says, "for the more speedy abolishing of a number of false and impious translations put forth by sundry sectes," is no less polemical than its Anglican rivals. In the New Testament, for instance, it replaces *repentance* — the proper translation of μετάνοια — with *penance*;[39] and, where the sacramental doctrine suggests it, substitutes *chalice* for *cup* as the rendering of ποτήριον.[rr] In the Old Testament it regularly insists, in contravention of Jewish cosmological teaching, upon rendering שׁאוּל [šeʾôL] not by *grave* or *pit*, as in the Authorized Version and Revised Version, but by *hell*.[ss] At Job xix. 25,

---

[pp] T. R.: κατέχωμεν τὴν ὁμολογίαν τῆς ἐλπίδος ἀκλινῆ. Goodspeed turns this into "the hope that we profess."

[qq] In the sole instance in the N. T. [Acts xiii. 43] where *congregation* occurs, it is a translation of συναγωγή.

[rr] *Cf.* Mt. xx. 22; Mk. x. 39; Lk. xxii. 20. In Ps. xxiii, also, where A. V. reads [v. 5] "my cup runneth over," Douay [1914 rev. ed.] renders: "my chalice which inebriateth me, how goodly it is!" Knox renders: *cup*.

[ss] *Cf.* Gen. xxxvii. 35; Job vii. 9; *et al.* To this, in current editions of Douay O. T., there are two exceptions: Job xvii. 16, *pit*; and, remarkably, Hos. xiii. 14, *death*. The A. V., deliberately inconsistent in this matter — see its

in company with the Authorized Version, it translates גאלי [GO'ALI]ᵗᵗ *my Redeemer*, a controversial reading which — though recognized by Jewish scholars since the time of Saadya as a reference, here, to a Defender other than God, and replaced accordingly in the Revised Version, and by J. M. Powis Smith in his *American Translation*, by *my Vindicator* — is retained by the American Jewish Version.

An even more tendentious mistranslation in which the Rheims New Testament and the Authorized and Revised Versions concur, repeated three times in the Gospel according to John and employed once in the first Johannine Epistle, is the expression "only begotten Son."[40] This locution occurs in no other Book of the New Testament. It is a faulty rendering of the Greek μονογενής, the use of which by both Aquila and Symmachus as the equivalent of the Hebrew word for *only* [יחיד — YAḤIDh] — by which Isaac, son of Abraham, is thrice designated in the Book of Genesis — sufficiently indicates its proper interpretation. Isaac, as one learns from the twenty-fifth chapter of Genesis, was at no time the only son of his father, being not even the first to be born of Abraham's numerous progeny. His denomination as *only son*, accordingly, can have meant nothing other than *favorite*, *dear*, *beloved*, and was so understood by the Septuagintal translators who rendered YAḤIDh, here and elsewhere,[41] by the very word ἀγαπητός, which is used in the New Testament at each passage where, in the English versions, Jesus is referred to as "*beloved* Son."[42] At two of the several places in the Old Testament, where the Septuagint translates YAḤIDh by ἀγαπητός,[43] both the Authorized and Revised Versions are impelled to make use of the unequivocal word *darling*.ᵘᵘ The Greek

---

Preface — makes use also of *hell*, but only in the Prophets. The A. S. V. consistently employs only *sheol*.

ᵗᵗ This participial form of the verb גאל is translated, in the A. V., thirteen times as *avenger* or *revenger*, and fourteen times as *redeemer*. Moffatt: *One to champion me*.

ᵘᵘ The A. J. V. abides here by *only one*. Douay, following the Vulgate, which renders μονογενής by *unicus*, also retains *only one*. This, however natural

μονογενής, moreover, is used not only by Aquila and Symmachus but also, before them, by Josephus to express something
other than uniqueness; for in his *Antiquities of the Jews*[44] he
makes use of this word in referring to Izates — whose mother,
as Josephus reports, had previously born another male child —
as the only-begotten, that is the favorite, the *best beloved* son of
his father.[vv] A like usage is found, again with reference to Isaac,
in the Epistle to the Hebrews [xi. 17]. It would appear, then,
that the current literal interpretation *only begotten* is a far cry
from the Scriptural authors' original intention, and, as one
commentator discreetly puts it,[45] "might be discontinued with
advantage." Well established ecclesiastical tradition, it might
once have been assumed, would have duly tempered any im-
pulse to carry out this suggestion; yet *only begotten* has been
abandoned not only by Goodspeed and Moffatt but by the less
untraditional Revised Standard Version.

Confirmed patterns of thinking continue to be influential
in discouraging scholarly modification of other theologically
crucial passages. The translators of the King James Version
were somewhat restricted, as we have seen, by the predilections
of their monarch; but royal prescription such as James could
dictate, irksome perhaps to some of his scholars, was less exacting
than the tyrannical compulsion, unfelt as such, of immemorial
Christian custom. To this influence, of course, the Jacobean
Hebraists and Hellenists were no more subject than were their
contemporaries, the learned Churchmen at Rheims and Douai,
or their successors of the nineteenth century, the scholarly theologians who produced the Revised Version. This influence, as

---

an interpretation of the Latin, is not obligatory; for *unicus* is used in other than
its primary sense *unique*; see Plautus, *Captivi*, I. 147 and 150, where the word is
applied by Hegio to *one* of his two sons. In English, also, this use of *only* to
indicate endearment rather than uniqueness may be seen in *The Comedy of
Errors*, V. 1. 309, where Ægeon speaks of one of his two sons as his *only* son.
This semantic extension of the word is implicit in such an expression as "I
love you only."

[vv] So, too, in Syr. S., Jn. iii. 18: τοῦ ἐκλεκτοῦ υἱοῦ τοῦ θεοῦ.

one would naturally expect, inevitably determined the hermeneutical sustenance to be sought in Scripture; and established,
with a flavor of finality, the one authoritative interpretation of
those crucial passages in the Old Testament the meaning of
which is disputed by Synagogue and Church. Exegetical decision, arrived at by ecclesiastical wisdom and fortified by popular
sanction, found prompt confirmation in Biblical translation.
Nowhere is this powerful influence more in evidence than at
Isaiah vii. 14, which, identical in the Douay and King James
Versions, achieves the superb English form: "Behold, a virgin
shall conceive, and bear a son . . . " A careful comparison of
this familiar reading of the "Messianic Prophecy" with its variants in other Bibles, English, Hebrew, and Greek, reveals at
least three features of this fragment of the sacred text in the
rendering of which the translators were obviously subject to
their particular cultural heritage. These three features, in the
order in which they are here considered, are the indefinite
article, the tense of the verbs, and the word *virgin*.

The word here translated *virgin* occurs just four times in the
Hebrew Old Testament — at Isaiah vii. 14 and Genesis xxiv. 43
with the definite article, and twice, in the Song of Songs, without
it. At the passage in Genesis, the Douay, King James, and Revised
Versions scrupulously concur with the American Jewish Version
in preserving the definite article *the* of the original. At the
passage in Isaiah, however, despite the identical use, in the
Hebrew, of this word with the definite article [העלמה — HA-
'ALMAH], and in face of the fact that Matthew, in quoting [διὰ
τοῦ προφήτου] this verse, carefully put the definite article into
his Greek,[ww] the Douay, King James, and Revised Versions —
these three — unscrupulously abandon fidelity to the original

---

[ww] M. T.: הנה העלמה הרה וילדת בן. Mt. i. 23: Ἰδού, ἡ παρθένος ἐν γαστρὶ
ἕξει [א, A, Q; λήψεται, B], καὶ τέξεται υἱόν. This article [ἡ] is rightly retained in the King James and Revised N. T., but, in bland disregard of the
Evangelist's Greek, is changed to the indefinite article *a* in the R. S. V. and
in the Rheims N. T., the latter to conform, presumably, with the Douay
reading of Isaiah. Westminster Version and Msgr. Knox: the virgin. Weymouth, Moffatt and Goodspeed: the maiden.

and replace the definite article with the indefinite form *a*.[xx]
The American Jewish Version correctly retains the definite
article of the Massoretic Text.

Correct, too, is the use of the future tense — with the identical
phraseology, "shall conceive, and bear a son" — of the Douay,
Authorized, and American Jewish Versions. Both of the verbs
in the translation by Matthew of this passage from Isaiah, it
will be observed, are likewise correctly in the future. The
Revised Version, with scant justification, turns these futures into
the present tense: "is with child, and beareth a son." This
highly questionable procedure has the merit — as some would
think — of obliterating the prophetic character of the verse,
and may have been so intended; that end could have been more
happily attained had not the weight of custom prevailed upon
the Revisers with respect to the word *virgin*.

Tradition with respect to this crucial word is of long standing.
Toward the close of the second century Irenaeus, in complaining
that the translations of Aquila and Theodotion failed at Isaiah
vii. 14 to conform to Christian doctrine, calls attention to the
fact that these early revisers of the Septuagint had rendered
the Hebrew עלמה by a Greek word [νεᾶνις] meaning young
woman or *maiden*, and even, in Euripides, a young *married* woman.
In the translation made by Symmachus, apparently unknown
to Irenaeus,[46] this same word, νεᾶνις, which does not mean
virgin, is employed. Matthew's word, παρθένος, although without doubt invested with the meaning *virgin*, is also used to signify
merely a *young woman*, a *maiden*. The authors of the Douay Old
Testament found it within their dogma to render the underlying עלמה, at both of its occurrences in the Song of Songs, by
maidens, to which, in each instance, with a charming nicety of
perception, they prefixed the extra-textual but appropriate at-

---

[xx] The legitimate disapproval by Jewish scholars of this disregard of syntactical accuracy is undermined by the authors of the A. J. V. who, at S. of
S. i. 3, conversely insert the definite article where none occurs in the M. T. —
a needless imitation of the mistaken R. V. and A. V. Douay here correctly
omits this article. At S. of S. vi. 8 all four Versions accurately follow the M. T.
in using the indefinite article.

tribute *young*. In Genesis and Isaiah, however, in accordance with the teaching of the Church,[47] Douay makes use of *virgin*. The King James scholars hewed to the line with *virgin* in all four passages. The Revisers, enlightened but apparently a little torn, compromised by departing from their predecessors with *maiden* in Genesis, and by retaining *virgin(s)* both in the Song of Songs, where it is of no doctrinal moment, and in Isaiah where its employment is theologically crucial. The compulsion of tradition is strong. The Smith-Goodspeed translation successfully eludes this cultural influence, as does Moffatt, with "a young woman" (is) with child. In the American Jewish Version, as one might expect, *virgin* is nowhere to be found. In Isaiah this Version gives us, with entire propriety, "*the young woman shall conceive, and bear a son*"; and in the remaining three places it can certainly not be condemned for its consistent use of *maiden(s)*.

The translation of this controversial passage, as it appears in the Douay and King James Bibles, gives no indication of any uncertainty which may have troubled some of the scholars responsible for these two Versions; nor was there, apparently, any doubt in the mind of their contemporary, Giovanni Diodati, who though employing *vergine* at Genesis xxiv. 16 and *la fanciulla* at Genesis xxiv. 43 in his Italian translation of 1603, scrupulously renders the Hebrew of Isaiah vii. 14 by *la giovane*. As this verse from Isaiah appears in Spanish, however, in the "Ferrara Bible" of half a century earlier, it clearly reveals the perplexity under which the sponsors of that celebrated version labored. Of the Ferrara Bible there was printed but a single edition.[yy]

[yy] *Biblia en Lengua Española, Traduzida Palabra por Palabra de la Verdad Hebrayca por Muy Excellentes Letrados, etc.*, Ferrara, 1553. In-folio. This volume, though often referred to as the first Spanish Version of the Old Testament, is, in reality, a revision of an earlier translation made in 1422 for the Duke of Alba. The common opinion that there were two editions — one for Jews, the other for Christians — is without justification. There were, however, two impressions, probably run off concurrently, one of which, a handsome volume, was on large paper. The variant renderings here recorded are common to both impressions, bibliographical features of which are examined by the present writer in a study now in preparation.

This edition is remarkable for several features, one of them being that at Isaiah vii. 14 the individual copies so vary among themselves as to exhibit three different readings. Two of these variants are, without question, successive corrections of the original setting-up made while the sheet [Z⁸; folio 186] was passing through the press. Which of these three readings was the original and in what sequence the two alterations were made, are interesting points which bibliographic examination may never fully determine. In any case, the reading of some copies — destined, it was formerly supposed, for Christian consumption — is that *a virgin shall conceive and bear a son*; in other copies *virgen* is replaced with *moça*, the uncompromising vernacular for *maiden*; and in still others — designed, some have maintained, for Jewish purchasers — the doctrinal difficulty is surmounted simply by transliterating the Hebrew העלמה into ornate capitals as *la A L M A.*[zz] The Spanish translators' perplexity, and the threefold Ferraran solution, must have been known to the scholarly servants of King James; for their leader, Lancelot Andrews, dean of Westminster, once owned, and annotated, a magnificent copy of the large-paper impression.[aaa]

At another disputed passage in Isaiah [ix. 6], not only the Ferrara Bible but also the American Jewish Version has recourse to transliteration. The Authorized Version renders this verse, with definite articles not found in the Hebrew,[bbb] as follows: "and his name shall be called Wonderful, Counsellor, The mighty God, The everlasting Father, The Prince of Peace." Douay varies this to read: "and his name shall be called, Wonderful, Counsellor, God the Mighty, the Father of the world to

[zz] Observe the definite article. Unfortunately for the theory of separate editions for Jews and Christians, each of these three readings is found in that portion of the edition which was dedicated to the Christian Duke of Ferrara, and likewise in the remainder dedicated to the wealthy Jewish patron of Arts and Letters, Doña Gracia Nasi. See Cecil Roth, in *Modern Language Review*, xxxviii, 307 ff.

[aaa] Andrews' volume, untrimmed, and in its original calf binding, is now at Pembroke College, Cambridge [I. 3. 18]. It reads la A L M A and is dedicated to Ferrara.

[bbb] M. T.: ויקרא שמו פלא יועץ אל גבור אבי־עד שר־שלום.

come, the Prince of Peace." In the Revised Version the definite articles are rightly omitted, and the punctuation is slightly modified to produce: "and his name shall be called Wonderful Counsellor, Mighty God, Everlasting Father, Prince of Peace." The Ferrara Bible, apparently without variants of any kind, puts all of this passage, and its intrusive articles, into the vernacular, except the two last controversial words which are transliterated.[ccc] The American Jewish Version, shifting to the present tense, and exploiting the Ferraran hint to the utmost, disfigures its text with an unparalleled transliteration[ddd] the intention of which it immediately counteracts by a marginal translation: "Wonderful in counsel is God the Mighty, the Everlasting Father, the Ruler of peace." Retention of the extraneous definite articles in this rendering is conceivably an unconscious tribute to the influence of the Authorized Version, but there can be nothing unconscious about the substitution of that unalliterative *Ruler* for the esthetically superior, lexicographically justified,[eee] but theologically tinged *Prince*. This, like the preceding reading from Isaiah, illuminates the misrepresentation of connotative values likely to inhere in a translation which abides by interpretations of a purely informative character; and, conversely, the potential falsification of denotative values in a translation controlled by influences predominantly emotional. Jewish theologians, traditionally free from any authoritative interpretation of the Scriptural text, are, it would appear, no more liberated than their colleagues of other faiths from the unfelt fetters of their cultural heritage. This comfortable bondage, like that of their neighbors — for whom occasionally, by their own admission,[48] "tradition and associations were too strong" — manifests itself, as doctrine compels, at crucial passages throughout the American Jewish Version.

[ccc] Ferrara: y llamo su nombre el marauilloso el consejero el Dio barragan el padre eterno Sar Salom.

[ddd] A. J. V.: "and his name is called Pele-joez-el-gibbor-Abi-ad-sar-shalom."

[eee] שר [sar] is rendered by *prince* about 200 times in the A. V.; by *ruler* only 22 times.

CHAPTER IX

The Higher Criticism

"It was said by them of old time, ... but I say unto you ... "
Matthew v. 21, *et al.*

INFORMED evaluation of the Bible, as of any ancient literary monument, is dependent upon an understanding of several inherent difficulties over and above those, essentially textual in nature, with which as we have seen, the translator is unavoidably concerned. Attempted solution of these additional Biblical problems has been known, ever since invention of the inauspicious designation late in the eighteenth century, [1] as "the Higher Criticism." More difficult in some respects than textual analysis, certainly broader in scope, higher criticism undertakes to determine, for each Book of the Bible, its author or authors, its sources and literary structure, the time and place of its composition, the resolution of its inconsistencies, its original intention and subsequent use, and, in general, the literary implications of its historical or cultural references.

Inquiry with such ends as these in view, startling though it appeared when first directed toward Scripture, is, of course, standard procedure in literary study. Orthodox Elizabethan scholarship, for example, does not blanch at the evidence that Fletcher wrote portions of Shakespeare's *Henry the Eighth*; recognizes with satisfaction the Danish, Italian and Latin sources respectively of *Hamlet*, *Othello* and *The Comedy of Errors*; triumphs in the demonstration, made within recent years, that a quarto edition of *The Merchant of Venice*,[2] dated on its title-page 1600, was actually printed in 1619; discovers in Prince Hamlet's age a problem no less baffling than that of Jehoiachin who, only eight years old according to the Chronicler [II Chr. xxxvi. 9] when he ascended the throne of Judah, is recorded in the Book of Kings [II Kgs. xxiv. 8] to have begun his reign at the age of eighteen; and freely admits that throughout the plays of the now established Shakespeare canon there are passages "which — from whatever cause —" as Driver says of the Books of Samuel, "defy, or elude, explanation."[3] Even false attribution of authorship — now a commonplace of Biblical criticism — has been demonstrated, for instance, in *Vortigern*, successfully palmed off for a time as Shakespeare's by the late eighteenth-century forger William Ireland; in the *Poems* assigned by Macpherson to "Ossian"; and, to return to ecclesiastical illustration, in the spurious *Donation* of Constantine — upon which papal pretension to temporal power was subsequently based — a notable document which, long credited to the first Christian Emperor, has been proved an eighth-century forgery.[4]

Application to the Biblical Books of established methods of literary criticism — a development, strictly speaking, of the eighteenth century — was more than once anticipated, early in the Common Era, especially with respect to considerations of date of composition and authorship. Anonymity being the rule, rather than as now the exception, among writers of antiquity,[a] identification of the original author of an ancient composition was a matter of no great assurance. The Gospel according to Matthew provides Biblical illustration of this literary uncertainty by attributing to Jeremiah a passage generally assigned to Zechariah.[b] Origen, repeatedly writing as if he accepted the

---

[a] In the O. T., Jonah and the eighteen Books from Genesis through Job are anonymous; in the N. T., the Gospels, Acts, Hebrews, I, II, III John. Pseudonymity is apparent in Song of Songs and II Peter, and the uncanonical Epistle of Jeremiah.

[b] Cp. Mt. xxvii. 9 and Zech. xi. 12, 13.

Pauline authorship of the Epistle to the Hebrews, is yet ingenuous enough to confess, in words none too circumspect,[c] that "God knows" who wrote that anonymous communication to first-century Christians of Jewish heritage. Determination of the identity of Biblical authors is further impeded by ascription of anonymous work, for the purpose presumably of securing a hearing, to some reverenced personality — king, prophet or law-giver — long since dead. A tradition of authorship, originating in this common practice, succumbs but slowly, if at all, to corrective evidence marshalled by later generations.

Traditional attribution of authorship, more characteristic of the Old Testament than the New, is recognized for the first time by Jewish scholars, so far as is known, in the fifth-century *Babylonian Talmud*,[5] which, in answer to the question, "Who wrote the Books of the Bible?" supplies (probably from a second-century *Baraita*) the following detailed answer: "Moses wrote his own book, and the section about Balaam and Job. Joshua wrote his own book and [the last] eight verses of the Pentateuch. Samuel wrote his own book and the books of Judges and Ruth. David wrote the book of Psalms by the ten venerable elders, Adam the first man, Melchezedek [see Ps. cx. 4], Abraham, Moses, Heman, Jeduthun, Asaph, and the three sons of Korah. Jeremiah wrote his own book, the books of Kings, and Lamentations. Hezekiah and his friends [see Prov. xxv. 1] wrote Isaiah, Proverbs, Song of Songs, and Ecclesiastes. The men of the Great Synagogue wrote Ezekiel, the Twelve [Minor Prophets], Daniel and Esther. Ezra wrote his own book and continued the genealogies of the books of Chronicles down to his own time . . . . But who completed them? Nehemiah ben Hachaliah."

Talmudic tradition, it will be observed, while at one with modern scholarship in denying to Moses the account [Deut. xxxiv. 5–12] of his death, accepts without question as Joshua's

---

[c] Τίς δὲ ὁ γράψας τὴν Ἐπιστολὴν, τὸ μὲν ἀληθὴς Θεὸς οἶδεν. Ex *Origenis homiliis in Epistolam ad Hebræos*, Migne, *Patrologiæ Cursus Completus, Series Græca Prior*, Tom. XIV, col. 1309. The Epistle to the Hebrews has been variously assigned to SS. Luke, Clement and Barnabas, to Apollos, and within recent years to Priscilla, wife of Aquila (*cf.* Acts xviii. 2, *et al.*).

the record [Josh. xxiv. 29] of his own burial in mount Ephraim, and casts no doubt on Samuel's ability to chronicle historical events subsequent to his yielding up the ghost [I Sam. xxv. 1] and being gathered unto his people. Multiple authorship of the Psalms, it should be noted, is here — as in the Psalms themselves — expressly conceded.[d] Untraditional though the attribution be of the late, post-exilic[6] Song of Songs — "which is Solomon's" — to King Hezekiah and his unspecified friends of the eighth century B. C., this unorthodox opinion is unfortunately no more conclusive than Talmudic denial of authorship to Ezekiel is warranted.[e] Discovery, it is seen, that the Book of Isaiah is the work of more than one writer, one of whom lived long after Hezekiah's reign and knew the Babylonian captivity,[7] was a critical revelation withheld from the Talmudists, the first to question the literary integrity of the Isaianic prophecies — to anticipate — being that same Ibn Ezra of the twelfth century who cryptically intimated his doubt of Mosaic authorship of portions of the Pentateuch with veiled allusions to inconsistencies, mainly historical, within the Biblical text.[f] The caution

[d] The "Davidic" Psalms, like the Proverbs of Solomon, before being gathered together into canonical Books, circulated in several independent collections, the literary product of many men, and the reflection of various epochs in the history of Israel from the tenth pre-Christian century to post-exilic times. *Cf.* S. R. Driver, *Introduction to the Literature of the Old Testament*, 9th ed., rev., Edinburgh, 1913, p. 377, and W. E. Addis in *Studies in the Synoptic Problem* (ed. W. Sanday), Oxford, 1911, p. 383.

[e] "If any book bears the impress of its author's hand, both in matter and arrangement, it is the Book of Ezekiel; and yet it is said here [*Baba Bathra* 14[b]] to have been 'written' [כתב] by members of a body which (*ex hypothesi*) did not come into existence till many years after the author's death." (Driver, *op. cit.*, pp. viii and ix).

[f] *Cf.* William Rosenau, *Jewish Biblical Commentators*, Baltimore, 1906, p. 86. Ibn Ezra's Biblical criticism, admitting the assimilation of Scriptural glosses, included the observations that Dan, mentioned at Gen. xiv. 14, could not have been known to a writer of Moses' time, that place-name having been given the city formerly called Laish in the much later period of Judges xviii. 29; that the statement, "the Canaanite was then in the land," of Gen. xii. 6, *et al.*, reveals an author aware of the post-Mosaic conquest of Canaan; and — this with profuse professions of regard for orthodox teachings — that to linguistic differences of frequent occurrence in the O. T. must be attributed the variants between the two versions of the Decalogue.

which Synagogal and Church tradition imposed upon Ibn Ezra in the medieval period was not felt in the third century by the neo-Platonist philosopher Porphyry, whose contention — foreshadowing an established conclusion of latter-day criticism — that the Book of Daniel was produced, not, as traditionally maintained, during the Jewish captivity in Babylon, but four centuries thereafter in the time of the Maccabees,[8] entirely escaped either the notice or the acceptance of the Talmudic authors.[g]

Toward the close of the fourth century, or early in the fifth, that greatest of Latin Fathers, Augustine (like Porphyry originally a neo-Platonist, but later, as Bishop of Hippo, an orthodox Churchman, subject, as Porphyry had never been, to theological discipline), was able to persuade himself that difficulties of authorship and date created in the Biblical record by phrases such as "Beforetime in Israel" or the recurrent "unto this day" — which, in the eleventh century invited the critical attention of Joseph Qara,[h] and, in the seventeenth, aroused the suspicion of Hobbes — could be overcome through an intellectual dexterity such as he, master of the art of rhetoric, could readily command and was willing to exercise. To him, and to those who are able to accept the subtleties of Augustine's reasoning, the Biblical historian who reports that the twelve stones set up by Joshua are still there in the midst of Jordan "unto this day" was not necessarily writing at a time considerably after Joshua's memorial pile had been erected;[9] nor to him was the conclusion inescapable that the Deuteronomic author, speaking of the sepulchre of Moses as unknown "unto this day," lived at a period subsequent to the lifetime of Moses. Augustine, delighting like other theologically determined commentators, in exegetical

[g] Porphyry's contention did not escape the notice, nor did it gain the approval, of Jerome, who cites it merely for the purpose of refutation in his commentary on Daniel (*Opera*, ed. Vallarsi, Vol. V, 619 ff.).

[h] Qara, because of I Sam. ix. 9, assigned the writing of Samuel to a later date than the traditional (*v. supra*, p. 252). *Cf.* Wilhelm Bacher, *Die Jüdische Bibelexegese vom Anfange des zehnten bis zum Ende des fünfzehnten Jahrhunderts*, Trier, 1892, p. 40.

ingenuity, and prepared, as were the authors of the *Midrashim*[i]
to exploit it as need required, unintentionally betrays his want
of confidence in the results obtained through his mental adroit-
ness by vilification of those who, failing to share his uncompromising interpretation, insist upon "heretical" admission of
textual incongruities.[10] Examination of historical discrepancies
revealed by expressions of which "unto this day" is representative, were acceptable and inoffensive to theologians of Church
and Synagogue just so long as they challenged neither the
ultimate infallibility of Scripture nor the capacity of the Doctors
of theology successfully to reconcile all apparent inconsistencies
of Holy Writ.

Unacceptable and offensive, accordingly, were many of the
opinions of Theodore, bishop of Mopsuestia in Cilicia, Augustine's able contemporary and his opponent in vital matters of
doctrine. Most modern in critical approach to the Bible of all
patristic writers, Theodore, in contrast to the Bishop of Hippo,
insisted, like the later scholar Saadya, upon adherence to the
literal, primary meaning of the Scriptures — the Pešaṭ [פשט],
as Jewish exegetes term it — and recognition of the historical
circumstances under which they were written. One of the
consequences of this insistence was Theodore's rejection of the
historical validity of the titles of the Psalms, and his anticipation
of the modern position that a portion of the Psalter is of Maccabean origin.[11]

Five centuries after Theodore of Mopsuestia offered his
pattern of rationalistic Bible criticism to fellow Churchmen,
Saadya,[j] at the Academy of Sura in Babylonia, instituted a

---

[i] The *Midrashim* [מדרשים — MIDRAŠIM], in their traditionalist, allegorical
interpretations [*Midrash Haggadah*] of the O. T. for moralizing or edifying ends,
exemplify, in the Synagogue, that Catholic *Regula Fidei* which rejects as
erroneous any explanation of Scripture contradictory to established doctrine
of the Church.

[j] Saadya ben Joseph [A. D. 892–942, *v. infra*, p. 321, note 15] whose
principal work was a translation of the O. T. into Arabic, flourished at a
period of developing Biblical criticism by scholars of the three dominant faiths.
Preceding him by half a century, Photius [c. A. D. 820–891], patriarch of

similar critical method, which, new to the world of Jewish
scholars, would have seemed familiar to Theodore except for
its improved philological foundation. Saadya's untraditional
interpretation — restricting itself, fortunately for its acceptance
by Jewish scholars, to a Scriptural exegesis strictly compatible
with his belief in the Divine inspiration of the Old Testament
Books and the verity of their miracles — introduced a Jewish
exegetical rationalism which, though undeveloped by his associates in the Orient, found fruition in the contributions of learned
Jews of Spain, foremost of whom was the linguistic scholar
Ibn Janaḥ,[12] and, subsequently, in the commentaries of Rashi
and his fellow-exegetes of northern France. Rashi [A. D. 1040–
1105], removed from Saadya a century and a half in time, and
the length of the Mediterranean world in space, rejected those
explanations from traditional rabbinical literature which he

Constantinople, addressed some three hundred questions concerning points
of Biblical difficulty, and his answers, to Amphilochius, archbishop of Cyzicus
[Migne, *Patr. Gr.*, Vol. CI], including one on the structure of Isaiah. Following
Saadya by a century, Rabbi Isaac of Toledo [A. D. 982–1057] came to the
conclusion that Gen. xxxvi. 31 — "before there reigned any king over . . .
Israel" — could not have been written prior to the time of Saul [*Ency. Brit.*,
11th ed., IX. 580]; and Ibn Ḥazm [A. D. 994–1064], the Islamic scholar of
Cordova, applying to Scripture the method of literal interpretation, pointed
out, in his *magnum opus*, *Faṣl, etc.* [Cairo, 5 vols., 1317–1321 A. H. (A. D.
1899–1903)], "difficulties in the biblical narratives which disturbed no other
minds till the rise of higher criticism." [Philip K. Hitti, *The History of the
Arabs*, 2nd ed., rev., London, 1940, p. 558]. Professor Hitti, in a private communication, kindly contributes, in illustration of the Muslim scholar's method,
the information that at p. 122 of Vol. I of *Faṣl* (ed. Cairo 1347–1348 A. H.),
Ibn Ḥazm computes the years of Israel's sojourn in Egypt to be less by an
even hundred than the 430 years given at Ex. xii. 40; that, at p. 18 of Vol. II,
he indicates contradictions at Mt. v. 17, 27, 28, 31, *seq.* in the statements of
Jesus; and that, at pp. 18–19 of Vol. II, in discussing the parable of the Mustard
Seed [Mt. xiii. 31, 32], he observes that the Evangelist must have been completely ignorant of agriculture, for, he writes, "We saw the mustard plant
ourselves; we also knew others who had seen it in distant countries. Yet we
never saw nor were we told by those who had seen anything of the plant that
a bird could dwell on it." [*Cf.* Israel Friedlander, *The Heterodoxies of the Shiites
according to Ibn Ḥazm*, New Haven, 1909, p. 14]. See further, M. Perlmann,
in *Proceedings of the American Academy for Jewish Research*, XVIII (1949), pp.
269 ff., and H. Hirschfeld in *Jewish Quarterly Review*, Vol. 13, pp. 222 ff.

was unable to reconcile with the literal significance of the Scriptural text. Most widely acclaimed of medieval Jewish commentators, this scholar of Troyes, quietly dissociating himself from *Midrashic* exposition of the Hebrew Bible, consistently accommodated his exegesis to the Talmudic doctrine that the Old Testament, in its every verse, may be read only with respect for its primary textual meaning. Rashi's outspoken grandson, Rashbam [Rabbi Samuel ben Meïr], reinforced this unorthodox position with his insistence that allegorical interpretation of Holy Writ was worthy of preservation only if it harmonized with the literal sense of the Hebrew text; and his illustrious contemporary, Ibn Ezra, with opinions such as those previously mentioned, continued the rationalist trend in Biblical criticism which, so far as medieval Jewish learning is concerned, culminated, toward the close of the twelfth century, with the recognition by Joseph Bekhor Shor that there are duplicate accounts in the Pentateuch, [13] and with the avowal both by David Kimchi at Narbonne, and at Cairo by the Spanish Aristotelian, Moses Maimonides, that certain of the Scriptural narratives, visionary in nature, were historically unsubstantial. [14]

Jewish Scriptural exegesis, decadent in the centuries after Maimonides, not only reverted to the ancient method of allegorical interpretation, but declined further into irrationalism through the mysticism of the *Cabala*,[k] particularly as it found expression in the *Zohar*;[l] Christian exegesis of the Bible, con-

---

[k] The *Cabala* [קבלה — QABBALAH] incorporates Jewish esoteric speculation — "hidden wisdom" [חכמה נסתרה — ḤOKHMAH NISTARAH] — concerning God and the universe, anciently revealed, it is held, to chosen spirits such as Ezra, and transmitted through the elect few, their disciples, some of whom, particularly in later times, obscured the original theosophic and cosmological doctrines by a mysticism centered upon the inherent creative powers which they attributed to the twenty-two characters of the Hebrew alphabet.

[l] The *Zohar* — the canonical book of the Cabalists — is a pseudepigraphic mystic commentary on the Pentateuch (proximately of Persian, ultimately of Hindu, origin), which, appearing first in Spain late in the thirteenth century, stimulated not only Jewish exegetes but Christians such as Pico della Mirandola [A. D. 1462–1494] and Johann Reuchlin [A. D. 1455–1522] to concentrate upon the "higher truths" rather than the primary meaning of the Old Testament.

forming on the whole to the dogmatism of the Church, pursued no further throughout this long period of critical stagnation the rationalistic tendencies of Theodore of Mopsuestia, which, dormant a millennium, were not to reappear in theological writings until the Reformation.

Rationalistic approach to the Scriptures, embryonic in Theodore, Saadya and Rashi, has matured in that which is known as "the higher criticism" only within the last three hundred years. Further back in time, to be sure, both Erasmus and Luther had given early indication of critical trends to come,[m] but it was not until the middle of the seventeenth century that Thomas Hobbes, in England, and Isaac de la Peyrère, in France, inaugurated, with untraditional analyses of Old Testament narratives, a critical method which, however crude in its initial employment, has become, with certain refinements, the staple of modern Biblical scholarship. In *Leviathan*, published at London in 1651, Hobbes not only cited verse after Pentateuchal verse which, from their very nature, could not have come from the pen of Moses,[15] but maintained that "the whole Scripture of the Old Testament" is a compilation the traditional arrangement of which was finally settled by Jewish authorities between the return from captivity in Babylon — after which Ezra-Nehemiah, Esther, and Psalms cxxvi and cxxxvii were written — and the reign of Ptolemy Philadelphus. Four years later, in 1655, La Peyrère[n] shocked ecclesiastical circles and got himself

---

[m] Erasmus, for example, differentiates the direct statements of Acts from inferences in the Pauline Epistles. Luther held that Solomon was not the author of Ecclesiastes, questioned the plausibility of Esther, maintained that later hands than those of Isaiah, Jeremiah and Hosea had put their prophecies into the received form, was openly indifferent to Mosaic or other authorship of the Pentateuch, and sufficiently doubted the canonicity of Hebrews, James (which he styled "an epistle of straw"), Jude and Revelation to place them apart, with explanatory prefaces, in an appendix to his translation of the Bible.

[n] Isaac de la Peyrère, born in 1594 into a Bordeaux family which, though of Jewish ancestry, had embraced Calvinism, became librarian to the Prince of Condé, with whom he was travelling in the Low Countries when arrested for his theologically unacceptable publications. Released after six months in prison, at either Brussels or Antwerp, on condition that he publicly recant, he

promptly into prison by publishing two works: one, *Praeadamitae*,[16] containing his novel theory that, in the light of Genesis itself, there must have been men upon earth before Adam; the other, *Systema theologicum*,[17] in which, having satisfied himself, with the very arguments of *Leviathan*, of the non-Mosaic authorship of the Pentateuch, La Peyrère undertakes to establish the incredibility of narratives in Genesis; and, with a rationalistic skepticism as to miracles, whether in Old Testament or New, assigns to purely natural causes or to local terrestrial disturbances such reportedly celestial manifestations as the retrogression of the shadow on the sun-dial of Ahaz, the interruption of the sun in its course at the command of Joshua, and even the advent of the star of Bethlehem, of which, had it actually appeared in the heavens, "all famous Historians would have spoken."

The arguments of Hobbes and La Peyrère reappear, without acknowledgment,° a few years later (1670) in the *Tractatus theo-*

---

set forth toward Rome ostensibly to throw himself upon the mercy of the Pope. Gui Patin, however, who encountered him *en route*, reports La Peyrère as "gai, gaillard et sain, fort passionné pour son opinion." [*Lettres de Gui Patin*, Paris, 1846, II. 264]. His contemporaries generally failed, no doubt with reason, to take La Peyrère's retractation seriously, their appraisal being epitomized by the epitaph [preserved in Bayle's *Dictionnaire critique*, Rotterdam, 1697, II. 767] prepared shortly after his death:

> La Peyrère ici gît, ce bon Israëlite
> Huguenot, Catholique, enfin Préadamite.
> Quatre Religions lui plurent à la fois;
> Et son indifférence étoit si peu commune,
> Qu'après quatre-vingts ans qu'il eut à faire choix;
> Le bon homme partit, & n'en choisit pas une.

° Pierre Daniel Huet, in his *Demonstratio evangelica* (Amsterdam, 1679), supports his accusation of Spinoza as a plagiarist from Hobbes and La Peyrère with nothing more than his detection of parallel passages. Father Richard Simon, in his *Histoire critique du vieux testament* (Paris, 1678), maintains that the non-Mosaic authorship of the Pentateuch, far from being a recent question, was raised even by ante-Nicene Fathers. Spinoza, accordingly, may have been quite independent of Hobbes and La Peyrère, the latter of whom, moreover, is unlikely to have originated his astro-physical explanations, *refraction* and *parhelia*, used also by Spinoza in connection with the solar miracles of Joshua and Ahaz. Certainly to neither Hobbes nor La Peyrère does the "God-intoxicated" philosopher owe his anticipation of modern criticism with respect

logico-politicus[18] of Spinoza (A. D. 1632-1677), who, learned in
the wisdom of his own people, attributes to Ibn Ezra his introduction to the non-Mosaic and contradictory elements in the
Pentateuch, and derives from the Jewish Aristotelians, Maimonides and Levi ben Gershon,[19] his inability to accept the miraculous aspects of Biblical narrative as history. Although Hobbes,
La Peyrère and Spinoza were followed in rapid succession by
numerous imitators[20] of their rationalistic but random inspection
of Scriptural passages, it was not until a full century after the
appearance of *Leviathan* that, in 1753 — a year memorable in
Biblical scholarship also for Bishop Lowth's illumination of
Hebrew poetry — Jean Astruc, a Roman Catholic physician,
coming as he thought to the defense of the Mosaic authorship
of the Pentateuch, discovered in the narratives of Genesis a
stylistic distinction which not only in the end controverted his
thesis but became the point of departure for Biblical criticism
of a systematic kind. What had escaped the observation, apparently, of all Biblical students but one[21] prior to Astruc was that
the two distinct names — 'ELOHIM (God) and YAHVEH (LORD) —
by which the Deity is most frequently designated in Genesis are
so distributed throughout the narrative as to suggest its compilation from more than one source. Publishing this brilliant
inference from stylistic differentiation in his anonymous *Conjectures*,[21] Astruc unintentionally made himself the inspiration
of modern, "scientific" higher criticism by his assumption of
two independent ancestral documents of which Moses, as he
believed, had made editorial use in composing Genesis. These
two inferential sources — one of which, in referring to the
Divine Being, habitually employed *Elohim*; the other, *Yahveh* —
scrutinized though they were by many later students,[22] occupied
an even century after Astruc's germinal discovery, to multiply,
through the penetrating analysis of Hupfeld,[22] into the currently
accepted three.

---

to the role of Ezra as definitive editor of the Pentateuch; or his conviction that
Joshua, Judges, Samuel and Kings were composed by other men than those
for whom they are named.

Of these three principal sources now commonly held to under-lie Genesis — and indeed, except for Leviticus, the entire Hexa-teuch — the latest to be detected, and the latest in date, is known, for reasons to which we shall subsequently come, as the Priestly Document. The more ancient of the two earliest sources to be discovered is conveniently identified, because of its predi-lection for the ineffable Tetragrammaton, Y H V H, as the name of the Creator, as the *Yahvistic* narrative or document, and its author as the *Yahvist*. The other, less ancient, major source of Genesis, probably produced in the early part of the eighth century B. C. within a century after its earlier counterpart,[23] is generally known, in view of its consistent choice of *Elohim* for the Divine Name, as the *Elohistic* narrative or document, and its composer is distinguished as the *Elohist*. This stylistic discrimi-nation in Genesis — a reflection probably of provenance rather than theology — is frequently paralleled elsewhere in the Old Testament, as, for a conspicuous illustration, in the literary twins, Psalms xiv and liii, which, differentiated principally by their divergence in the selection of Divine names, sufficiently establish the fact that Biblical writings, like the Judaeo-German folk song and other popular forms of literature,[24] acquire lin-guistic and cultural variants attributable to the peoples among whom they circulate. In the case of Genesis, certain indications within the narrative — emphasis upon Hebron as the home of Abraham; designation of Judah rather than his elder brother, Reuben, as the leader of Joseph's brethren — point to the Yahvist as a man of Judah, the southern kingdom; other features within the same narrative — emphasis upon Beersheba, rather than Hebron, as the center of Abraham's activities; prominence of other northern places such as Shechem and Bethel; mention of Ephraimite (northern) localities noteworthy for their reputed remains of a Joseph or a Joshua — suggest that the Elohistic document was transmitted in conformity with the tradition of the northern kingdom.

The use of two Hebrew words for the Deity, whether or not of regionally distinct origin, is, in itself, of course, no indubitable evidence of multiple sources. Suggestive though *Yahveh* and *Elohim* were to Astruc, their concurrent employment in Genesis, it should be borne in mind, may have been originally no more than an attempt by the author — the sole author — of the Book to enhance its style with a little "elegant variation." Stylistic reassurance of this type, however, vanishes upon rigorous analysis; for, discernible even in the vernacular versions, the narrative is remarkable for its pairs of interchangeable expressions other than *God* and *Lord*, in each of which one of the two verbal equivalents is peculiar to passages associated with *Yahveh*, and the other characteristic of sections in which *Elohim* appears.[p] *Canaanites*, as the Yahvist prefers to record them, are *Amorites* to the Elohist; *Israel*, predominantly used in the Yahvistic text as the name of the third Hebrew patriarch after its conferment upon him [Gen. xxxii. 28] by his Divine Antagonist, customarily appears, in the Elohistic narrative, as *Jacob*. The Yahvistic etymology of *Joseph* at Genesis xxx. 24 differs from that of the Elohist in the verse preceding; and at xviii. 12–15 the explanation of Isaac's name in the Yahvistic context is not in agreement with the derivation, at xxi. 6, by the Elohist.[q] Such concomitant usages — deliberately chosen, not to overtake Astruc, from Genesis alone, and, not to anticipate Hupfeld's discovery in this Book of a second major source which also employs *Elohim*, from no Elohistic passage prior to the twentieth chapter — are, in their cumulative effect, undeniably compelling.[r] Even within the limits to which our examination has thus

[p] The Yahvist, for example, employs שפחה [šiphḥah] for *maid* [Gen. xii. 16]; the Elohist prefers אמה ['amah (Gen. xx. 17)]. The Yahvist uses ארח נשים ['oraḥ našim] for *manner* or *custom of women* [Gen. xviii. 11]; the Elohist, דרך נשים [derekh našim (Gen. xxxi. 35)]. A *sack* in the Yahvistic text [Gen. xlii. 27] is אמתחת ['amtaḥath]; whereas in the Elohistic [Gen. xlii. 25] it is שק [saq].

[q] Still another etymology of *Isaac* occurs, in the Priestly narrative, at Gen. xvii. 16–19.

[r] Conspicuous examples, beyond the limits of Genesis, are the Yahvist's preference for *Sinai* as the name of the "mountain of God," and *Hobab* as the name of the father-in-law of Moses; whereas in the Elohist's narrative these designations are supplanted by *Horeb* and *Jethro* (or *Jether*) respectively.

far been confined, the Biblical narrative gives marked indication
of composite structure.

The major documents which coalesce into this Eloh-Yahvistic
union[8] may be either, as some scholars hold,[25] two originally
separate versions of the same, or nearly the same, historical
and legendary accounts; or, as others believe,[26] and as seems
more credible, two recensions of an ancestral narrative which,
as they circulated in different districts of Palestine, accumulated,
and preserved in transmission, more and more divergent features of their own. These sources — the Yahvistic and Elohistic
— sometimes confused through superficial similarities in their
presentation of practically identical material, are further differentiated by certain characteristics of their style. One of the
authors — the Yahvist — has an anthropomorphic conception
of the Deity which, graphic and picturesque, is unexcelled in
vividness. For him God walks in the garden, threatens more
than He carries out, punishes disobedience like any irate parent,
plays favorites, regrets past action, is grieved at heart, performs
a major operation, and even retreats in His purpose before the
importunate pleading of a man. The Elohist, in contrast, tem-
pering his anthropomorphism with dreams and visions, gives
to his Supreme Being an extra-terrestrial quality. Poetically less
gifted than his rival, the Elohist, elsewhere than in Genesis,
draws repeatedly upon earlier lyric sources like The Book of the
Wars of the LORD [Num. xxi. 14] or The Book of Jashar [Josh.
x. 13]; and, not so luxuriant in imagery, is prone to prosy par-
ticulars, especially those which, like his several references to
things Egyptian, manifest a degree of learning. Characteristic
of the Elohist is his recurrent "God of my (thy, their) father"
[אלהי אבי], the wordiness of his typical formula, "And it came
to pass after these things" [Gen. xxii. 1, *et al.*], and numerous
expressions, distinctive in the original Hebrew, such as "face
to face," "to all generations," and "the man Moses."[27]

[8] Commonly referred to — where the Yahvist [Jahwist] and his text is
symbolized by J, and the Elohist and his text by E — as JE.

Compilation from two or more sources — sufficiently apparent in Chronicles or such later works as the *Diatessaron* of Tatian or the Gospels according to both Matthew and Luke — was the historical method of antiquity.[28] Biblical historiographers assembled their material from earlier documents, often incorporating lengthy, and unacknowledged, excerpts; now and then abridging or paraphrasing the original; occasionally deleting unwanted portions or effecting juncture of the fragments with contributions of their own. Such, it is clear, was the technique of the compiler of Genesis; and such is the persistent stylistic individuality not only of the excerpts but also of the editorial insertions that, with a reasonable degree of confidence, they can still be segregated and the excerpted portions sometimes reassembled into their original form. That this is practicable, *even in a portion of the Eloh-Yahvistic narrative where neither* God *nor* Lord *occurs as a clue,* may be demonstrated by restoration of a section of each of the two major sources from which the story of Joseph and his brethren is derived. A specimen reconstruction of the narrative as originally presented by the Yahvist is effected, beginning at Genesis xxxvii. 17[b], by omitting selected passages and by reading consecutively the remaining portions of the Biblical text:

"And Joseph went after his brethren... (18) And they saw him afar off, and before he came near unto them, they conspired against him to slay him. (21) And Judah[t] heard it, and delivered him out of their hand; and said, Let us not take his life. (25) And they sat down to eat bread: and they lifted up their eyes and looked, and, behold, a travelling company of Ishmaelites came from Gilead, with their camels bearing spicery and balm and myrrh, going to carry it down to Egypt. (26) And Judah said unto his brethren, What profit is it if we slay our brother and conceal his blood? (27) Come, and let us sell him to the Ishmaelites, and let not our hand be upon him; for he is our brother, our flesh. And his brethren hearkened unto him (28[b]) and sold Joseph to the Ishmaelites for

---

[t] M. T. reads *Reuben*. The emendation, endorsed by many critics, is obviously essential to the context. See verse 26.

twenty pieces of silver.[u] (31) And they took Joseph's coat, and killed a he-goat, and dipped the coat in the blood; *etc.*"

If, now, the Scriptural passages omitted to obtain the foregoing reconstruction be in their turn read consecutively, they will be seen to comprise another consistent and effective tale — the Elohist's — as follows:

(xxxvii. 19) "And they [Joseph's brethren] said one to another, Behold, this dreamer cometh. (20) Come now therefore, and let us slay him, and cast him into one of the pits, and we will say, An evil beast hath devoured him: and we shall see what will become of his dreams. (22) And Reuben said unto them, Shed no blood; cast him into this pit that is in the wilderness, but lay no hand upon him; that he might deliver him out of their hand, to restore him to his father. (23) And it came to pass, when Joseph was come unto his brethren, that they stript Joseph of his coat, the coat of many colors that was on him; (24) and they took him, and cast him into the pit; and the pit was empty, there was no water in it. (28) And there passed by Midianites, merchantmen; and they drew and lifted up Joseph out of the pit, (28c) and they brought Joseph into Egypt.[v] (29) And Reuben returned unto the pit; and, behold, Joseph was not in the pit; and he rent his clothes. (30) And he returned unto his brethren, and said, The child is not; and I, whither shall I go? (36) And the Midianites sold him into Egypt unto Potiphar, an officer of Pharaoh's, the captain of the guard."

Inexpert editorial interweaving of these two self-sufficient reports of fraternal jealousy and revenge — each an admirable example of coherent narrative — is responsible, it is reasonable to suppose, for such inconsistencies and confusion in the traditional Biblical version as Reuben's surprise at the disappearance of Joseph or the inexplicable transmogrification of Midianites into Ishmaelites. Further incongruities which mar the tale — apparent to any reader who attentively pursues the narrative in its composite form, through subsequent chapters — are like-

---

[u] This transaction is confirmed by the Yahvist at xlv. 4, 5.

[v] This account is substantiated further on in the Elohist's narrative, at Gen. xl. 15, where Joseph supplies the information that he had been *stolen away* — not *sold* — out of the land of the Hebrews.

wise traceable to the imperfect manner in which the compiler of the Eloh-Yahvistic redaction has merged his parallel but disparate sources.[29] Differentiation of the two principal elements in this composition is no longer possible in every detail, but, though the line of demarcation cannot always be drawn between portions of the text plainly marked with the stamp of the Yahvist and portions equally identifiable as the work of the Elohist, utilization of the two sources to produce a large part of the narrative of the received text of Genesis is an established tenet of Biblical criticism.

Concentration by Astruc and subsequent scholars upon Divine names as evidence of a twofold documentary ancestry of Genesis, blinded them to the possibility — and the fact — that the "signature" *Elohim* is not necessarily that of an isolated pre-Scriptural author. The Elohist, indeed — it was Hupfeld's fortune to discover — is not unique in the use of *Elohim*, that designation of the Deity being characteristic also of another ancient record, now embodied in portions of the Massoretic Text, distinct from, but interwoven with, the Eloh-Yahvistic composition.

Differentiation of this third Scriptural source — the Priestly document[w] — from the Elohistic, despite their common employment of *Elohim*, is indicated by a marked distinction between their theosophies, and is attested by distinguishing peculiarities of their substance, vocabulary and style. These idiosyncrasies of the Priestly source differentiate it also, and with equal impressiveness, from the narratives of the Yahvist. Contrasting conspicuously, for instance, with the frankly anthropomorphic treatment of the Divine Being in the Eloh-Yahvistic narratives is the Priestly supra-mundane conception of the Eternal, who, though his voice be occasionally heard by men, never emerges, in the Priestly representation, from either his nebulous or his fiery manifestation. A further advance on the

[w] Symbolized by "P." This source — the *legislative* portions of which [Leviticus and parts of Exodus and Numbers] are known as the Priests' Code — though a composite work of multiple authorship and various dates, is conveniently referred to as if it came from a single pen.

concepts of the Yahvist and the Elohist is the Priestly narrator's
exclusion of their intermediating angels, their dreams and their
theophanies. He is concerned less with their "prophetic" problems of justice and righteousness than with ritualistic proprieties
of the Israelite theocracy. To him may be confidently assigned
the whole of Leviticus and many portions of the remaining
Books of the Hexateuch devoted to legalistic matters such as
commutation of vows or the Sabbatical year, and to such ceremonial institutions as sacrifice, circumcision, purification rites,
the Sabbath, Passover and the Day of Atonement.

On subjects of this legalistic nature the Eloh-Yahvistic document has little to offer. Where, however, the substance of the
text is not peculiar solely to the Priestly document, and, as at
several places in Genesis, it is paralleled by the Yahvist, discrepancies in the duplicate accounts tend to confirm the multiplicity of sources. The naming of *Bethel* is inconsistently reported
[Gen. xxviii. 19 and xxxv. 15] by these two sources. The
Priestly account [Gen. xxxv. 10] of the circumstances under
which the third patriarch acquired the name *Israel* conflicts
with that of the Yahvist [Gen. xxxii. 28]. To the divergent
Eloh-Yahvistic folk-etymologies of *Isaac* previously noted, the
Priestly narrator contributes a variant of his own [Gen. xvii.
16–19]. The motivation of Rebekah in proposing that Jacob
journey forth from his home in Canaan is, in the one source
[(P) Gen. xxvii. 46], that he find a wife acceptable to his parents;
in the other [(J) Gen. xxvii. 42–45], that he save himself from
Esau's murderous anger.

Existence of a Priestly source — evidenced not only by the
foregoing but by other conflicting representations — is further
confirmed by the writer's distinctive diction. Prior to the disclosure in Exodus [vi. 3] that the God of Israel calls himself
Yahveh, the Divine appellation in passages for which neither
Yahvist nor Elohist is held responsible is consistently *Elohim*.[x]

---

[x] Only twice [Gen. xvii. 1 and xxi. 1[b]] has *Yahveh* crept into this portion of
P, possibly through scribal or editorial inadvertence. In four verses of Genesis
[xvii. 1, xxviii. 3, xxxv. 11, xlviii. 3] P uses the ancient Divine Name, אל שדי
['ēL šaDDay].

Preferred throughout the Eloh-Yahvistic record, the longer form of the first personal pronoun *I* [אנכי — 'ānoĸhi] is used but once [Gen. xxiii. 4] by the Priestly writer, who, in some hundred and thirty instances, impresses his individuality into the text by employing an equivalent pronominal form — the shorter אני ['ani].[y] Only once does the Elohist employ [Ex. xxii. 28 (M. T. 27)] the exceedingly common Priestly term for *prince* or *ruler* among the Israelites [נשיא — nasi']. Twice only in the Yahvistic text [Ex. xii. 21; Num. xi. 10] does the oft-repeated phrase *after their families* [למשפחתם — Leмišpeḥoтhām] appear beyond the limits of the Priestly narrative.[z] Priestly diction, however, is often *sui generis*, as in its invariable employment, when using the verb *to beget*, of an inflectional variation other than the basic conjugational form regularly selected for that verb in genealogical passages by the Yahvist.[aa] Exclusive occurrence within the Priestly portion of the Pentateuch is further illustrated by repeated locutions such as *for food* [לאכלה — Le'oĸhlah], or *an everlasting covenant* [ברית עולם — Berith 'ôlam]; and by iterated nouns like *congregation* [עדה — 'ēdah], or *hosts* [צבאות — ṣeвha'ôth; *i. e., armies* (of Israelites)], or *generations* [תולדות — tôleдhôth] which, recurring in the stereotyped Priestly introduction *These are the generations of*, and elsewhere, is never employed in place of its well-known synonym דורות [dôrôth] either by Yahvist or Elohist.

Accompanying these representative verbal peculiarities of the text — indicative of the individuality of the source in which they occur — are characteristic mannerisms of style which impressively supplement the foregoing evidence of subject-matter and linguistic usage that a document, distinct from the Eloh-

[y] A similar discrimination between these two forms of the pronoun is elsewhere an index of authorship: the Deuteronomist regularly employs אנכי; and Ezekiel, with a single exception in 139 occurrences, אני.

[z] *Rare* occurrences of phrases such as these are, of course, to be expected outside the Priestly document, of which, owing to their frequency within that source, they are none the less typical.

[aa] In the Perfect 3rd sg. masc., P uses the *Hiph'il* form הוליד [hôlid]; J, the *Qal* ילד [yālad].

Yahvistic, made generous contribution to the received Hexateuchal narratives. The Priestly source, indeed, once it has been
isolated, is seen to possess a quality, juristic rather than literary,
suitable to its function of structural skeleton upon which the
mythological, legendary and heroic aspects of Patriarchal and
later history are hung. It is precise and orderly, prosaic and
formal. Its specifications of ark and tabernacle suggest ship-
wright and architect; its genealogies and statistics, the archivist.
Chronological features of the Priestly narrative support, whenever possible, its historicity, at whatever cost to its lustre.
Repetitious expansion of its generalizations, lest they be incom-
pletely understood, is practised to the point of pedantry.[30] Its
frequent enumerations begin and end methodically with a formula, and stereotyped expressions repeatedly introduce or
conclude other unitary divisions of its text. Above all, it is
conspicuous for the organization and systematic development of
its material, the mark, unquestionably, of an experienced and
disciplined mind.

The account of Creation with which the Old Testament opens
[Gen. i. 1–ii. 3] owes much of its impressiveness to these stylistic
characteristics of the Priestly writer.[bb] Literature has nothing
more methodical to show than the rhythmic repetition of his
structural phrasing: "And God said," "And it was so," "And
God saw that it was good," "And there was evening and there
was morning, [a] . . . day." Systematically he unfolds the process
of creation from its beginning in watery chaos to its culmination,
on the sixth day, in dominion-having man, after which, with
deft rhetorical variation, he reports the Creator (referred to here

---

[bb] The impressiveness of the first three verses is enhanced in the A. V.,
R. V., and A. J. V. through mistranslation of the Hebrew text as pointed by
the Massoretes. Greater fidelity to the traditional punctuation requires: "In
beginning to create the heavens and the earth — the earth being unformed and
void, and darkness upon the face of the deep, and the spirit of God hovering
over the face of the waters — God said, 'Let there be light.' And there was
light." Similarly, both Moffatt and Smith-Goodspeed. The Babylonian story
of creation begins with a like parenthetical construction. *Cf.* R. W. Rogers,
Cuneiform Parallels to the Old Testament, 2nd ed., Abingdon, © 1926, p. 3.

only as Elohim) as seeing, at least for the time being, that everything He had made was *very* good. In his careful ordering of this
account the Priestly narrator records, with circumstantial precision, the exact sequence in which Earth, emerging from the
waters on the third day, was divinely provided with living
things: vegetation first — grass, herb, and fruit-tree; then, on
the fifth day, fish of the sea and fowl of the air; on the sixth day,
cattle and creeping things and beasts of the earth; and finally —
male and female — God's image, man. This accomplished, God
rests — not, however, without first blessing the man and the
woman, instructing them to be fruitful and to multiply, and
giving them for food every herb yielding seed and, *without re-
striction*, every fruit-tree which is upon the face of all the earth.

In contrast — stylistic and substantial — with this superbly
planned portion of the Priestly narrative, is the noticeably different version of the Creation which immediately follows. Introduced [Gen. ii. 4] by the formula "These are the generations
of"[cc] which, prefacing no less than nine other discrete divisions
of the Book of Genesis, conspicuously indicates the beginning of
a constituent unit of the text, this second story of the Creation,
closer to the folk than is its sophisticated predecessor, dispenses
with its companion's structural formality and captivates the
reader with the liveliness of its representation and its dramatic
vitality. This is the creation-tale lodged in the consciousness of
Judaeo-Christian man. This is the creation-tale through which
John Milton, in *Paradise Lost*, sought to illumine, if not to redeem,
post-Puritan and dissolute England; this, the familiar story
through which Bernard Shaw, in *Back to Methuselah*, delights
and instructs the contemporary world. Here, from the hand of
the Yahvist, comes a human tragedy — forbidden fruit-trees of
marvelous powers, a beguiling serpent more subtle than any

[cc] This stereotype — somewhat analogous to "Once upon a time" — elsewhere characteristic of P, is held by some critics to have been misplaced by an
ancient compiler, its original position having been in the text of P at the head
of Ch. i., where it is placed by Moffatt.

other beast, temptation to the like of which unprofited descendants of Eve still yield, disobedience and punishment in which all mankind may, unto this day, vicariously participate. In this immortal legend no mention is made of the number of days of God's labor, nor is the reported order of events in the least compatible with that of the Priestly narrative. There, to recapitulate, creation of living forms on earth, in a sequence of several days, was: vegetation, fish and fowl, beasts of the earth, and — male and female — man. Here, in the Yahvistic chronicle, the Lord God otherwise manifests His omnipotence — inferentially in the course of a single momentous day — first by forming man, a solitary male, out of the dust of the yet barren ground, yielding neither shrub nor herb;[dd] then by planting a garden in which He put His prime creature to work; next by making an arboretum in the midst of which grow two supernatural trees, the fruit of one of which is denied the man; then by creating beasts of the field and fowls of the air — with the singular omission, be it noted, of fish[ee] — to all of whom the man gave names;[ff] and finally — climax to all His endeavor — by making for the lonesome man in Eden, not out of earth this time but from one of the man's own ribs, a help meet for him, the first woman.

[dd] Herbs of the field, expressly noted in ii. 5 as yet to be created, are not again mentioned until iii. 18, where, together with thorns and thistles, they are punishments meted out to Adam for his disobedience.

[ee] Fishes are "frankly omitted," according to Skinner, *Genesis* [*I. C. C.*], "as inappropriate to the situation." In Driver's opinion [*Westm. Comm.*] "fishes are not mentioned; the possibility of their proving a 'help' to man being out of the question."

[ff] Rationalists from La Peyrère to Voltaire exercised themselves considerably over the enormity of Adam's lexicographical achievement during the latter part of the sixth day [Voltaire, *Dictionnaire philosophique*, *s. v. Genèse*: "si Adam eût ainsi connu toutes les propriétés des animaux, ou il avait déjà mangé du fruit de la science, ou Dieu semblait n'avoir pas besoin de lui interdire ce fruit; il en savait déjà plus que la Société royale de Londres et l'Académie des sciences"], and openly ridiculed the prodigious feat of logistics by which was accomplished the rapid transportation of, say, elephants, which are slow and heavy [*lentus & gravis*] from India and Africa into Eden, to say nothing of the innumerable species from America ["Quid porro dicam de

Supplementing these obvious discrepancies of style, substance and arrangement, indicative of divergent creation-stories ultimately of distinct provenance, is the contrasting usage of the two versions in their designation of the Creator. In the six-day account with which Genesis begins, the Divine appellation, as previously noted, is invariably *Elohim*. One reads to the close of the narrative, where God rests from creative labor [ii. 3], without the slightest intimation that the Deity is known by other names. With the opening verse, however, of the one-day version [ii. 4], *Yahveh* makes initial appearance as the name of the Lord; whereafter it is consistently employed throughout the account of Paradise and the Fall of Man. Peculiar to this, the second creation-story [ii. 4ᵇ–iii. 24], is the regular union of *Yahveh* with *Elohim*, the standard English rendering of which conjoined form is the Lᴏʀᴅ God. Responsibility for this special combination of the sacred names is assigned, as a rule, to an unknown redactor, who, in amplifying the formal Priestly account with the less spectacular but more human material of the Yahvistic source, thought by this simple editorial device to identify the anthropomorphic Deity of the Yahvist with the transcendental Creator of All Things presented in the Priestly narrative. Not entirely to be excluded from consideration is the alternative explanation that, among the compiler's sources for the Creation story, there was also a third document — the Elohistic — vestigial remains of which, discernible here and there in the Yahvist's story, lurk in the second element of the "hyphenated" Yahveh-Elohim.ᵍᵍ

---

innumeris fere animalium & volatilium speciebus . . . ut ex America in Meso-potamiam venirent." La Peyrère, *Systema theologicum* (n. p., 1655), pp. 154–155; *cf.* also Bayle's *Dictionnaire critique*, 1697, *s. v. Adam*].

ᵍᵍ This interpretation of the compound Name as of Elohistic origin, is admittedly without substantial support, no considerable evidence of the Elohist's pen appearing prior to the twentieth chapter of Genesis. Inasmuch as this evidence presupposes an antecedent chronicle, of which, it may be, a few items still manifest themselves in chapter fifteen [B. W. Bacon, in *Hebraica*, VII (1890), pp. 75 ff.], it is not unthinkable that the Elohistic source, were it recoverable in its entirety, would be found to start, like the accounts of the rival historiographers, with a version of how the world began. Mythological

of which is scarcely to be questioned,[32] the Decalogue of Exodus [xx. 3–17],[ii] in all probability from earlier, and less elaborated, sources,[jj] is, with the exception of the Priestly verse eleven, from the hand of the Elohist alone.[33]

Comparison of the Elohistic Decalogue in Exodus with the variant form in which, expanded and slightly altered, it appears in Deuteronomy, introduces another major source of the Hexa-

---

[ii] The Philonic verse-enumeration of the Commandments, followed by Josephus and adopted by the Anglican Church, differs (as set forth in the subjoined table) from that of Talmudic authority retained by the Synagogue, and even more from that of Augustine, which is adhered to by the Roman Catholic Church and the Lutherans.

	I	II	III	IV	V	VI	VII	VIII	IX	X
Philo	3	4–6	7	8–11	12	13	14	15	16	17
Talmud	2	3–6	7	8–11	12	13	14	15	16	17
Augustine	3–6	7	8–11	12	13	14	15	16	17^a	17^b

The Augustinian enumeration, found also in Codex A, divides verse 17 into two Commandments, the Ninth and the Tenth, adopting here the reading of Deut. v. 21 (A. J. V. 18), which, replacing *covet* [חמד — ḤAMADh] in its second half by *desire* [*Hithpaʻel* of אוה — ʼAVAH], lends some support to the Roman division. The Talmudic enumeration is anticipated in Codd. B and, in Deut. only, F. The A. J. V., following Hebrew tradition, counts vv. 13–16 as a single verse, the final verse [v. 17] of the Decalogue, accordingly, being 14 in the Jewish edition.

[jj] The number of words in the first five Commandments, as they now stand in the M. T., so far exceeds those in the second five as to preclude the possibility of their equal division between the two tablets. Commandments I–V, however, relieved of their presumed amplifications, total only 28 Hebrew words, VI–X containing a comparable 26. The Decalogue, thus conceived, originally approximated the following form, the likelihood being that all ten Words, rather than the present eight, were uniformly negative: I. Thou shalt have none other gods before me. II. Thou shalt not make to thyself any graven image. III. Thou shalt not take the name of Yahveh in vain. IV. Thou shalt not labor on the sabbath day. V. Thou shalt not be disrespectful of thy father or thy mother. VI. Thou shalt do no murder. VII. Thou shalt not commit adultery. VIII. Thou shalt not steal. IX. Thou shalt not bear false witness. X. Thou shalt not covet. *Cf.* G. H. A. Ewald, *Geschichte des Volkes Israel*, 3rd ed., Göttingen, 1865, Vol. II, p. 231; H. L. Strack, in *Kurzgefasster Kommentar zu den heiligen Schriften, etc.*, München, 1894, p. 242; A. Dillmann, in *Kurzgefasstes ... Handbuch zum Alten Testament*, 3rd ed., Leipzig, 1897, p. 225.

teuch. To the characteristics of this, the fourth and last of our major Hexateuchal sources, we shall come presently. The Decalogue, in the Deuteronomic version [Deut. v. 7–21], though purporting [vv. 5, 22] to be the very words of the Lord — and all of them — uttered in the mount from out the midst of the fire and recorded by the Elohist in Exodus, is remarkable rather for revision than for exactness of quotation. The first three Commandments in the Deuteronomic text are, to be sure, scrupulously faithful to the earlier narrative. With the Fourth Commandment, however, unmistakable discrepancies both of substance and form manifest themselves upon collation of the two recensions. The sabbath day, originally to be no more than *remembered*, is now [v. 12] to be *observed* as holy; and this starkly apodictic injunction of Exodus is gratuitously amplified with the apologetic — though in the context inappropriate — insertion: *as the LORD thy God commanded thee*. Further Deuteronomic expansion of the ancestral text is seen in the non-Elohistic *thine ox, nor thine ass, nor any of* thy cattle, and, in the same verse [14], the elucidating addition: *that thy manservant and thy maidservant may rest as well as thou*. Just prior to these textual augmentations is to be noted an intrusive *nor*, the first of several polysyndetic modifications of the original. Of Deuteronomic departures from the Exodus reading of the Fourth Commandment the most extensive, and the most striking, is in verse fifteen, which, rejecting the Elohistic reason for sabbath-observance—"For in six days the LORD made heaven and earth, the sea, and all that in them is, and rested the seventh day; wherefore the LORD blessed the sabbath day, and hallowed it" — substitutes the altogether different motivation: *And thou shalt remember that thou wast a servant in the land of Egypt, and the LORD thy God brought thee out thence by a mighty hand and by a stretched out arm: therefore the LORD thy God commanded thee to keep the sabbath day*. Similarly, in the Fifth Commandment, the Deuteronomist again inserts the contextually unsuitable *as the LORD thy God commanded thee*, and adds to longevity — the sole incentive of Exodus for honoring one's father and mother — the further inducement *and that it may go well with thee*.

The Sixth Commandment is identical in the two representations, and numbers Seven through Nine differ, in the Hebrew, only in the stylistic variation which, in English, yields the Deuteronomic *neither* against the Elohistic *not*.[kk] More elaborate, again, are the alterations, artistic and substantial, made by the Deuteronomic redactor in the last of the Commandments: reapportionment of co-ordinating conjunctions; substitution of *desire* [אוה — 'avaн] for the second *covet* [חמד — ḤAMADh] of the Exodus version; augmentation of the items not to be coveted in Exodus by the *field* of one's neighbor; and, most remarkable of all, transposition of *house* and *wife* — a modification of the Exodus version indicative, it may be inferred, of improved social status for women. Multifold variations such as these in so basic a section of the Biblical text as the Decalogue — a phenomenon paralleled in numerous duplicate passages[34] — establishes the composite nature of the Biblical text, as a consequence of which there can be no reasonable doubt as to the evolutionary character of portions, if not all, of Scripture.

Contributory to this Scriptural evolution is the genius of the principal compiler of the Fifth Book of the Law, conventionally identified, from the Septuagintal title of the Book which is almost entirely his, as the Deuteronomist.[11] Indebted in consid-

[kk] Thou shalt *not* (Ex. xx. 14–16); *Neither* shalt thou (Deut. v. 18–20). For centuries, moreover, the sequence of the Commandments now numbered VI, VII, and VIII [Douay: V, VI, and VII] was variable. The established order — accepted at Mt. v. 21, 27; xix. 18; Mk. x. 19 (R. V.); by Josephus and by several Fathers — is that of the M. T., Codd. A, *F*, *M*, and many minuscules, and the Syr. Hexapla. Codex Vaticanus, in Exodus, has the unique sequence: VII, VIII, VI; and, in Deut., departs again from the received order with still another variant — VII, VI, VIII — duplicated by the Nash Papyrus and by Brit. Mus. Copt. MS. of Deut. No. 7594, and adopted at Mk. x. 19 (A. V.), Lk. xviii. 20, Rom. xiii. 9, and by Philo and certain Fathers. The Decalogue survives in none of the early uncials other than those cited.

[11] Symbolized by "D." A few sections near the end of the Book, possibly not from D's hand, are assigned to a second Deuteronomic editor, D[2]. The Greek title of the Book, though not inappropriate in view of its structure, derives from a mistranslation of Deut. xvii. 18, *a copy of this law* [משנה התורה הזאת], erroneously rendered in LXX *this repetition of the law* [τὸ Δευτερονόμιον (Deuteronomion) τοῦτο].

erable measure to the Eloh-Yahvistic redaction, but wholly
independent of the Priestly document, the Deuteronomist, like
the other major Pentateuchal sources, displays idiosyncrasies of
diction and peculiarities of style by which he may be readily
distinguished. Even where his characteristic expressions may
have been borrowed from Yahvist or Elohist — as *within thy
gates* [Ex. xx. 10], or *the land which the* LORD *thy God is giving thee*
[Ex. xx. 12] — the Deuteronomist, by frequent repetition, makes
them his own. Where, as often, his iterated phraseology is unquestionably original, the individualistic quality of his discourse
is unmistakable. Although Old Testament passages are not
wanting containing either *a mighty hand* or *a stretched out arm*,
their effectiveness in juxtaposition was first realized by the chief
author of Deuteronomy. Peculiar to him is the injunction,
uttered five times, *And remember that thou wast a bondman in the
land of Egypt.* His, too — with the exception of a single instance in
I Chronicles [xxviii. 8] — are the references to Canaan as *the
good land*; and his exclusively are the four occurrences of the ad-
monitory assertion *And* [all the people] . . . *shall hear, and fear.*
None but the Deuteronomist employs the locution *observe and do*;
nor is it possible to find, outside of his Book, the command *and
thou shalt put away the evil from the midst of thee* (or *of Israel*). [35] More
readily perceived than these distinctive usages of the Deuteronomic writer is the strikingly oratorical flavor of his exhortations.
Obviously an ardent personality, he develops, in sustained and
compelling cadences suitable to the parenetic purpose of his
Book, a persuasive eloquence, new to Hebrew literature, which,
resembling that of his contemporary, Jeremiah, and greatly in-
fluencing the style of later Old Testament writers, such as
the compilers of the Books of Kings, is properly designated
prophetic.

The Fifth Book of the Pentateuch, thus hortatory in character,
is a lively reflection of the period of reform in which it appears
to have been written. If it be true, as first suggested by Jerome, [36]
and unanimously concurred in by critics of the modern school,
that Deuteronomy — at least most of its central portion [xii–xxvi

and xxviii] — is identical with the Book of the Law discovered by Hilkiah, the high priest [II Kgs. xxii. 8 *seq.*], during reparation of the Temple in the eighteenth year of King Josiah [621 B. C.], then the probability is strong that it was composed in the seventh pre-Christian century, either in the time of the blood-shedding King Manasseh [698–643 B. C.], as a declaration — unpublished of course — against that monarch's "abominations of the heathen," or early in the reign of Josiah as a manifesto of religious reformation conceivably produced in anticipation of its dramatic promulgation later on. Less generally held, though not impossible, is the opinion that the core of Deuteronomy, supporting Hezekiah's policy [II Kgs. xviii. 1–8] of suppression of Canaanite sanctuaries, was written very late in the century preceding, but that, during the evil years of Manasseh, it was naturally "lost" and forgotten until the middle of Josiah's reign when conditions were favorable to its public reception. Under whichever of these three Kings of Judah Deuteronomy made its appearance, it is certainly, by many centuries, post-Mosaic.^{mm}

^{mm} Certain passages — beginning with i. 1, *beyond Jordan*, the author manifestly writing from that side of the river, the west, which Moses never reached; and concluding with xxxiv. 5–12, the account of Moses' death — cannot reasonably be thought of as penned by the Law-giving Prophet himself [A. S. Peake, *The Servant of Yahweh*, Boston, 1931, p. 153]. Although earlier Eloh-Yahvistic legislation — embodied, with some amplification, in the Fifth Book of the Law — may well have originated under Mosaic guidance, its adaptation in Deuteronomy to a society more advanced than that of the people of the Exodus is but one of several indications [Driver, *Lit. of the O. T.*, pp. 86 ff.] that the Deuteronomist and Moses are different personalities of widely separated epochs. The apologetic position [*Jew. Ency.*, IV. 545] not only rejects this critical view as "exposed to the insuperable objection that the religion which brought truth into the world can not have been founded upon a deception," but condemns as "inconceivable" the claim "that this fundamental book of religion . . . could be pseudographic, and that the whole nation should have considered as of Mosaic origin . . . a book which was a forgery." Deuteronomic ascription to Moses of its seven eloquent discourses — reflecting a tradition, one is tempted to conjecture, of a Mosaic valedictory — is, of course, like ascription of Proverbs to Solomon [*v. supra*, p. 253], a typical literary device of antiquity; its use elsewhere in the Bible may be verified, for example, at Joshua xxiii–xxiv or II Chr. xviii *seq.* Designation of the method

Assignment of Deuteronomy to the seventh century B.C. permits relative dating of the three remaining major Hexateuchal sources: the Elohistic, Yahvistic and Priestly. The Deuteronomic code, as comparison of the two versions of the Decalogue makes plain, is, in part at least, an *amplification* of Eloh-Yahvistic legislation. Seniority being conceded, as a canon of textual criticism, to the shorter rather than to the expanded form of an ancient work, the Eloh-Yahvistic compilation must be accorded temporal priority. The Elohistic document, moreover, preserving, as previously noted, the tradition of the northern kingdom, can hardly have originated after that kingdom's collapse — to which, significantly, it makes no reference — with the fall of Samaria, its capital, in 722 B. C.; nor, considering its reference to Abraham as a *prophet* [Gen. xx. 7] and its superlative precative "would God that all the LORD's people were prophets" [Num. xi. 29], can it be earlier than the beginnings of prophecy in the eleventh pre-Christian century [I Sam. ix. 9]. The Elohist, furthermore, in view of his less anthropomorphic representation of deity, and his recognition of three successive developments in religious thinking,[nn] appears to be more advanced, and therefore perhaps a century later, than the Yahvist, whose more primitive work was probably produced early in the ninth century B. C.[37] Both narratives of the Patriarchal period, anticipating as they do in their present form the occupation of the promised land by a *united nation* such as only Saul and his successors of the tenth century knew, cannot, in any case, antedate the early years of the monarchy.

---

as a *forgery* — a regrettable anachronistic imposition of modern standards of copyright upon ancient historiographical practice — an alleged literary piracy, that is, of which the Deuteronomist, by virtue of his ethical purpose, was incapable, recommends itself rather as pietistic asseveration than as effective refutation. Deuteronomy, it should be noted, referring to Moses invariably *in the third person*, nowhere claims him as its author.

[nn] (1) Idolatrous polytheism — note the "strange gods" of Jacob's wives [Gen. xxxv. 2–4], and cp. Josh. xxiv. 2; (2) Patriarchal worship of Elohim; (3) Mosaic Yahveh-worship [Ex. vi. 2 *seq.*].

These narratives of Elohist and Yahvist are the foundation upon which the Deuteronomist built. It is to them — and not to the Priestly narratives of Genesis and Exodus nor to the legislation of the Priests' Code — that he consistently alludes. His work reflects nothing, for instance, of the Priestly School's Levitical cities, and recognizes neither the Levitical year of Jubilee nor the Priestly Day of Atonement. Not once does the Deuteronomist open a discourse with the recurrent Priestly formula, *speak . . . and say*. To him, *Horeb* — not the Priestly *Sinai* — is the name of the mountain upon which Moses received the Ten Words; to him, *the priests, the Levites*, perform sacerdotal functions which are regularly assigned in the later code of the Priests to *the sons of Aaron*. To the Deuteronomist, accordingly, it is reasonable to hold, the Priestly document was unavailable. That source, as his freedom from its influence indicates, had not yet been integrated with the Eloh-Yahvistic to form the familiar Patriarchal narratives of Genesis. The assumption, indeed, may safely be made that, at the time of Hilkiah's discovery of the Book of the Law, writers of the Priestly School were still to compose their Document. A generation after the Reformation of Josiah, however, at least that distinctive portion of the Priestly legislation known as the Code of Holiness [Lev. xvii–xxvi] seems, from its apparent exploitation by the prophet Ezekiel [Ezek. xl–xlviii], to have been current when, with the destruction of Jerusalem [586 B.C.] by Nebuchadrezzar, he and his fellow Jewish survivors were driven into exile at Babylon. Other sections of the Priests' Code — particularly parts of Exodus and Numbers — incorporating sacerdotal practices of undoubted antiquity, presumably acquired approximately their present form, either at the hands of exilic compilers or within a few decades following the half-century of Babylonian captivity.[38] Combined with the Code of Holiness and earlier sacerdotal regulations, but lacking certain subsequent provisions,[oo] these compilations comprised,

---

[oo] Notably, at Neh. viii. 14 *seq.*, procedures for the Day of Atonement specified at Lev. xvi.

in all probability, the post-exilic book of the Law of Moses which, from early morning to midday, was read, allegedly by Ezra the scribe,[pp] before all the people of Jerusalem [Neh. viii. 3] in 444 B. C. Incorporating this Nehemian version of the Mosaic Law, the completed Priestly document, though unquestionably elaborated from earlier ritualistic and chronological material — some of which may have come to the compilers in written form — is, from all the evidence, latest of the four major Scriptural sources which, fused none too skillfully by successive redactors, supplied the Hebrew people with an acceptable historical legend, and codified their slowly-evolved social and ceremonial legislation into its ultimate expression, a *"Diatessaron* of the Old Testament," the Pentateuch.[qq]

*   *   *

This primary and theologically fundamental division of the Old Testament is revealingly paralleled, in its literary evolution from antecedent documents, by the first four Books of the New. Whereas, however, the independent existence of Pentateuchal

---

[pp] Should the Artaxerxes of Ezra iv prove to be not the first of that name — called Longimanus (465–424 B. C.) — but, as has been proposed, Artaxerxes II — Mnemon (404–361 B. C.) — then Ezra's dates will have to be advanced into the fourth century B. C.

[qq] Numerous O. T. sources other than these major four, within the Pentateuch and beyond, are acknowledged by Scriptural authors either by citation of title or by quotation of excerpts. Lost works known only by title are *The Book of the Acts of Solomon* [I Kgs. xi. 41]; *The Book of the Chronicles of the Kings of Israel* [I Kgs. xiv. 19, *et al.*]; and *The Book of the Chronicles of the Kings of Judah* [I Kgs. xiv. 29, *et al.*]. Songs quoted include those of Lamech [Gen. iv. 23–24]; of Moses [Ex. xv. 1–18], verses 12–17 of which presuppose the post-Mosaic conquest of Canaan; of the *Well* [Num. xxi. 17–18]; of the *Triumph over Sihon* [Num. xxi. 27–30]; and of Deborah [Judg. v. 1–31]. Excerpted sources include *The Book of the Wars of the LORD*, a title which, though cited in Numbers [xxi. 14], could hardly have been penned prior to the post-Mosaic entry into Palestine; and *The Book of Jashar*, which, first mentioned and quoted in Joshua [x. 12–13], cannot have been completed, in view of the poetic quotation therefrom at II Sam. i. 18, before the reign of David. To literary sources such as these, must be added the special interpolation [ch. xiv] in Genesis, and connective passages, such as that of Gen. xxii. 14–18, by the various editors.

sources now lost can only be inferred from the internal evidence of the surviving Scriptural text, it is clearly demonstrable, as will shortly appear, that the Gospel according to Mark — or something closely resembling it — itself constitutes one of the principal written sources[rr] of the Gospels attributed to Matthew and Luke; and sufficiently apparent, furthermore, in the Gospel according to John, is its author's unhesitating appropriation of previous Christian material, particularly items supplied by the second and third Gospels — those of Mark and Luke. The Gospels, to be certain, required for their full development an interval of time considerably briefer than that required for evolution of the completed Pentateuch, but the process of compilation was in both instances very much the same. Insofar, on the one hand, as the Gospels according to Matthew and Luke are in part derived from no document now in existence but from a source or sources purely inferential, their interrelationships and those conjectured for the Pentateuchal Books are in large measure comparable. Insofar, on the other hand, as these two Gospels, again in part, palpably derive from the still extant Gospel of Mark, their mutual relationships are analogous less to those inferred for the Pentateuchal Books than to those which demonstrably subsist between Chronicles and the four antecedent Books of Samuel and Kings. Incorporation by the Chronicler into his own narrative of large sections of the surviving text of the Former Prophets — frequently word for word; sometimes with alterations or editorial deletions — is exactly paralleled by the assimilative literary methods of the first and third Evangelists.

Unacknowledged assimilation of a preceding author's work being, it is to be remembered, the customary practice of Old Testament and other ancient historiographers, surprise need not be felt that this technique was also exploited in Christian writings — notably in portions of the Gospels and, as marked by Erasmus, in the Acts of the Apostles, and in the late second-

---

[rr] That Mark was *written* is indicated — if the passage be not a later gloss — within the Gospel itself at xiii. 14 (cp. Mt. xxiv. 15): "let him that readeth understand."

century Harmony of the Gospels of the missionary Tatian. That illuminating document, the *Diatessaron*, compiled from the four separate Gospels originally in Greek, it is thought, and then translated into Syriac, but preserved for the most part only in Arabic and Latin translation,[39] is the earliest known attempt to harmonize the accounts of the Evangelists. Based upon the Gospel according to John, from which both its opening and closing passages were culled, the *Diatessaron* is evidently a pioneer undertaking to coalesce into a single document, by eclectic gleaning of the editor's four principal sources, all available items contributory to a complete and integrated record of the beginnings of Christianity. Although the compiler's apparent intention was to incorporate in the *Diatessaron* one representative version, and only one, of each event or discourse in the Gospels, neglecting nothing of importance and reproducing his excerpted passages without serious alteration, Tatian's finished redaction is nevertheless remarkably instructive as an exhibition of the multifarious modifications of source material — duplication, substitution, conflation, inept amalgamation, and every variety of transposition[40] — through which an ancient editor inadvertently produced those undetected incongruities which subsequent investigation reveals in his text. From this composite work of Tatian, had none of the Gospels survived, segregation of excerpted passages typical of the distinctive writing and substance of John might, with some confidence, be in large measure accomplished; in the case of the remaining three Evangelists, however, the winnowing out of their contributions to the *Diatessaron* could be effected, if at all, only partially and with disconcerting uncertainty. Possession of the Gospels, of course, not only eliminates any doubt as to the compilatory nature of Tatian's "Harmony" but fortunately makes possible the illumination of related problems by analysis of the manner in which the editor utilized each of his four sources.[41]

Recognition that the compendious literary method of Tatian and the Chronicler is likewise employed, as will appear, by the authors "Matthew" and Luke, is fundamental in successful analysis of the interrelationship of the Synoptic Gospels[ss] — those according to Matthew, Mark and Luke — and in the attempted recovery of their source or sources. This analysis and theoretical reconstruction constitutes the Synoptic Problem. Solution of this intricate literary enigma begins with the realization that the first three Gospels, though varying considerably in content and in length, and characterized by inexplicable minor discrepancies,[tt] frequently, in reporting one and the same incident, commonly phrase their accounts in language which is strikingly similar and often identical.[uu] The vocabulary of Mark in such narrative portions of the Gospel is usually reproduced with considerable fidelity in both Matthew and Luke; or, when that is not the case, in one or the other of them. The language of slightly more than half of Mark is approximated by Luke; "Matthew's" proportion is about nine-tenths. Such similarity or identity of phrasing in these documents, which there is reason to believe were prepared at different times for churches widely separated both in location and in theological tendencies, is strong indication of at least one written source common to all three. Memorial transmission — to which the Synoptists' similarity of narrative style was formerly attributed — being inconsistent with divergent methods of handling some of the source-material to be seen in Matthew and Luke, is generally rejected by modern scholars as an explanation of stylistic uniformity in the narrative sections of the first three Gospels.

[ss] The use of *Synoptic* to identify — because of their similarity in content, arrangement and literary form — the first three Gospels, was initiated, it seems, in 1841, by Frederic Myers, in *Catholic Thoughts on the Bible and Theology*, Vol. III, § 17. 45.

[tt] Illustrative of such discrepancy, perplexing to the scribes, is the variation in the name of one of the Apostles, who, though invariably called Judas son of James in early uncial MSS. of Luke (except Codex C in which the name is wanting), appears as Thaddaeus in Mt. and Lk. of both ℵ and B and in Mk. alone of Θ; as Lebbaeus in Mt. and Mk. of D; and as Lebbaeus called Thaddaeus in Mt. of W and Θ. In Mk., W omits the name entirely. The *Diatessaron* exhibits the conflate form James of Lebbaeus. *V. supra*, *Gerasenes*, p. 120.

[uu] Cp., for example, the cure of the leper at Mt. viii. 1, Mk. i. 40, and Lk. v. 12; or the accounts of the woman with an issue of blood at Mt. ix. 19, Mk. v. 24, and Lk. viii. 42.

The written Synoptic source of the *narratives* — in contra-distinction to the parables and sayings — may be provisionally held to have been one of the Gospels themselves. Any one of the three may, hypothetically, have served as the foundation of the remaining two. Detailed examination, however, precludes either the Gospel according to Matthew or the Gospel according to Luke from consideration as a Marcan source; for Mark, had he been copying either Evangelist, could not conceivably have omitted, as he does, Matthaean or Lucan masterpieces such as the parables of the Talents and the Good Samaritan, or the Sermon on the Mount. Imbedded in the texts of Matthew and Luke, indeed, are more than two hundred verses of strictly non-Marcan but superlative material, a large measure of which could hardly have escaped inclusion by Mark had his Gospel been derived from the work of either the first or the third Evangelist. Furthermore, the Gospel according to Matthew, omitting exclusively Lucan features like the Adoration of the Shepherds or the parable of the Prodigal Son, is surely out of the question as a source for Luke; and, reciprocally, the Gospel according to Luke, lacking peculiarly Matthaean parables such as the Laborers in the Vineyard or the Ten Virgins, is inconceivable as a source for the Gospel which bears Matthew's name. The residual possibility, then, under the assumption that one of the Synoptics underlies the other two, is necessarily that, of the three, Mark's is the only Gospel possible as a source; and, consequently, that the major portion of the narrative core common to both the first and the third Gospels, if derivative, is patterned upon material essentially Marcan. Pertinent, in this connection, is the observation that of the 661 verses of Mark — by far the shortest of the Synoptic Gospels — only thirty are wanting from one or the other of Mark's two fellow-Evangelists, and all but fifty-five[vv] are reproduced in Matthew alone. The conclusion, furthermore, that "Matthew" and Luke elaborated their predecessor's Gospel — a conclusion now of nearly univer-

[vv] Even fewer, according to B. H. Streeter, *The Four Gospels*, London, 1930, p. 169. The number of verses in Mt. is 1068; in Lk., 1149.

sal acceptance — is fortified by the important consideration that each of these two Evangelists repeatedly improves not only the grammar and style of Mark but also his tone, assuredly an indication that, of the three versions, the Marcan is the most primitive.[ww]

The Gospel according to Mark, whether or not itself employed as a source by either "Matthew" or Luke, was, in any case, available, chronologically speaking, to both the Evangelists. Generally accepted dating of the Gospels, though at best only approximate, recognizes Mark's as the first of the four to be written. If not all of his Gospel, presumably the first thirteen chapters,[xx] in the last of which destruction of the Temple is prophesied, must have been set down for his Gentile readers prior to that Jewish calamity, A. D. 70. How much earlier the Gospel may have been composed is an unresolved question. According to the testimony of Papias, bishop of Hierapolis in Asia Minor, about A. D. 125, Mark, who had neither heard Jesus nor followed him, later became the interpreter of Peter, writing down faithfully, albeit unsystematically [οὐ μέντοι τάξει], all he remembered of Peter's oral account of the sayings and deeds of Christ.[yy] Whether the Petrine memoirs were com-

---

[ww] Typical of such refinement by Luke is his compression of Mark's redundancy, "at even, when the sun did set" [i. 32], into the entirely adequate "when the sun was setting" [Lk. iv. 40]. Revision by "Matthew" of Mark's "Why callest thou me good?" [x. 18] results in the less provocative "Why askest thou me concerning that which is good?" [Mt. xix. 17]. For Mark's *Rabbi* or *Teacher* (διδάσκαλη), used in addressing Jesus, "Matthew" substitutes *Lord* (Κύριε) nineteen times; Luke, either *Lord*, sixteen times, or *Master* (ἐπιστάτα) six times. Mark employs *Lord* in but a single instance. *Cf.* Sir John Hawkins, *Horae Synopticae*, 2nd ed., rev., Oxford, 1909, pp. 117–153. For refinements in which "Matthew" and Luke concur, *v. infra*, note zz.

[xx] Mk. xiii — the so-called "Little Apocalypse" — may, of course, have been written prior to the twelve chapters which now precede it.

[yy] Condensed from Eusebius, *Hist. Eccl.*, III. 39 [Migne, *Patr. Gr.*, XX, col. 300], who, on the authority of a certain John "the Elder," thus reports Papias: Μάρκος μὲν ἑρμηνευτὴς Πέτρου γενόμενος, ὅσα ἐμνημόνευσεν, ἀκριβῶς ἔγραψεν, οὐ μέντοι τάξει, τὰ ὑπὸ τοῦ Χριστοῦ ἢ λεχθέντα ἢ πραχθέντα· οὔτε γὰρ ἤκουσε τοῦ Κυρίου, οὔτε παρηκολούθησεν αὐτῷ, ὕστερον δὲ, ὡς ἔφην, Πέτρῳ, ὃς πρὸς τὰς χρείας ἐποιεῖτο τὰς διδασκαλίας, ἀλλ' οὐχ ὥσπερ σύνταξιν τῶν κυριακῶν ποιούμενος λόγων. ὥστε οὐδὲν ἥμαρτε Μάρκος, οὕτως ἔνια γράψας

posed by Mark, as Clement of Alexandria claims,[42] during the lifetime of Peter, or, as Irenaeus, c. A. D. 177, maintains,[43] and Streeter, on the basis of Mark xiii, agrees,[44] after his martyrdom at Rome, A. D. 64–65, is an unsettled point of no immediate moment. In either case, the second Evangelist's recollection of Peter's eye-witness narrative, put into written form, in all likelihood at Rome, prior to A. D. 70, antedates the Gospels according to Matthew and Luke — for which, indeed, it seems to have served as Synoptic outline—by more than a decade. The first and third Gospels, intended, if not to supersede Mark at Rome, then to be used elsewhere in churches unfamiliar with the Marcan tradition, were most probably produced, in recent scholarly opinion,[45] Matthew at Antioch in Syria approximately A. D. 80, and Luke either at Ephesus or Corinth not many years thereafter.

The Synoptic Gospels, then, so far as their narratives resemble one another, are generally thought to owe their similarities to the circumstance that "Matthew" and Luke, working independently, assimilated most of the literary substance of their predecessor, John Mark, into their own more comprehensive versions of the same eventful story. Omission of Marcan passages from the first and third Gospels — most conspicuous of which is Luke's exclusion of sixty-four consecutive verses [Mk. vi. 45–viii. 26] — suggests, at first thought, the further possibility that our second Gospel is itself an expansion of an earlier and of course shorter document — a prototypic Mark, or, in German idiom, an *Ur-Marcus* — upon which both "Matthew" and Luke are likewise, in part, dependent. This hypothesis — which cannot be lightly dismissed — has the advantage of requiring no explanation for the deletion, apparently deliberate, of portions of Mark by his fellow Evangelists. Motivation, indeed, for these textual excisions is not always to be found, and, although some-

---

ὡς ἀπεμνημόνευσεν. Ἑνὸς γὰρ ἐποιήσατο πρόνοιαν, τοῦ μηδὲν ὧν ἤκουσε παραλιπεῖν, ἢ ψεύσασθαί τι ἐν αὐτοῖς... Cf., further, Jerome, *Ep. ad Hedibiam* [*Opera*, ed. Vallarsi, Vol. I, 844]: Habebat ergo Titum interpretem: sicut, & beatus Petrus Marcum, cujus Evangelium, Petro narrante, & illo scribente, compositum est.

times obviously apologetic, may frequently be nothing other than the personal predilection of the writer, or his obligation — a practical matter — to contain his assembled material, Marcan and other, within the limits of a single papyrus roll.[46] Nevertheless — unfortunately for the hypothesis — minute examination of linguistic and stylistic features peculiar to all of Mark, convincingly identifies the sixty-four consecutive verses overlooked by Luke as an integral part of the Marcan document,[47] necessitating the conclusion that they — and, if they, even more certainly the shorter Lucan or Matthaean omissions from Mark — were, for whatever motive, deliberately dropped out of the narrative to satisfy the editorial needs of the third Evangelist. Contravening the *Ur-Marcan* theory even more decisively is the insurmountable objection that no two documents, such as our Mark and its hypothetical ancestor, are in the least likely exactly to have duplicated their loss of essential concluding verses, both breaking off unfinished at precisely the same point, as Mark does,[48] in the middle of a sentence. Had a prototype of Mark come to the hands of either "Matthew" or Luke — as the theory requires — something of the Galilean Appearances of the Risen Christ expected in its conclusion [see Mk. xvi. 7] would surely have been appropriated by one or the other Evangelist. Rejection, however, of an *Ur-Marcus* as neither acceptable nor demonstrable, involves no assumption that the common source available to "Matthew" and Luke was precisely the Gospel according to Mark *as it now appears in Scripture*. The cumulative effect, in fact, of well over two hundred grammatical and other improvements in the Marcan text *concurrently* made in the superior Greek of the Lucan and Matthaean versions, dictates the conjecture that the Biblical recension of Mark is itself the primitive Greek form of the text, which, prior to its utilization by either "Matthew" or Luke, had undergone a certain amount of revision.[zz]

[zz] Mt. and Lk. frequently agree against Mk. in a substituted synonym, in removal of a redundancy, in replacement of an historical present — one of Mark's mannerisms — by an aorist. *Cf.* Hawkins, *op. cit.*, p. 210.

The Gospels according to Matthew and Luke, while embracing approximately an identical two-thirds of the substance of Mark, incorporate also, as previously noted, some two hundred verses[aaa] of other than Marcan origin. Distribution of these non-Marcan verses throughout Matthew and Luke — primarily, it would appear, in deference not to historical but to literary considerations — varies in so mutually inconsistent a manner as to require, in explanation, the inference, a perfectly natural one, that the two authors, dissatisfied with what they considered the insufficient nature of the Marcan biographical outline, expanded it — "Matthew's" if not Luke's[49] primary source — with enriching features of current Christian tradition, each in accordance with a system peculiarly his own.[50] These amplifications of the second Evangelist's pioneering sketch were derived, as will appear, partly from a source to which both biographers had access and partly from sources available to, or exploited by, only one or the other.

Identification of these conjectural sources, from which "Matthew" and Luke presumably derive their many enrichments of the Marcan Gospel, is, of course, entirely a matter of inference. The possibility of documentary rather than oral sources is suggested by Luke's own statement, in the prefatory verses of his Gospel, that, when he took up his pen, there had already been several attempts to draw up a narrative of "matters . . . fully established" as they had been orally delivered by eyewitness "ministers of the word." Eusebius, furthermore, on the authority of Papias in passages previously quoted,[51] attributes to Matthew — not, of course, the unknown author of the first Gospel, but the customs-collector who became an Apostle — the composition in Aramaic [πατρίῳ γλώττῃ γραφῇ] not only of a Gospel ['Εναγγέλιον], but, in the same language ['Εβραΐδι διαλέκτιῳ . . . συνεγράψατο], of something so different in character as to be called "the oracles" [τα λόγια], which, he continues, each one interpreted as he was able ['Ηρμήνευτε δ'αὐτά ὡς

[aaa] Streeter, *op. cit.*, p. 150, increases this count by more than a third to 270 plus.

ἠδύνατο ἕκαστος]. This latter expression, surely inapplicable
to a Gospel — a biographical study — is appropriate rather to
a collection of the sayings or discourses of Jesus — a written
record of his memorable words, or *Logia*. Probable though a
"Logian"[bbb] document of this kind seem, either in Aramaic or in
Greek translation, early Christian literature contains no acceptable indication of its existence other than that of the second-
century Epistle of Barnabas, which, at iv. 14, introduces the
non-Marcan aphorism from Matthew [xxii. 14], "many are
called, but few chosen," with the significant phrase, *as it is
written*. Slight though such external evidence be, it lends support
to the generally accepted inference that, for the discursive and
allegorical non-Marcan matter similarly treated by both "Matthew" and Luke, there was ultimately a single written source,
possibly — even probably — the Aramaic document referred to
by Papias. This theory, leaving something to be desired, as will
be seen, with respect to Luke's direct use of this source — the
Logia, whose customary symbol, "Q," is derived from the initial
of *Quelle*, the German word for *source* — is satisfactorily consistent
with the conclusion previously reached that likeness of the narrative in all three Synoptic Gospels is the result of "Matthew's"
and Luke's common, but different, utilization of *a written document*
— something, that is, closely resembling, if not identical with,
the Gospel according to Mark.

If, as may be reasonably assumed, "Matthew" and Luke put
each to his particular Evangelical use not only the Marcan
narratives but also the aphorisms and allegories of the *Logia*,
their methods of exploiting the latter document exhibit striking
dissimilarities. Luke's inclination is for few but extensive insertions of large blocks of the foreign substance[ccc] into the Marcan
matrix, each insertion being augmented with a comparable
quantity of discursive matter peculiar to Luke himself. "Matthew's" tendency — like the Deuteronomist's — is to reassemble

---

[bbb] The convenience of this adjectival form is offered in extenuation of its
morphological impropriety.

[ccc] Notably Lk. vi. 20–viii. 3, ix. 51–xviii. 14, and xix. 1–27.

scattered but topically related passages into formal discourses,[ddd] introducing them at whatever point in the Marcan narrative they seem most appropriate, the parable, peculiar to the Matthaean account, of the Laborers in the Vineyard [Mt. xix. 30–xx. 16] being, for instance, used obviously to exemplify the Marcan dictum "But many that are first shall be last, and the last first" [Mk. x. 31], and even his longest interpolation, the Sermon on the Mount — itself an agglomeration — serving as an elaborate prelude to Mark's observation [i. 22]: "And they were astonished at his teaching; for he taught them as having authority, and not as the scribes."

Non-Marcan portions of the text, which, being similar in the Gospels according to Matthew and Luke, can be readily recognized as of common and therefore presumably of Logian origin, whatever their disposition in Luke, are throughout the first Gospel distributed with seeming indifference to chronological consideration. Attention to temporal sequence cannot, of course, be safely predicated of a pre-Evangelical compiler whose reverential but presumably unhistorical concern, like that of the publican Levi who became the Apostle Matthew, was chiefly the gathering and preservation of the memorable sayings of his Master; and it may well be that the *Logia*, like the Torah, "did not" as the Talmud[52] says of that earlier Palestinian document, "arrange facts chronologically." Indeed, outside of the Marcan text there is within the two Gospels little, if any, assignment of incident or sayings to specific occasions, and, possibly as a consequence, few instances can be found (all of them prior to the story of the Temptation) in which the authors "Matthew" and Luke insert a Logian excerpt in an identical Marcan context. Consistent with the Evangelists' treatment of the Marcan document is the assumption that Luke adheres to the Logian

---

[ddd] This compilatory practice was occasionally "Matthew's" also in his treatment of the Marcan document, as at Mt. x. 1–20 where he gathers together excerpts from Mark as separated from each other as iii. 13–19, vi. 6–11, and xiii. 9–13. This literary technique, of course, is not confined to the first Book of the N. T., dispersed selections from the LXX being quoted consecutively, for example, at Rom. iii. 10–18, ix. 33, and I Pet. ii. 7, 8.

outline, and that "Matthew" is the editor who disregards the chronological or other arrangement of material in his source, fitting excerpted fragments together in accordance with his own agglomerative practice. It is furthermore not at all unlikely that, in the arrangement of the Matthaean *memorabilia*, the unknown author of the first Gospel incorporated almost the whole of the Apostle's *Logia* — in all probability from a current Greek translation[53] — making it altogether fitting and proper that his should have come to be known as the Gospel *according to Matthew*.[eee]

The postulate that Matthew and Luke share, as their major written sources, to the exclusion of any others, the canonical Mark and the conjectural *Logia* — conveniently designated the Two-Document Hypothesis — necessitates either the complementary assumptions, sufficiently plausible in themselves, that, undetected in non-Marcan matter peculiar to Matthew, lurk Logian passages rejected by Luke, and in non-Marcan passages peculiar to Luke there survive, undetected, Logian items rejected by "Matthew,"[fff] or the alternative supposition that preservation of non-Marcan sections by only one of the two Evangelists is attributable to his special familiarity with, and utilization of, a localized oral tradition. These two assumptions, it need hardly be said, are neither implausible nor mutually exclusive. Oral tradition no doubt is a factor to be taken into consideration, as, it may well be, in transmission of the popular Beatitudes or the Lord's Prayer, the Matthaean and Lucan versions of which are conspicuously divergent; and sundry Logian excerpts, to be certain, may have been preserved by one of the Evangelists alone. Of the non-Marcan matter, however, the portions peculiar to either Matthew or Luke are so extensive —

[eee] Neither the attribution to Matthew [κατὰ Ματθαῖον] nor the term *Gospel* ['Ευαγγέλιον] was supplied by the original author or his contemporaries, the familiar title being — like the titles of the three other Gospels and of Acts [Πράξεις] — inventions of a later period.

[fff] Portions of the *Logia*, it may be assumed, having, like a few verses of the Marcan document, been assimilated by neither "Matthew" nor Luke, are lost beyond possibility of recovery.

particularly the Jerusalem-centered portion of those Gospels [54] — that their derivation from a single written source exceeds the limits of reasonable conjecture. Although the inference of common documentary origin, whether single or multiple, [55] is inescapable with respect to numerous non-Marcan parallel passages in which "Matthew" and Luke employ nearly identical verbal patterns, certain of these extensive non-Marcan accounts of the two Evangelists — as the Nativity, the Passion and the Resurrection — are so noticeably at variance as to make it immediately apparent that their Gospels, composed under the influence of diverse Christian traditions, presumably Palestinian and Syro-Antiochéne, were conditioned only in part by loyalty to identical written traditions. Deviation in treatment, indeed, by "Matthew" and Luke of non-Marcan material plainly indicates the critical obligation to add to the Sayings collected by Matthew the Apostle an extra-Logian source or sources — documentary or oral — for those portions of their Gospels having no counterpart in Mark.

The existence of supplementary sources is inferable, to begin with, even where in the second Gospel parallels occur to Matthew and Luke; for in Mark — independent though it presumably be of the *Logia* — there are some fifty scattered verses[ggg] the substance of which, but neither the form nor the extent, is duplicated in Logian passages of Matthew and Luke. Derivation of these fifty verses by Mark, assuming his independence of the *Logia*, is necessarily referred, it will be appreciated, to some unidentified tradition, divergent from the Logian document *but overlapping it*, and less elaborately developed. [56] With all the more assurance, then, may inferred sources be sought for those parallel portions of Matthew and Luke which, unrecorded in Mark, exhibit widely dissimilar features.

Conspicuous among such dissimilar non-Marcan parallels are the Sermon on the Mount [Mt. v. i–vii. 27] and its much shorter

[ggg] John's preaching, the Baptism and Temptation, the Beelzebub controversy, the parables of the Leaven and the Mustard Seed, the Mission Charge, and briefer sayings.

analogue in Luke [vi. 20–49], the Sermon on the Plain. Of the
thirty verses which comprise the Lucan version of the Sermon,
no less than twenty-six find their equivalent in some three dozen
comparable verses of Matthew, and may, therefore, be considered of Logian origin. Deletion of these thirty-six Matthaean
verses from the one hundred and nine which constitute the
Sermon on the Mount isolates seventy-three verses — almost
exactly two-thirds of the Matthaean original — which, read in
uninterrupted sequence, produce a piece of writing sufficiently
coherent to have stood by itself in an independently circulating
document. This residual matter — two-and-a-half times the
length of the Sermon on the Plain, and in the main peculiar to
Matthew — having escaped, as it appears, the notice of Luke,
must have come into the hands of "Matthew" either through
oral tradition with which the third Evangelist was unfamiliar or
through a document or documents unavailable to him when he
wrote his Gospel. This unidentified Matthaean source — estimated by Streeter to consist of two hundred and thirty verses,
and conveniently symbolized by him with the appropriate initial
"M" — contains, in addition to the seventy-three verses of the
Sermon on the Mount, distinctive versions of numerous non-
Marcan passages so divergent from their Lucan parallels that
they and their counterparts cannot both be held to have originated in a common source, the *Logia* or any other. In these
instances, then, the received text of the first Evangelist was
produced by an interweaving of the available materials. The
ultimate in this process of conflation is the Sermon on the Mount,
in which "Matthew" has effectively welded together the related
subject-matter of two distinguishable traditions, one of which —
most probably, though not necessarily, the *Logia* — supplied
the abbreviated Lucan version of Christ's discourse to his followers, and the other of which — the putative "M" — fortunately provided the substance of that memorable Sermon in a
more generous and rewarding version. This second tradition —
whether or not its place of origin be, as Streeter suggests, Jerusalem, and its date as early as A. D. 65 — is accounted, in recent

scholarly opinion, a major source of the discourses and parables of the Gospel according to Matthew, occupying about the same position relative to Mark, its narrative source, as is accorded the Logian document. [57]

For Luke, even more abundantly than for Matthew, the evidence of the text itself points to a major source supplementary to the generally recognized two — Mark for the narrative portions, and, for parables and discourse, the *Logia*. Something more than one-half of the content of Mark was compressed by Luke into less than a third of his Gospel, the greater portion being, accordingly, of Logian or other origin. Not only does Luke achieve this compression by omission of as many as one hundred and twenty-seven complete Marcan verses [58] which "Matthew" saw fit to assimilate, but, frequently — as in the Call of Peter, the Great Commandment, or the Rejection at Nazareth — when he does incorporate matter included in the second Gospel his presentation varies markedly in form from that of Mark and is placed in a non-Marcan context. In such circumstances, re-writing of one's sources being alien to ancient historiographical method, it is certainly reasonable to attribute the modified "Marcan" matter to still another Lucan source, which, at the suggestion of Streeter, may be appropriately referred to as "L." The Rejection at Nazareth, for specific illustration, separated from the Temptation, in Mark, by one hundred seventy-eight verses, is advanced in Luke to follow immediately after the Temptation; and, besides this change of location, to the substance of its seven Marcan verses [Mk. vi. 1–6] are added another eleven [Lk. iv. 17–21, 25–30] entirely different in character and peculiar to the third Gospel. This, it would seem, can have no explanation other than Luke's use, at this point, of some independent source — a source, moreover, presumably extra-Logian, inasmuch as there is no parallel Rejection by "Matthew," even when, at the close of his thirteenth chapter, the first Evangelist reports the preaching of Jesus in the Synagogue at Nazareth. The extra-Logian nature of Luke's second major non-Marcan source is further apparent in his account of John's preaching [Lk. iii. 7–16], to which Mark devotes but two verses [Mk. i. 7, 8]. Augmentation of these two verses by "Matthew" and Luke is in part identical, both Evangelists adding to Mark's brief notice the pronouncement that "God is able of stones to raise up children to Abraham," and the observation that "the axe is laid to the root of the trees." Thus far, accordingly, the non-Marcan source may well have been the *Logia*. Luke, however, not content with these additions, borrows six verses [10–15] from some unidentified source — our hypothetical "L" — used here by neither Mark nor "Matthew," which amplified John's discourse with several injunctions: to the multitudes, "He that hath two coats, let him impart to him that hath none"; to the publicans, "Extort no more than that which is appointed to you"; and to the soldiers, "Do violence to no man . . . and be content with your wages."

Luke's ability thus to supplement his Marcan material is more than equalled by his capacity to dispense with it. Comparison of the content of the Gospels discloses the undeniable and revealing fact that Luke repeatedly makes no use of Mark even when Mark is available. Particularly in two extended passages does Luke depart from reproduction of his Marcan prototype — with the substance, phrasing and order of which he is in reasonable accord — apparently to interpolate matter from some other source. In these departures the substance of Mark is almost entirely ignored. Whatever the peculiarly Lucan weight of the lesser of these two lengthy "interpolations" [111 verses: Lk. vi. 20–viii. 3], the greater [Lk. ix. 51–xviii. 14 — often misleadingly referred to as the Peraean Section] is no mean contribution, its three hundred and fifty-one verses — a third of the total in Luke — constituting the very heart of the third Gospel. These and some shorter "interpolations" of Luke,[hhh] together with his non-Marcan beginning and end,[iii] being considerably

---

[hhh] Lk. iii. 1–iv. 30; less certainly xxii. 14–xxiv. 12. *Cf.* Streeter, *op. cit.*, pp. 201–207.

[iii] Were the lost conclusion to Mark's Gospel ever to be recovered, it would assuredly contain neither of the two Resurrection Appearances at Jerusalem

greater in bulk than the Marcan matter in his Gospel, the inference recommends itself that, contrary to established opinion,
the passages in Luke which may logically be termed "interpolations" are, if there be any such, those which derive from
Mark, Luke having selected as fundamental in the creation of
his Gospel material essentially non-Marcan. This is to say that
Luke, finding the Marcan narratives, though indispensable as
a source, secondary to his purposes, based his Gospel primarily
upon the Logian document — "Q" — and upon extra-Logian
traditions — "L" — opportunity for the collection of which was
amply afforded by his two years' residence at Caesarea [59]
awaiting the imprisoned Paul's release by the Roman authorities. If, as Streeter proposes, [60] these two non-Marcan sources,
"Q" and "L," had been united into one impressive document
— a "Proto-Luke" [jjj] — by some earlier compiler, possibly Luke
himself, then the subsequent product, the received Gospel according to Luke, may be looked upon, so to speak, as a "second
edition, newly enlarged and revised."

Whether or not this suggestive conjecture be true, the major
sources of Luke, as of Matthew, are now seen to be three. Two
of these sources — Mark and the *Logia* — being common to
both Evangelists, the total of major Synoptic sources — as, by
curious coincidence, of the Pentateuch — is obviously four:

---

with which Luke terminates his Gospel. The Appearances anticipated for the
missing end of Mark were indubitably Galilean. *Cf.* Mark xvi. 7.

[jjj] The maximum extent of "Proto-Luke" is determined by deletion from
the third Gospel of the introductory Infancy narrative [Lk. i. 5–ii. 52] and all
passages of Marcan origin. The remainder, if combined in a single document,
constitutes a sufficiently complete, though non-biographical, Gospel, longer
indeed than Mark's, and, in Streeter's opinion, likely to have impressed Luke
as "more important and valuable an authority than Mark," to whom he turned
chiefly for details of a strictly biographical character. First among Jewish-
Christian writers to apply the biographical technique of the contemporary
Gentile community to a Life of Jesus was Mark. In the evolution of the biographical Gospel, "Proto-Luke," if a reality, was an intermediate form between
amorphous collections such as "Q" or Jeremiah and the sculptured biographies
of Greek and Roman authors.

Mark, "M," "L," and the Logian document.[kkk] The Synoptic Gospels, whose structure is thus explained, in the main, by a "Four-Document Hypothesis," reveal themselves upon analysis as both composite and evolutionary. No doubt independently written, each of the Synoptic Gospels is in part indebted to a source or sources available to, and exploited by, one or both of the others. Each, at the hour of composition, appears to have embodied the Evangelical traditions — the "primitive Gospels" — current at one or more of four focal points of the developing Church: Antioch, Jerusalem, Caesarea and Rome.[111]

*   *   *

The authors of the Gospels, it may be taken as certain, wrote with no conscious intention of augmenting the Law and the Prophets. That their works when first issued were invested with nothing of Scriptural sacredness is evident equally from the use made of Mark by "Matthew" and Luke, and from the freedom with which John, in his — "the Ephesian" — Gospel (c. A. D. 90 –110), utilized the writings of his predecessors Mark and Luke.[61] The Synoptic Gospels, and subsequently other Christian writ-

---

[kkk] Minor sources include probably the core of the thirteenth chapter of Mark [*cf*. Streeter, in *Studies in the Synoptic Gospels*, p. 183]; more probably the Matthaean and Lucan versions of the genealogy of Jesus, which, interpolated by both Evangelists between the Baptism and Temptation passages of the Marcan narratives, are constructed on plans so dissimilar, and differ so patently in details, as to preclude their derivation from a common source; and certainly both the first two chapters of Matthew, peculiar to its unknown author, and apparently derived from an independent Antiochene tradition, and the first two chapters of Luke, which, peculiar to the third Gospel, seem on internal evidence to have been composed originally in Hebrew. *Cf*. C. C. Torrey, *The Translations made from the Original Aramaic Gospels*, New York, 1912, pp. 290 ff.; and R. A. Aytoun, "The Ten Lucan Hymns of the Nativity in their Original Language," in *Journal of Theological Studies*, Vol. XVIII (July, 1917), pp. 274–278.

[111] The Ephesian tradition being represented, according to scholarly consensus, in the Gospel according to John, no considerable body of early Christian tradition sponsored by any of the five leading churches of the first century fails of representation in at least one of the four Gospels.

ings, achieved the Scriptural position they now enjoy by a gradual historical process, an illuminating parallel to which is afforded by the earlier development of discrete units of Jewish literature into the canon — the recognized and authoritative content — of the Old Testament.

Acceptable external evidence as to when, where, how or by whom the Old Testament canon was established is unavailable. The well-known Jewish legend, published in 1538 by Elias Levita and advanced in Protestant circles of the seventeenth century by Johannes Buxtorf the elder,[62] that the "Men of the Great Synagogue," Ezra the scribe presiding,[mmm] first collected the Books of the Old Testament into a single volume and indicated its three main divisions, has no foundation in the records of antiquity,[63] and runs counter both to the ascertained period of codex-invention[64] and to such internal evidence as resides within the Old Testament itself. The concept of a Biblical canon — an authentic list of the sacred Books — is, indeed, a late development, the Greek word κανών being used with that particular meaning only after the middle of the fourth century,[nnn] and the Hebrew language possessing no equivalent until medieval times when Jewish exegetes, among them Ibn Ezra, introduced the expression "Holy Books" [ספרי הקדש — siphrE haq-qodeš]. In the pre-Christian centuries all Jewish books were, so to speak, sacred, and required no term of differentiation from profane writings. Of these holy books, however, only a designated

---

[mmm] The institution of a Great Synagogue, or Religious Sanhedrin, sitting continuously in Ezra's time or in any other prior to the destruction of the Temple, has been thoroughly discredited; special religious synods, short-lived as a constitutional convention, were apparently assembled at very infrequent intervals and at various centers as occasion required. One such special convocation may have been called at Jerusalem in 444 B. C. in connection with the public reading of the Book of the Law recorded at Neh. viii–x. *Cf.* Solomon Zeitlin, "Origin of the Synagogue," in *Proceedings of the American Academy for Jewish Research*, Vol. II (1930–1931), pp. 79, 80; and "The Canonization of the Hebrew Scriptures," *id.*, Vol. III (1931–32), pp. 155, 156.

[nnn] A. D. 363 [*v. infra*, note eeee], in the sixtieth, probably spurious, decree of the Council of Laodicea; A. D. 367, by Athanasius, in *Ep. Festalis*, xxxix. 1; A. D. 380, by Amphilochius (?) in *Iambi ad Seleucum*.

few — ultimately twenty-four — might be read with rabbinical approval in public; that is, in the Synagogue. The remainder, at first without the slightest implication of inferiority or rejection, were known in the Mishnaic period simply as "outside books."[ooo] Books which were sanctioned for Synagogal ritual had the property, according to Pharasaic doctrine, of "defiling the hands."[65] This surprising application of the ritual law of cleanliness [Lev. xi–xv] to sacred Scripture, the underlying import of which may baffle, if not altogether elude, those unaccustomed to its peculiarly Levitical significance, apparently necessitated ceremonial ablution by the officiating priest upon conclusion of his ritual reading. Whether lavation of hands or some other end was the intention of the rule, resultant priestly practice must have emphasized the special sacredness of rolls publicly read in the Synagogue, and, as a corollary, minimized the possibility of endowing additional books with Synagogal sanctity. Thus Jewish authority approached the concept of canonization.

Rabbinical controversy as to the hand-defiling virtue of certain of the Hagiographical Books flourished, it seems, well into the first century. Credibility need not be denied the Tannaitic tradition[66] of a celebrated debate, about A. D. 65, between the followers of Hillel, who favored "canonization" of Ecclesiastes, and the followers of Shammai who, victoriously maintaining the inability of that Book of Wisdom to render the hands unclean, prevented its inclusion, at least for some years following destruction of the Temple, among the books acceptable for reading in the Synagogue. Admission of Ecclesiastes — together with other disputed books: Esther, Proverbs, Ezekiel, Song of Songs[ppp] —

[ooo] *I. e.,* ספרים חיצונים — sePhāRIM ḤIṢÔNIM [*Mish. Sanh.* x. 1]. The Hebrew verb *to set aside, to store away* [גנז — GāNAZ], originally applied to esoteric works which were especially esteemed [*cf.* S. Zeitlin, *op. cit.,* Vol. III (1931–32), pp. 126–128], came to be used in the less complimentary sense of *conceal* [*v. supra,* p. 5, n. g], and, with reference to "outside books," *excluded,* or, in the Greek equivalent, *apocryphal.* The invidiousness of this latter word has at times been tempered with the Roman Catholic Church by substitution of *deutero-canonical,* a term created in 1566 by Pope Sixtus Senensis.

[ppp] The disputed books are themselves disputed. Rabbi Judah held that Song of Songs defiles [*i. e.,* is sacred] and the sacredness of Ecclesiastes alone is

seems to have been finally authorized, near the beginning of the second century, at Jabneh (Jamnia) in Judaea, at which city, after the fall of Jerusalem, Hillel's famous disciple Jochanan ben Zakkai had established a college, to which a specially convened religious synod was summoned about A. D. 100. That the Old Testament "canon" was then brought to its completion is substantiated by the contemporaneously written Apocalypse of Ezra,[qqq] which, at xiv. 37–45, for the first time in literary history, indicates, through a palpable fiction,[rrr] that twenty-four is the number of Books approved for public reading.

---

questionable. When Rabbi Simon ben Azzai specified the precise date of "canonization" of these two Books, Rabbi Akiba's brother-in-law concurring, Rabbi Akiba remonstrated: "God forbid! No Jew has ever questioned that the Song defiled ... The Song is most holy; if there was any dispute it concerned only Ecclesiastes." Although tradition has it that Ezekiel, because of its contradictions of Pentateuchal doctrine, was unable to render the hands unclean, and was released from that disability only by Hananiah ben Hezekiah ben Garon's championship [*Shab.* 13[b], *et al.*] and expenditure of three hundred jars of oil, Professor S. Zeitlin maintains [*Proc. A. A. J. R.*, III, 126–128] that in "the entire Tannaitic literature there is no inkling that Ezekiel was threatened with withdrawal from the canon."

[qqq] *I. e.*, II Esdras, "The Fourth Book of Ezra," the confusing relation of which to the other Ezra Books — themselves perplexingly interrelated — is exhibited in the subjoined table.

Contents	*A. V.*	*Vulgate*	*LXX*
Ezra (M. T.)	Ezra	I Esdras ⎫	II Esdras (B)
Neh. (M. T.)	Nehemiah	II Esdras ⎭	
"Greek Ezra": II Chr. xxxv–xxxvi, most of Ezra, Neh. vii. 72–viii. 12, misc. vv.	I Esdras (A)	III Esdras	I Esdras (A)
Fourth Bk. Ezra, in main apocalyptic.	II Esdras	IV Esdras	III Esdras

[rrr] In forty days, according to this legend, Ezra, under Holy inspiration, dictated from memory ninety-four Scriptural Books lost at the fall of Jerusalem in 586 B. C., the first twenty-four of which to be given immediate publication

Although Josephus,[67] for whatever reason, and Melito of Sardis[68] both discover but twenty-two Books in the Hebrew Bible, the larger number, implicit in the *Baraita* previously cited from the *Babylonian Talmud*,[69] is authenticated many times in Midrashic literature by its learned authors, the *tannaim* and *amoraim*. These twenty-four Books are co-extensive with the thirty-nine of the Old Testament in Protestant English Bibles, the twelve Minor Prophets, according to Jewish enumeration, being a single Book, Ezra and Nehemiah being united, and each of the three divided Books, Samuel, Kings and Chronicles, counting — as they did universally until the sixteenth century — as one. Incorporation of the Old Testament Books into two perfected canonical divisions — the Law and the Prophets — and a third category of uncertain title and content, which was still in progress, had been effected several centuries before Talmudic and even before Christian times. This threefold division, probably referred to both by Luke — xxiv. 44: "the law of Moses, and the prophets, and the psalms" — and, a little earlier, in similar fashion, by Philo,[70] is clearly recognized as early as 132 B. C.; for thrice in the brief Preface to Ecclesiasticus, written that year for the Greek version of the Hebrew Wisdom of Jesus ben Sirach, does the translator unmistakably indicate his familiarity with the tripartite canon, "the law itself, and the prophecies, and the rest of the books." Although identification of the last of the three groups, as will be observed, here lacks in precision, and, equally indeterminate, finds variant expression in the two companion references,[sss] no doubt may be entertained that, "in the eight and thirtieth year of Euergetes the king"[ttt] canonization of

---

are obviously "canonical," and the remainder of which, to be transmitted secretly to men of wisdom only, as erudite and highly prized works of esotericism [גנוזים — GeNUZIM], are plainly "apocryphal."

[sss] (1) "and by the others that have followed in their steps"; (2) "the other books of our fathers."

[ttt] The second Ptolemy to bear that name [Ptolemy VII, 170–116 B. C.]; not, as has been proposed [*cf.* R. G. Moulton, *The Modern Reader's Bible*, New York, 1948, p. 1630], Ptolemy III, Euergetes I, c. 247–221 B. C., a total of *twenty-six* years.

Hebrew Scriptures, all but the third division complete, left little opportunity for amplification.[uuu]

That the second division, the Prophets, had been brought to completion by the period [c. 200 B.C.] in which the Hebrew Wisdom of Jesus ben Sirach was originally composed is apparent not only from the fact that all of the Former and Latter Prophets are cited in Ecclesiasticus [xlvi–xlix] in their currently received Massoretic sequence but from the circumstance that Daniel, written during the persecution of the Jews under Antiochus Ephiphanes, about 165 B. C.,[71] and significantly ignored in Ecclesiasticus, is denied by Jewish tradition its customary Septuagintal classification as one of the Prophets, being regularly placed in the third part of the Hebrew Old Testament among the "Writings." For this arrangement no better explanation is likely to be offered than that Daniel, assuredly prophetic in character, was composed subsequent to closure of the second major division of the Jewish Scriptural canon. At the very end of the Prophets, moreover, Malachi — if it be he — concludes his Book with three verses whose reminder of the Mosaic Law and whose comforting promise of an Elijah[vvv] — that is, of Prophetic intervention — serve well enough, and may have been so intended, as colophon to "The Twelve," being, in that case, an unofficial canonization, so to speak, of all that precedes — that is, the Law and the Prophets.

The Prophetic portion of this twofold canon — completion of which may be assigned, at the latest, to the beginning of the second pre-Christian century — appears to have assumed its present form by stages. Whereas the order of Books in its earlier

---

[uuu] See also, II Mac. ii. 13–15, in which the Jewish brethren in Egypt (presumably possessed of the Torah) are offered "books about the kings and the prophets, and the books of David" which had been gathered together after the war by Judas Maccabeus. *Cf.* R. H. Charles, *Apocrypha and Pseudepigrapha of the Old Testament*, Oxford, 1913, Vol. I, p. 134.

[vvv] Elijah seems here to be representative of the Prophets in general, other examples of which "typical" use may be seen, for instance, at Mt. xvii. 11 and Lk. i. 17. *Cf.* Shakespeare's "*A* Daniel come to judgement," *The Merchant of Venice*, IV. i. 223.

section — Joshua, Judges, Samuel, Kings — maintains, to the remotest record, a constancy characteristic of canonization, in its latter part the sequence of the three Major Prophets, even in Talmudic times, is variable.[72] Uncertainty as to their order — understandable in view of the fact that each Book originally circulated, like the recently discovered "Dead Sea Scrolls" of Isaiah, as an independent document — indicates a "canonization" of Isaiah, Jeremiah and Ezekiel later than that of the Former Prophets.

To whatever remote date canonization of the Former Prophets must be referred, Synagogal acceptance of the special sanctity of the Pentateuch must be assigned to a time even earlier. If it be beyond critical warrant to claim, with some authorities, that promulgation of the Deuteronomic Code in 621 B. C. marked the beginning of the Old Testament canon, scholarly approval is not likely to be withheld from the conclusion that canonization of the greater portion, if not all, of the Torah was the dominant motive and the chief accomplishment of those who, in 444 B. C., assembled the people of Jerusalem to attend public reading of the book of the Law. Evidence, however, is not lacking that, subsequent to this initial canonization, the Pentateuch underwent further development to achieve its present canonic form. Discussion, particularly of matters concerning the calendar, in the late fourth-century Book of Jubilees — itself "apocalyptic to the Pentateuch"[73] — plainly indicates that certain sections of "Mosaic" legislation were still subject to modification more than a century after Ezra's memorable convocation.[74] When, after Alexander's defeat of the Persians in 333 B. C., and his advance upon Jerusalem, Manasseh, the disaffected Samaritan, obtained royal permission to build a Temple in which his sect might worship upon Mt. Gerizim,[75] it was imperative that he possess himself of a copy of the Law complete with the latest regulations essential to the cult. The Samaritan Pentateuch, accordingly, unchanged from that time unto this day, closely conforming as it does — with a few sectarian variations previously noticed[76] — to the Five Books of Moses of the Massoretic Text, establishes the date subsequent to which nothing other than exceedingly minor alterations of, or additions to, the Pentateuchal canon could be effected.

Such evidence, in summary, as is available points to the conclusion that something more than half a millennium was required for completion of the Old Testament canon. From the middle of the fifth pre-Christian century, when canonization confined its initial phase to the nearly completed Law, down to the close of the first century of the Common Era when the last of the disputed Books was admitted to the Writings, the Jewish people, naturally reflecting in their accumulating literature something of the historical and cultural influences to which they were subjected, gradually set apart a small collection of books, peculiarly theirs, for use in public worship. The process, thus protracted, no doubt reduced the number of Hebrew works preserved for posterity. Those few which, rather by force of tradition than by official action, were saved through investiture with special sanctity have established themselves, immutably, as the Holy Scriptures of the Jews — "The People of the Book" — the world over, and as the older of the two inspired Covenants which together constitute the Bible of Christianity.[www]

The canon of the New Testament, like that of the Old, required several centuries for its consummation; and, again like that of the Old, was the result not so much of administrative initiative or theological dictation as of an instinctive feeling, slowly developed by the Christian community, of the inspired nature of Apostolic and Evangelistic communication. Of such inspired writings as ultimately comprised the New Testament canon, none was produced until the first Christian century had completed half its course. Christians of the generation subsequent to the Crucifixion, living in momentary expectation of the Coming of the Messiah, had no immediate need of additions to

[www] Books rejected by the Jews as uncanonical, but included by Jerome in the Vulgate "for example of life and instruction in manners . . . not to establish doctrine," were officially incorporated into the O. T. canon of the Roman Catholic Church at the Council of Trent, A. D. 1545–1563.

their sacred literary inheritance. Sufficient unto their worship — as it had been for Jesus and his Disciples — was the traditional public reading from the Law or the Prophets or the Writings; and for doctrinal purposes oral instruction by itinerant spiritual leaders was the natural rule. Only at a later period, when eschatological hopes suffered indefinite postponement, and deviations such as Gnosticism and Montanism[xxx] arose to plague the scattered churches, did provisional guidance of the faithful in matters mundane and practical compel Christian founding Fathers, notably Paul, to take up the pen.

The letters of Paul, written in response to immediate organizational needs, were penned, of course, with no thought of matching the sacred Books of the Septuagint or of adding to their number. Their purpose in the earlier instances, far from offering extra-Scriptural instruction to those who might survive the anticipated wrath to come [I Thess. i. 10], was partly to admonish Paul's converts against abuses of which he had learned, partly to answer their questions as to conduct, partly to allay the fever with which the Messianic Advent continued to be awaited. Paul's communications, addressed for the most part not to individuals but to churches he had founded, were made known to the youthful Christian communities, at his particular direction [I Thess. v. 27], by public reading at religious assemblies. Thus associated with the solemnity of Christian worship, the Pauline epistles inevitably acquired at an early period something of the liturgical flavor of Old Testament selections regularly read as part of the ritual. This circumstance, coupled it

---

[xxx] Gnosticism — the reaction to which was a determining factor in establishing homogeneity of procedures within the early Church — was an anti-Jewish, dualistic religious movement, which, rejecting the authority of the O. T., and claiming for itself a mystical revelation ($\gamma\nu\hat{\omega}\sigma\iota\varsigma$), added to an Iranian concept of two powers, good and evil, contending within the material world, the Hellenic idea of salvation through separation of the corporeal and spiritual beings. Although no earlier account has survived of this religion, whose sacraments and mysticism persevere in its Christian rival, than that of Irenaeus [*Adv. Haer.*, c. 180], the movement is known to have been thriving at the beginning of the second century and is probably several decades older. *Cf.* I Tim. vi. 20. For Montanism, *v. infra*, p. 311, note cccc.

can hardly be doubted with the compelling personality of Paul, resulted in careful preservation of his communications, which though of peculiar authority were by no means considered sacred. These epistles, even when addressed to a single church or individual, were, as we learn from the "Muratorian fragment,"[yyy] of such value to the Church as a whole in matters of practice or doctrine that they came at an early period into general circulation, and were quoted — but not as "Scripture" — by writers like Clement of Rome and Polycarp of Smyrna about the dawn of the second century long before they acquired a sacrosanct status and were definitely elevated to liturgical use.

A collection of the Pauline letters — the first such collection of which there is record, but probably not the first to be made — was treasured by the Gnostic Marcion who, about A. D. 140, listed ten out of the thirteen Epistles, not in their established order, and omitting the three Pastorals.[77] Inasmuch as these three — I and II Timothy and Titus — are referred to among other Pauline epistles a generation earlier by Ignatius and Polycarp, it is reasonably inferred that all thirteen of the letters of Paul were included in the collections in circulation during the first quarter of the second century. Marcion, whose only acceptable Gospel was that according to Luke, intended in drawing up his list to exclude all those books which, generally accepted by Christians as authoritative with respect to apostolic doctrine, were not so considered by him and his sect.[zzz] Determination

---

[yyy] The "Muratorian fragment" — so designated in recognition of its first publication, A. D. 1740, by the Italian historian, Ludovico Muratori — is a badly mutilated MS., invaluable for its register of Writings comprising what amounts to the N. T. "canon" of the western churches at the close of the second century. The fragment, of eighty-five lines, formerly the property of the Irish Monastery of St. Columban at Bobbio, in Lombardy, now in the Ambrosian Library at Milan, preserves a translation, in barbarous Latin of the second century, of a private document, written, it is thought, originally in Greek, at Rome, possibly by Hippolytus, shortly before A. D. 200. *V. infra*, p. 310.

[zzz] *E. g.*, Clement of Rome's epistle to the Corinthians; the letters of Polycarp, Ignatius, Barnabas; and non-epistolary writings like the *Shepherd* of Hermas, the *Didaché*, and the numerous Apocryphal Gospels and Apocryphal *Acts of the Apostles*.

of the canon of the New Testament, as of the Hebrew Scriptures, was, from the outset, primarily a process of exclusion in the interest of doctrine.

Early substantial testimony to emergence of the New Testament canon is that of Irenaeus who, writing from his episcopal seat at Lugdunum (Lyons), Gaul, about A. D. 185, not only accepts as authoritative Gospels no fewer and no more than the now customary four, but quotes — for the first time known as "Scripture" — Acts of the Apostles, each of the Pauline Epistles except Philemon, three of the seven Catholic Epistles, and the Apocalypse.[78] Less than a decade earlier, not even the four Gospels had attained "Scriptural" standing; for Tatian, had such been their recognized position, would never have presumed to obscure their individual distinctiveness in his *Diatessaron*. The Evangelists themselves, of course, had motives other than literary renown, and no suspicion that they were producing a "Scriptural" literature which would ultimately become as sacred to their followers as the Books of the Hebrew Bible had long since been. Their writings, had Scriptural status immediately been claimed for them, could never have been subjected to such editorial rearrangement, interpolation and excision as created the Synoptic Problem. The author of Revelation, alone among New Testament writers to protect his text from alteration with threat of Divine punishment for him who augments or diminishes his prophecies, cannot be held, on the basis of this conventional imprecation, to have looked upon his Apocalypse as "Scriptural."[aaaa]The New Testament from its first to its last Book, was endowed, so far as evidence is available, with no vestige of its subsequent canonicity until about the middle of the second century when Justin, master of Tatian, seems, in the light of his disciple's *Diatessaron*, to have restricted the Gospels of which he approved to the present canonical four. The purpose of this restrictive selection was apparently not so much the posi-

---

[aaaa] *Cf*. Rev. xxii. 18. The conventional character of this imprecation may be seen in the *Letter of Aristeas*, § 311, and the blessing and curse at the end of the *Code of Hammurabi*. Cp. Deut. iv. 2.

tive one of achieving "Scriptural" status for the Synoptic Gospels and John as the negative one of denying authority to rival
Gospels such as those according to the Hebrews and to the
Egyptians, or that incorrectly ascribed to Peter, or especially
those of the Gnostics, some twenty-three of which, though for
the most part now lost, are known through citation or attestation
by the Fathers or through condemnation, toward the close of
the fifth century, in the so-called Gelasian Decree.ᵇᵇᵇᵇ Controversy with the Gnostics, it seems reasonable to believe, was a
dominant factor in propelling leaders of the growing Church to
nearly universal dependence upon a recognized selection of
Christian writings, approximating that of Irenaeus, through
which apostolic doctrine might be best defended. Inclusion in
this select group of writings was largely conditioned by the
period of their composition, nothing "late" in the history of the
Church being acceptable, and by the apostolic rank — or, exceptionally for Mark and Luke, apostolic discipleship — of the
authors. The first of these two conditions makes its appearance
in the previously mentioned "Muratorian fragment" the original
of which, written at Rome probably a little later than the Gallic
Irenaean "canon," specifically excludes the *Shepherd* of Hermas
from its catalogue of authoritative and acceptable writings not
because of its substance, which it commends for private reading,
but because of its late date, probably the second quarter of the
second century.⁷⁹ Included in the "Muratorian canon" are the
Gospels according to Luke and John, and, only by inference
owing to the corrupt state of the manuscript, those according to
Matthew and Mark. Additional apostolic and sufficiently early
Christian writings admitted to this canon are altogether eighteen:
Acts, thirteen Pauline Epistles [Hebrews missing], I and II John,
Jude and Revelation. Besides Hebrews the Muratorian list wants
four other Epistles: James, I and II Peter, III John. Indicative

---

ᵇᵇᵇᵇ *Decretum Gelasi de libris recipiendis et non recipiendis.* The contribution of
Pope Gelasius I [A. D. 492–496] to this Roman compilation of earlier documents which bears his name is conjectural. This Decree is known only through
transcription not earlier than the sixth century.

of the still slightly fluid state of the crystallizing canon is the inclusion in the Muratorian list of a work soon to be universally acclaimed apocryphal, the Apocalypse of Peter. The content of the Old Latin Version, prepared for the churches of North Africa presumably some time prior to the third century, is, as we learn from Tertullian of Carthage, identical, in its post-Septuagintal portion, with the canon of the "Muratorian fragment" except for deletion of the Apocalypse of Peter and addition of I Peter and III John. Gaul, Rome and Carthage, it is now clear, converge in their independent testimony to the widespread and very close agreement among the churches of the west at the close of the second century as to what constituted their authoritative, if not yet officially proclaimed, sources of apostolic doctrine.

The original author of the "Muratorian fragment," in addition to enumerating the "canonical" Books in their accepted sequence in advance of all others, and limiting the period in which Books of the "canon" could have been written, indulged in some comparative evaluation of the Gospels, condemned the works of Valentinus and Basilides, Gnostics associated with Marcion, and rejected the writings of Montanus.[cccc] In all this, even within the brief compass of the fragment, he conveys his feeling that between the Books of the Hebrew Bible and the Christian works of his select list there is a distinction perhaps best expressed by the overtones which distinguish *prophetic* from *apostolic*. The concept of a New Covenant — a collection of

[cccc] Montanus, founder and spiritual head of an "heretical" sect — known as Montanists, or, place of origin emphasized, Kataphrygians — whose disturbing influence most seriously competed with that of Gnosticism, appeared about A. D. 156 in Phrygia, where his frenzied protest against the rapidly developed secularism of the Church, his insistence upon reversion to earlier and more stringent Christian discipline, and his demand for a thoroughgoing renunciation of the world so effectively invigorated the latent eschatological expectations of his audiences, assembled in non-conformist conventicles, as to create a new religious movement, formidable enough to attract the support of Tertullian in Africa and to extend its power even unto Gaul. The annihilation of Montanism, together with the extirpation of Gnosticism, brought to an end one of the most critical periods in ecclesiastical history and was, indeed, the making of the Catholic Church. *Cf.* G. N. Bonwetsch, *Die Geschichte des Montanismus*, Erlangen, 1881.

Scriptural Books — equal in inspiration and authority with the Old had yet to arise. Certainly there could have been no such concept in the mind of Tatian when, after long residence at Rome, he undertook his mission, about A. D. 170, to his native land. Collections of Christian writings, similar to that of Marcion, were no doubt available to Tatian and his Roman colleagues, yet up to the time of his departure for Syria no one, it is obvious, had entertained the idea that such a collection constituted a definitive and ultimate embodiment of apostolic doctrine, establishing anew a spiritual agreement between man and his Creator of no less import than that of the Septuagint. The New Testament, so conceived, came into being without official benefit of the Roman or of any other Christian Church.

First employment of the term *New Testament* [ἡ καινὴ διαϑήκη], so far as surviving records disclose, occurs in a polemic against the Kataphrygians, addressed, about A. D. 192, to Abircius, bishop of Hierapolis, by some unsung presbyter or bishop whose very name, despite his notable contribution, is unknown. [80]

Although Origen, in the first half of the following century, refers to "canonical" Christian documents in the aggregate as a New Testament comparable, in authority, to the Old, he is not inflexible as to its contents. Hebrews, though failing to meet his criterion of universal acceptance, he is willing to receive into the canon. He has doubts about accepting some of the Catholic Epistles, but is confident of II Peter, the genuineness of which is still questioned by some modern authorities, and the admission of which into the canon was apparently the result rather of critical indifference than of positive evidence of Petrine authorship. He does not hesitate, while limiting the Gospels of his New Testament to the canonical four, to establish his point or to illustrate his meaning by reference to the apocryphal Gospel of Peter or the Gospel according to the Hebrews. Another apocryphal Book, the Preaching of Peter, he explicitly rejects. Revelation, most disputed of the major canonical works, and to this day, in conformity with the judgment of Cyril of Jerusalem and

Gregory of Nazianzus, rejected by the Greek-speaking Church, Origen freely admits into his New Testament.[dddd] Even the great authority of Origen, however, did not remove the Johannine Apocalypse from the realm of dispute, one of his own disciples, Dionysius of Alexandria, attempting to assign Revelation not to the Apostle but to an Elder of Ephesus of the same name.

A century later, c. A. D. 363,[eeee] reading of uncanonical but unspecified books was forbidden by the last of the fifty-nine regulations issued by the Synod of Laodicea in Asia Minor.[81] To these Laodicean regulations there is sometimes added a sixtieth, which, though probably spurious, is interesting for its designation as canonical all of the Books of the present New Testament with the conspicuous exception of Revelation.

Detailed application of the fifty-ninth Laodicean regulation, offered to the churches of his diocese by Athanasius, the far-travelled bishop of Alexandria, in his Easter letter of A. D. 367, practically terminated the uncertainties concerning the New Testament canon. The Athanasian solution of the questionable authority of the *Didaché* and the *Shepherd* of Hermas was to relegate their reading, together with apocryphal Books of Hebrew Scripture, to catechumens — those receiving elementary oral religious instruction. The canon proposed by Athanasius — identical with the twenty-seven Books of the Western Church today — was duplicated by the Synod held at Rome in A. D. 382 at the call of Pope Damasus and under the powerful domination of Jerome. Subsequently, adoption of the Athanasian New Testament list for the Church in Africa by a Council at Hippo in A. D. 393, was confirmed at Carthage four years later, under the vigilant eye of Augustine, and, as if that were insufficient, was reaffirmed again at Carthage, and again with Augustine in control, by the Council of A. D. 419. The canon

---

[dddd] MSS. of Revelation, reflecting its uncertain position, are scarce. Among the early uncials it is present only in Codd. ℵ, A, and C. The Vatican MS. of Revelation, No. 046, is a tenth-century uncial. *Cf.* Table B.

[eeee] The date of the Synod of Laodicea, placed between A. D. 343 and 381 by Karl Joseph von Hefele, *Conciliengeschichte*, 2nd ed., Freiburg, 1873–1890, Vol. I, p. 746, is uncertain.

approved by the Synod under Damasus was ratified for Rome more than a century later by Pope Gelasius I; and, after a lapse of two more centuries, at the "Trullan" Synod of Constantinople[ffff] in A. D. 692, was formally recognized as authoritative for the Church in the East as well as in the West.

* * *

Modification of the Scriptural canon, the substance of which has been acquiesced in by innumerable millions of men, is the last imaginable result of increasing Biblical scholarship. The complete Old Testament canon is now secure in an immutability of eighteen centuries, and any irregularities in the canon of the New have been localized and negligible in the Western Church since the time of Augustine. Stability of the content of Holy Writ is greater, however, than its uniformity of excellence. No attentive reader of the Bible can fairly deny the unevenness of literary quality and moral tone of its parts. This variability of artistic and ethical level is in some measure due, it would seem, to the fact that, in the final analysis, the instinct of the folk rather than ecclesiastical rule determined the selection of the sacred writings. The Book of Esther, for a conspicuous instance, long withheld from the Old Testament canon, was finally admitted, according to a modern scholar, only in response to public opinion. [82] Conciliar regulations, whether Jewish or Christian, were frequently the work of men who, in their wisdom, ratified the conclusions of the community, and the canon adopted by Synagogue and Church, though no doubt officially determined by their leading spirits, was to a large degree a reflection of popular tradition. In this determination of the constituent writings of Holy Scripture neither Synagogal nor Ecclesiastical judgment

---

[ffff] So called because the Synod convened in the *dome of the Imperial Palace*: ΚΑΝΟΝΕΣ ΤΩΝ ΕΝ ΚΩΝΣΤΑΝΤΙΝΟΥΠΟΛΕΙ ΕΝ ΤΩΙ ΤΡΟΥΛΛΩΙ ΤΟΥ ΒΑΣΙΛΙΚΟΥ ΠΑΛΛΑΤΙΟΥ ΣΥΝΕΛΘΟΝΤΩΝ ΑΓΙΩΝ ΠΑΤΕΡΩΝ [H. T. Bruns, *Canones apostolorum et conciliorum, etc.,* Berlin, 1839, Pars Prior, p. 32]. This Synod is also known as the "Quinisextine," the Greek view being that it was supplementary to the fifth and sixth ecumenical councils.

was, from the modern point of view, infallible. Twentieth-century scholarship, though in the main concurring in the content of the New Testament canon, is by no means reconciled to II Peter; and is willing to entertain the opinion that, appraised theologically, some of the excluded Epistles, such as I Clement, are of no less value than, say, the Epistle of Jude.[83] The Old Testament, while including passages whose moralistic intent is so dimmed by indelicacy of expression as to move the editors of the American Jewish Version to euphemistic translation,[84] rejects the admirably written and ethically significant Ecclesiasticus; and, while chronicling events none too edifying under king after king of Israel and Judah, excludes a book which records the memorable deeds, celebrated to this day throughout Jewry, performed by the heroic Judas Maccabeus. Compensatory, it may be, for all such regrettable decisions with respect to Scriptural canonization is the surprising inclusion of Ruth, the perfection of whose idyllic narrative apparently outweighed its tractarian presentation of successful religious intermarriage. Surprising, too, would have been the inclusion of Job had not the original text of that masterpiece been accommodated, as previously suggested, to orthodox doctrine. The Scriptural canon, in any case, however its evolution appear in the light of the higher criticism, and whatever the artistic or religious disparity of its several parts, is no longer liable to alteration. Fixed and immutable it stands, a monument, in its thirty centuries of history and in its diverse ethical and esthetic qualities, to its human origin — of all records since stylus first chronicled on bricks of clay the culture of Mesopotamian man, undoubtedly the most influential in its impact upon the many generations descended from those who wrote it, and, of all anthologies, beyond question the most enduring, the most universal, the most revealing yet compiled.

NOTES TO CHAPTERS I–IX

NOTES TO CHAPTER I

[1] S. R. Driver, *An Introduction to the Literature of the Old Testament*, 9th ed., rev., New York, 1914, *passim*; H. E. Ryle, *The Canon of the Old Testament*, 2nd ed., London, 1925, *passim*; H. L: Strack, in Hastings' *Dictionary of the Bible*, IV. 726; *et al.*

[2] See Tables A and B.

[3] *Biblia Sacra tam Veteris quam Novi Testamenti cum Apocryphis secundum fontes Hebraeos et Graecos*, ed. C. B. Michaelis, 2 vols., Züllichau, 1740–41. The *polyglots* (*q. v.*) are in a category of their own.

[4] *Cf. Jewish Encyclopedia*, VIII. 304. Several items of the Hebrew manuscript collection of Cambridge University were exhumed from a graveyard.

[5] *Jewish Encyclopedia*, III. 178. "Open" sections begin flush with the right-hand margin, the preceding line being partially or completely blank; "closed" sections are marked either by an indention at the beginning of a line or by a preceding blank space left in the line.

[6] Stefano Evodio Assemani and Giuseppe Simone Assemani, *Bibliothecae Apostolicae Vaticanae Codicum manuscriptorum Catalogus*, Pars I, Tomus I, Rome, 1756; reprinted, Paris, Maisonneuve frères, 1926. The number of Hebrew MSS. now at the Vatican Library is 659.

[7] Modifications of the Scriptural "square" alphabet [see p. 29] which, though more freely written, tolerate no ligature. *Cf.* Carlo Bernheimer, *Paleographia Ebraica*, Firenze, 1924, p. 40.

[8] The colophon, fol. 224ᵃ, dates the MS. the month of *Tishri*, an. 1228 Sel. ["auctumno anni 916 p. Chr."]. *Cf.* A. Harkavy and H. L. Strack, *Catalog der hebräischen Bibelhandschriften in St. Petersburg*, Leipzig, 1875, Vol. I, p. 224; and D. A. Chwolson, *Corpus Inscriptionum Hebraicarum*, St. Petersburg, 1882, col. 215.

[9] Assemani, *op. cit.*, No. V: "Is Codex scriptus dicitur anno Christi 840."

[10] Giovanni Bernardo de Rossi, *MSS. codices Hebraici biblioth. I. B. de Rossi . . .* 3 vols., Parmae, 1803, Vol. I, pp. 114–115: "Erutum ex ghenizà Luci, et non tam vetustate, quam ipsius loci humiditate corrosum. Membrana rudis, atra-

mentum evanescens, antiquus et intermedius character, puncta desunt, alicubi tamen recentius apposita, litterae obsoletae et aliis antiquioribus superscriptae, plagulae mutilae, nullum masorae vel keri vestigium, nullum ante majores sectiones spatium, aliquando inter verba, quod in vetustissimis aliis codicibus fit, puncta quaedam inserunter... ad IX forte vel X sec., vel saltem ad remotiorem vetustatem referendum. Unic. Lev. XXII 4."

[11] Christian D. Ginsburg, *Introduction to the Massoretico-critical Edition of the Hebrew Bible*, London, 1897, p. 242.

[12] For vowel-pointing *v.* p. 40.

[13] G. Margoliouth, *Catalogue of the Hebrew and Samaritan Manuscripts in the British Museum*, London, 1899, Part I, pp. 36–39. MS. Or. 4445 (imperfect at the beginning and the end, and with some folios — 122–124, 126, 127, 158 — sadly mutilated) begins (fol. 29[a]) with Gen. xxxix. 20 and ends (fol. 158[b]) at Deut. i. 33 (לראתכם). Fifty-eight leaves — fols. 1–28, the conjoint 125 and 128, and 159–186 — of the original vellum which are missing were supplied, on paper, in A. D. 1540. Mention of Ben Asher in the margin [at 40[b] and 106[a]; see facsimile (Plate I) in *Catalogue*] without euphemism for the dead, indicates that the marginalia were written while he was still living, perhaps a century later than the text itself.

[14] *V.* p. 20.

[15] *Cf.* Solomon Zeitlin, "'A Commentary on the Book of Habakkuk' Important Discovery or Hoax?" in *Jewish Quarterly Review*, XXXIX (Jan. 1949), pp. 235–247; and "Scholarship and the Hoax of the Recent Discoveries," *op. cit.* (April 1949), pp. 337–361.

[16] W. F. Albright, "Editorial Note on the Jerusalem Scrolls," in *Bulletin of the American Schools of Oriental Research*, 111 (Oct. 1948), pp. 2, 3.

[17] Solomon A. Birnbaum, "The Date of the Isaiah Scroll," in *B. A. S. O. R.*, 113 (Feb. 1949), p. 35.

[18] John C. Trever, "A Paleographic Study of the Jerusalem Scrolls," in *B. A. S. O. R.*, 113, p. 23. Trever's italics. See p. 20.

[19] Gerald Lankester Harding, of the Department of Antiquities of the Hashemite Kingdom of Jordan, and Père René de Vaux of Dominican École Biblique. *Cf.* R. Tournay, "Les anciens manuscrits hébreux récemment découverts," in *Revue Biblique*, Vol. 56, No. 2 (April 1949), pp. 204 ff.; also O. R. Sellers, "Excavation of the 'Manuscript' Cave at 'Ain Fashkha," in *B. A. S. O. R.*, 114 (April 1949), pp. 6, 7.

[20] *V.* p. 27.

[21] Lev. xix. 31–34; xx. 20–23; xxi. 24–xxii. 3; xxii. 4–5. *V.* p. 281. *Cf.* R. de Vaux, "La grotte des manuscrits hébreux," in *Revue Biblique*, Vol. 56, No. 4 (Oct. 1949), p. 602.

[22] *V.* Chapter IX.

[23] For Septuagint and other Versions *v.* Chapter VI.

[24] *Bibliorvm Ss. graecorvm Codex vaticanvs 1209 (cod.* B) *denvo phototypice expressvs ivssv et cvra praesidvm Bybliothecae Vaticanae*... [ed. G. Cozza-Luzi] Mediolani, 1904–07. *Codex Sinaiticvs Petropolitanvs; the New Testament, the Epistle of Barnabas and the Shepherd of Hermas... reproduced in facsimile from photographs*

by *Kirsopp Lake and Helen Lake*, Oxford, 1911. *Codex Sinaiticvs Petropolitanvs et Friderico-Avgvstanvs lipsiensis. The Old Testament . . . reproduced in facsimile from photographs by Kirsopp Lake and Helen Lake*, Oxford, 1922.

[25] For specific details *v.* p. 21, and Table A.

[26] *V.* p. 163.

[27] [British Museum], *The Mount Sinai Manuscript of the Bible*, 4th ed., rev., for the trustees, Oxford, 1935, p. 17. A similar note is found in this MS. at the end of Ezra (at Leipzig), and at two places in the Vatican MS. of the Minor Prophets, Codex Marchalianus.

[28] Published by Tischendorf, *Codex Ephraemi Syri rescriptus . . .* Leipzig, 1845.

[29] *V.* p. 22, and Table C.

[30] F. Kenyon, *Our Bible and the Ancient Manuscripts*, New York, 1941, pp. 64, 65.

[31] See descriptive Table E.

[32] C. H. Roberts, *Two Biblical Papyri in the John Rylands Library*, Manchester, 1936, p. 24.

[33] *V.* p. 11.

[34] See footnote v, p. 13.

[35] *V.* p. 313, note eeee.

[36] *V.* p. 148, note w.

[37] F. H. A. Scrivener, *A Plain Introduction to the Criticism of the New Testament for the Use of Biblical Students*, 4th ed., rev. by E. Miller, 2 vols., London, 1894, p. 97.

[38] The surviving parts are Mt. xxv. 2–xxiii. 20; Jn. i. 1–vi. 49, and viii. 53–xxi. 25; II Cor. i. 1–iv. 12, and xii. 7–xiii. 13;

[39] Published by Tischendorf, *Codex Ephraemi Syri rescriptus . . .* Leipzig, 1843; O. T. portion published 1845.

[40] P 46, with a line or two missing from the bottom of each page, contains Romans (except i. 1–v. 17; vi. 14–viii. 15), Hebrews, I and II Corinthians, Ephesians, Galatians, Philippians, Colossians, and I Thessalonians (except ii. 3–v. 4).

[41] First published by H. A. Sanders, *University of Michigan Studies*, Vol. XXXVIII. Both portions edited by Sir Frederic Kenyon, *The Chester Beatty Biblical Papyri*, London, 1939.

[42] xviii. 31–33 and 37–38.

[43] C. H. Roberts, ed., *An Unpublished Fragment of the Fourth Gospel in the John Rylands Library*, Manchester, 1935.

[44] Kenyon, *Our Bible and the Ancient Manuscripts*, New York, 1941, p. 128. Of approximately the same date is another specifically Christian, though non-Biblical MS., Egerton Papyrus 2, consisting of portions of three leaves of a codex; *cf.*, H. I. Bell and T. C. Skeat, *Fragments of an unknown Gospel and other early Christian Papyri*, London, 1935, p. 1.

NOTES TO CHAPTER II

[1] *Cf.* Robert W. Rogers, *A History of Babylonia and Assyria*, 6th ed., 2 vols., New York and Cincinnati, [c. 1915].

[2] Albright, *From the Stone Age to Christianity*, Baltimore, 1940, p. 193.

[3] *Cf. Babylonian Talmud*, ed. by I. Epstein, London, 1935–1949, *Menachot* 29ᵃ.

[4] *Cf.* Falconer Madan, *Books in Manuscript*, 2nd ed., rev., New York, 1927, p. 28.

[5] *Cf.* T. H. Weir, *A Short History of the Hebrew Text of the Old Testament*, London, 1899, p. 129; also Nicholas de Lyra as quoted by Margaret Deanesly, *The Lollard Bible and other mediaeval Biblical versions*, Cambridge, 1920, pp. 166–7. *V.* pp. 67 ff. and 98 ff.

[6] *Erubin* 13ᵃ.

[7] *V.* pp. 50 ff.

[8] *Cf.* D. Chwolson (tr. T. K. Abbott), "The Quiescents (or vowel-letters) הוי in Ancient Hebrew Orthography," in *Hebraica*, VI, 2 (Jan. 1890), pp. 89–108.

[9] *Cf.* Alexander Roberts, *Old Testament Revision*, London, 1883, p. 146; cp. also Zech. i. 8; Ps. lxviii. 22 (M. T. 23); Mic. vii. 19.

[10] *Cf.* Chwolson, *op. cit., passim.*

[11] Some of the O. T. authors themselves made some use of the vowel-letters; *cf.* G. B. Gray, in *Encyclopaedia Britannica*, 11th ed., III. 859.

[12] *Cf.* A. B. Davidson, *An Introductory Hebrew Grammar*, ed. J. E. McFadyen, 24th ed., rev., Edinburgh, 1932, p. 11. *Aleph* [א] as a vowel-letter is a later development.

[13] *V.* p. 40.

[14] S. R. Driver, *Notes on the Hebrew Text of the Books of Samuel*, 2nd ed., rev., Oxford, 1913, p. xxxiv.

[15] *Cf.* J. F. Stenning, in *Encyclopaedia Britannica*, 11th ed., III. 856.

[16] *V.* p. 164.

[17] Driver, *op. cit.*, p. lii.

[18] Compare II Sam. xxii with Ps. xviii; II Kgs. xviii. 13–xx. 19 with Is. xxxvi–xxxix; Ps. xiv with Ps. liii; I and II Sam. with I and II Kgs. and with I and II Chr.

[19] *Jewish Encyclopedia*, VIII. 366. The *Tannaim* were sages of the Oral Law whose teachings, written down, occur in *Mishna* and *Baraita*.

[20] Abraham Geiger, *Urschrift und Übersetzungen der Bibel*, Breslau, 1857, p. 260, trans. by Edward Robinson, in *Journal of Near Eastern Studies*, II, 1, p. 35. See p. 43, note ff.

[21] *Cf.* I Kgs. xxi. 10, 13; Ps. x. 3; Job i. 5, 11 and ii. 5, 9.

[22] *V.* p. 161.

[23] *Cf.* J. F. Stenning in *Encyclopaedia Britannica*, 11th ed., III. 855–6.

[24] *Cf.* Louis H. Gray, *Foundations of Language*, New York, 1939, p. 285.

[25] Max L. Margolis, *The Story of Bible Translations*, Philadelphia, 1917, p. 51.

[26] Second edition, Venice, 1524–25. *V.* p. 176.

[27] *Cf. Jewish Encyclopedia*, VIII. 360.

NOTES TO CHAPTER III

[1] *Cf.* J. Dover Wilson, *The Manuscript of Shakespeare's "Hamlet" and the Problems of its Transmission*, Cambridge, 1934, Vol. II, pp. 307 ff.; also *Shakespeare, Twenty-three Plays*, ed. by Thomas Marc Parrott, N. Y. [c. 1938], p. 680.

[2] *Cf.* W. W. Greg, "Principles of Emendation in Shakespeare," in *Proceedings of the British Academy*, Vol. XIV (1928), p. 4.

[3] *Cf.* Greg, *op. cit.*, p. 5. M. T.: ‏רעי האליל‎.

[4] "And when Pharaoh drew nigh,
    the children of Israel lift up their eyes,
    and behold, the Egyptians marched af-
    ter them, and they were sore afraid: and
    the children of Israel lift up their eyes,
    and beholde, the Egyptians marched
    after them, and they were sore afraid:
    and the children of Israel cried out un-
    to the LORD."

[5] MS. Harl. 6395, No. 348; *cf.* F. S. Merryweather, *Bibliomania in the Middle Ages*, London, 1849, pp. 23, 24. Italics added.

[6] James Kennedy, *The Note-line in the Hebrew Scriptures*, Edinburgh, 1928, pp. 5–6.

[7] *Cf.* Romain Butin, *The Ten Nequdoth of the Torah, etc.*, Baltimore, 1906, p. 117.

[8] *Jewish Encyclopedia*, III. 186.

[9] *V.* pp. 36 ff.

[10] *V.* p. 44.

[11] The marginalia, of course, serve numerous other purposes — such as noting the differences between the Babylonian and Palestinian textual traditions, or condemning certain earlier Massoretic annotations (*sebirin*) as misleading. *Cf. Jewish Encyclopedia*, VIII. 368.

[12] *Cf. Encyclopedia Biblica*, IV, col. 5014.

[13] *Cf.* Max L. Margolis, *The Story of Bible Translations*, Philadelphia, 1917, pp. 126–7.

[14] A. J. V., *Preface*, pp. ix–x.

[15] See, for outstanding examples, the tenth-century head of the Jewish Academy at Sura in Babylonia, Gaon ben Joseph Saadya, of whose *Book on Language*, written in Arabic, only fragments are preserved; the eleventh-century Cordovan scholar, Abu al' Walid Merwan ibn Janaḥ, whose *Kitab al-Luma* has been translated from the Arabic both into Hebrew [sēpheR hariꞯmah, translated by B. Goldberg and R. Kirschheim, Frankfort, 1855] and into French [*Le Livre des Parterres Fleuris*, translated by M. Metzger, Paris, 1889]; and the prolific twelfth-century scholars Abraham ben Meïr ibn Ezra (from Toledo), and the Kimchis (father and son) from Narbonne.

[16] [Paul] Kleinert, in *Revision of the Old Testament. Opinions of Eminent German Hebraists, etc.*, New York, 1886, pp. 22 and 44.

[17] Moses Buttenwieser, *The Psalms, chronologically treated, with a new translation*, Chicago, [c. 1938], p. viii.

[18] B. H. Streeter, *The Four Gospels, etc.*, 4th impression, revised, London, 1930, p. 147.

[19] *V.* pp. 81 ff.

[20] Giovanni Bernardo de Rossi, *Variae lectiones Veteris Testamenti ex immensa mss. editorumq. codicum congerie haustae et ad samar. textum, ad vetustiss. versiones, ad accuratiores sacrae criticae fontes ac leges examinatae, opera ac studio Johannis Bern. de Rossi* . . . . 4 vols., Parmae, 1784–88. Also *Supplement*, 1798.

[21] Falconer Madan, *Books in Manuscript*, 2nd ed., rev., New York, 1927, p. 48.

[22] *Cf.* Morris Jastrow, *A Gentle Cynic*, Philadelphia, 1919. Jastrow's analysis, however, must be accepted with caution, his assumptions being extreme.

[23] *Cf.* F. H. A. Scrivener, *A Plain Introduction to the Criticism of the New Testament*, 4th edition, London, 1894, Vol. I, p. 9.

[24] *Cf.* G. B. Gray, *The Forms of Hebrew Poetry*, London and New York, 1915, p. 295.

[25] I Chr. vi. 69. According to the numbering of the M. T., which here, as occasionally elsewhere, differs from that of the several English versions, Gath-rimmon is cited in I Chr. vi. 54.

[26] *Die Psalmen*, Freiburg, Leipzig, Tübingen, 1899, p. 189.

[27] *Cf.* QERE: I Sam. xxiv. 8; I Kgs. ix. 18; Lam. iv. 3.

[28] *Cf.* W. A. Copinger, *The Bible and its Transmission*, London, 1897, pp. 4–5.

[29] *Cf.* Millar Burrows, W. H. Brownlee, and J. C. Trever (eds.), *The Dead Sea Scrolls of St. Mark's Monastery*, New Haven, 1950, Vol. I, p. xii: "While the Isaiah manuscript has two quite distinct forms [of *vav* and *yodh*], they are in general used quite interchangeably for both letters. In the Habakkuk scroll there is no perceptible distinction at all in the writing of these two consonants." The scribe of the Hebrew University Isaiah scroll is, with respect to these two consonants, equally undiscriminating; note, for example, in the column herewith reproduced [frontispiece], his יהוה at lines 3, 11, 13, 17 (twice), 19, 25, 26 (twice), and his יום (l. 12), ביום (l. 9), ויום (l. 11).

[30] *Cf.* S. R. Driver, *Notes on the Hebrew Text of the Books of Samuel*, 2nd ed., Oxford, 1913, p. xv.

[31] Ex. xvi. 7; Num. xiv. 36; xvi. 11; xxvi. 9; xxxii. 7; Deut. v. 10. Correction of the pointing, rather than the *vav*, at Gen. viii. 17 yields *Hiph'il imp.* הוֹצֵא, as at Lev. xxiv. 14, *et al.*

[32] *Loc. cit.*; Gen. xiv. 2; xxiv. 33; xxxvi. 5; Ex. xvi. 2; Num. i. 16; xxi. 32; Deut. xxix. 23 (M. T. 22).

[33] *Cf.* M. T. Gen. xxii. 13; I Sam. xiv. 40; II Sam. vii. 23; Jer. xxxii. 39; *et al.*

[34] *Cf.* James Kennedy, *An Aid to the Textual Amendment of the Old Testament*, Edinburgh, 1928, p. 112. This book, though convenient as a collection of emendations of various types, is unfortunately marred by serious defects — especially its numerous typographical errors — and is to be employed only with caution and discrimination.

NOTES TO CHAPTER IV

¹ *Cf.* William F. Albright, *From the Stone Age to Christianity*, Baltimore, 1940, p. 210.

² *Cf.*, for example, Job ii. 10 *seq.*

³ *Cf.* Albright, *From the Stone Age to Christianity*, p. 249; and Driver, *Notes on* : : *. the Books of Samuel*, 2nd ed., Oxford, 1913, p. xxxix.

⁴ For some of these, see the margin of R. V.; see, further, the *Variorum Bible*, 3rd ed., London, 1889.

⁵ *Cf.* Paul de Lagarde, *Librorum Veteris Testamenti Canonicorum pars prior Graece*, Göttingen, 1883; also S. R. Driver, *Notes on the Hebrew text of the Books of Samuel*, 2nd ed., Oxford, 1913, p. xlix; also C. F. Burney, *Notes on the Hebrew Text of the Books of Kings*, Oxford, 1903, p. xxxi. *V.* p. 84, footnote i.

⁶ προσάγαγε τὸ ἐφούδ. *Cf.* R. V. margin.

⁷ *Cf.* Israel Abrahams in *Essays on Some Biblical Questions of the Day*, ed. by H. B. Swete, London, 1909, pp. 171–2.

⁸ *Pesachim* x. 4. *Cf.* Abrahams, *loc. cit.*, p. 175.

⁹ *Cf.* Driver, *op. cit.*, pp. xi–xii; G. B. Gray, in *Encyclopaedia Britannica*, 11th ed., vol. III p. 860; and *Encyclopedia Biblica*, IV, col. 4980 ff.

¹⁰ *Cf.* William Rosenau, *Jewish Biblical Commentators*, Baltimore, 1906, p. 20; and James Kennedy, *An Aid to the Textual Amendment of the Old Testament*, Edinburgh, 1928, pp. 5 ff.

¹¹ *Cf.* Kennedy, *op. cit.*, p. 4.

¹² *Cf.* Gesenius, *Hebrew Grammar*, Ch. III, § 81, Rem. 2.

¹³ *Cf.* Job, *International Critical Commentary*, pt. II, p. 18.

¹⁴ LXX: ἀφροσύνη. *Cf.* Job (*I. C. C.*), pt. II, pp. 10 ff.

¹⁵ Ibn Ezra's emendation is concurred in by Beer, Budde, Hitzig, Wright and Moffatt. Cp. Prov. vii. 20 and Ps. lxxxi. 3 (M. T. 4).

¹⁶ Gen. xlix. 11 (twice); Ex. xxii. 4, 26; xxxii. 17; Lev. xxi. 5; xxiii. 14; Num. x. 36; xxxiv. 4; Deut. xxi. 7; Josh. xi. 16; xv. 4; xviii. 12, 14, 19. In the two instances from Genesis, as in many other cases, the replaced *he* is the older form of the pronominal suffix, 3rd sg. masc. This older suffix, however, is sometimes retained, as in שירה [*his* song] at Ps. xlii. 8 (M. T. 9).

¹⁷ As at Judg. xix. 3 where להשיבו [*bring him back*] is read להשיבה [*bring her back*], and at Jer. ii. 24 where נפשו [*his pleasure*] is understood to be נפשה [*her pleasure*]. At Jer. xxvi, indeed, the terminal letter of Shiloh is *he* in verse six and *vav* a few lines further on in verse nine.

¹⁸ The M. T. is here defended, however, by A. Sperber, "Biblical Hebrew," in *Proc. Amer. Acad. Jew. Research*, XVIII, p. 337, § 29.

¹⁹ *Cf.* Julius Wellhausen, *The Book of Psalms*, Leipzig, 1895, p. 89.

²⁰ II Sam. xxi. 19 is analogous; see p. 78, note c.

²¹ *Cf.* Job xlii. 16: M. T. וירא; QₑRE ויראה.
　　Ex. iv. 2: M. T. מזה; QₑRE מה זה.
　　I Sam. ix. 26: M. T. הגג; QₑRE הגגה.
　　I Sam. xviii. 1: M. T. ויאהבו; QₑRE ויאהבהו.

²² *Cf.* Josh. vii. 21: M. T. וארה; QₑRE וארא. Josh. xxiv. 8: M. T. ואביאה; QₑRE ואביא.

[23] Gen. xxx. 11: M. T. בגד; Qᴇʀᴇ בא גד. I Sam. xxv. 8: M. T. בנו; Qᴇʀᴇ באנו. Jer. xix. 15: M. T. מבי; Qᴇʀᴇ מביא, et al.

[24] Cf. Driver and Gray, *Job* (*I. C. C.*), pt. II, p. 185.

[25] M. T.: ותחפנס; Qᴇʀᴇ, ותחפנחס.

[26] Kennedy, *op. cit.*, pp. 138–9.

[27] Cf. Ex. vi. 3; xxxi. 2; xxxv. 30; Is. xliv. 5.

[28] *Das Buch Hiob, übersetzt und erklärt*, 2nd ed., Göttingen, 1913, p. 237. Cp. Ps. cv. 39.

[29] *V.* pp. 70 ff.

[30] Cf. G. B. Gray, *The Book of Isaiah* (*I. C. C.*), p. 93. Note restoration of the second *yodh* in גריים.

[31] Felix Perles, *Analekten zur Textkritik des Alten Testaments*, Munich, 1895, p. 60.

[32] *Emendationes in plerosque Sacrae Scripturae Veteris Testamenti libros*, Breslau, 1894, fasc. II, p. 31. Observe the supplied *yodh* in the emendation.

[33] *Op. cit.*, fasc. III, p. 16. Note the concurrent replacement of the second *vav* by a *yodh*.

[34] See, for example, Qᴇʀᴇ at Josh. iv. 18; vi. 5; vi. 15; Judg. xix. 25; I Sam. xi. 6; xi. 9; Job xxi. 13; and the converse at II Sam. xii. 31; Prov. xxi. 29.

[35] Cf. II Sam. vi. 3: M. T. אבינדב [Abinadab]; LXX Ἀμιναδαβ. See Qᴇʀᴇ at Josh. iii. 16; xxiv. 15; II Kgs. v. 12; and the converse at Josh. xxii. 7. See also Qᴇʀᴇ at I Kgs. i. 47.

[36] Cf. *Job* (*I. C. C.*), pt. I, p. 37.

[37] Is. xxxvii. 25 and l. 2.

[38] Cf. *Job* (*I. C. C.*), pt. II, p. 90.

[39] *V.* pp. 62 ff.

[40] Cf. Solomon Frensdorff, *Ochlah we Ochlah*, Hanover, 1864, § 91: *V.* p. 63, note s.

[41] *Cf.*, for example, Jer. xxxii. 41; Ps. xlii. 1; lxxxiv. 2.

[42] *Cf.* I Kgs. vii. 2; x. 17; x. 21; II Chr. ix. 16; ix. 20.

[43] *Op. cit.*, fasc. II, pp. 28–9. Cf. Ps. xxv. 5; xxvi. 3; lvii. 10; *et al.*

[44] "Although he should kill me, I will trust in him."

[45] *V.* p. 68.

[46] A. B. Ehrlich, *Randglossen zur hebräischen Bibel, etc.*, Leipzig, 1908 seq., Bd. 6, 232; and M. Jastrow, *The Book of Job*, Philadelphia, 1920, p. 244.

NOTES TO CHAPTER V

[1] As Msgr. Knox puts it [*Trials of a Translator*, New York, 1949, p. 41], "The New Testament was written, mainly, by people who thought in Aramaic and used Greek as a kind of Esperanto"; and [*ibid.*, p. 108] "Most of the New Testament authors knew Greek as a foreign language." *Cf.*, among the more recent studies, C. F. Burney, *The Aramaic Origin of the Fourth Gospel*, Oxford, 1922; C. C. Torrey, *Our Translated Gospels; some of the evidence*, New York and

London, 1936; Matthew Black, *An Aramaic Approach to the Gospels and Acts*, Oxford, 1946. Among ancient authorities this tradition was well established. As early as the second century Irenaeus stated [*Adv. Hæreses*, III. i. 1 (Migne, *Patrologiæ Cursus Completus, Series Prior Græca*, Tom. VII, col. 844): Ματθαῖος ἐν τοῖς Ἑβραίοις τῇ ἰδίᾳ διαλέκτῳ αὐτῶν, καὶ Γραφὴν ἐξήνεγκεν Εὐαγγελίου] that Matthew was written in Hebrew (*i. e.*, Aramaic). Eusebius, on the authority of Papias, asserts of Matthew that he wrote down the oracles in the Hebrew (Aram.) language [*Hist. Eccl.* III. 39 (Migne, *Patr. Gr.*, XX, col. 300): Ματθαῖος μὲν οὖν Ἑβραΐδι διαλέκτῳ τὰ λόγια συνεγράψατο]; and [*ibid.* III. 24 (Migne, *Patr. Gr.*, XX, col. 265): Ματθαῖος μὲν γὰρ πρότερον Ἑβραίοις κηρύξας, . . . πατρίῳ γλώττῃ γραφῇ παραδοὺς τὸ κατ' αὐτὸν Εὐαγγέλιον, τὸ λεῖπον τῇ αὐτοῦ παρουσίᾳ] also that, after preaching to the Hebrews, . . . he committed to writing in his native tongue (Aram.) the Gospel that bears his name. Jerome, who held that the apocryphal *Gospel according to the Hebrews* — which he had himself translated into Greek and Latin from the Aramaic [*De viris illustribus*, Cap. II; *Opera*, ed. Vallarsi, Tom. II, pars 2, 831] — was the prototype of the canonical Mt. [*Dialogus Contra Pelagianos* III. 2; *op. cit.*, II, 2, 782; also *Comm. in Matthaeo*, xii. 13; *op. cit.*, VII, 1, 77], goes out of his way, in addressing himself to Pope Damasus [*op. cit.*, X, iii, 661–2], to relate the first Gospel to an Aramaic ancestor: "De Novo nunc loquor Testamento: quod Graecum esse non dubium est, excepto Apostolo Matthaeo, qui primus in Judaea Evangelium Christi Hebraicis literis edidit." *Cf.*, further, *De viris illustribus*, Cap. III [*op. cit.*, II, 2, 833]: "Matthaeus . . . primus in Judaea . . . Evangelium Christi Hebraicis literis verbisque composuit: quod quis postea in Graecum transtulerit, non satis certum est. Porro ipsum Hebraicum habetur usque hodie in Caesariensi bibliotheca quam Pamphilus Martyr studiosissime confecit." Of this book no trace remains. Since the Reformation, scholarly opinion has been inclined to discount the foregoing medieval opinions with an inferential Aramaic document, the *Logia* of the Apostle Matthew, conjectured to have been, in Greek translation, the underlying text of large parts both of the first Gospel and of Luke, and even of a small portion of Mark. *V.* Ch. IX, *passim*.

[2] *Cf. The Biblical Archaeologist*, XII, 2 (May 1949), New Haven, pp. 46–52.

[3] Gen. xxxi. 47; Ezra iv. 8–vi. 18; Jer. x. 11; Dan. ii. 4–vii. 28. See also II Kgs. xviii. 26 and Is. xxxvi. 11.

[4] *V.* p. 211, note b.

[5] *Cf.* R. H. Charles, *The Book of Enoch, etc.*, Oxford, 1912, pp. lvii–lxx:

[6] *V.* p. 134.

[7] *V.* p. 136.

[8] *V.* p. 146.

[9] *V.* p. 44.

[10] *Cf.* Kirsopp Lake, "The Sinaitic and Vatican Manuscripts and the copies sent by Eusebius to Constantine," in *Harvard Theological Review*, IX. 1 (Jan. 1918), pp. 32–35.

[11] Nos. 13, 69, 124, 346. *Cf.* Rendel Harris, *The Ferrar Group*, Cambridge, 1900. Also 230, 543, 788, 826, 828, 983, 1689, 1709.

[12] *V.* p. 142.

[13] Nos. 1, 118, 131, 209. *Cf.* Kirsopp Lake, "Codex 1 and its Allies," in *Texts and Studies*, vii. 3 (1902).

[14] *V.* pp. 150 ff.

[15] *Cf.* David Daiches, *The King James Version of the Bible*, Chicago, © 1941, pp. 92–3.

[16] Also, for Mk., in C *et al.*; Psh., Hkl., Gth. For Lk., in W, Ψ, *et al.*; Syr. S., Psh., Hkl.

[17] Also of C, M, Δ, Θ, Σ, *et al.*; and of Syr. S., Psh., and Hkl.; and of Epiphanius. This part of Mt. has been lost from A. A. V.: Gergesenes; *v. infra*, n. 19.

[18] In Mt. this reading is supported by no known Greek MS., but is said by Origen to be found in many MSS.; it is confirmed by O. Lat., Sah., and Hkl. (margin); also by Hilary *et al.* In Mk. it is corroborated by ℵ and D, and Sah.; in Lk., by C and D; O. Lat., Hkl. (margin), Sah., and the Syriac version of Cyril.

[19] Gergesenes. In Lk., supported by L, X, Θ, Ξ; minuscules Fam. 1, 33, 157, 251, 700; Syr. H., Boh., Arm., Eth. In Mt., supported by L, W, a corrector of C, *et al.*; minuscules Fam. 1; Boh., Arm., Eth., Gth. In Mk., supported by L, U, Δ, Θ, *et al.*; Syr. S., Hkl. (mg), Boh., Arm., Eth.; Epiphanius. A unique variant γεργυστηνων ["Gergustenes"], occurs in Mk. in W. A. V., at Mt. viii. 28: Gergesenes.

[20] O. Lat. MSS. a, b, c, ff², *et al.*; Justin, Clement, Methodius, Iuvencus, 'Ambrosiaster,' Tichonius, Augustine.

[21] B. H. Streeter, *The Four Gospels, etc.*, 4th impression rev., London, 1930, pp. 143, 188.

[22] P. Oxy. 2. *Cf.* B. P. Grenfell and A. S. Hunt, *The Oxyrhynchus Papyri*, London, 1898–1941, Vol. I.

[23] *Adversus Helvidium*, "De perpetua virginitate Beatae Mariae," *Opera* (ed. Vallarsi), Tom. II, pars 1, 205–230.

[24] Including the Latin text of D, in which, at this point, the Greek text is deficient.

[25] *Cf.* Streeter, *op. cit.*, pp. 590–597.

[26] Constantine Tischendorf, *The Mount Sinai Manuscript of the Bible* [translated anonymously], printed for the British Museum by order of the trustees, Oxford [1934], p. 19.

[27] *Cf.* James Moffatt, *The New Testament, a new translation*, new ed., New York [1935], pp. 80, 246.

[28] *V.* p. 74.

[29] B. F. Westcott and F. J. A. Hort, *The New Testament in the original Greek*, 2 vols., Cambridge, 1881.

[30] A fragment — some 14 lines in Greek, written prior to A. D. 256 — was found at Dura. *Cf.* C. H. Kraeling, "A Greek Fragment of Tatian's Diatessaron from Dura," in *Studies and Documents*, ed. by K. and S. Lake, No. III, London, 1935.

[31] *Cf.* F. C. Burkitt, *Evangelion da-Mepharreshe*, 2 vols., Cambridge, 1904. See pp. 127 and 284.

³² Falconer Madan, *Books in Manuscript*, 2nd ed., rev., 1927, p. 72. Specimen instances, all from John, may be found in the Vaticanus (xvii. 15) or the Sinaiticus (iii. 20, 21) or Washingtonianus I (vi. 56). *Cf.* H. A. Sanders, *The New Testament Manuscripts in the Freer Collection*, New York, 1918, p. 26.

³³ Evidence of abbreviation of the ineffable Name even in Biblical texts of pre-Massoretic times has been adduced by Felix Perles (*Analekten zur Text-kritik des Alten Testaments*, Munich, 1895, pp. 12–16; Neue Folge, Leipzig, 1922, Ch. I, *passim*). In earliest copies of the LXX, long antedating those extant, the Tetragrammaton, not rendered, as it was subsequently, by κύριος, but transcribed in its Hebrew form, was erroneously taken by Greek readers for its graphic resemblant Π I Π I (*cf.* F. Field, *Origenis Hexaplorum quæ supersunt*, 2 vols., Oxford, 1875, Vol. I, p. 90). Abbreviation of יהוה takes an astonishing variety of forms — 83 have been recorded — those most commonly employed being two *yodhs* accompanied by various arrangements of dots or a vestigial *vav* [*cf.* Jacob Z. Lauterbach, "Substitutes for the Tetragrammaton," in *Proceedings American Academy Jewish Research*, II (1930–31), pp. 39–67; and W. F. Albright, "Further Observations on the Name Jahwe and its modifications in proper names," in *Journal of Biblical Literature*, 1925, p. 159]. יָהּ [yāh], Ex. xv. 2, *et al.*, is held by L. Blau (*Jewish Encyclopedia*, XII, 120) to be יהוה abbreviated.

³⁴ *Cf.* H. I. Bell and T. C. Skeat, *Fragments of an unknown Gospel and other early Christian Papyri*, London, 1935, pp. 2–3.

³⁵ Supported by minuscules 33, 442; Epiphanius, Theodore of Mopsuestia, Cyril, Jerome, *et al.*

³⁶ Supported by the correctors of C and D, by Ψ and many others; Gregory of Nyssa, Didymus, *et al.*

³⁷ Supported by 061; O. Lat., Vulg.; Hilary, Augustine, 'Ambrosiaster,' *et al.*; followed by both R. S. V. and Goodspeed.

³⁸ *Cf.* Gunnar Rudberg, *Neutestamentlicher Text und Nomina Sacra*, Uppsala, 1915, p. 60; Ludwig Traube, "Nomina sacra. Versuch einer Geschichte der christlichen kürzung," in *Quellen und Untersuchungen zur lateinischen Philologie des Mittelalters*, Bd. 2, München, 1907; F. G. Kenyon, "Nomina Sacra in Chester Beatty Papyri," in *Ægyptus*, XIII, pp. 5–10.

³⁹ *Cf.* Burkitt, *op. cit.*, Vol. ii, p. 277.

⁴⁰ Also inserted by a corrector in 299, and found in Syr. S., Syr. H., and Arm.

⁴¹ This emendation, proposed independently, in 1901, by Rendel Harris and Montague R. James (*cf. Expositor*, Sixth Ser., IV, 346 ff.; V, 317 ff.; VI, 318, 377 ff.), was anticipated by Bowyer in his Greek N. T., London, 1763, and approved by Spitta (1890) and Cramer (1891). *Cf.* R. F. Weymouth, *The New Testament in modern speech*, etc., 5th ed., rev., London, 1930, p. 694, note; and Edgar J. Goodspeed, *Problems of New Testament Translation*, Chicago, [1945], pp. 196–7.

⁴² *Cf.* R. H. Charles, *op. cit., passim*; Charles, *Apocrypha and Pseudepigrapha of the Old Testament*, Oxford, 1913, Vol. II, p. 180. See Jude 14 ff.; Mt. xix. 28; Jn. v. 22, 27; *et al.*

⁴³ Also in 33, and by a corrector in 424; Boh., Eth.; concurred in by Origen

et al. The omitted words have been restored by a corrector to ℵ, and are included in D, G, and many others; O. Lat., Vulg., Psh., Hkl., Arm., with the approval of Irenaeus, Chrysostom, Theodore of Mopsuestia, 'Ambrosiaster,' *et al.*

[44] Supported by U, X, 700, *et al.*; also by Hkl. and Eth.

[45] Supported by L, N, Fam. 1, *et al.*; O. Lat., O. Syr., Psh., Syr. H., Egypt., Arm., Gth.

[46] *V.* p. 117. Also MSS. 28 and 86.

[47] Syr. H., Arm., Eth.

[48] Nor in L, Δ, 28, 102, and most of the Boh. MSS.

[49] Also in L, W, Δ, Ψ; 700 and a few other minuscules; the Breslau and Turin O. Lat.; Syr. S., Egypt., Arm., Eth.

[50] Also N, Θ, and many others; most O. Lat., Vulg., Psh., Hkl., with the partial support of Cyprian.

[51] O. Lat., Psh., Hkl., some Boh., Arm., Gth., Eth.

[52] Nor in X, Y, Ψ, 047; 1078, 1080, 1444, 1485, 1510, and many other minuscules.

[53] O. Lat. (Turin), Syr. S., Sah., some Boh.

[54] Nor in Δ, Ψ, Fam. 1, 28, 251, 565; O. Lat. (Turin), Syr. S., Arm., Egypt.

[55] Including N; supported by O. Lat., Vulg., Psh., Hkl., Gth., Eth.; and Augustine.

[56] See p. 126, note m.

[57] It is wanting, also, in 33, 1604; O. Lat. (cod. e), Syr. S., Syr. C., Syr. H., some Boh., Sah., Eth.

[58] Also in Psh., Hkl., Arm., some Boh. Origen notes it in his *Comm. in Matthaeo.*

[59] *V.* p. 143.

[60] Nor in Chester Beatty Papyrus I; L, *et al.*; 28, 1424, *et al.*; O. Lat. (Breslau *et al.*), Syr. S., Sah., some Boh., Eth.; Basil, Cyril, Jerome.

[61] O. Lat., Syr. C., Psh., Hkl., some Boh., Arm., Gth., Eth. (1 MS.).

[62] Clement, Epiphanius, Chrysostom, Cyprian, 'Ambrosiaster,' *et al.*

[63] N, R, T, Fam. 13, and others. In Ω, 1071, 1080, these verses occur but are marked with asterisk or obelus as questionable.

[64] Included in most O. Lat., Syr. C., Psh., Syr. H., several Boh., one Sah., several Arm., and Eth. Omitted by Syr. S., Hkl. mg., most Egypt., most Arm.

[65] Some O. Lat., Syr. C., Psh., Hkl., Syr. H., *Diat.*, some Boh., Eth., Arm.

[66] Eusebius, Clement, Basil, Hilary, 'Ambrosiaster,' Irenaeus (Lat.), Origen (Lat.), and others.

[67] MSS. 38, 435, and 579. O. Lat. (Vercelli and Verona MSS.), Syr. S., and Egypt.

[68] ὅτι σοῦ ἐστιν ἡ βασιλεία καὶ ἡ δύναμις καὶ ἡ δόξα εἰς τοὺς αἰῶνας· ἀμήν [with slight variants also in certain versions: O. Lat. (f, g, q), Psh., Hkl., Syr. H., some Boh., Arm., Gth., Eth.]; without ἡ βασιλεία in Sah. and the *Didaché*; without ἡ δύναμις in Syr. C.; in *Constitutiones 'Apostolicae'*; in Chrysostom, *et al.* The passage is lost from the Alexandrinus.

⁶⁹ *Cf.* Thomas Turton, *A Vindication of the literary character of the late Professor Porson, from the animadversions of the Right Reverend Thomas Burgess, etc.*, Cambridge, 1827; also *The Correspondence of Richard Porson, M. A., formerly regius professor of Greek in the University of Cambridge*, ed. by Henry Richards Luard for the Cambridge Antiquarian Society, Cambridge, 1867; E. Nestle, *Introduction to Textual Criticism of the New Testament*, English translation by William Edie, ed. by Allan Menzies, London and New York, 1901, p. 5; Alexander Roberts, *Companion to the Revised Version of the New Testament*, New York, [c. 1881], pp. 69–72; Caspar René Gregory, "The Greek Text in 1611," in *Biblical World*, Chicago, April 1911, p. 256; Preserved Smith, *Erasmus, etc.*, New York and London, 1923, p. 164; *Catalogue of John Rylands Exhibition illustrating the history of the transmission of the Bible, etc.*, Manchester, 1925, p. 73.

⁷⁰ *Cf.* Desiderius Erasmus, *Opera omnia emendatiora et auctiora, etc.*, ed. by Jean Le Clerc, London, 1703–06, IX, 353.

⁷¹ Codex A has lost John. vi. 50–viii. 52; in the missing folios, however, space was insufficient for inclusion of the *Pericope Adulterae*. The story is wanting also in codices N, W, Y, Θ, Ψ, 22, 565, 1424 *et al.*, 2193, *et al.*; also in O. Lat. a, f, q; and Arm.

⁷² Minuscules 1, 118, 131, 209, 1076, 1582, *et al.* MSS. 1 and 1582 each mark the *Pericope* with a warning note.

⁷³ At end of Luke in minuscules 1 and 1582; following Lk. xxi. 38 in the Ferrar Group of minuscules [*v.* p. 117].

⁷⁴ *V.* pp. 150 ff.

⁷⁵ Missing from O. Syr., Psh., Gth. and Arm., and from some of the Egypt. and O. Lat. MSS. (a, f, q). Included in Syr. H., Eth., some MSS. of O. Lat. (b, e, *al.*), 1 Sah., several Boh.

⁷⁶ Streeter, *op. cit.*, pp. 71, 88, and, for a full discussion of the passage, pp. 335 ff.

⁷⁷ Also minuscule 579 and two uncial fragments, 099, 0112.

⁷⁸ O. Lat., Syr. C., Psh., Hkl., Syr. H., Sah. (several MSS.), Boh. (1 MS.), Arm., Gth., Eth.

⁷⁹ Justin, Irenaeus (Lat.), Hippolytus, Tatian (*Diat.*), Marinus (*ex* Eusebius), Epiphanius, Didymus and others, as well as in *Constitutiones 'Apostolicae.'*

⁸⁰ *Dialogus Contra Pelagianos*, II. 15 [*Opera*, ed. Vallarsi, II, 758]: "Et illi satisfaciebant dicentes: Saeculum istud iniquitatis & incredulitatis substantia [Unus Vatican: *sub satana*] est, quae non sinit per immundos spiritus veram Dei apprehendi virtutem: idcirco jam nunc revela justitiam tuam."

⁸¹ *Op. cit.*, Vol. X, pars 3, 663–4.

⁸² This, it may be noted, is but part of a longer passage of uncertain manuscript authority: Mt. xvi. 2 (from "When it is evening")–xvi. 3, which — though omitted by the uncials א, B, V, X, Γ, 047; by the minuscules Fam. 13, 1078, 1080, and, according to Jerome, many others; by O. Syr., Sah., some Boh., Arm.; and by Origen in his *Comm. in Matthaeo* — is included in C, D, W; Fam. 1 and others; O. Lat., Vulg., Psh., Hkl., *Diat.*; some Boh., Eth.; Eusebius, Chrysostom, *et al.*

⁸³ Also a few other MSS.; supported by Syr. H. (some MSS.) and Eth.; Chrysostom, and Severus of Antioch; but prohibited by several commentators.

[84] A, D, W, Θ, Fam. 1 and many minuscules; O. Lat., Vulg., Syr. S., Psh., Hkl., some Syr. H., *Diat.*, Egypt., Arm., Gth.; Origen (Lat.), Eusebius, Hilary, Jerome, *et al.*

[85] Thus also L; minuscules Fam. 1 and Fam. 13, 22 and a few others, including the twelfth-century British Museum MS. 700 which, however, supported by Marcion and Gregory of Nyssa, replaces ἐλθέτω ἡ βασιλεία σου [thy kingdom come] with ἐλθέτω τὸ πνεῦμά σου τὸ ἅγιον ἐφ᾽ ἡμᾶς καὶ καθαρισάτω ἡμᾶς [thy Holy Spirit come upon us and cleanse us]; so Vulg., Syr. S., Arm.; Origen, Tertullian, Cyril, Augustine.

[86] Also A, C, D, W, Θ and many others; O. Lat., Psh., Hkl., Boh., Eth.; Titus, bishop of Bostrenus, Arabia. "Thy will be done," with no further addition, in O. Lat. (Vercelli MS.), Sah., some Boh.

[87] Also in O. Lat., Syr. C., Psh., Hkl., some Boh., Eth.

[88] Additional instances of assimilation may be seen in the Greek text at Mt. xxiii. 14 (*ex* Mk. xii. 40, Lk. xx. 47); Mt. xviii. 11 (*ex* Lk. xix. 10); Mk. xii. 26 (*ex* Mt. vi. 15); Lk. vi. 48 (*ex* Mt. vii. 25); Lk. xvii. 36 (*ex* Mt. xxiv. 40); Lk. xxii. 19–20 (*ex* I Cor. xi. 23b–25); and of interpolation at Mt. x. 8; xvii. 11; xxi. 44; Lk. xxiii. 17; xxiv. 12, 40; Jn. v. 4; Acts viii. 37; xv. 34; xxiv. 7; xxviii. 29.

[89] *V.* p. 129.

[90] Basil, Didymus, Epiphanius, Gregory of Nyssa, Cyril, Irenaeus (1 Lat.), some Clement.

[91] *V.* p. 243.

[92] O. Lat., Vulg., Syr. C., Hkl., Syr. H., Eth., Arm.; Chrysostom, Hilary, some Clement, Athanasius, nearly always in Eusebius, Gregory of Nazianzus, Theodore of Mopsuestia, Tertullian, Gaius Marius Victorinus, some 'Ambrosiaster,' some Irenaeus (Lat.), *et al.*

[93] Nestorius, Nonnus Panapolitanus, Cyril of Jerusalem.

[94] *Cf.* Westcott and Hort, *op. cit.*, Vol. II, *passim.*

[95] Streeter, *op. cit.*, p. 130.

[96] *V.* p. 21.

[97] Streeter, *op. cit.*, *passim. Cf.* also Kirsopp Lake, "Codex 1 and its Allies," in *Texts and Studies*, VII. 3; and his further discussion in *Harvard Theological Review*, XXI, 207–404.

NOTES TO CHAPTER VI

[1] *Cf.* Humphrey Hody, *Contra historiam Aristeae de LXX interpretibus dissertatio*, Oxford, 1684; and I. Abrahams, "Recent Criticism of the Letter of Aristeas," in *Jewish Quarterly Review*, XIV, London, 1902, pp. 321–342. The *Letter*, ed. by H. St. J. Thackeray in Swete's *Introduction to the Old Testament in Greek*, 2nd ed., Cambridge, 1914, is available in English translation by Thackeray in *J. Q. R.*, XV, London, 1903, pp. 337–391; also, ed. and tr. by Moses Hadas, *Aristeas to Philocrates*, New York, 1951. *Cf.* Josephus, *Antiquities of the Jews*, XII. 2, *passim.*

[2] *V.* p. 210.

³ S. R. Driver, *An Introduction to the Literature of the Old Testament*, rev. ed., New York, 1914, p. 514.

⁴ *Cf.* D. Chwolson, "The Quiescents . . . in Ancient Hebrew Orthography" (tr. by T. K. Abbott) in *Hebraica*, Jan. 1890, VI. 2, pp. 89–108.

⁵ Although much of Baruch is Greek, there is no doubt that its beginning (i–iii. 8) was originally composed in Hebrew. *Cf.* C. H. Toy in *Jewish Encyclopedia*, II. 556.

⁶ *V.* Chapters III and IV *passim. Cf.* E. F. Kautzsch, C. F. Keil, A. Kamphausen, *et al.*, in *Revision of the Old Testament. Opinions of Eminent German Hebraists, etc., publ. for use of the American Committee* [on Revision], New York, 1886, pp. 16–17.

⁷ *Cf.* Joseph Perles, *Meletemata Peschittoniana*, Breslau, 1859.

⁸ Bar Hebraeus, a thirteenth-century Syrian, of Jewish descent, embraced Christianity and rose high in its service. *Cf.* his Commentary on Psalm x, in J. Göttsberger, *Barhebräus, und seine Scholien zur heiligen Schrift*, Freiburg i. B., 1900.

⁹ Josephus, *op. cit.*, XX. iv. 2.

¹⁰ *Cf.* Graetz, *Geschichte der Juden*, 2nd ed., Leipzig, 1902, V. 435.

¹¹ *Cf.* Jerome, *Praefatio in Danielem, Opera*, ed. Vallarsi, V, 619. The LXX Daniel survives in only two MSS.: the vellum Codex Chisianus, and the Chester Beatty papyrus fragment, P 968. See Tables A and E.

¹² *Comm. in Epistolam ad Titum, Opera*, ed. Vallarsi, Vol. VII, pars I, col. 734.

¹³ Paul's translation of the poetical Books and the Prophets, preserved in the eighth-century Codex Ambrosianus at Milan, has been published by Antonio Maria Ceriani in *Monumenta Sacra et Profana, etc.*, Milan, 1874; the remaining parts of the other Books, by Paul de Lagarde, *Bibliothecae Syriacae, etc.*, Göttingen, 1892.

¹⁴ Edited (as far as Esther) from MSS. 19, 82, 93, 108 and 118 by Paul de Lagarde, *Librorum Veteris Testamenti Canonicorum pars prior Graece*, Göttingen, 1883.

¹⁵ *V.* pp. 80 and 84, note i.

¹⁶ *V.* p. 127.

¹⁷ *Cf.* F. C. Burkitt, "S. Ephraim's quotations from the Gospel" in *Texts and Studies*, VII. 2, Cambridge, 1901.

¹⁸ Augustine, *De Doctrina Christiana*, Bk. II, Cap. XI ff.; *cf.* Migne, *Patr. Curs. Compl. Ser. Lat.*, Vol. XXXIX, col. 42 ff. For Jerome, *v. supra*, p. 124, n. l; also *Praefatio in Librum Josue Ben Nun, Opera*, ed. Vallarsi, IX, 355.

¹⁹ The Apocryphal Books, however — other than Judith and Tobit — are completely preserved in their O. Lat. form in the Vulgate. Codex Bobiensis (k) of the fourth or fifth century, at Turin, and Codex Palatinus (e), fifth century, at Vienna and Dublin, preserve the African text of the Gospels in mutilated condition. Parts of Acts and Catholic Epistles are extant in Codex Floriacensis (h), a sixth century (fifth?) palimpsest at Paris. The European text of the Gospels is best preserved in the fifth-sixth century Codex Veronensis (b) and in the fourth-century Codex Vercellensis (a); of Catholic Epistles, in the tenth-century Leningrad Codex Corbeiensis (f or ff); of Acts and Revelation, in Codex Gigas (g or gig), thirteenth century, Stockholm.

[20] *Cf.* Petrus Sabatier, *Bibliorum Sacrorum Latinae versiones antiquae, seu vetus Italica et ceterae quaecumque in codd. MSS. et antiquorum libris reperiri potuerunt, &*, 3 vols., Rheims, 1743–9.

[21] Represented, in mutilated condition, by the seventh-century Codex Monacensis (q), which, as its name indicates, is at Munich.

[22] *V.* p. 124, note l.

[23] *V.* p. 195, note gg.

[24] *V.* p. 210.

[25] MS. Douce 369, part i. *Cf.* Margaret Deanesly, *The Lollard Bible and other mediaeval Biblical versions*, Cambridge, 1920, pp. 253–4.

[26] *Cf.* J. Forshall and F. Madden, *The Holy Bible, containing the Old and the New Testaments, with the Apocryphal Books, in the Earliest English Versions made from the Latin Vulgate by John Wycliffe and his followers*, 4 vols., Oxford, 1850.

NOTES TO CHAPTER VII

[1] *V.* p. 55. *Cf.* C. D. Ginsburg, *Jacob ben Chajim's Introduction to the Rabbinic Bible; Hebrew and English; with explanatory notes*, London, 1865. A third edition of Bomberg's Rabbinic O. T. was printed in 1546–1548.

[2] *V.* p. 183, note r. In the same year this N. T. was reprinted in England in a quarto edition (three variant issues) and an octavo edition (three [four?] variant issues).

[3] *V.* p. 173, note u.

[4] *V.* p. 190, note bb.

[5] *Cf.* B. F. Westcott, *A General View of the History of the English Bible*, 3rd ed., rev. by W. A. Wright, New York, 1927, p. 172, note.

[6] *The Prophete Isaye translated into englysshe by George Ioye.* Attributed — despite the colophon "Printed in Straszburg by Balthassar Beckenth in the year of our lorde 1531. the . x. daye of Maye" — to the press of Martin de Keyser at Antwerp.

Unacknowledged by Joye, but probably his, is the first known printed English Psalter: *The Psalter of Dauid in Englishe purely and faithfully translated aftir the texte of Feline* [Martin Bucer's *Latin Psalter*], etc., printed, according to its probably false colophon, at Argentine [Strassburg], 1530. Now attributed to press of de Keyser. *Cf.* Charles C. Butterworth, *The Literary Lineage of the King James Bible*, Philadelphia, 1941, p. 64.

[7] *Ieremy the Prophete translated into Englisshe: by George Ioye: . . . Anno . M.D. and .xxxiiii. in the monethe of Maye.* Lamentations included. Antwerp?

Dauids Psalter diligently and faithfully translated by George Ioye with Breif Arguments before euery Psalme declaringe the effecte therof. Colophon: "Martyne Emperowr. 1534." *Cf.* Butterworth, *op. cit.*, pp. 87 ff.

[8] This attribution derives from the mark "G-H" on the inner title-page.

[9] *Cf.* B. F. Westcott, *op. cit.*, p. 163.

[10] Formerly thought to have been printed at Antwerp, then at Zurich, Coverdale's Bible has recently been credited to Johannes Soter and Eucharius Cervicornus of Cologne and Marburg. *Cf.* L. A. Sheppard, "The Printers of

the Coverdale Bible, 1535," in *The Library*, Ser. 4, vol. 16, p. 280, London, 1935.

[11] David Wilkins, *Concilia Magnae Britanniae et Hiberniae*, 4 vols., fol., London, 1737, III, 770: "quod sacra Scriptura in vulgarem linguam Anglicanam, per quosdam probos et doctos viros per dictum illustrissimum regem nominandos transferatur, et populo pro eorum eruditione deliberetur et tradatur." Quoted by A. W. Pollard, *Records of the English Bible, etc.*, London and New York, 1911, p. 176.

[12] *Biblia: The Bible / that is, the holy Scripture of the Olde and New Testament, faithfully and truly translated out of Douche and Latyn in to Englishe. M. D. XXXV.* Colophon: "Prynted in the yeare of oure Lorde M. D. xxxv. and fyneshed the fourth daye of October."

[13] *Cf.* J. F. Mozley, *William Tyndale*, New York, 1937, pp. 354–5. The title-page reads: *The Byble, which is all the holy Scripture: In whych are conteyned the Olde and Newe Testament truly and purely translated into Englysh by Thomas Matthew . . . . M. D. XXXVII. Set forth with the Kinges most gracyous lycence.*

[14] *Cf. Works of Thomas Cranmer*, ed. for the Parker Society by John Edmond Cox, Cambridge, 1844–1846, letters of August 4 and August 13, 1537; also Pollard, *op. cit.*, pp. 214–215. Grafton's letter of August 28, 1537 to Cromwell, soliciting the king's licence (preserved in MS. Cott. Cleopatra E v, 325), is reproduced by Pollard, *op. cit.*, p. 218. *Cf.* also *Letters and Papers of the Reign of Henry VIII* arranged and catalogued by James Gairdner, London, 1891, Vol. 12, pt. 2, p. 220, item 593.

[15] *The Most Sacred Bible, Whiche is the holy scripture, conteyning the old and new testament, translated in to English, and newly recognised with great diligence after most faythful exemplars, by Rychard Taverner . . .* Prynted at London in Flete Strete at the sygne of the sonne by Iohn Byddell, for Thomas Barthlet . . . M. D. XXXIX.

[16] *The Byble in Englyshe, that is to saye the content of all the holy scrypture, bothe of ye olde and newe testament, truly translated after the veryte of the Hebrue and Greke textes by ye dylygent studye of dyuerse excellent learned men, expert in the forsayde tonges . . .* Prynted by Rychard Grafton & Edward Whitchurch . . . 1539.

[17] *Cf.* Pollard, *op. cit.*, quoting from Foxe's 4th ed., p. 1191.

[18] *Hebraica Biblia, Latina planeque, nova Sebast. Munsteri translatione*, 2 vols., fol., Basle, 1534–5.

[19] *The Byble in Englyshe, that is to saye the content of al the holy scripture, both of ye olde, and newe testament, with a prologue therinto, made by the reuerende father in God, Thomas archbyshop of Cantorbury.* This is the Byble apoynted to the vse of the churches . . . Prynted by Edward whytchurche . . . M. D. xl. The colophon gives the date April 1540.

Some title-pages of this edition bear the imprint of Richard Grafton instead of that of Whitchurch.

Competing for the position of "second edition" is a reprinting of the 1539 Great Bible, slightly reduced in size, "by Thomas Petyt, and Roberte Redman for Thomas Berthelet: Prynter vnto the Kynges grace . . . 1540," the colophon of which dates the issue as of April 1540.

[20] According to Francis Fry, *Bibliographical Description of the New Testament*,

Tyndale's Version, in English, London, 1878, twenty-one editions of Tyndale's N. T. were printed between 1536 and 1550. This, however, does not complete the tally; for Richard Jugge, who (like John Daye and William Seres) had issued a folio edition in 1548, produced at least three editions in quarto: 1552 (used as a basis for the first Geneva N. T., 1557), 1553 and 1566.

21 *The Nevve Testament of ovr Lord Iesus Christ. Conferred diligently with the Greke, and best approued translations. VVith the arguments, as wel before the Chapters, as for euery Boke & Epistle, also diuersities of readings, and moste proffitable annotations of all harde places: wherunto is added a copious Table* . . . At Geneva printed by Conrad Badius M. D. LVII.

22 Chiefly Anthony Gilbey, pastor of the English congregation at Geneva, later rector at Ashby-de-la-Zouch in Leicestershire; and Thomas Sampson, subsequently dean of Christ Church, Oxford.

23 *The Bible and Holy Scriptvres Conteyned in the Olde and Newe Testament. Translated According to the Ebrue and Greke, and conferred With the best translations in Diuers languages. With moste profitable annotations vpon all the hard places, and other things of great importance as may appeare in the Epistle to the Reader* . . . At Geneva Printed by Rouland Hall. M. D. LX.

24 *Cf.* Butterworth, *op. cit., passim.*

25 An octavo Geneva N. T., "Imprinted at London by T. V. [Thomas Vautrolier?] for Christopher Barker. 1575," was apparently the earliest printing of any portion of the Genevan Version in England.

Christopher Barker, who, after Jugge's death in 1577, held the monopoly, as "Printer to the Queenes Maiestie," of Scriptural publication in England, started the astonishing flood of Geneva Bibles, in 1576, with two small-folio editions: (1) "*The Bible and Holy Scriptvres conteined in the Olde and Nevve Testament. Translated according to the Ebrewe and Greeke,* . . . Imprinted at London by Christopher Barkar, dwelling in Povvles Churchyard at the sign of the Tygers Head. 1576. (2) .*The. Bible. That Is, The Holy Scriptvres,* [*etc.,* as above]. 1576.

In the same year, Barker published a revision of the N. T. portion of the 1560 Geneva Bible by Laurence Tomson, Fellow of Magdalen College, Oxford, in accordance with the Greek text of Beza: *The New Testament of our Lord Iesus Christ Translated out of Greeke by Theod. Beza: Whereunto are adioyned brief Summaries* . . . *And also short expositions* . . . Englished by L. Tomson . . . Imprinted at London by Christopher Barkar dwelling in Poules Churchyeard at the signe of the Tigres head. 1576. Slightly revised in an edition of the following year, Tomson's N. T. was adopted by nearly all subsequent editions of the Geneva Bible.

26 *The. holie. Bible. conteynyng the olde Testament and the newe.* London, 1568. Some copies have only *The. holie. Bible* on title-page. Black letter, with roman replacing italic type.

27 A quarto, published at London, by Richard Watkins, not earlier than 1572.

28 *V.* p. 242.

29 *The Nevv Testament of Iesvs Christ, Translated faithfvlly into English, out of the authentical Latin, according to the best corrected copies of the same, diligently conferred vvith the Greeke and other editions in diuers languages: Vvith Argvments of bookes*

and chapters, *Annotations, and other necessarie helpes, for the better vnderstanding of the text, and specially for the discouerie of the Corrvptions of diuers late translations, and for cleering the Controversies in religion, of these daies: In the English College of Rhemes* . . . Printed at Rhemes, by Iohn Fogny. 1582. Cvm Privilegio.

³⁰ *The Holie Bible Faithfvlly Translated into English, ovt of the Avthentical Latin. Diligently conferred with the Hebrew, Greeke, and other Editions in diuers languages* . . . *By the English College of Doway* . . . Printed at Doway by Lavrence Kellam, at the signe of the holie Lambe. M. DC. IX.

³¹ These rules — preserved in Gilbert Burnet's *History of the Reformation in England*, Vol. II, p. 368, London, 1681 — are available in B. F. Westcott, *op. cit.*, and in *Encyclopaedia Britannica*, 11th ed., III, pp. 902-3.

³² *Cf.* J. G. Carleton, *The Part of Rheims in the Making of the English Bible*, Oxford, 1902. Also Pollard, *op. cit.*, p. 37.

³³ F. H. A. Scrivener, *The Authorized Version of the English Bible*, Cambridge, 1884, p. 3.

³⁴ W. Kilburne, *Dangerous Errors in Several late printed Bibles*, London, 1659; Robert Gell, *An Essay toward the Amendment of the last English translation of the Bible*, London, 1659.

³⁵ R. C. Trench, *On the Authorized Version of the New Testament in connexion with some recent proposals for its revision*, 2nd ed., London, 1859 [Trench, the theological philologist of Dublin — soon to be its archbishop — was the initiator of the Oxford *Dictionary* (N. E. D.), but not the first English philologist to interest himself in Biblical translation. *V.* p. 200 and *infra*, note 44]; J. Tomlin, *Improved Renderings and Explanations of many passages in the Authorized Version, etc.*, Liverpool, 1865; J. B. Lightfoot [bishop of Durham], *On a fresh revision of the English New Testament*, Cambridge, 1871; C. J. Ellicott [bishop of Gloucester and Bristol], *Considerations on the revision of the English version of the New Testament*, London, 1870.

³⁶ In 1834, Solomon Bennett published at London his *Critical Remarks on the Authorized Version*; and five years later appeared Selig Newman's study — undertaken, according to the author, "to point out and correct the mistranslations which exist in the authorized version of the Old Testament": *Emendations of the Authorized Version of the Old Testament*, London, 1839. In 1840, D. A. de Sola, M. J. Raphall and J. L. Lindenthal jointly published a proposal (in Julius Fürst's *Litteraturblatt des Orients*) for an improved English translation of the O. T. which, within four years, found fruition in their revised *Genesis* (London, 1844). No more of this projected O. T. appeared. Abortive, too, was a previous attempt by Solomon Bennett to produce a new translation of the O. T., only chapters i–xli of his *Genesis* being published at London in 1841. At Dublin, in 1846, Benjamin Marcus published still another contribution to the same subject: *Mykur Hayim . . . Mistranslations and Difficult Passages of the Old Testament*.

³⁷ At the request of a Convocation of 1699, William Lloyd, bishop of Worcester, undertook the preparation of an improved King James Version. This revision — a folio published at London in 1701 — dates events B. C. and A. D. A similar folio issued at Oxford the same year is attributed by some bibliographers to Lloyd.

[38] [William Mace], *The New Testament in Greek and English . . . corrected from the Authority of the most Authentic Manuscripts*, London, 1729; [William Whiston], *Mr. Whiston's Primitive New Testament*, Stamford and London, 1745 (Whiston, bishop of Norwich, best remembered for his translation of Josephus, is immortalized — for his advocacy of clerical monogamy — in Goldsmith's *Vicar of Wakefield*); John Wesley, *The New Testament with explanatory notes*, "for plain, unlettered men," London, 1755; E[dward] Harwood, *A Liberal Translation of the New Testament, etc.*, London, 1768; John Worsley, *The New Testament . . . translated from the Greek*, London, 1770; Gilbert Wakefield, *A Translation of the New Testament*, London, 1791; William Newcome [archbishop of Armagh], *An attempt toward revising our English translation of the Greek Scriptures . . .*, Dublin, 1796; Nathaniel Scarlett, *A Translation of the New Testament from the original Greek: humbly attempted by Nathaniel Scarlett, assisted by men of piety and literature*, London, 1798.

[39] *V. infra*, note 43.

[40] *V. infra*, note 44. An unauthorized *New and Corrected Version of the New Testament*, published by Rodolphus Dickinson the same year (1833) at Boston, had been preceded by George Campbell's *Gospels*, Boston, 1811, later incorporated in Alexander Campbell's *The Sacred Writings*, Buffalo, Va., 1826. Subsequent *New Testaments* included those of Granville Penn, London, 1836–1837; George Townsend, Boston and Philadelphia, 1836; George R. Noyes, trans. from the Greek Text of Tischendorf, Boston, 1869; and Henry Alford, "Newly compared with the original Greek and revised," London, 1871.

[41] Those portions of the M. T. never issued by Baer and Delitzsch, or published after 1884, and therefore unavailable to the revisers, include eighteen of the thirty-nine Books: Exodus through II Chronicles; Esther, Eccl., S. of S., Jer. and Lam.

[42] Christian David Ginsburg, a Jew by birth, whose *Introduction to the Massoretico-critical Edition of the Hebrew Bible*, published at London in 1897 by the Trinitarian Bible Society, and for some time the standard edition, has been superseded by that of Kittel: Rudolf Kittel and Paul Kahle (eds.), תורה נביאים וכתובים *Biblia Hebraica adjuvantibus W. Baumgartner, G. Beer, J. Begrich . . . [et al.] edidit Rud. Kittel; textum Masoreticum curavit P. Kahle. Editionem tertiam denuo elaboratam ad finem perduxerunt A. Alt et O. Eissfeldt.* Stuttgart, 1937.

[43] Julius Bate, *A New and Literal Translation from the original Hebrew, of the Pentateuch of Moses, and of the Historical Books of the Old Testament . . . by . . . Julius Bate*, London, 1773; Anselm Bayly, *The Old Testament, English and Hebrew, . . . by Anselm Bayly*, London, 1774; Robert Lowth [bishop of London], *Isaiah. A new translation, etc.*, London, 1778; William Hopkins, *Exodus. A corrected Translation, . . .* London, 1784; Benjamin Blayney, *Jeremiah and Lamentations. A new translation, etc.*, Oxford, 1784; A. Alexander (ben Judah Loeb) [sic] חמשה חומשי תורה והפטורת *The First [— Fifth] Book of Moses* [with *Haphtaroth* and *Megilloth*] *in Hebrew and English . . .* 6 vols., London, [1785]; William Newcome [archbishop of Armagh], *An attempt toward an improved version . . . of the Twelve Minor Prophets*, London, 1785; David Levi, תקון סופרים *The first [second — fifth] book of Moses* [with the *Haphtaroth* and *Megilloth*] *. . . in Hebrew, with the English translation . . . by Lion Soesmans. Corrected, and translated, by*

David Levi, 6 vols., London, c. 1787 [only volume two has the date upon its title-page]; William Newcome, *An attempt toward an improved version . . . of the prophet Ezekiel*, Dublin, 1788; Isaac Delgado, *A new English Translation of the Pentateuch . . . by Isaac Delgado*, London, 1789; Thomas Wintle, *Daniel, an improved version attempted, etc.*, Oxford, 1792; George Benjoin, *Jonah, a faithful translation from the original, etc.*, Cambridge, 1796; Benjamin Blayney, *Zechariah; a new translation, etc.*, Oxford, 1797.

⁴⁴ John Bellamy, *Holy Bible, newly translated from the original Hebrew . . .* [Gen. — S. of S. only], London, 1818–[1842]; Levy Alexander, *The Holy Bible* [Gen. and Ex. only appeared] *in Hebrew and English*, London, 1824; Noah Webster, *The Holy Bible, containing the Old and New Testaments, in the Common Version, with Amendments of the language*, New Haven, 1833; Solomon Bennett and H. A. Henry, *The Hebrew and English Holy Bible*, London, 1841; Abraham Benisch, ספר עדות ה' *Jewish School and Family Bible*, London, 1851–56; Isaac Leeser, *The Twenty-four Books of the Holy Scriptures*, Philadelphia, 1853; Samuel Sharpe, *The Hebrew Scriptures . . . being a revision of the authorized English Old Testament*, 3 vols., London, 1865 (other eds. 1871, 1876). Michael Friedländer's כתבי הקדש *The Jewish Family Bible*, officially sanctioned by the Chief Rabbi of England, published in 1884, was too late to be of use to the revisers.

⁴⁵ *V.* p. 178, note h.

⁴⁶ The American Committee of Revision consisted of thirty-two members under the chairmanship of Professor Philip Schaaf of the Union Theological Seminary of New York. See the Committee's *Documentary History of the American Committee on Revision* and their *Historical Account of the Work of the American Committee of Revision of the Authorized English Version of the Bible*, both New York, 1885.

⁴⁷ Arthur T. Quiller-Couch, *On the Art of Writing*, Cambridge, 1923, p. 129.

⁴⁸ The dean of Peterborough, J. J. S. Perowne, held the Revisers "too unmindful of the claims of their own language," and Charles H. Spurgeon, the celebrated Baptist preacher, pronounced the R. V. "strong in Greek, weak in English." See George W. Moon, *The Revisers' English*, London, 1882; and, for criticism of wider scope, John W. Burgon [dean of Chichester], *The Revision Revised*, London, 1883.

⁴⁹ *Cf.* B. P. Grenfell and A. S. Hunt, *The Oxyrhynchus Papyri*, London, 1898–1941.

⁵⁰ *V.* p. 115. *Cf.* Adolf Deissman, *Light from the ancient East* (tr. by Lionel R. M. Strachan), New York and London, 1911, *passim*; R. F. Weymouth, *On the Rendering into English of the Greek Aorist and Perfect*, London, 1894.

⁵¹ Pioneer modernizations of Biblical English were made by Ferrar Fenton, *St. Paul's Epistles in Modern English, etc.*, London, 1884; E. Bilton, *The Four Gospels translated into Modern English from the Authorized and Revised Versions*, Paisley and London, 1888; William Norton, *A Translation, in English daily used, of the seventeen Letters forming part of the Peshitto-Syriac books of the New Covenant writings . . .* , London, 1890; [Ralph Sadler], *The Gospel of Paul the Apostle. Being an attempt to render into modern English the principal writings of St. Paul . . . etc.*, London, 1892; George Barker Stevens, *The Epistles of Paul in Modern English, etc.*, New York, 1898; F. A. Spencer, *The Four Gospels: a new*

translation, etc., New York, 1898; F. S. Ballentine, *The Four Gospels*, New York, 1899; John Edgar McFadyen, *Isaiah in modern speech*, London, 1918; *Jeremiah in modern speech*, London [1919]; National Adult School Union, *Books of the Old Testament in Colloquial speech*, edited by G. Currie Martin and T. H. Robinson, London, [1920–   ]; and C. C. Torrey, *The Four Gospels: A new translation*, New York, 1933.

New Testaments in modern translation include: Ferrar Fenton, *The New Testament . . . translated . . . into current English*, London, 1896; *The Twentieth Century New Testament: a Translation into Modern English Made from the Original Greek* [Westcott and Hort's text], London, 1898–1901; James Moffatt, *The Historical New Testament*, Edinburgh, 1901; F. S. Ballentine, *The American Bible . . . in modern English for American Readers* [N. T., 4 vols.], Scranton, Pa., 1902; R. F. Weymouth, *The New Testament in modern speech, etc.*, edited and partly revised by Ernest Hampden-Cook, London, 1903 [5th ed., rev. by J. A. Robertson, London, 1930]; Ferrar Fenton, *The Holy Bible in Modern English* [N. T. . . . 2nd ed. of Gospels, and 6th of Paul's Epistles translated afresh], London, [1903]; James Moffatt, *The New Testament, a new translation*, London, 1913 [new ed., rev. 1934]; William G. Ballantine, *The Riverside New Testament: A Translation from the Original Greek into the English of To-day*, Boston and New York, 1923 [rev. ed. 1934]; F. S. Ballentine, *A Plainer Bible for Plain People in Plain American* [N. T. only], Jersey City, N. J., 1922; Edgar J. Goodspeed, *The New Testament, an American Translation*, Chicago, 1923; F. A. Spencer [*ob.* 1913], *The New Testament . . . from the Original Greek*, ed. by Charles C. Callan, O. P. and John A. McHugh, O. P., New York, 1937; *The New Testament in Basic English*, Cambridge, 1941; Ronald Knox, *The New Testament . . . a new translation*, New York and London, 1944.

The Old Testament, modernized, appears as part of five complete Bibles: Ferrar Fenton, *The Bible in Modern English, etc.* [4 vols., O. T. only, no more of this ed. published], London, [1901–03]; James Moffatt, *The Holy Bible, a New Translation*, Chicago, 1922; J. M. Powis Smith *et al.*, in Smith-Goodspeed, *The Bible, an American Translation*, Chicago, 1931; *The Bible in Basic English*, Cambridge, 1949; Ronald Knox, *The Old Testament . . . a new translation*, New York and London, 1948–1949.

[52] *The Holy Scriptures* — sponsored by the Central Conference of American Rabbis and the Jewish Publication Society of America — frequently reissued since its first publication at Philadelphia in 1917; *v.* p. 45, note jj.

[53] As at Ps. lxxviii. 4; *v.* p. 96.

[54] *Cf. An Introduction to the Revised Standard Version of the New Testament by Members of the Revision Committee. Luther A. Weigle Chairman*, n. p., © 1946, by the International Council of Religious Education.

[55] *Cf.* Oswald T. Allis, *Revision or new translation? "The revised standard version of 1946," a comparative study*, Philadelphia, 1948; and Allen Paul Wikgren, "A Critique of the Revised Standard Version of the New Testament," in *The Study of the Bible Today and Tomorrow*, ed. by Harold R. Willoughby, Chicago, [c. 1947].

[56] Mt. v. 18; vii. 3.

[57] *V.* p. 237, note jj, pp. 134–144, and p. 245, note ww.

NOTES TO CHAPTER VIII

[1] Nicolaus, a Minorite of the convent of Lire in Normandy, died in 1340 about ten years after he had completed his commentary on the Bible, which was ultimately published at Antwerp in 1634. *Cf.* Margaret Deanesly, *The Lollard Bible, etc.*, Cambridge, 1920, pp. 166–7.

[2] *Cf.* Max Margolis, *The Story of Bible Translations*, Philadelphia, 1917, p. 58.

[3] *Cf.* Preserved Smith, *Life and Letters of Martin Luther*, Boston, [1911], p. 266.

[4] *Cf.* Stanley Cook, *An Introduction to the Bible*, Harmondsworth, 1945, p. 41.

[5] Max Margolis, *op. cit.*, pp. 53–54.

[6] *Ibid.*, p. 126.

[7] S. R. Driver, *Notes on the Hebrew Text of the Books of Samuel*, 2nd ed., Oxford, 1913, p. lxi.

[8] *Cf.* Preserved Smith, *loc. cit.*

[9] *Cf.* S. I. Hayakawa, *Language in Action*, New York, [1941], pp. 191–2.

[10] L. H. Gray, *Foundations of Language*, New York, 1939, pp. 140–1.

[11] Theodor Nöldeke in *Encyclopaedia Britannica*, 11th ed., XXIV, 623.

[12] *The Book of Genesis* (*Westminster Commentaries*), 1904, p. x.

[13] *Ibid*

[14] T. K. Cheyne, *Founders of Old Testament Criticism*, London, 1893, p. 6.

[15] The only extant MS. of this treatise, in Arabic, is at the Bodleian Library (Neubauer, No. 1448, 2). It has been available since 1844 in translations by L. Dukes and A. Geiger.

[16] *Cf.* Margolis, *op. cit.*, p. 128.

[17] *Cf.* T. H. Weir, *The Variants in the Gospel Reports*, Paisley, 1920, pp. 101–2. For the inscriptions found at Zingirli, in N. Syria, see *Ausgrabungen in Sendschirli, Ausgeführt und Herausgegeben im Auftrage des Orient-Comite's zu Berlin*, I, Berlin, 1893; J. Halévy, "Deux Inscriptions Sémitiques de Zindjirli," in *Revue Sémitique d'épigraphie et d'histoire ancienne*, I. 77 ff., Paris, 1893; M. Lidzbarski, *Handbuch der Nordsemitischen Epigraphik, etc.*, I. 440 ff., Weimar, 1898.

[18] *Cf. Jewish Encyclopedia*, VI, 226 ff.

[19] *The Holy Bible*, Benziger Brothers, New York, *etc.*, [1914], p. xxx.

[20] Solomon Schechter, quoted by Margolis, *op. cit.*, pp. 122–3.

[21] *V.* p. 335, note 31.

[22] See II Sam. xvi. 12; II Chron. iii. 1; xxii. 6; Job xxxvii. 7; Ezek. xlvi. 10; Am. v. 26; Hag. i. 2.

[23] *V.* p. 66.

[24] Ex. xxxiv. 13; Deut. xvi. 21; *et al.* Moffatt and Smith-Goodspeed: *sacred poles*.

[25] Ex. xxxviii. 25–29; II Chron. iii. 8–9; ix. 9–13.

[26] Douay: Ezra (I Esdras) ii. 69 renders *solids*.

[27] I Chron. xxix. 7; Ezra viii. 27.

[28] Gen. xvii. 17 and xxi. 6. In contrast with this folk etymology, cp. W. Albright (*From the Stone Age to Christianity*, 1940, p. 186), who derives Isaac from yiṣḥaq-'ēl; *i. e., May God smile*.

[29] Gen. xxv. 26. The name in Hebrew is עקב [YA'AQOBH]. *Cf.* Albright, *loc. cit.*: YA 'QOBH- 'ĒL; *i. e.*, *May God protect*.

[30] Mt. xvi. 18; cp. pun on Onesimus (*profitable*) at Phm. 10, 11.

[31] *V.* pp. 82 ff.

[32] F. G. Kenyon, *Our Bible and the Ancient Manuscripts*, 4th ed., London, 1939, p. 233. Italics supplied.

[33] *The Union Prayerbook for Jewish Worship*, rev. ed., Cincinnati, 1947, p. 109.

[34] *Liber Quaestionum Hebraicarum in Genesim* (ii. 8), *Opera*, ed. Vallarsi, III, Pt. 1, col. 307.

[35] William H. Saulez, *The Romance of the Hebrew Language*, New York and London, 1913, p. 99.

[36] For this interpretation, adapted from Ehrlich [*Randglossen*, Bd. V, p. 286], see J. H. Hertz, *Jewish Translations of the Bible in English*, London, 1920, p. 22.

[37] For a fuller treatment of this passage, see R. G. Moulton, *The Literary Study of the Bible*, 2nd ed., Boston, 1899, pp. 88 ff.

[38] *Cf.* Preserved Smith, *op. cit.*, p. 267.

[39] *Cf.* Mt. iii. 2 and 11; Mk. i. 4; Lk. iii. 3; Acts xiii. 24; *et al.* Knox restores *repentance.*

[40] *Cf.* John i. 18; iii. 16 and 18; I Jo. iv. 9.

[41] *Cf.* Judg. xi. 34 [A]; Jer. vi. 26; Am. viii. 10; Zech. xii. 10; Ps. xxii. 20; xxxv. 17.

[42] Mt. iii. 17; xvii. 5; Mk. i. 11; Lk. iii. 22.

[43] Ps. xxii. 20; xxxv. 17.

[44] *Antiquities* XX. ii. 1. *Cf.* also I. xiii. 1.

[45] T. H. Weir, *op. cit.*, pp. 111 ff. *Cf.*, further, C. F. Burney, *The Aramaic Origin of the Fourth Gospel*, Oxford, 1922, p. 40; and Matthew Black, *An Aramaic Approach to the Gospels and Acts*, Oxford, 1946, p. 10.

[46] *Cf.* Friedrich Bleek, *An Introduction to the Old Testament*, 2nd ed., translated by G. H. Venables, London, 1875, vol. II, p. 415.

[47] *Cf.* Jerome, *Prolegomenon III in Isaiam, De Canone Hebraicae Veritatis, Opera*, ed. Vallarsi, Vol. IX. *V.* p. 326, note 23.

[48] *Cf. An Introduction to the Revised Standard Version of the New Testament* by Members of the Revision Committee. Luther A. Weigle, Chairman. n. p., [c. 1946], p. 24.

NOTES TO CHAPTER IX

[1] By Johann Gottfried Eichhorn — pioneer in applying established methods of literary criticism to the Old Testament — who first published his *Einleitung in das Alte Testament* at Göttingen in 1780. [Vierte Original-Ausgabe, 1823–1824].

[2] The "Pavier" quarto. *Cf.* W. J. Neidig, "The Shakespeare Quartos of 1619," in *Modern Philology*, Vol. VIII (Oct. 1910), pp. 145 ff.

[3] *Notes on the Hebrew Text of the Books of Samuel*, 2nd ed., Oxford, 1913, Preface, p. 1, note.

4 *Cf.* Laurentius Valla, *De falso credita et ementita Constantini donatione declamatio*, 1439; a French edition of this MS. was published at Lisieux, 1879.

5 *Baba Bathra*, 14[b].

6 *Cf.* S. R. Driver, *Introduction to the Literature of the Old Testament*, 9th ed., rev., New York, 1914, pp. 448 ff.

7 *Cf.* Driver, *op. cit.*, pp. 230 ff.

8 *Cf.* J. D. Prince, *A Critical Commentary on the Book of Daniel*, New York, 1899, pp. 15 ff., and Driver, *op. cit.*, pp. 497 ff.

9 Augustine, *In Heptateuchum Locutionum Libri Septem*, Book VI, *ad* Jos. iv. 9 and vi. 25 [Migne, *Patr. Curs. Compl.*, Ser. Lat., XXXIV, col. 537]. For additional occurrences of *unto this day* see Deut. xxxiv. 6, Judg. x. 4, I Sam. vi. 18, I Kgs. viii. 8, *et al.*

10 As, for example, in his *De Consensu Evangelistarum;* *cf.* Migne, *Patr. Curs. Compl.*, Ser. Lat., Vol. XXXIV, col. 1042 ff.

11 *Cf.* Fr. Bäthgen, "Der Psalmen-commentar des Theod. v. Mops. in Syr. Bearbeitung," in *Zeitschrift für Alt-Testament Wissenschaft*, V. 53 ff., VI. 261 ff., VII. 1–60. Theodore's conclusion as to Maccabean contributions to the Psalms is shared by Theodoret, bishop of Cyrrhus in Syria [c. A. D. 386–c. 458].

12 *V.* p. 321, note 15.

13 *Cf.* Wilhelm Bacher, *Die Jüdische Bibelexegese vom Anfange des zehnten bis zum Ende des fünfzehnten Jahrhunderts*, Trier, 1892, pp. 41, 50.

14 *Cf.* Maimonides, *Guide of the Perplexed*, trans. from the Arabic by M. Friedländer, 2nd ed., rev., London, 1928, pp. 234 ff.; also William Rosenau, *Jewish Biblical Commentators*, Baltimore, 1906, p. 105.

15 *E. g.*, Gen. xii. 6, Num. xxi. 14, Deut. xxxiv. 6. See *Leviathan*, Pt. 3, Ch. xxxiii.

16 *I. e.*, *Praeadamitae sive exercitatio super versibus duodecimo, decimo tertio, et decimo quarto capitis quinti Epistolae Pauli ad Romanos, quibus inducuntur primi hominis ante Adamum conditi*, n. p., 1655. This book, ordered to be burned by the Paris Parliament, enjoyed immediate popularity, going through four editions in the year of publication, and being translated into English the year following, and into Dutch in 1661.

17 *I. e.*, *Systema theologicum ex prae-Adamitarum hypothesi*, n. p., 1655. Three editions in 1655, and an English translation the same year.

18 The full title of this celebrated work, published anonymously in 1670, under the protectively false imprint *Hamburgi apud Heinricum Künraht*, runs as follows: *Tractatus theologico-politicus, continens dissertationes aliquot, quibus ostenditur libertatem philosophandi non tantum salva pietate et reipublicae pace posse concedi sed eandem nisi cum pace reipublicae ipsaque pietate tolli non posse*. See Ch. vi for miracles; Chs. viii and ix for Pentateuchal criticism.

19 Levi ben Gershon (A. D. 1288–1344) is known also both as Gersonides and as RALBAG. For his discussion of Biblical miracles see § vi, pt. 2 of his major work, MILḤAMÔTH 'ADONAY, first printed at Riva di Trenta, 1560.

20 Seventeenth century followers include: Richard Simon, the first edition of whose *Histoire critique du vieux testament* (Paris, 1678) was confiscated and burned; Jean Le Clerc, a Dutch scholar who, noticing that the epithet *prophet*

with which Abraham is honored [Gen. xx. 7] is a word of late origin [I Sam. ix. 9], inferred, in *Sentimens . . . sur l'histoire critique . . . par le P. Richard Simon* (Amsterdam, 1685), that the Pentateuch could have assumed its final form only in the monarchical period; Compegius Vitringa, of the Reformed Church of Holland, whose *Sacrarum Observationum Libri Sex* (Freneker, 1683-1708) maintained that Moses had made use of earlier documents in writing the Pentateuch; Thomas Burnet, author of *Archaeologiae philosophicae* (London, 1692), the seventh and eighth chapters of which criticized rather provocatively the Mosaic account of Creation and the Fall of Man; Charles Blunt, who, in his *Oracles of Reason* (London, 1693), not only plagiarized the *Praeadamitae* but incorporated the sensational seventh and eighth chapters of Burnet; and Pierre Bayle who published his *Dictionnaire critique* at Rotterdam in 1697.

[21] Herminghus Bernhard Witter, whose anticipation of Astruc's analysis [*Jura Israelitarum in Palæstinam terram Chananæam commentatione in Genesin . . . demonstrata . . . Accedit . . . textus Hebræus cum versione Latina* (ch. i–xvii) autore H. B. Witter, Hildesheim, (1711)] was without discoverable influence upon the French physician's stimulating work, which, published at Brussels in 1753, was boldly entitled *Conjectures sur les Mémoires Originaux dont il paroît que Moyse s'est servi pour composer le Livre de la Genèse.*

[22] Reference should be made especially to J. G. Eichhorn (v. p. 340, note 1), whose Pentateuchal criticism — limited, like Astruc's, by the tradition of Mosaic authorship — included valuable studies in linguistic usage, and admitted, besides two primary sources for Genesis, several original documents, many *fragmentary*; to Karl David Ilgen, *Die Urkunden des Jerusalemischen Tempelarchivs*, 1798, who first maintained that *Elohim* was characteristic of more than one source of Genesis; to Alexander Geddes, *Critical Remarks on the Hebrew Scriptures, etc.*, 1792-1800; to W. M. L. De Wette, of whose *Lehrbuch der historischkritischen Einleitung in die . . . Bücher des Alten Testaments*, Berlin, 1817 (available in English translation by Theodore Parker, 2nd ed., 1858), an edition by Eb. Schrader (the 8th) appeared in 1869; to J. F. Bleek, *Einleitung in das Alte Testament*, 1822; to G. H. A. Ewald, who in 1831 published his contention that the Elohistic and Yahvistic sources were traceable throughout the Pentateuch; to Wilhelm Vatke, *Biblische Theologie wissenschaftlich dargestellt*, 1835; to J. F. George, *Die ältern jüdischen Feste, mit einer Kritik der Gesetzgebung des Pentateuch*, Berlin, 1835; to H. Hupfeld, who, in *Die Quellen der Genesis*, 1853, refined Ilgen's hypothesis and applied it to the Hexateuch; to Eduard Riehm, *Die Gesetzgebung Mosis im Lande Moab*, 1854; to J. W. Colenso, *The Pentateuch and Book of Joshua critically examined*, 1862-1879; to A. Dillmann, *Hexateuch Komentar*, 1875, and *Die Genesis erklärt*, 1892; to Édouard Reuss, *Die Geschichte der heiligen Schriften des alten Testaments*, 1881; to A. Kuenen, *An historico-critical inquiry into the origin and composition of the Hexateuch* (trans. by P. H. Wicksteed), 1886; to Julius Wellhausen, whose conclusions, in *Die Komposition des Hexateuchs, etc.*, 1889, if not altogether acceptable, are yet the point of departure for modern criticism; to C. H. Cornill, *Einleitung in das Alte Testament*, 1891; to W. E. Addis, *The Documents of the Hexateuch*, 1892; to H. Holzinger, *Einleitung in den Hexateuch*, 1893; to C. A. Briggs, *The Higher Criticism of the Hexateuch*, 1897; to J. E. Carpenter and G. Harford-Battersby, *The Composition of the Hexateuch,*

1902; to S. R. Driver, *Introduction to the Literature of the Old Testament*, rev. ed., 1913; to J. Skinner, "The Divine Names in Genesis," in *The Expositor*, 1913; to Ernst Sellin, *Einleitung in das Alte Testament*, 7th ed., rev., 1935.

²³ *V.* p. 280.

²⁴ *Cf.* Saul M. Ginzburg and P. S. Marek, ЕВРЕЙСКІЯ НАРОДНЫЯ ПѢСНИ ВЪ РОССІИ, St. Petersburg, 1901, and Leo Wiener, *The History of Yiddish Literature in the nineteenth Century*, New York, 1899.

²⁵ *Cf.* S. R. Driver, *The Book of Genesis (Westminster Commentaries)*, pp. xii and xvi.

²⁶ *Cf.* W. F. Albright, *From the Stone Age to Christianity*, pp. 189, 190.

²⁷ האיש משה; לדר דר לדר; פנים אל פנים. For additional examples see H. Holzinger, *Einleitung in den Hexateuch*, Freiburg, 1893, pp. 181 ff.

²⁸ *V.* p. 127. *Cf.* B. H. Streeter, *The Four Gospels, etc.*, London, 1930, p. 156; Albright, *op. cit.*, p. 46; Driver, *Introduction to the Literature of the Old Testament*, pp. 4, 5; F. G. Kenyon, *The Bible and Archaeology*, London, [1940], p. 23.

²⁹ *Cf.* J. Skinner, *Genesis (I. C. C.)*, *passim*; Driver, *Genesis (Westm. Comm.)*, *passim*.

³⁰ See Gen. i. 27; xlix. 29ᵇ–30; Ex. xxv. 19; Num. ii. 2; *et al.*

³¹ *Cf.* Driver, *Genesis*, p. 107; R. W. Rogers, *Cuneiform Parallels to the Old Testament*, 2nd ed., Abingdon, © 1926, pp. 80–113.

³² Ch. xix, analysis of which yields the following. P: vv. 1–2ᵃ; J: vv. 3ᵇ–9, 11ᵇ–13, 18, 20–25; E: vv. 2ᵇ–3ᵃ, 10–11ᵃ, 14–17, 19. *Cf.* Driver, *Literature of the O. T.*, p. 31.

³³ *Cf.* Driver, *Lit. of the O. T.*, p. 33.

³⁴ Representative duplicate passages in the O. T. are II Sam. xxii and Ps. xviii; Ps. xiv and Ps. liii; I Chr. xvi. 8–22 and Ps. cv. 1–15; I Chr. xvi. 23–33 and Ps. xcvi; Ps. xl. 13–17 and Ps. lxx; Ps. lvii. 7–11 plus Ps. lx. 5–12 and Ps. cviii; II Kgs. xix–xx and Is. xxxvii–xxxix; II Kgs. xxv and Jer. lii; Judg. i. 10ᵇ–15 and Josh. xv. 14–19. Typical of this duplication in the N. T. is the Lord's Prayer: Mt. vi. 9–13 and Lk. xi. 2–4.

³⁵ For further illustration of D's usage, see Driver, *Lit. of the O. T.*, pp. 100 ff.

³⁶ *Adv. Jovinianum*, I. 6, *Opera*, ed. Vallarsi, II. 244: ". . . Josiam . . . sub quo in Templo Deuteronomii liber repertus est, . . ."

³⁷ *Cf.* Driver, *Genesis*, p. xvi; also his *Lit. of the O. T.*, p. 123; and W. F. Albright, *op. cit.*, p. 189.

³⁸ *Cf.* Albright, *op. cit.*, pp. 265, 266.

³⁹ *Cf. Tatiani Evangeliorum Harmoniae arabice . . . edidit . . .* P. Augustinus Ciasca, Rome, 1888. A Latin version of the *Diatessaron* was translated into Old German [East Franconian] by monks of the Benedictine monastery at Fulda, c. A. D. 835. *Cf.* E. Sievers, *Tatian, Lateinisch und altdeutsch*, Paderborn, 1892.

⁴⁰ *Cf.* E. D. Burton, *Some Principles of Literary Criticism and their Application to the Synoptic Problem*, Chicago, 1904, pp. 21–22.

⁴¹ *Cf.* Burton, *op. cit.*, *passim*.

⁴² *Cf.* Eusebius, *Hist. Eccl.*, VI. 14 [Migne, *Patr. Gr.*, XX, col. 552]: Τοῦ Πέτρου δημοσίᾳ ἐν Ῥώμῃ κηρύξαντος τὸν Λόγον . . . , τοὺς παρόντας πολλοὺς

ὄντας παρακαλέσαι τὸν Μάρκον . . . ἀναγράψαι τὰ εἰρημένα, ποιήσαντα δὲ τὸ Εὐαγγέλιον . . . Ὅπερ ἐπιγνόντα τὸν Πέτρον, προτρεπτικῶς μήτε κωλῦσαι μήτε προτρέψασθαι.

43 *Adv. Haer.*, III. 1: Μετὰ δὲ τὴν τούτων ἔξοδον, Μάρκος ὁ μαθητὴς καὶ ἑρμηνευτὴς Πέτρου, καὶ αὐτὸς τὰ ὑπὸ Πέτρου κηρυσσόμενα ἐγγράφως ἡμῖν παραδέδωκε [Migne, *Patr. Gr.*, VII, col. 845].

44 B. H. Streeter, *op. cit.*, p. 494.

45 *Cf.* Streeter, *op. cit.*, pp. 524, 540; and Edgar J. Goodspeed, *Formation of the New Testament*, Chicago, © 1926, p. 34.

46 Conceivable is the explanation that missing material, far from being deleted, has been lost through accidental mutilation of the original manuscript. *Cf.* Streeter, *op. cit.*, p. 175, and W. Sanday, in *Studies in the Synoptic Problem*, (ed., W. Sanday), Oxford, 1911, pp. 25 ff.

47 *Cf.* Sir John Hawkins, in *Studies in the Synoptic Problem*, pp. 61 ff.

48 *V.* p. 144, note u.

49 *V.* pp. 296 ff.

50 *Cf.* Streeter, in *Studies in the Synoptic Problem*, pp. 156, 157:

51 *V.* p. 324, note 1.

52 *Yer. Soṭah.*

53 *Cf.* Carl S. Patton, *Sources of the Synoptic Gospels*, New York, 1915, pp. 123 and 164.

54 *Cf.* E. D. Burton, *op. cit.*, p. 48.

55 For multiple sources see Burton, *op. cit.*, p. 53.

56 *Cf.* Carl S. Patton, *op. cit.*, pp. 234 ff.; and Streeter, *The Four Gospels*, pp. 186 and 201. Cp., for example, Mk. vi. 7–11 with Mt. x. 1–16ᵃ and Lk. x. 1–12.

57 *Cf.* Streeter, *op. cit.*, ch. VIII, *passim.*

58 Mk. i. 6, iv. 33, vi. 17–29, vi. 45–viii. 26, ix. 9–13, 43–47, x. 1–10, 35–41, xi. 12–14, 20–22, 24, xiv. 26–28.

59 Acts. xxiv. 27.

60 *Cf.* Streeter, *op. cit.*, p. 211.

61 *Cf.* Goodspeed, *op. cit.*, p. 14.

62 *Cf.* C. D. Ginsburg, *The Massoreth ha-Massoreth of Elias Levita*, London, 1867, pp. 107, 108; and J. Buxtorf, *Tiberias, sive Commentarius Masorethicus, etc.*, Basel, 1620, "Preface," p. [7].

63 *Cf.* H. E. Ryle, *The Canon of the Old Testament*, 2nd ed., London, 1925, pp. 269 ff.

64 *V.* p. 4.

65 מטמאין את הידים [*Mish. Yad.* iii. 2–5; iv. 5, 6]. *Cf.* S. Zeitlin, "The Canonization of the Hebrew Scriptures," in *Proceedings of the American Academy o r Jewish Research*, Vol. III (1931–2), pp. 135–141.

66 *Meg. Yad.* iii. 5.

67 *Contra Apionem*, i. 8; c. A. D. 100.

68 Melito's list — drawn up c. A. D. 170 — occurs in his Ἐκλογαί, cited by Eusebius, *Hist. Eccl.*, IV. 21, and edited by Martin J. Routh, *Reliquae sacrae*, Vol. i, Oxford, 1814.

69 *V.* p. 341, note 5.

70 Περὶ βίου θεωρητικοῦ ἢ ἱκετῶν ἀρετῶν [*De Vita Contemplativa*], § 3: "*νόμους καὶ λόγια θεσπισθέντα διὰ προφητῶν καὶ ὕμνους . . .*" This work [*cf.*, *Philonis Alexandrini Opera qvae svpersvnt*, Vol. VI (ed. Leopold Cohn and Siegfried Reiter), Berlin, 1915, p. 52], thought spurious by Graetz and others, is held to be genuinely Philo's by L. Massebieau (*Revue de l'histoire des religions*, Vol. xvi, Paris, 1887) and F. C. Conybeare (*Philo: About the Contemplative Life*, Oxford, 1895).

71 *Cf.* J. D. Prince, *A Critical Commentary on the Book of Daniel*, New York, 1899, p. 13; and Driver, *Lit. of the O. T.*, pp. xxxiv–xxxviii and 508, 509.

72 *Cf.* C. D. Ginsburg, *Introduction to the Massoretico-critical Edition of the Hebrew Bible*, London, 1897, p. 6.

73 *Cf.* S. Zeitlin, *op. cit.*, p. 144. *V.* p. 38, note w.

74 *Cf.* Albright, *op. cit.*, p. 267.

75 *Cf.* Josephus, *Antiquities of the Jews*, xi. 8, § 2–4.

76 *V.* p. 157, note c.

77 *Cf.* Tertullian, *Adv. Marcionem*, V. xxi. [Migne, *Patr. Lat.* II, col. 524].

78 *Adv. Haer.* III. 11. 8. [Migne, *Patr. Gr.* VII, col. 885].

79 See further on this point Eusebius, *Hist. Eccl.*, V. 16. 3.

80 The term appears here in the genitive case: ". . . τῷ τῆς τοῦ 'Εναγγελίου Καινῆς Διαθήκης λόγῳ." *Cf.* Eusebius, *Hist. Eccl.*, V. 16. 3. [Migne, *Patr. Gr.* XX. col. 465].

81 ὅτι οὐ δεῖ ἰδιωτικοὺς ψαλμοὺς λέγεσθαι ἐν τῇ ἐκκλησίᾳ οὐδὲ ἀκανόνιστα βιβλία, ἀλλὰ μόνα τὰ κανονικὰ τῆς καινῆς καὶ παλαιᾶς διαθήκης. *Cf.* H. T. Bruns, *Canones apostolorum et conciliorum, etc.*, Berlin, 1839, Pars Prior, p. 79.

82 *Cf.* S. Zeitlin, "The Canonization of the Hebrew Scriptures," in *Proc. A. A. J. R.*, III (1931–32), pp. 132–134.

83 *Cf.* W. Sanday, in *Ency. Brit.*, 11th ed., III, 876.

84 Cp., *e. g.*, A. J. V. and R. V. at Ex. xxxiv. 15; Lev. xvii. 7.

SELECT BIBLIOGRAPHY

NOTE. This abbreviated list of works of general interest is supplemented by full bibliographical reference in the *Notes* to all sources consulted: specialized studies, standard authorities and the various editions of the Bible.

Albright, William Foxwell, *Archaeology and the Religion of Israel*, Baltimore, 1942.
—— *The Archaeology of Palestine and the Bible*, 3rd ed., New York, 1937.
—— *From the Stone Age to Christianity*, Baltimore, 1940.
Ancient Records of Assyria and Babylonia, W. R. Harper, ed., Chicago, n. d.
Ancient Records of Palestine, Phoenicia, and Syria, W. R. Harper, ed., Chicago, n. d.
Babylonian Talmud translated in English, The, I. Epstein, ed., London, 1935–1949.
Bewer, Julius A., *The Literature of the Old Testament*, rev. ed., New York, 1933.
Biblia Hebraica adjuvantibus W. Baumgartner, G. Beer, J. Begrich . . . [et al.] edidit Rud. Kittel; textum Masoreticum curavit P. Kahle. Editionem tertiam denuo elaboratam ad finem perduxerunt A. Alt et O. Eissfeldt, Stuttgart, 1937.
Bleek, J. Friedrich, *Einleitung in das Alte Testament*, 4th ed., Berlin, 1878.
Briggs, C. A., *General Introduction to the Study of Holy Scripture, etc.*, New York, 1899.
Charles, R. H., *Apocrypha and Pseudepigrapha of the Old Testament*, Oxford, 1913.
Cheyne, T. K., *Bible Problems and the New Material for their Solution*, New York, 1904.
Copinger, W. A., *The Bible and its Transmission, etc.*, London, 1897.
Cornill, C. H., *Introduction to the canonical books of the Old Testament*, G. H. Box, tr., New York, 1907.
Darlow, T. H. and Moule, H. F., *Historical Catalogue of the Printed Editions of Holy Scripture in the Library of the British and Foreign Bible Society*, London, 1903.
Dead Sea Scrolls of St. Mark's Monastery, The, Vol. I, Millar Burrows, ed., New Haven, 1950.
Deanesly, Margaret, *The Lollard Bible and other mediaeval Biblical versions*, Cambridge, 1920.
Driver, S. R., *The Book of Genesis (Westminster Commentaries)*, New York, 1904.
—— *An Introduction to the Literature of the Old Testament*, 9th ed. rev., Edinburgh, 1913.
—— *Notes on the Hebrew Text of the Books of Samuel*, 2nd ed., Oxford, 1913.

Eichhorn, Johann G., *Einleitung in das Alte Testament*, 4th ed., Göttingen, 1823–1824.

Eissfeldt, Otto, *Einleitung in das Alte Testament*, Tübingen, 1934.

Ewald, G. H. A., *Geschichte des Volkes Israel bis Christus*, 3rd ed., Göttingen, 1865.

Frazer, J. G., *Folklore in the Old Testament*, 3rd ed., New York, 1935.

Ginsburg, C. D., *Introduction to the Massoretico-critical Edition of the Hebrew Bible*, London, 1897.

Goodspeed, Edgar J., *The Formation of the New Testament*, Chicago, 1926.

———— *The Making of the English New Testament*, Chicago, 1925.

———— *New Solutions of New Testament Problems*, Chicago, 1927.

———— *Problems of New Testament Translation*, Chicago, 1945.

Gray, George Buchanan, *A Critical Introduction to the Old Testament*, New York, 1919.

———— *The Forms of Hebrew Poetry*, London, 1915.

Gregory, C. R., *Textkritik des Neuen Testaments*, Leipzig, 1900–1902.

Gressman, Hugo, *Altorientalische Texte und Bilder zum Alten Testament*, Berlin, 1926–1927.

Harnack, Adolf, *The Origin of the New Testament*, New York, 1925.

Harper, R. F., *The Code of Hammurabi, King of Babylon about 2250 B. C.*, Chicago, 1904.

Hawkins, John Caesar, *Horae Synopticae, etc.*, 2nd ed. rev., Oxford, 1909.

Hieronymus, Sophronius Eusebius [St. Jerome], *Opera omnia studia ac labore Dominici Vallarsi*, Venice, 1766–1771.

International Critical Commentary on the Holy Scriptures of the Old and New Testaments, S. R. Driver, A. Plummer, *et al.*, eds., New York, 1896–1929.

Jastrow, Morris, *The Book of Job, etc.*, Philadelphia, 1920.

———— *The Civilization of Babylonia and Assyria*, Philadelphia, 1915.

———— *A Gentle Cynic*, Philadelphia, 1919.

———— *Hebrew and Babylonian Traditions*, New York, 1914.

Kenyon, F. G., *The Bible and Archaeology*, London, 1940.

———— *Handbook to the Textual Criticism of the New Testament*, 2nd ed., London, 1912.

———— *Our Bible and the Ancient Manuscripts*, rev. ed., New York, 1941.

———— *The Text of the Greek Bible*, London, 1937.

Knox, Ronald, *The Trials of a Translator*, New York, 1949.

Loisy, Alfred, *Les Mythes Babyloniens et les Premiers Chapitres de la Genèse*, Paris, 1901.

———— *Les Mythes Chaldéens de la Création et du Déluge*, Amiens, 1892.

———— *Origins of the New Testament*, New York, 1950.

Margolis, Max L., *The Hebrew Scriptures in the Making*, Philadelphia, 1922.

———— *The Story of Bible Translations*, Philadelphia, 1917.

Marston, Charles, *The New Knowledge about the Old Testament*, London, 1933.

Maspero, G., *History of Egypt, Chaldea, Syria, Babylonia, and Assyria*, A. H. Sayce, ed., M. L. McClure, tr., London, n. d.

Montefiore, Claude, G., *The Old Testament and After*, London, 1923.

Montefiore, Claude, G., *The Synoptic Gospels, etc.*, 2nd ed. rev., London, 1927.

Nestle, E., *Introduction to the Textual Criticism of the New Testament*, Allan Menzies, ed., William Edie, tr., London, 1901.

Old Testament in Greek according to the text of Codex Vaticanus, The, A. E. Brooke, Norman MacLean, H. St. John Thackeray, eds., Cambridge, 1906–1940.

Patton, Carl S., *Sources of the Synoptic Gospels*, New York, 1915.

Peake, A. S. (ed.), *A Commentary on the Bible*, London, 1920.

—— *The People and the Book*, Oxford, 1925.

Pollard, A. W., *Records of the English Bible, etc.*, London, 1911.

Queen's Printers' Bible [The Variorum Bible], Cheyne, Driver, Clarke, Godwin, Ball, eds., 3rd ed., London, 1889.

Rahlfs, Alfred (ed.), *Septuaginta, id est Vetus Testamentum Graece juxta LXX interpretes*, Stuttgart, 1935.

Rogers, Robert William, *Cuneiform Parallels to the Old Testament*, 2nd ed., Abingdon, 1926.

—— *A History of Babylonia and Assyria*, 6th ed., New York, 1915.

—— *The Religion of Babylonia and Assyria*, New York, 1908.

Rosenau, William, *Jewish Biblical Commentators*, Baltimore, 1906.

Rossi, Giovanni Bernardo de, *Variae lectiones Veteris Testamenti ex immensa mss. editorumq. codicum congerie haustae et ad samar. textum, ad vetustiss. versiones, ad accuratiores sacrae criticae fontes ac leges examinatae opera ac studia Johannis Bern. de Rossi*, Parmae, 1784–1788. Supplement, 1798.

Rushbrooke, W. G. and Abbott, E. A., *The Common Tradition of the Synoptic Gospels*, London, 1884.

Ryle, H. E., *The Canon of the Old Testament*, 2nd ed., London, 1925.

Scrivener, F. H. A., *A Plain Introduction to the Criticism of the New Testament, etc.*, 4th ed., E. Miller, ed., London, 1894.

Sellin, Ernst, *Einleitung in das Alte Testament*, 7th ed., Leipzig, 1935.

Sitterly, Charles Fremont, *The Canon, Text and Manuscripts of the New Testament*, New York, 1914.

Soden, Hermann Freiherr von, *Griechisches Neues Testament*, Göttingen, 1913.

Souter, Alexander, *Novum Testamentum Graece*, Oxford, 1910.

Stevens, Henry, *The Bibles in the Caxton Exhibition MDCCCLXXVII, etc.*, London, 1878.

Strack, H. L., *Einleitung in das Alte Testament*, 6th ed., Munich, 1906.

—— *Prolegomena critica in Vetus Testamentum Hebraicum*, Leipzig, 1873.

Streeter, B. H., *The Four Gospels, a study of Origins, etc.*, 4th impr. rev., London, 1930.

Studies in the Synoptic Problem By Members of the University of Oxford, W. Sanday, ed., Oxford, 1911.

Swete, H. B., *An Introduction to the Old Testament in Greek, etc.*, 2nd ed., Cambridge, 1914.

—— *The Old Testament in Greek*, 4th ed., Cambridge, 1909 *et seq.*

Thompson, E. M., *Introduction to Greek and Latin Palaeography*, Oxford, 1912.

Tischendorf, L. F. Constantin, *Novum Testamentum Graece*, 8th ed., Leipzig, 1869–1872.

Torrey, Charles C., *Our Translated Gospels some of the evidence*, New York, 1936.

Weigle, Luther A., *The English New Testament from Tyndale to the Revised Standard Version*, New York, 1949.

Wellhausen, Julius, *Die Composition des Hexateuchs und der historischen Bücher des alten Testaments*, 3rd ed., Berlin, 1899.

────── *Einleitung in die drei ersten Evangelien*, Berlin, 1905.

────── *Prolegomena to the History of Israel*, J. S. Black and Allan Menzies, trs., Edinburgh, 1885.

Westcott, B. F., *A General View of the History of the English Bible*, 3rd ed. rev. by W. A. Wright, New York, 1927.

Westcott, B. F. and Hort, F. J. A., *The New Testament in the Original Greek*, Cambridge, 1881–1882.

Wilde, Laura H., *A Literary Guide to the Bible*, New York, 1922.

Wildeboer, G., *Origin of the Canon of the Old Testament*, G. F. Moore, ed., London, 1895.

TABLE A

CONTENTS OF PRINCIPAL GREEK UNCIAL MANUSCRIPTS OF THE SEPTUAGINT

	א	Θ[1]	A	B	C	E	F	G	L	M	N	Q	R	T
Genesis	frags[1]		whole[10]	frag[18]		parts[27]	parts[32]	frag[37]	parts[44]	parts[45]				
Exodus			whole	whole		whole[28]	parts[33]	frags[38]		whole				
Leviticus			whole[11]	whole		whole[28]	parts[34]	frags[39]		whole	part[51]			
Numbers	frags[2]		whole	whole		whole[28]	whole	frags[40]		parts[46]	parts[52]			
Deuteronomy		whole[65]	whole	whole		whole[28]	part[35]	parts[41]		whole	parts[53]			
Joshua		whole[66]	whole	whole		whole[29]	parts[36]	part[42]		parts[47]	whole			
Judges			whole	whole		whole[30]		frags[43]		whole	parts[54]			
Ruth*			whole	whole		whole[30]				whole[48]	whole			
I Samuel			parts[12]	whole		whole[28]				parts[49]	parts[55]			
II Samuel			whole	whole[19]		whole[28]				whole	whole			
I Kings			whole	whole		parts[31]				part[50]	parts[56]			
II Kings			whole	whole							whole			
I Chron.**	parts[3]		whole	whole							whole			
II Chron.**			whole	whole							whole			

351

TABLE A (continued)

	ℵ	Θ/Ι	A	B	C	E	F	G	L	M	N	Q	R	T
Ezra***	frag[4]		whole	whole							part[57]			
Nehemiah†	whole[5]		whole	whole							part[58]			
Esther	whole[5]		whole	whole							whole			
Job	whole		whole	whole	parts[21]						part[59]			
Psalms	whole		parts[13]	parts[20]									parts[63]	parts[64]
Proverbs	whole		whole	whole	parts[22]						whole[60]			
Eccl.	whole		whole	whole	parts[23]						whole[60]			
Song of S.	whole		whole	whole	part[24]						whole[60]			
Isaiah	whole		whole	whole			frag				whole[60]	whole		
Jeremiah	whole[6]		whole	whole							whole[60]	whole		
Lam.††	frag[7]		whole	whole							whole[60]	whole		
Ezekiel			whole	whole							whole[60]	whole		
Daniel†††			whole	whole							whole[60]	whole		
Hosea			whole	whole							whole[60]	whole		
Joel	whole		whole	whole							whole[60]	whole		
Amos			whole	whole							whole[60]	whole		

	ℵ	Θ	A	B	C	E	F	G	L	M	N	Q	R	T
Obadiah	whole		whole	whole							whole [60]	whole		
Jonah	whole		whole	whole							whole [60]	whole		
Micah			whole	whole							whole [60]	whole		
Nahum	whole		whole	whole							whole [60]	whole		
Habakkuk	whole		whole	whole							whole [60]	whole		
Zephaniah	whole		whole	whole							whole [60]	whole		
Haggai	whole		whole	whole							whole [60]	whole		
Zechariah	whole		whole	whole							whole [60]	whole		
Malachi	whole		whole	whole			frag				whole [60]	whole		
Old Testament Apocrypha														
I Esdras§			whole	whole							part [61]			
II Esdras§§§														
Esther§ §§	whole [5]		whole	whole	frags [25]						whole [62]			
Wisdom	whole		whole	whole	parts [26]						whole [60]			
Ecclus.	whole		whole [14]	whole							whole [60]			
Baruch			whole	whole							whole [60]	whole		

	ℵ	Θ	A	B	C	E	F	G	L	M	N	Q	R	T
Epistle of Jeremiah#				whole								whole		
Three Children##			whole[15]	whole							whole[60]	whole		whole
Susanna##			whole[16]	whole							whole[60]	whole		
Bel & Dragon##			whole[17]	whole							whole[60]	whole		
Prayer of Manasses###			whole											whole
Tobit	whole[8]		whole	whole							whole[60]			
Judith	whole[9]		whole	whole							whole[60]			
I Maccabees	whole		whole								whole[60]			
II Mac.			whole								whole[60]			
III Mac. ‡			whole								whole[60]			
IV Mac. ‡	whole		whole								whole[60]			

NOTES TO TABLE A OF MANUSCRIPTS

* Ruth, in the Jewish canon, is included in the Hagiographa (κeΤΗuΒΗιΜ — the Writings), and follows Song of Songs.

** I Chron. and II Chron., in the Jewish canon, follow Nehemiah, being thus the two concluding books of the Hagiographa.

*** Ezra, in the Vulgate and Douay O. T., is titled I Esdras.

† Nehemiah, in the Vulgate and Douay O. T., is titled II Esdras.

†† Lamentations, in the Jewish canon, is included in the Hagiographa, and follows Ruth.

††† Daniel, in the Jewish canon, is included in the Hagiographa, and follows Esther. This is Theodotion's version; only two Septuagintal MSS. of Daniel are extant — Codex Chisianus, a cursive at Chigi Library, Rome, and the fragmentary third-century (?) papyrus, 968 (Chester Beatty X).

§ The apocryphal I Esdras of A. V. and R. V. — consisting of parts of II Chron. (xxxv–xxxvi), most of Ezra, Nehemiah (vii. 72–viii. 12), and certain verses of unknown provenance — is, in the Septuagint, also called I Esdras, but in the Vulgate is titled III Esdras.

§§ The apocryphal II Esdras of the A. V. and R. V. is known in the Roman Catholic tradition as IV Esdras. This book, included in Latin MSS., is not found in the Greek Septuagint, only a few Greek verses being known in quotations. It was probably originally in Hebrew. The Latin translation, and the Ethiopic and two Arabic translations, were made from the lost Greek version. The English translation, and the Armenian, are from the Latin.

§§§ This book is Jerome's arrangement of disconnected interpolations (unknown to the Massoretic Text, but common in MSS. of LXX) in the canonical Esther. In A. V. and M. T. Esther ends at x. 3; in the Douay Version the additions constitute Esther x. 4–xvi. 24 (end).

\# The Epistle of Jeremiah, an independent work, is sometimes mistakenly considered to be chapter vi of Baruch.

\#\# These books, unknown to the Massoretic Text but occurring in the Septuagint, supplement the narrative of the Book of Daniel. Fragments of Bel and the Dragon are preserved also in a fifth-century (earlier?) MS. (Δ — Western MS. 31074) in the Bodleian Library.

\#\#\# First included in a printed English Bible in "Matthew's" Version, Antwerp [?], MDXXXVII.

‡ III and IV Maccabees are preserved in the Septuagint only.

¹ Gen. xxiii. 19–xxiv. 14 (with some lacunae); xxiv. 17–19 (only one or two initial letters of twenty lines); xxiv. 25–27 (only one or two final letters of twenty lines); xxiv. 30–33; xxiv. 36–41 (with lacunae); xxiv. 43–46. These fragments are preserved at Leningrad in a book binding. Of the original four columns only parts of three remain.

² Num. v. 26–30; vi. 5, 6, 11, 12, 17, 18, 22, 23; vii. 4, 5, 12, 13, 15–20. Preserved at Leningrad in a book binding. Of the four columns of 48 (?) lines each, only fragments of the first 34 lines remain.

³ At British Museum (a single leaf): I Chron. ix. 27–xi. 22. At Leipzig: I Chron. xi. 22–xix. 17.

⁴ At Leipzig: Ezra ix. 4–x. 44.

⁵ At Leipzig.

⁶ At British Museum: Jer. i. 1–x. 25. At Leipzig: Jer. x. 25–lii. 34 (end).

⁷ At Leipzig: Lam. i. 1–ii. 20.

⁸ At Leipzig: Tob. i. 1–ii. 2. At British Museum: Tob. ii. 2–xiv. 17 (end).

⁹ British Museum: Judith i. 1–xi. 13; xiii. 9–xvi. 31 (end). All but one leaf, of which a portion (the first 33 lines — of an original 48 — of two badly blurred columns — of an original four — on both sides of leaf) containing, with the indicated lacunae, Judith xi. 23–xii. 9, is at the Society for Ancient Literature at Leningrad.

¹⁰ Complete except for parts of 21 or 22 lines torn away from lower right-hand corner of fol. 1 (Gen. i. 20–25; i. 30–ii. 3), and lower portion of fol. 12 (15–17 lines) containing Gen. xiv. 14–17; xv. 1–5, 16–19; xvi. 6–9.

¹¹ Complete except for 3½ lines torn away from upper right-hand corner of fol. 67 containing parts of Lev. viii. 6–7; viii. 16.

¹² I Sam. i. 1–xii. 17; xiv. 10–xxxi. 13 (end).

¹³ Ps. i. 1–xlix. 18; lxxix. 11–cl. 6 (end). In Cod. A Psalms are preceded by the Epistle of Athanasius to Marcellinus, the ὑποθέσεις of Eusebius, a table, and the canons of the Morning and Evening Psalms; and are followed by an apocryphal psalm (Ps. cli; found also in Cod. R) and 14 "Canticles" (*cf.* codices R, T, and the ninth-century Bodleian MS. I): 1. Ex. xv. 1–19; 2. Deut. xxxii. 1–43; 3. I Sam. ii. 1–10; 4. Is. xxvi. 9–20; 5. Jon. ii. 3–10; 6. Hab. iii. 1–19; 7. Is. xxxviii. 10–23; 8. Prayer of Manasses (No. 9 in list of "Canticles" in MS. T); 9. Dan. iii. 23; 10. ὕμνος τῶν πατέρων ἡμῶν; 11. Magnificat (προσευχὴ τῆς θεολόκου); 12. Nunc dimittis (προσευχὴ Συμεών); 13. Benedictus (προσευχὴ Ζαχαρίου); 14. ὕμνος ἑωθινός (morning hymn).

¹⁴ Complete except for Ecclus. l. 21, 22; and li. 5.

¹⁵ Inserted immediately after Dan. iii. 23 (fol. 407ʳ, col. 1, line 21).

¹⁶ Immediately precedes the canonical text of Daniel (fol. 403ʳ, col. 1).

¹⁷ Immediately follows the canonical text of Daniel (fol. 416ʳ, col. 2).

¹⁸ Gen. xlvi. 29–l. 26 (end).

¹⁹ Complete except II Sam. ii. 5–7, 10–13.

²⁰ Ps. i. 1–cv. 26; cxxxvii. 7–cl. 6 (end).

²¹ Job ii. 12–iv. 12; v. 27–vii. 7; x. 9–xii. 2; xiii. 18–xviii. 9; xix. 27–xxii. 14; xxiv. 7–xxx. 1; xxxi. 6–xxxv. 15; xxxvii. 5–xxxviii. 17; xl. 20–xlii. 17 (end).

²² Prov. i. 2–ii. 8; xv. 29–xvii. 1; xviii. 11–xix. 23; xxii. 17–xxiii. 25; xxiv. 22–56; xxvi. 23–xxviii. 2; xxix. 48–xxxi. 31 (end).

²³ Eccl. i. 2–14; ii. 18–xii. 14 (end).

²⁴ S. of S. i. 3–iii. 9.

²⁵ Wisd. viii. 5–xii. 10; xiv. 19–xvii. 18; xviii. 24–xix. 22 (end).

²⁶ Ecclus. Prologue; i. 1–vii. 14; viii. 15–xi. 17; xii. 16–xvi. 1; xvii. 12–xx. 5; xxi. 12–xxii. 19; xxvii. 19–xxviii. 25; xxx. 8–xxxi. 6; xxxii. 22–xxxiv. 22; xxxvii. 11–xxxviii. 15; xxxix. 7–xliii. 27; xlv. 24–xlvii. 23; xlviii. 11–xlix. 12.

²⁷ At Bodleian: Gen. i. 1–xiv. 6; xviii. 24–xx. 14; xxiv. 54–xlii. 18. At U. L. C.: Gen. xlii. 18–xliii. 14 (a single leaf; *cf.* Table C, note 5). At Leningrad: Gen. xliii. 14–xlvi. 12; xlvii. 23–l. 26 (end).

²⁸ At Leningrad.

²⁹ At Leningrad: Jos. i. 1–xxiv. 26; at British Museum: xxiv. 27–33 (end).

³⁰ At British Museum.

³¹ At Leningrad: I Kgs. i. 1–xiii. 17; xv. 19–xvi. 28.

³² Gen. xxxi. 15–37; xlii. 14–21; xlii. 28–xlvi. 6; xlvii. 16–xlviii. 3; xlviii. 21–li. 14.

³³ Ex. i. 10–viii. 19; xii. 31–xxx. 29; xxxi. 18–xxxii. 6; xxxii. 13–xxxvi. 3; xxxvii. 10–xl. 38 (end).

³⁴ Lev. i. 1–ix. 18; x. 14–xxvii. 34 (end).

³⁵ Deut. i. 1–xxviii. 63; xxix. 14–xxxiv. 12 (end).

³⁶ Jos. i. 1–ii. 19; ii. 15–iv. 5; iv. 10–v. 1; v. 7–vi. 23; vii. 1–ix. 27; x. 37–xii. 12.

³⁷ At Leyden: Gen. xxxi. 53–xxxvi. 18.

³⁸ At Bibl. Nationale: Ex. xxxvi. 8–29; xxxvii. 3–6; xxxviii. 1–18; xxxix. 1–11; xxxix. 16–19. At Leyden: Ex. xl. 2–xl. 38 (end).

³⁹ At Bibl. Nat.: Lev. i. 1–iv. 26; xiii. 49–xiv. 6; xiv. 33–49; xv. 24–xvii. 10; xviii. 28–xix. 36. At Leyden: Lev. iv. 27–xiii. 17; xxiv. 9–xxvii. 16.

⁴⁰ At Leyden: Num. i. 1–vii. 85; xi. 18–xviii. 2; xviii. 30–xx. 22; xxix. 34–xxxvi. 13 (end). At Bibl. Nat.: Num. xxv. 2–xxvi. 3; xxix. 12–33.

⁴¹ At Leyden: Deut. iv. 11–26; vii. 13–xvii. 14; xviii. 8–xix. 4; xxviii. 12–xxxi. 11.

⁴² At Leyden: Jos. ix. 33–xix. 23.

⁴³ At Leningrad: Judg. ix. 48–x. 6. At Leyden: Judg. xv. 3–xviii. 16; xix. 25–xxi. 12.

⁴⁴ Gen. iii. 4–24; vii. 19–viii. 20; ix. 8–15, 20–27; xiv. 17–20; xv. 1–5; xix. 12–26, 29–35; xxii. 15–19; xxiv. 1–11, 15–20, 22–31; xxv. 27–34; xxvi. 6–11; xxx. 30–37; xxxi. 25–34; xxxii. 1–18, 22–32; xxxv. 1–4, 8, 16–20, 28, 29; xxxvii. 1–19; xxxix. 9–18; xl. 14–xli. 2; xli. 21–32; xlii. 21–38; xliii. 2–21; xlviii. 16–xlix. 3; xlix. 28–30; l. 1–4.

⁴⁵ Gen. i. 1–xxxiv. 2; xxxviii. 24–l. 26 (end).

⁴⁶ Num. i. 1–xxix. 23; xxxi. 4–xxxvi. 13 (end).

⁴⁷ Jos. i. 1–x. 6; xxii. 34–xxiv. 33 (end).

⁴⁸ Ruth i. 1–iv. 19.

⁴⁹ I Sam. i. 1–iv. 19; x. 19–xiv. 26; xxv. 33–xxxi. 13 (end).

⁵⁰ I Kgs. i. 1–viii. 40.

⁵¹ Lev. xiii. 59–xxvii. 34 (end).

⁵² Num. i. 1–xxi. 34; xxii. 19–xxxvi. 13 (end).

⁵³ Deut. i. 1–xxviii. 40; xxx. 16–xxxiv. 12 (end).

⁵⁴ Judg. i. 1–xiv. 16; xviii. 2–xxi. 25 (end).

⁵⁵ I Sam. i. 1–xvii. 12; xvii. 31–xxxi. 13 (end).

⁵⁶ I Kgs. i. 1–viii. 8; xi. 17–xxii. 53 (end).

⁵⁷ Ezra v. 10–x. 44.

⁵⁸ Neh. i. 1–vii. 3.

⁵⁹ At Venice: Job xxx. 8–xlii. 17 (end).

[60] At Venice.

[61] At Vatican: I Esdras i. 1–ix. 1.

[62] At Vatican.

[63] Complete except for four lacunae (Ps. i. 1–ii. 7; lxv. 20–lxviii. 3; lxviii. 26–33; cv. 43–cvi. 2) which have been supplied by a later hand which also added the apocryphal Psalm cli. The Psalms are followed (in the original hand) by eight "Canticles": 1. Ex. xv. 1–21; 2. Deut. xxxii. 1–44; 3. I Kgs. ii. 1–10; 4. Is. v. 1–9; 5. Jon. ii. 3–10; 6. Hab. iii. 1–10; 7. Magnificat; 8. Dan. iii. 23 ff.

[64] Ps. xxvi. (xxvii.) 1–xxx. 1; xxxvi. 21–xli. 5; xliii. 4–lviii. 23; lix. 4–8, 11, 12; lx. 2–lxiv. 11; lxx. 5–xcii. 2; xciii. 8–xcvi. 11; xcvii. 9–cl. 5 (end). Psalms are followed by "Canticles" [all that remains of an original twelve: 6. I Kgs. ii. 6–10; 7. Magnificat; 8. Is. xxxviii. 10–20; 9. Prayer of Manasses (*cf.* Cod. A); 10. Dan. iii. 23 ff.; 11. Benedictus; 12. Nunc dimittis].

[65] Complete except for Deut. v. 16–vi. 18.

[66] Complete except for Jos. iii. 3–iv. 10.

TABLE D

CONTENTS OF PRINCIPAL GREEK UNCIAL MANUSCRIPTS OF THE NEW TESTAMENT

	ℵ	Ξ	Θ	A	B	C	D	D_2	E_1	E_2	F_2	I	L	W
Matthew	whole		whole[3]	frag[4]	whole	parts[10]	parts[29]		whole				parts[55]	whole
Mark	whole[1]	part[2]	whole	whole	whole[1]	parts[11]	whole		whole				parts[56]	whole[58]
Luke	whole		whole	whole	whole	parts[12]	parts[30]		whole[36]				whole	whole
John	whole#		whole#	parts[5]	whole#	parts[13]	parts[31]		whole#				part[57]	whole[59]
Acts	whole			whole	whole	parts[14]	parts[32]			parts[37]				
Romans	whole			whole	whole	parts[15]		parts[34]			part[38]			
I Cor.	whole			whole	whole	parts[16]		parts[35]			parts[39]	frags[42]		
II Cor.	whole			parts[6]	whole	part[17]		whole				frags[43]		
Gal.	whole			whole	whole	part[18]		whole			whole	frags[44]		
Eph.	whole			whole	whole	part[19]		whole			whole	frags[45]		
Philip.	whole			whole	whole	part[20]		whole			whole	frags[46]		
Col.	whole			whole	whole	whole		whole			parts[40]	frags[47]		
I Thess.	whole			whole	whole	part[21]		whole			whole	frags[48]		
II Thess.	whole			whole	whole			whole			whole	frags[49]		
I Tim.	whole			whole		part[22]		whole			whole	frags[50]		

TABLE B (continued)

	$\aleph$	Ξ	Θ	A	B	C	D	D_2	E_1	E_2	F_2	I	L	W
II Tim.	whole			whole		part[23]		whole			whole	frags[51]		
Titus	whole			whole		whole		whole			whole	frags[52]		
Philemon	whole			whole		whole		whole			whole	parts[53]		
Hebrews	whole			whole	part[9]	parts[24]		whole			[41]	parts[54]		
James	whole			whole	whole	part[25]								
I Peter	whole			whole	whole	part[26]								
II Pet.	whole			whole	whole	whole								
I John	whole			whole	whole	part[27]								
II John	whole			whole	whole									
III John	whole			whole	whole	whole	frag[33]							
Jude	whole			whole	whole	whole								
Rev.	whole			whole		parts[28]								
Non-canonical														
Barnabas*	whole													
Hermas**	part													
I Clem.				part[7]										
II Clem.***				part[8]										

360

NOTES TO TABLE B

*Pericope adulterae* omitted. See also *infra*, notes 57, 59.

* See note ***.

** Of the Shepherd of Hermas only about one-fourth survives.

*** Not an Epistle, but a homily, as shown by the conclusion, wanting in A. Now known from MS. discovered 1875 by Archbp. Bryennios of Nicomedia in a monastery at Istanbul. This MS. contains also the Didaché and Barnabas.

[1] Except Mk. xvi. 9–20.

[2] Lk. i. 1–9; 19–23; 27 frag.; 30–32; 36–66; 77–ii. 19; 21 frag.; 33–39; iii. 5–8; 11–20; iv. 1 frag.; 6–20; 32–43; v. 17–36; vi. 21–vii. 6; 11–37; 39–47; viii. 4–21; 25–35; 43–50; ix. 1–28; 32 frag.; 35; 41–x. 18; 21–40; xi. 1–4; 24–33.

[3] Mt. i. 9–21; iv. 4–17 (lacunae); v. 4–xxviii. 20 (end).

[4] Mt. xxv. 7–xxviii. 20 (end).

[5] Jn. i. 1–vi. 49; viii. 53–xxi. 25 (end). Space in missing folios insufficient for inclusion of *pericope adulterae*.

[6] II Cor. i. 1–iv. 12; xii. 7–xiii. 13 (end).

[7] All but one leaf, containing I Clem. 57, 6–63, 64. Many interior corners missing; badly stained; considerable damage through the use of galls.

[8] II Clem. i. 1–xii. 5. The lost portion (xii. 5–xx. 5) was contained on a leaf conjoint with the leaf missing from I Clem.

[9] Heb. i. 1–ix. 13.

[10] Mt. i. 1–v. 15; vii. 7–xv. 26; xviii. 28–xxii. 20; xxiii. 17–xxiv. 10; xxiv. 45–xxv. 30; xxvi. 22–xxvii. 11; xxvii. 47–xxviii. 14.

[11] Mk. i. 17–vi. 31; viii. 5–xii. 29; xiii. 19–xvi. 20 (end).

[12] Lk. i. 1–ii. 5; ii. 42–iii. 21; iv. 25–vi. 4; vi. 37–vii. 16; viii. 28–xii. 3; xix. 42–xx. 27; xxi. 21–xxii. 19; xxiii. 25–xxiv. 7; xxiv. 46–53 (end).

[13] John i. 1–41; iii. 33–v. 16; vi. 38–vii. 3; viii. 34–ix. 11; xi. 8–46; xiii. 8–xiv. 7; xvi. 21–xviii. 36; xx. 26–xxi. 25 (end).

[14] Acts i. 1–iv. 3; v. 35–x. 42; xiii. 1–xvi. 36; xx. 10–xxi. 30; xxii. 21–xxiii. 18; xxiv. 15–xxvi. 19; xxvii. 16–xxviii. 4.

[15] Rom. i. 1–ii. 5; iii. 21–ix. 6; x. 15–xi. 31; xiii. 10–xvi. 27 (end).

[16] I Cor. i. 1–vii. 18; ix. 6–xiii. 8; xv. 40–xvi. 24 (end).

[17] II Cor. i. 1–x. 8.

[18] Gal. i. 21–vi. 18 (end).

[19] Eph. ii. 18–iv. 16.

[20] Phil. i. 22–iii. 5.

[21] I Thess. i. 1–ii. 8.

[22] I Tim. iii. 9–v. 19.

[23] II Tim. ii. 14–iv. 22 (end).

[24] Heb. ii. 4–vii. 26; ix. 15–x. 24; xii. 16–xiii. 25 (end). Heb. follows Thess. as in Washingtonianus II.

[25] Jas. i. 1–iv. 2.

[26] I Pet. i. 1–iv. 5.

[27] I Jo. i. 1–iv. 2.

[28] Rev. i. 1–iii. 19; v. 14–vii. 14; vii. 17–viii. 4; ix. 17–x. 10; xi. 3–xvi. 13; xviii. 2–xix. 5.

[29] Mt. i. 12–vi. 20; ix. 2–xxvii. 1; xxvii. 12–xxviii. 20 (end).

[30] Lk. i. 1–iii. 23; iii. 31–xxiv. 53 (end).

[31] John i. 1–i. 16; iii. 26–xxi. 25 (end). *Pericope adulterae* included.

[32] Acts i. 1–viii. 29; x. 14–xxi. 2; xxi. 10–15; xxi. 18–xxii. 10; xxii. 20–29.

[33] Of III Jo., 12 lines of the Latin text only (i. 11–14) survive.

[34] Rom. i. 8–26; i. 31–xvi. 27 (end). Rom. i. 27–30 supplied by a second, but very early, hand.

[35] I Cor. i. 1–xiv. 12; xiv. 23–xvi. 24 (end). I Cor. xiv. 13–22 supplied by a second, but very early, hand.

[36] Complete except for Lk. iii. 4–15; xxiv. 47–53 (end).

[37] Acts i. 1–xxvi. 28; xxviii. 26–31 (end).

[38] Rom. iii. 19–xvi. 27 (end).

[39] I Cor. i. 1–iii. 7; v. 15–vi. 6; vi. 15–xvi. 24 (end).

[40] Col. i. 1–29; ii. 9–iii. 18 (end).

[41] Only the Latin text of Heb. has survived. In the Greek text there is preserved a Prologue to this Epistle.

[42] I Cor. x. 29–xii. 13 (lacunae).

[43] II Cor. i. 1–xiii. 11 (lacunae).

[44] Gal. i. 1–iv. 23 (lacunae); four folios, containing remainder of Gal. and beginning of Eph., are wanting.

[45] Eph. ii. 16–vi. 21 (lacunae).

[46] Phil. i. 1–iv. 15 (lacunae).

[47] Col. i. 1–iv. 12 (lacunae).

[48] I Thess. i. 1–v. 27 (lacunae).

[49] II Thess. i. 1–iii. 10 (lacunae).

[50] I Tim. i. 1–vi. 19 (lacunae).

[51] II Tim. i. 1–iv. 20 (lacunae).

[52] Tit. i. 1–iii. 9 (lacunae).

[53] Phm. i. 1–16 (lacunae).

[54] Heb. i. 1–xiii. 25 (lacunae); follows II Thess. in this MS.

[55] Mt. i. 1–iv. 21; v. 15–xxviii. 16.

[56] Mk. i. 1–x. 15; x. 31–xv. 1; xv. 21–xvi. 20 (end).

[57] John i. 1–xxi. 14. Blank space sufficient for *pericope adulterae* after vii. 53.

[58] Mk. i. 1–xv. 12; xv. 38–xvi. 20 (end). A single leaf has been lost. A unique insertion follows Mk. v. 14. *V. supra*, p. 143.

[59] John i. 1–xiv. 25; xvi. 7–xxi. 25 (end). Two leaves missing. *Pericope adulterae* omitted.

PRINCIPAL BIBLICAL GREEK UNCIAL MANUSCRIPTS

Symbol	Name	Century	Location	LXX Contents	N. T. Contents
A	Alexandrinus	V	British Museum	All but frags of Gn, I Sa, Ps.	All but parts of Mt, Jn, II Cor.
B	Vaticanus	IV	Vatican Libr	All but most of Gn, I Sam(pt), Ps (pt).	All but I, II Tim, Tit, Phm, Rev, Heb (pt).
C	Ephraemi [1]	V	Bibl. Nationale	Pts. Jb, Eccl, Wisd, Ecclus, Song, Prov.	Pts. all bks. exc. II Th and II Jo.
D	Cotton Genesis [2]	V	British Museum	Genesis	
D	Bezae	V[3]	Univ. Libr. Cambridge		Gospels, Acts, 3 small frags III Jo.
D₂	Claromontanus [4]	VI	Bibl. Nationale		Paul. Epp, few lacunae
E	Bodleian Gen. [5]	X	Bodl., U. L. C., Leningrad, B. M.	Gn — I Kgs xvi. 28; some lacunae	
E	Basiliensis [6]	VIII	Univ. Libr. Basle		Gospels; small lacunae
E₂	Laudianus [7]	VII	Bodleian		Acts exc. xxvi. 29–xxviii. 26
E₃	Sangermanensis [8]	IX	Leningrad		Pauline Epistles
F	Ambrosianus	V	Ambrosian Libr, Milan	Gn xxxi. 15–Jos xii. 12 mutilated; frags Is, Mal.	
F	Boreeli	IX	Utrecht		Gospels; many lacunae

TABLE C (continued)

Symbol	Name	Century	Location	LXX Contents	N. T. Contents
F₂	Augiensis[9]	IX	Trin. Coll. Camb.		Pauline Epp; lacunae
G	Sarravianus	V	Leyden, Leningrad, Bibl. Nat.	Frags Gn, Ex, Nu, Lv, Dt, Jos, Judg.	
G₃	Boernerianus	IX	Dresden[10]		Paul. Epp exc. Heb and lacunae. See note 10.
H	Petropolitanus[11]	VI	Leningrad	Frags of Numbers	
H₃	Coislinianus	VI	Bibl. Nat., Kiev, Leningrad, Turin, Mt. Athos, Moscow		Paul. Epp: (frags) of I, II Cor, Gal, I Th, Heb, I, II Tim, Tit.
I		IX	Bodleian	Psalms, "Canticles"	
I	Washington. II	VII[12]	Smithsonian		Paul. Epp (parts)
K[11]		VII	Leipzig	Frags Nu, Dt, Jos, Judg.	
K	Cyprius	X[13]	Bibl. Nationale		Gospels
K	Moscuensis	IX	Moscow		Acts, Epistles (lacunae)
L	Vienna Genesis[14]	VI	Vienna	Parts of Genesis	
L	Regius[15]	VIII	Bibl. Nationale		Gospels; lacunae
L	Angelicus	IX	Bibl. Angelica		Acts-Jude; lac. Acts i. 1–viii. 10; Heb xiii. 10–25 (end)
M	Coislinianus I	VII	Bibl. Nationale	Gn–I Kgs; mutilated	

364

TABLE C (continued)

Symbol	Name	Century	Location	LXX Contents	N. T. Contents
M	Campianus	IX	Bibl. Nationale		Gospels
$\mathcal{N}$	Basiliano-Vaticanus[16]	VIII–IX	Vatican, St. Mark's Venice	Lv xiii. 59–Mal exc. Ps and lacunae	
N	Purpureus Petropolitanus[17]	VI	Leningrad, Lerma, Vatican, B. Mus., Vienna, Patmos		About half the Gospels; see note 17
O	Dublinensis[18]	VI	Trin. Coll. Dubl.	Two frags Isaiah	
O	Sinopensis[19]	VI	Bibl. Nationale		Matthew, 43 leaves
P	MS. III. 3. 22	XII	Emmanuel, Camb.	Parts of Psalms	
P	Guelpherbytanus A[11]	VI	Wolfenbüttel		Frags of Gospels[20]
P₂	Porphyrianus[11]	IX	Leningrad		Acts, Epp, Rev; many lacunae
Q	Marchalianus	VI	Vatican	Prophets, Lam, Dan, Bar, Ep. Jer.	
Q	Guelpherbytanus B[11]	V	Wolfenbüttel		Lk iv. 34–xxiii. 49; Jn xii. 3–xiv. 22; many lacunae
R	Verona Psalter[21]	VI	Verona, Chpt. Lib.	Psalms, "Canticles"	
R	Nitriensis[11]	VI	British Museum		Luke (fragments)[22]
S	Vaticanus 354	X	Vatican		Gospels

365

TABLE C (continued)

Symbol	Name	Century	Location	LXX Contents	N. T. Contents
T	Zurich Psalter[23]	VII	Zurich, Stadtbibl.	Psalms, "Canticles," 3 Child, Manasses.	Lk xxii. 20–xxiii. 20; Jn vi. 28–67; vii. 6–viii. 31
T	Borgianus	V	Vatican		Gospels
U	Nanianus	X	Venice		Gospels
V	Venetus[24]	X	St. Mark's Venice	*V. supra, N* and Table A	Gospels (lacunae)[25]
V	Moscuensis	IX?	Moscow	Frags of Psalms	
W	Parisiensis	IX	Bibl. Nationale		Gospels[27]
W	Washington. I	V[26]	Smithsonian		Gospels[27],[28]
X	MS. Gk. 749	IX	Vatican	Major part of Job	
X	Monacensis	X	Munich		Gospels (lacunae)[29]
Υ	Taurinensis	IX	Turin, Bibl. Naz.	Minor Prophets	
Y	Macedonianus	IX	Banbury		
Z	Dublinensis[11]	VI	Trin. Coll. Dubl.		Frags Mt i. 17–xxvi. 71
ℵ	Sinaiticus	IV	British Museum Leipzig Leningrad[30]	Frags Gn, Nu, I Ch, Ezr. Neh-Mal exc. Lam (pt), Ezek, Dn, Ho, Am, Mic.	Complete, plus Barnabas and ¼ Shepherd of Hermas
Γ	Cryptoferratensis[11]	VIII–IX	Grotto Ferrata, Basilian mnsty.	Frags of Prophets	

TABLE C (continued)

Symbol	Name	Century	Location	LXX Contents	N. T. Contents
Γ	Tischendorf. IV	IX–X	Bodl., Leningrad	Frags Bel and Dragon	Parts Mt, Mk; Lk, Jn.[31]
Δ̱	West. MS. 31074.	V[32]	Bodleian		Gospels[33] exc. Jn xix. 17–35
Δ	Sangallensis	IX	St. Gall		
Θ	Washington. I	V–VI[34]	Smithsonian	Dt, Jos (lacunae)	
Θ	Koridethianus	IX?	Tiflis		Gospels exc. Mt i. 1–8; i. 22–iv. 3; iv. 17–v. 3
Λ	Tischendorf. III	IX–X	Bodleian[35]		Luke, John
Ξ	Zacynthius[11]	VI	London, Brit. and For. Bible Soc.		Luke, 342 vv. See Table B, note 2
Π̱		IX	Leningrad	Frags IV Maccabees	
Π	Petropolitanus	IX	Leningrad		Gospels (exc. about 77 vv.)[36]
Σ	Rossanensis[37]	VI	Rossano, Calabria		Matthew, Mark (lacunae)
Φ	Beratinus[38]	VI	Berat, Albania		Mt, Mk (mutilated)[39]
Ψ	Laurensis	VIII–IX	Monastery of the Laura, Mt. Athos		Mk ix. 5–end, Lk, Jn, Acts, Epistles
Ω	Dionysiacus	VIII–IX	Mt. Athos		Gospels
1219	Washington. II	VI[40]–VII	Smithsonian	Frags Ps i.–cxlii	
046[41]		VIII[42]	Vatican		
87			Rome, Chigi Bibl.	Dan, LXX version	Revelation

NOTES TO TABLE C

[1] A palimpsest, the superior text (12th century?) being a copy of the writings of the Syrian St. Ephraem. In the inferior text the order of the Biblical books is unorthodox, 42 folios are inverted, and an interchange of two sections of Ecclus. (xxx. 25–xxxiii. 13ª and xxxiii. 13ᵇ–xxxvi. 16ª) restores sense to the customarily confused sequence.

[2] Shriveled and disfigured by fire in 1731, before which, however, it had been carefully collated by Grabe.

[3] "Not later than the fifth century" (Kenyon). The earliest known bilingual Bible, the Greek text occupying the versos and a Latin version the rectos. Characterized by notable departures from the accepted text, one of which is a long addition (found also in Φ) following Mt. xx. 28, and another of which is the inclusion of the story of the Woman taken in Adultery (John vii. 53–viii. 11) found in sundry Old Latin MSS. and the Vulgate but lacking in א, A, B, C, L, N, W, Y, Ψ, Θ, *et al.*, and relegated to the margin in the R. V. Once the property of Theodore Beza, by whom it was presented, in 1581, to University Library Cambridge.

[4] Bilingual: Greek on versos, Latin on rectos. The missing Greek verses of Rom. and I Cor. have been supplied by a second, but very early, hand. The Latin text lacks Rom. i. 27–30; I Cor. xiv. 8–18; Heb. xiii. 21–25. Rom. i. 24–27 (Latin) supplied by a very early hand.

[5] Bodleian: Gen. i. 1–xlii. 17 (lacunae) in uncial letters; U. L. C.: a single leaf, the recto of which (Gen. xlii. 18–xlii. 30) is in the uncial hand of the Bodleian portion, and the verso of which (Gen. xlii. 31–xliii. 14) is in the minuscule hand of the Leningrad and British Museum portions. (See Table A, Notes). The minuscule portion is designated No. 509, or, in the Cambridge LXX, a₂. Tischendorf is responsible for this dismemberment of the codex. Attempts by the Bodleian to recover the single leaf from U. L. C. have proved unavailing, a suggested exchange "for some volume abstracted from [that] library and deposited in the Bodleian" never having been effected. See letter, dated Jan. 11, 1892, attached to Western MS. 28644.

[6] Folios 160, 207, 214 are palimpsests, "et ont été refaits."

[7] Bilingual, two columns to a page, each line of the left-hand column containing one to three words only of the Latin text, and each corresponding line of the right-hand column containing the equivalent word or words of the Greek, so that the MS. appears like an unalphabetized glossary. This is the earliest known MS. to include the eunuch's confession of faith (Acts viii. 37). It was apparently used by Bede for his commentary upon Acts. Souter dates it sixth century.

[8] A copy of D₂, of no independent critical value.

[9] Bilingual, two columns to a page, the versos containing the Latin text (minuscule) in the left-hand column and the Greek in the right, the rectos reversing this arrangement. This MS., once at the Belgian monastery Augiae, is closely allied to D₂.

Table C. Principal Biblical Greek Uncials 369

¹⁰ Once a part of Codex Sangallensis, Δ, at monastery of St. Gall, Switzerland. Lacks: Rom. i. 1–5; ii. 16–25; I Cor. iii. 8–16; vi. 7–14; Col. ii. 1–8; Phm. 21–25 (end); Heb. Interlineated in Latin.

¹¹ Palimpsest.

¹² This date is assigned by Kenyon with a cautioning "probably." Sanders: VI.

¹³ Possibly of the ninth century.

¹⁴ Silver letters on purple vellum.

¹⁵ Following Jn. vii. 52, on fols. 119ᵛ and 120ʳ sufficient blank spaces left for inclusion of the story of the Woman taken in Adultery, which occurs, at that point, among the Uncials, only in D and (with asterisks) M. Mk. xvi. 9–20 preceded (as in Ψ, ٦, ק) by shorter interpolation.

¹⁶ One MS. in two volumes, much mutilated. The first vol. (Vatican Gk. 2106) now contains, with lacunae, Lev. xiii. 59–Esther, and I Esdras i. 1–ix. 1. The second volume, at St. Mark's Library, Venice (formerly known as Codex Venetus and designated as *V*), containing, with lacunae, the remainder of LXX except Psalms, was used, together with B, as the basis of the Roman edition of LXX, 1587.

¹⁷ Silver letters on purple vellum. Gold letters used for the abbreviated sacred names, and occasionally elsewhere. Originally 462 leaves. At Leningrad, 182 leaves; at Patmos, 33; at Vatican, 6; at B. M., 4; at Vienna, 2; at Lerma, 1 (Jn. iii. 14–21). Altogether, approximately half of Mt. i. 24–xxvii. 34; Mk. v. 20–xv. 42; Lk. ii. 23–xxiv. 49; Jn. i. 21–xxi. 20.

¹⁸ Palimpsest. Bound up with Codex Z.

¹⁹ Gold letters on purple vellum.

²⁰ Mt. i. 11–21; iii. 13–iv. 19; x. 7–19; x. 42–xi. 11; xiii. 40–50; xiv. 15–xv. 3; xv. 29–39; Mk. i. 2–11; iii. 5–17; xiv. 13–24; xiv. 48–61; xv. 12–37; Lk. i. 1–13; ii. 9–20; vi. 21–42; vii. 32–viii. 2; viii. 31–50; ix. 26–36; x. 36–xi. 4; xii. 34–45; xiv. 14–25; xv. 13–xvi. 22; xviii. 13–39; xx. 21–xxi. 3; xxii. 3–16; xxiii. 20–35; xxiii. 45–xxiv. 1; xxiv. 14–37; Jn. i. 29–40; ii. 13–25; xxi. 1–11.

²¹ Bilingual. The Greek text is written in Roman characters.

²² Lk. i. 1–13; i. 69–ii. 4; ii. 16–27; iv. 38–v. 5; v. 25–vi. 8; vi. 18–31; 32; 34–40; vi. 49–vii. 22; vii. 44; 46; 47; 50; viii. 1–3; 5–15; viii. 25–ix. 1; ix. 12–43; x. 3–16; xi. 4–27; xii. 4–15; 40–52; xiii. 26–xiv. 1; xiv. 12–xv. 1; xv. 13–xvi. 16; xvii. 21–xviii. 10; xviii. 22–xx. 20; xx. 33–47; xxi. 12–xxii. 6; xxii. 8–15; 42–56; xxii. 71–xxiii. 11; 38–51.

²³ Silver, vermilion, gold on purple vellum. The 233 leaves (out of an original 288) of this codex, like those of B, have been individually mounted between glass sheets.

²⁴ See note 16.

²⁵ Lacks Mt. v. 44–vi. 12; ix. 18–x. 1; xxii. 44–xxiii. 35; Jn. xxi. 10–25 (end).

²⁶ Possibly late fourth century.

²⁷ In the Western order: Matthew, John, Luke, Mark.

²⁸ Mt. vi. 6; vii. 1–ix. 20; x. 1–xi. 24; xii. 9–xvi. 28; xvii. 14–xviii. 25; xix. 22–xxi. 13; xxi. 28–xxii. 22; xxiii. 27–xxiv. 2; xxiv. 23–35; xxv. 1–30; xxvi. 69–xxvii. 12; Mk. vi. 47–xvi. 20 (end — many lacunae); Lk. i. 1–37;

ii. 19–iii. 38; iv. 21–x. 37; xi. 1–xviii. 43; xx. 46–xxiv. 53 (end); Jn. i. 1–v. 41; vii. 1–viii. 5; xiii. 20–xv. 25; xvi. 23–xxi. 25 (end).

²⁹ Lacks Mt. i. 1–ix. 11; x. 35–xi. 4; Lk. i. 26–36; xv. 25–xvi. 5; xxiii. 22–34; Jn. xx. 27–xxi. 17.

³⁰ B. M.: 347 leaves. Leipzig: 43 leaves, known as Codex Friderico-Augustanus (see Table A). Leningrad: 1 leaf (33 lines out of original 48) of Judith, at Society of Ancient Literature; and two mutilated fragments of leaves in manuscript bindings.

³¹ Mt. i. 1–v. 31; vi. 16–29; vii. 26–viii. 27; ix. 6–xxi. 19; xxii. 25–xxviii. 20 (end); Mk. i. 1–iii. 34; vi. 21–xvi. 20 (end); Lk.; Jn.

³² Possibly earlier.

³³ These nearly complete Gospels are interlineated in Latin. See note 10.

³⁴ Kenyon's dating. New Palaeographical Society assigns this MS. to the sixth century; H. A. Sanders, editor of this MS., to the fifth, and even to the first half of that century. The Smithsonian authorities, in a private communication, consider fifth century a "conservative opinion," and entertain the possibility of dating this codex as far back as the fourth.

³⁵ This codex, like *E*, was begun in uncials and finished in minuscules. The minuscule portion, thanks to Tischendorf, is at Leningrad (No. 566).

³⁶ Lacks Mt. iii. 12–iv. 17; xix. 12–xx. 2; Lk. i. 76–ii. 18; Jn. vi. 15–35; viii. 6–39; ix. 21–x. 3.

³⁷ Silver letters on purple vellum.

³⁸ Silver letters on purple vellum. Contains the addition after Mt. xx. 28 found in D.

³⁹ Mt. vi. 4–vii. 25; viii. 8–xviii. 23; xix. 4–xxiii. 3; xxiii. 14–xxviii. 20 (end); Mk. i. 1–xiv. 61.

⁴⁰ The dating here given is Kenyon's. H. A. Sanders, editor of this MS., places it in the fifth century, and gives it the designation Λ.

⁴¹ Formerly known as B₂, this MS. has no connection with Codex Vaticanus.

⁴² Kenyon's dating. Tischendorf: VIII "exeuntis." Von Soden and Gregory: tenth century.

TABLE D

ALPHABETICAL LIST OF MOST IMPORTANT BIBLICAL MANUSCRIPTS

Name	Symbol	Location
Alexandrinus	A	British Museum
Ambrosianus	*F*	Milan, Bibl. Ambrosiana
Angelicus	L	Rome, Bibl. Angelica
Augiensis	F$_2$	Trin. Coll. Cambridge
Basiliensis	E	Basle, University Library
Basiliano-Vaticanus	*N*	Vatican; St. Mark's, Venice
Beratinus	Φ	Berat, Albania
Bezae	D	Univ. Library Cambridge
Bodleian Genesis	*E*	Bodleian, B. M., U. L. C., Leningrad
Boernerianus	G$_3$	Dresden
Boreeli	F	Utrecht
Borgianus	T	Rome, Coll. Propaganda (Vatican)
Campianus	M	Paris, Bibl. Nat.
Chisianus	87	Rome, Chigi Library
Claromontanus	D$_2$	Paris, Bibl. Nat.
Coislinianus	*M*	Paris, Bibl. Nat.
Coislinianus	H$_3$	Paris, Turin, Leningrad, Mt. Athos, Moscow, Kiev.
Cotton Genesis	*D*	British Museum
Cryptoferratensis	Γ̄	Grotto Ferrata, Italy
Cyprius	K̄	Paris, Bibl. Nat.
Dublinensis	Z	Trin. Coll. Dublin
Dublinensis rescriptus	O	Trin. Coll. Dublin
Ephraemi	C	Paris, Bibl. Nat.
Friderico-Augustanus	ℵ	Leipzig
Guelpherbytanus A	P	Wolfenbüttel
Guelpherbytanus B	Q	Wolfenbüttel
Koridethianus	Θ	Tiflis
Laudianus	E$_2$	Bodleian
Laurensis	Ψ	Mt. Athos, Monastery of the Laura
Marchalianus	*Q*	Vatican
Moscuensis	K	Moscow
Moscuensis	V	Moscow
Nanianus	U	Venice
Nitriensis	R	British Museum
Petropolitanus	*H*	Leningrad

TABLE D (*continued*)

Name	Symbol	Location
Petropolitanus	II	Leningrad
Porphyrianus	P₂	Leningrad
Purpureus Petropolitanus	N	Brit. Mus., Leningrad, Vatican, Lerma (Italy), Vienna, Patmos
Regius	L	Paris, Bibl. Nat.
Rossanensis	Σ	Rossano, Calabria
Sangallensis	Δ	St. Gall
Sangermanensis	E₃	Leningrad
Sarravianus	G	Leyden, Paris, Leningrad
Sinaiticus	א	British Museum, Leipzig, Leningrad
Sinopensis	O	Paris, Bibl. Nat.
Taurinensis	Υ	Turin, Bibl. Naz. Univ.
Tischendorfianus III	Λ	Bodleian
Tischendorfianus IV	Γ	Bodleian and Leningrad
Vaticanus	B	Vatican
Vaticanus	S	Vatican
Venetus (=*N*)	V	Venice, St. Mark's
Verona Psalter	R	Verona, Chapter Library
Vienna Genesis	L	Vienna
Washingtonianus I	Θ̲	Smithsonian, Freer Gallery
Washingtonianus II	*1219*	Smithsonian, Freer Gallery
Washingtonianus I	W	Smithsonian, Freer Gallery
Washingtonianus II	I	Smithsonian, Freer Gallery
Zacynthius	Ξ̲	London, Brit. & For. Bible Soc.
Zurich Psalter	*T*	Zurich, Stadtbibliothek
	I	Bodleian
	K	Leipzig
	P	Emmanuel Coll. Cambridge
	W	Paris, Bibl. Nat.
	X	Vatican
	Δ̲	Bodleian
	II̲	Leningrad

TABLE E

PRINCIPAL GREEK PAPYRI OF THE SEPTUAGINT

Designation	Century	Location	No. leaves	Contents
U	VII (?)	Brit. Mus.	32	Ps. xi. 2–xix. 6; xxi. 14–xxxv. 6.
X	late III (?)	Smithsonian (Freer, Gk. V)	parts of 33	Am. i. 10–Mal. iv, 4 (minor mutilations; a few letters of Hos. and 1st vv. of Am.)
905 (Oxy. P. 656)	early III	Bodleian, MS. Gr. bibl. d. 5 (P)	parts of 4	Gen. xiv. 21–23; xv. 5–9; xix. 32–xx. 11; xxiv. 28–47; xxvii. 32, 33, 40, 41.
911	early IV	Berlin, Staatsbibl.	30	Gen. i. 16–xxxv. 8 (many mutilations)
919	VII	Heidelberg, Univ. Bibl.	27	Zech. iv. 6–v. 1; v. 3–vi. 2; vi. 4–15; vii. 10–x. 7; xi. 5–xiv. 21; nearly all of Mal. (all pages mutilated)
952	early IV	Brit. Mus. (2486)	2	One leaf: S. of S. v. 12–vi. 10; second leaf: Ch. xv of Apology of Aristides.
957	II B. C.	Manchester, Rylands Library (458)	frags	Deut. xxiii. 24–xxiv. 3; xxv. 1–3; xxvi. 12, 17–19; xxviii. 31–33.
961 (Ch. Beatty IV)	IV	Brit. Mus.*	56	Gen. ix. 1–xliv. 22 (many mutilations)
962 (Ch. Beatty V)	2nd half III	Brit. Mus.*	27	Gen. viii. 13–ix. 1; xxiv. 13–xxv. 21; xxx. 24–xlvi. 33. (17 lvs nearly perfect; 10 mutilated)
963 (Ch. Beatty VI)	not later mid. II	Brit. Mus.;* U. Mich (frags)	parts of 50	Parts of Num. beg. v. 12 (chiefly xxv–xxxvi); Deut. i. 20–xii. 17; xviii. 22–xxxiv. 12.

* On loan from Chester Beatty, Esq.

TABLE E (*continued*)

Designation	Century	Location	No. leaves	Contents
964 (Ch. Beatty XI)	IV (?)	Brit. Mus.*	2 (1 incomplete)	Ecclus. xxxvi. 28–xxxvii. 22; xlvi. 6–11, xlvi. 16–xlvii. 2.
965 (Ch. B. VII)	1st half III (?)	Brit. Mus.;* Lib. W. Merton**	frags of 33	Scattered fragments between Is. viii. 18–xix. 13; xxxviii. 14–xlv. 5; liv. 1–lx. 22. Merton: parts Is. xvii. 5–7; 9–12; liv. 14–17; lv. 3–6.
966 (Ch. B. VIII)	end of II (?)	Brit. Mus.*	pts of 2	Jer. iv. 30–v. 1; v. 9–14, 23, 24.
967*** (Ch. B. IX)	1st half III (?)	Brit. Mus.;* Princeton U.	pts of 37	B. M. (about 3/5 each pg): pts. Ezek. xi. 25–xvii. 21; Esther ii. 20–viii. 6. Princeton (21 lvs, 19 nearly perfect): Ezek. xix. 12–xxxix. 29 (large lacunae)
968*** (Ch. B. X)	1st half III (?)	Brit. Mus.*	pts of 13	Dan. iii. 72–vi. 18; vii. 1–viii. 27 (about ½ each leaf missing)
2013	late IV	Leipzig (39)	pts of roll 13ft. 6in.	Pss. xxx–lv (1st 5 badly mutilated)
2019	late III	Brit. Mus. (230)	2 cols of a roll (?)	Pss. xii. 7–xv. 4.
2055	late III or IV	Rome, Società Italiana (980)	2	Pss. cxliv. 14–cxlviii. 3.
Baden 56	II			Pt. of Ex. viii.
Amherst P. III	1st half IV	Amherst	1	Gen. i. 1–5 acc. to both LXX and Aquila.

* On loan from Chester Beatty, Esq.

** Private collection W. Merton, Esq.

*** The 50 leaves of Nos. 967 and 968 are parts of the same codex.

TABLE F

PRINCIPAL GREEK PAPYRI OF THE NEW TESTAMENT

Designation	Century	Location	No. leaves	Contents
P⁵	III	Brit. Mus. (782)	2 (conjoint pair)	Jn. i. 23–31, 33–41; xx. 11–17, 19–25.
P¹³ (Oxy. P. 657)	late III–early IV	Brit. Mus. (1532)	roll	Heb. ii. 14–v. 5; x. 8–22, 29–xi. 13; xi. 28–xii. 17.
P³⁸	IV earlier?*	U. Mich. (1571)	1	Ac. xviii. 27–xix. 6; xix. 12–16 (Western type, concurring often with Bezae)
P⁴⁵ (Ch. Beatty I)	III	Brit. Mus.#	30 (parts only)	Parts of Mt. xx. 24–32; xxi. 13–19; xxv. 41–xxvi. 3; xxvi. 6–10, 19–33; Mk. iv. 36–ix. 31; xi. 27–33; xii. 1–28; Lk. vi. 31–41; vi. 45–vii. 17; ix. 26–xiv. 33; Jn. x. 7–xi. 57; Ac. iv. 27–xvii. 17.
P⁴⁶ (Ch. Beatty II)	beginning (?) III	Brit. Mus.# 56 lvs; U. Mich. 30 lvs	86	B. M. (1 or 2 lines lost at ft. of each pg): Rom. v. 17–vi. 14; viii. 15–xvi. 27; Heb.;** I Cor.; II Cor.; Eph.; Gal.; Phil.; Col.; I Th. i. 1–ii. 2; v. 5–28. Mich. (with lacunae): Rom. xi. 35–Heb. ix. 26;** I Cor. ii. 3–iii. 5; II Cor. ix. 7–xiii. 13; Eph. i. 1–vi. 24; Gal. i. 1–vi. 8.
P⁴⁷ (Ch. Beatty III)	III (?)	Brit. Mus.#	10	Rev. ix. 10–xvii. 2 (1–4 lines lost at top of each pg)
P⁴⁸	III (?)	Rome, Società Italiana (1165)	frag.	Ac. xxiii. 11–16, 24–29 (mutilated)
P⁵²	1st half II	Manchester, Rylands Library (457)	frag.	Jn. xviii. 31–33, 37, 38.
?	IV	U. Mich.	1	Mt. xxvi. 19–52.

*Sanders (*Harv. Theol. Rev.*, xix, 215) dates this papyrus first half III.
** In this papyrus Hebrews follows immediately after Romans.
# On temporary loan from Chester Beatty, Esq.

EARLY SEMITIC ALPHABETS

Hebrew alphabetical names	Transliteration	Hebrew "Square" script	Phoenician 9th Cent. B. C.	Moabite stone c. 850 B. C.	Zingirli c. 800 B. C.	Siloam c. 700 B. C.	Seals 8th – 5th Cent. B. C.	Maccabean coins 2nd Cent. B. C.	Palmyrene 1st – 3rd Cent.
Aleph	ʼ								
Beth	b, bh								
Gimel	g, gh								
Daleth	d, dh								
He	h								
Vav	v								
Zayin	z								
Cheth	ḥ								
Teth	ṭ								
Yodh	y								
Kaph	k, kh								
Lamedh	l								
Mem	m								
Nun	n								
Samekh	s								
Ayin	ʻ								
Pe	p, ph								
Tsadhe	ṣ								
Qoph	q								
Resh	r								
Shin	š								
Tav	t, th								

TABLE H

VARIANT ORDERS OF THE OLD TESTAMENT BOOKS

Massoretic Text	Douay Version	Revised Version
Genesis	Genesis	Genesis
Exodus	Exodus	Exodus
Leviticus	Leviticus	Leviticus
Numbers	Numbers	Numbers
Deuteronomy	Deuteronomy	Deuteronomy
Joshua	Josue	Joshua
Judges	Judges	Judges
	Ruth	Ruth
I Samuel	I Kings (=I Sam.)	I Samuel
II Samuel	II Kings (= II Sam.)	II Samuel
I Kings	III Kings (=I Kings)	I Kings
II Kings	IV Kings (=II Kings)	II Kings
	I Paralipomenon (=I Chron.)	I Chronicles
	II Paralipomenon (=II Chron.)	II Chronicles
Isaiah	I Esdras (=Ezra)	Ezra
Jeremiah	II Esdras alias Nehemias	Nehemiah
Ezekiel	Tobias	
	Judith	
The Twelve (Amos — Malachi)		
	Esther (+Apocryphal adds.)	Esther
	Job	Job
Psalms	Psalms	Psalms
Proverbs	Proverbs	Proverbs
Job		
	Ecclesiastes	Ecclesiastes
Song of Songs	Canticle of Canticles	Song of Solomon
Ruth		
	Wisdom	
	Ecclesiasticus	
	Isaias	Isaiah
	Jeremias	Jeremiah
Lamentations	Lamentations	Lamentations
Ecclesiastes		
	Baruch	
Esther		
	Ezechiel	Ezekiel
Daniel	Daniel (+Apoc. adds.)	Daniel
	The Twelve Minor Prophets (Osee — Malachias)	The Twelve Minor Prophets (Hosea — Malachi)
Ezra		
Nehemiah		
I Chronicles		
II Chronicles		
	I Machabees	
	II Machabees	

INDEX OF
SCRIPTURAL PASSAGES CITED

GENERAL INDEX

NOTE. Subject entries, capitalized only as usage requires, are in roman; titles of books and names of Hebrew letters, in italics. Hebrew items cited from the Massoretic Text may be located by reference in this Index to their Revised Version English equivalents. Individual words quoted from English versions are in SMALL CAPITALS; Biblical phrases or clauses — located, for the most part, under their most significant words — are within single quotation marks. A virgule [/] separates alternative readings, textual or conjectural; a colon [:], interchangeable Scriptural usages. Page references in italics indicate main entries within a series.

Aaron ben Moses ben Asher, *see* Ben Asher
Aaron, sons of, 281
ABBA (Father), 114, n. a
ABIAH, 77
ABINADAB / Aminadab, 324, n. 35
Abircius, bp. of Hierapolis, 312
abbreviation, sacred names, 128 — 131
abridgment, Codd. א and B, 146
Abyssinia, 167
accents in M. T., 237 — 239
accusative particle (את) emended, 78, 93
ACRES, 220
acrostics, Olivétan, 180; pattern violated, 59; Prov. *xxxi. 10 — 31*, 229; Ps. *xxv. 2*, 64; Ps. *cxlv*, 59 — 60; restoration of M. T. by, 64, 82; translation of, 224 — 225
Acts of the Apostles, Aramaisms in, 113; compilatory practice, 283; Erasmus, 258, n. m; misprint, 199, n. kk; MS. Laud. E2, 23, n. mm; O. Lat. "African" text of, 331, n. 19; O. Lat. "European" text of, 331, n. 19; title of, 293, n. eee
Acts of Solomon, The Book of the, 282, n. qq
A. D., first Biblical use, 335, n. 37; inapplicable to centuries, 6, n. l
ADAM, achievements of, *see* Bayle, La Peyrère, Voltaire

additions to N. T., 134 — 147; "Appendix" to Mk., 143; Col. *ii. 18*, 136; doxology, 140; *pericope adulterae*, 141 — 143; Three Witnesses, 140, 141; unique interpolation in Cod. W, 143; *see* assimilation, editorial alteration in MSS., marginalia
Adoration of the Shepherds, 286
'adversaries are all before thee, mine,' 96
Ælfric, archbp. of Canterbury, Anglo-Saxon LXX, 171; on translation, 210
African (Bengel) classification N. T. MSS., 148, n. y.
"African" text, *see* Old Latin versions
'after their families,' 268
Agapiou, 165, n. l
AHAB, king of Israel, 28
Ahiram, king of Byblos, 28
AI, 96
'Ain Fashkha cave, excavation, 9, n. q; 11; *see* Dead Sea Scrolls, *Jubilees*
Akiba (Palestinian *tanna*), 161; on Eccl., 302, n. ppp
Albright, W. F., cities of refuge, 77, n. a; folk etymology, 339, n. 28, 340, n. 29; Isaiah Scroll, 318, n. 16; Nash Papyrus, 8, n. p; Phoenician alphabet, 27, n. b; Tetragrammaton, 327, n. 33
Alcalá de Henares, 177

389